BREAKING OUT OF THE WEB BROWSER WITH ADOBE AIR

JEFF TAPPER &
MICHAEL LABRIOLA

WITH PETER DILILLO, TOM KACZANKO, ANDRIY KUPRIYENKO, LOUIE PENAFLOR, MIKE NIMER, NATHAN WEBER, AND STEVE ZIMMERS

Breaking Out of the Web Browser with Adobe AIR
Jeff Tapper and Michael Labriola with Peter DiLillo, Tom Kaczanko, Andriy Kupriyenko, Louie Penaflor, Mike Nimer, Nathan Weber, and Steve Zimmers

Published by Peachpit Press. For information on Peachpit Press books, contact:

New Riders
1249 Eighth Street
Berkeley, CA 94710
(510) 524-2178
(510) 524-2221 (fax)
Find us on the Web at: www.newriders.com

To report errors, please send a note to errata@peachpit.com

New Riders is an imprint of Peachpit, a division of Pearson Education

Project Editor: Nancy Peterson
Editor: Robyn G. Thomas
Technical Editor: Angela Nimer
Production Coordinator: Lisa Brazieal
Copy Editor/Proofreader: Joanne Gosnell
Compositor: Maureen Forys, Happenstance Type-O-Rama
Marketing Manager: Glenn Bisignani
Indexer: Karin Arrigoni
Cover Design: Charlene Charles-Will
Cover Compositor: Mike Tanamachi

ISBN 13: 978-0-321-50356-5
ISBN 10: 0-321-50356-2

987654321
Printed and bound in the United States of America

To my wife Lisa and children Kaliope and Kagan—
without you to inspire me, this just wouldn't be possible.

To the memory of my recently departed grandmother Elizabeth Farrelly—
your words of wisdom will always live with me.

—Jeff Tapper

To my wife Laura and my daughter Lilia—you both make me smile.

To my grandmother and grandfather who provided
inspiration, guidance, and love for so long.

To my family and friends who provide the encouragement
and support to accomplish the craziest projects.

—Michael Labriola

Acknowledgments

I would like to thank Mike L. for writing this book with me and helping to keep me sane in the process. Thanks to Louie, Pete, Mike N., Tom, Andriy, Nathan, and Steve Z. for their contributions. Thanks to our editorial staff: Nancy, Robyn and Angie—here's hoping your efforts to keep us coherent were not in vain. Special thanks to Steve L., while not officially an editor on this book, his proofreading resulted in hundreds of positive adjustments, making this book as accurate as possible. As always, thanks to the Adobe team, who have brought these technologies to you and me.

—Jeff Tapper

Thanks to Jeff for his humor and relative insanity when approaching these projects. Thanks to Louie, Pete, Mike, Tom, Andriy, Nathan, and Steve for all their contributions, research, and content. Special thanks to: Robyn for keeping us on track with humor, Nancy for working so hard to balance schedule with quality, Angie for navigating the changing waters of AIR to ensure our accuracy, and Steve for taking on the final crazy continuity challenge. Final thanks are shared by the all the hardworking folks that made AIR a real product, the hardworking folks at Digital Primates who take up the slack when Jeff and I engage in these types of projects, and my wife whose hard work gives me the time to work on these books.

—Michael Labriola

Bios

Jeff Tapper is a senior technologist at Digital Primates IT Consulting Group. He has been developing Internet-based applications since 1995 for a myriad of clients including Morgan Stanley, Conde Nast, Toys R Us, IBM, Dow Jones, American Express, Verizon, and many others. He has been developing Flex applications since the earliest days of Flex 1. As an instructor, Jeff is certified to teach all of Adobe's courses on Flex, ColdFusion, and Flash development. He is also a frequent speaker at Adobe Development Conferences and user groups. Digital Primates IT Consulting Group provides expert guidance on Rich Internet Application development and empowers clients through mentoring.

Michael Labriola is a founding partner and senior consultant at Digital Primates IT Consulting Group. He has been developing Internet applications since 1995 and has been working with Flex since its 1.0 beta program. Michael is an Adobe Certified Instructor, Community Expert, Flex Developer Champion, and international speaker on Flex and AIR topics who has consulted for three of the world's 10 most recognized brands.

As a consultant, he mentors software development teams using emerging technologies and designs enterprise applications with high business impact. His free time is spent escaping from technology through wine and food.

Contents

Foreword

The web browser is my favorite application. As the Internet has evolved from sites of static text and images to a landscape of powerful Rich Internet Applications and experiences, I'm surprised that the browser icon on my desktop doesn't have wear marks from daily double-clicking.

Today, if I navigate to my preferred auction site, I can search for and check on the status of an item for sale. I can dig into the details of the item to see if it was paid for, and I can explore even deeper to check the shipping status with the carrier.

When using our web-based customer management application, I can see the IM status of both coworkers and a number of customers. I can even click into a contact record to initiate a quick videoconference with someone without leaving the site.

Developers are dreaming up connected applications that were just not fathomable in the client/server days. Combining web technologies like Flash, HTML/JavaScript, and PDF, as well as web services from several sources, more and more Rich Internet Applications (RIAs) are becoming critical tools in our daily lives.

But what if you could take a web experience and enable it to run as a local application on the desktop? What if a Rich Internet Application worked when a user was connected to the Internet and also when the user was disconnected? Finally, what if the application could receive and display status updates and notifications, even when the user's browser was on a different page or when the browser was closed?

These are some of the inspirations that influenced Adobe AIR, a runtime that lets developers use proven web technologies to build Rich Internet Applications that deploy to the desktop and run across operating systems.

AIR is about more than just putting an icon on the desktop and letting your web application run locally; it's a consistent way to bridge a web application with local desktop resources and data using technologies like Flash, Flex, and HTML/JavaScript. This enables some powerful new capabilities not possible when running inside a web browser. Now your RIA can implement file drag/drop events, integrate with the system clipboard, access local files, or trigger system notification bubbles.

Additionally, AIR enables persistence of local data, leveraging a SQLite database built into the AIR runtime. Manipulating information in the SQLite database is made easy with the rich APIs exposed to ActionScript, Flex, and JavaScript developers.

Without question, one of the most powerful ways to develop applications for AIR is to use Adobe Flex. Flex enables developers to quickly build applications that are responsive, engaging, and visually compelling. In the short time since we introduced Flex, it has already become the key technology behind a number of immersive consumer experiences and enterprise applications on the web today.

If you're new to Flex, getting started is easy! The Flex SDK is a free and open-source framework with a strong engaged community. Flex has a declarative markup language called MXML to help structure your application, and it uses ActionScript 3.0 (an implementation of ECMAScript 4) to define logic, data binding, and smooth effects. While Flex applications for AIR can be built using only the open-source SDK and your favorite text editor, developers can use Adobe Flex Builder 3 to dramatically accelerate AIR development, debugging, and packaging.

AIR applications built with Flex leverage the high-performance, cross-operating system virtual machine in the Adobe Flash Player, so you can deliver the same behavior and many of the same features on the desktop as in the browser.

Just as Adobe Flash Player is installed on 98 percent of Internet-connected desktops in the world today, we are putting our energy behind making sure that the AIR runtime is on just as many Mac, Windows, and Linux desktops. You can be assured that the applications you build for Adobe AIR will have the furthest market reach of any technology platform today.

You can also expect that the pace of innovation around Flash, Flex, and AIR will continue at a rapid pace. We've never been happy with the status quo, and we do everything we can to help developers like you venture into new territory.

As we embark on future versions of AIR and Flex, we constantly ask ourselves what kinds of applications developers could create if they had new capabilities. Some of the feedback you've communicated already has inspired upcoming design tools, advanced effects, and new components in Flex. Keep the feedback coming, and we'll help provide the best tools for your development journey.

It's fitting that the guys who brought you *Adobe Flex 3, Training from the Source* introduce AIR development using Adobe Flex. You now have the tools and knowledge to build next-generation desktop applications. All you need to add is imagination!

Steven Heintz
Adobe Flex Principal Product Manager
Adobe Systems, Inc.

THE GENESIS OF AIR

With the release of Adobe Integrated Runtime (AIR), Adobe has suddenly enabled millions of web developers around the world to develop desktop applications using the same technologies they already know. A whole generation of developers has been building applications to run in web browsers, simply because that was the required platform for the technologies they knew. With AIR, those same technologies can now be used to build desktop applications, with no need to house the applications within a web browser. In fact, that is what AIR is, a cross-platform runtime for web applications, without the need for a browser.

To fully understand what AIR is and why it is important, it helps to understand the history of computer applications and the progression they have made over the past 50 plus years. Many readers of this book are likely to have years of development experience (most likely as web developers), yet have no hands-on knowledge of computer applications before the Internet era.

Legacy Era

Computers have played a role in the business environment for nearly five decades. Between their introduction to business in the late 1950s, until the heyday of the Internet era (late 1990s), there has been a fluctuation between centralizing processing power on one or a cluster of servers and distributing the processing across the clients.

Mainframe Era

While there were dozens of computers produced and used before 1955, much of that usage was limited to military and other governmental organizations. The true age of business computing seems to have started in 1955, when the IBM 704 was the first commercially available computer system. This started the age of mainframe computing, in which all processing power was centralized in a powerful, centralized machine. Throughout the mainframe era, there were a number of improvements, such as the addition of terminals, spread throughout the business, which could allow multiple users to simultaneously connect and interact with the mainframe; however, all the processing power continued to remain at the server, with the terminals simply being a tool to allow users to view and interact with that data.

Microcomputers

Over the years, as memory and processing power became cheaper and more available, the microcomputer (sometimes referred to as the personal computer) began to emerge. These computers had the resources to run stand-alone applications, and soon most business needs could be handled from the desktop, as opposed to requiring the use of the mainframe. Another benefit of microcomputers was that they were frequently easier to use, as user interfaces continued to improve (it was during the age of the microcomputer that graphical user interfaces [GUIs] were first commercially available). While microcomputers offered many improvements, they specifically lacked some of the best features of the mainframe era, in that there was little or no centralization of data, nor of business rules.

Client/Server

The paradigm shift from mainframes to microcomputers solved many issues, but, as previously mentioned, it created a series of new problems. Responding to these issues, a number of software vendors began designing solutions that harnessed both benefits of a centralized server with the power of the desktop computer. This led to the birth of the client/server era. These applications usually had one or more powerful centralized servers, which stored the application data and housed all the business rules, and a number of independent desktop clients, each running an easy-to-use interface (often a GUI). This style of application was immensely useful to the business community, taking the greatest benefits and mitigating the greatest weaknesses of both the mainframe and microcomputer era. However, a weakness the client/server applications shared with the microcomputer era became far more apparent—distribution; it was extremely difficult to keep a vast number of clients up-to-date. As large businesses sought to update the software on hundreds or thousands of individual desktops, they found that a large staff was required to merely keep each machine up-to-date.

Internet Era

In the mid 1990s, the Internet began to find its way into everyday homes and businesses. Many of the early protocols of the Internet, such as FTP and GOPHER, were specifically designed for sharing files across distributed networks. This had a number of applicable business uses, but it was the introduction of the Hypertext Transfer Protocol (HTTP) that allowed for development of Internet applications. The idea of applications housed on a central web server and accessed through ultra-thin clients (web browsers) was very appealing to businesses in solving the distribution problem. Each time a user sought to use an application, the most up-to-date application downloaded from the server, so that the only maintenance needed for the desktop was updating the web browser.

Early Browser Applications

The early Internet applications adequately solved the problem for which they were designed; companies' IT staffs were free from the pains of constant software installations and could focus on other IT needs for the business. Throughout the last decade, more and more business applications migrated from client/server applications to web-based applications. In reality, the web-based applications were similar to mainframe applications: The central server (now a group of several servers, such as web server, application server, database server, and so on) housed all the logic, and the clients merely presented the data, as dictated by the server, and allowed for users to interact with that data.

While the similarities to mainframe applications were great for solving the distribution problems, early browser applications lacked much of the ease of use of client/server applications. The page-based model (that is, each user action sent a request to the server, which responded with a new page to render) frequently made it slower and more difficult for users to do the same work they had previously done with a client/server application.

Rich Internet Applications

The transition from client/server to web-based applications allowed businesses to save a tremendous amount of money on the costs of desktop support for their applications. It was no longer necessary to have a large staff move from desktop to desktop, installing the latest updates to each application; instead, the latest version of the application downloaded from the server each time it was needed.

Like most trade-offs, this one too had its cost. While web-based applications without the need to distribute software throughout the company saved money, employee productivity decreased, and users became increasingly frustrated. Web applications traditionally had a page-based model, that is, a user would interact with a web page. Each time a user clicked a link or submitted a form, a new page from the server replaced the current page. Even on very fast networks, it is far less efficient to re-render each page over and over again. Client/server applications were generally capable of updating data on the screen without the need to re-draw the whole screen each time. Even though it often took less than a second for screens to re-draw on web applications, over the course of a 40-hour workweek, those seconds rapidly added up, often costing an hour or more a week in lost productivity.

Looking to regain the loss in productivity, developers attempted several variations of rich Internet clients. The early Internet days saw a number of applications built in Java applets; however, these didn't catch on as expected, due to a combination of large file size and issues with compatibility of different Java Virtual Machines (JVM) available in varying operating systems and browsers. Developers wrote a number of browser-based applications using Microsoft's ActiveX technologies; these however suffered from a fierce platform dependency, often only working in the latest version of Internet Explorer on Windows.

Today, there are two main technologies used to create RIAs—AJAX (Asynchronous JavaScript and XML) and Flash.

AJAX-based applications

AJAX is a technique for building interactive web applications. Using the browser's scripting language (JavaScript), web pages became more responsive by exchanging small amounts of data (via XML) with the server behind the scenes, so that the entire web page does not reload each time the user requests a change. This is meant to increase the web page's interactivity, speed, and usability.

AJAX recently came into popular use in the Internet community, but in reality, the ideas behind AJAX (using JavaScript to dynamically load data and change the data rendered on a web page) have been around for over a decade.

There are a number of highly successful AJAX applications that are popular on the web today, including Google Maps and the GMail email client. While AJAX development can be difficult because of different levels of support for JavaScript in various browsers and operating systems, a number of worthwhile frameworks are available that greatly ease the process of building applications that work across a variety of browsers.

There are currently dozens of different AJAX frameworks available, including SPRY, a framework released by Adobe, to ease AJAX application development.

Flash Player-based applications

The other technology that has been extensively used for building RIAs in recent years is Flash Player. Originally written as a plug-in to run animations, Flash Player has evolved over the years, with each new version adding new capabilities while still maintaining a very small footprint. Over the past decade, Flash Player has gained near ubiquity, with some version of it installed in more than 97 percent of all web browsers on the Internet. Since 2002, Macromedia (now part of Adobe) began focusing on Flash as more than an animation tool. And with the Flash 6 release, Macromedia began to provide more capabilities for building applications. Macromedia found that with the combination of the ubiquity of the player and the power available from its scripting language (ActionScript), developers could build full browser-based applications and get around the limitations of HTML.

By targeting Flash Player, developers could also free themselves from browser and platform incompatibilities. One of the many nice features of Flash Player is that if a browser or platform will run a particular version of Flash Player, then it will run any content and application developed for that Flash Player version. With very few exceptions, it remains true today.

Historically, the biggest drawback of building applications for Flash Player was the authoring environment, which was clearly built as an animation tool for users creating interactive content. Many developers who wanted to build RIAs for Flash Player were thwarted by the unfamiliarity of the tools. This, coupled with the scant materials available in 2002 for learning to use Flash as an application platform, kept many serious developers from successfully building Flash applications.

Although Flash Player remains an excellent platform for RIAs, the introduction of solutions such as Laszlo and Flex have greatly simplified the development process and reduced the number of RIAs developed directly in Flash Studio.

Break Out of the Browser

AIR continues this evolutionary process, taking all the advantages of RIAs, and solving their key weakness—the inability to interact with a user's operating system. With the introduction of the Internet era in the 1990s, people began porting desktop applications to run in a web browser to help solve the distribution problems of desktop applications. However, today, with desktop Internet applications such as AIR, users can install applications by clicking a web page and automatically update them each time they run, offering the best of both worlds—all the power and interactivity of a desktop application, with the distribution of an Internet application.

Many developers, upon first hearing about AIR, ask the question "Why would I want to build an application that runs outside the browser?" This of course is the wrong question to ask. What developers should be asking is "What container is most appropriate for the application I'm trying to build?" Web developers usually build applications for the web browser simply because that is the only container they know. The reality is that web developers have been working around browser limitations for years, whether or not they realize it.

Limitations of Browser-Based Applications

While many web developers do not necessarily realize it, there are limitations to browser-based applications that other desktop applications do not have. For instance:

- Browsers do not allow applications to interact with the file system.
- Browser-based applications have very limited choices for storing client-side data: cookies in HTML applications, and Shared Objects in Flash Player applications.
- Browser-based applications cannot run as background services; if running, they are always running in an open browser.
- Browser-based applications offer only a very limited offline application; they rely heavily on being connected to the Internet.
- Browsers intercept many keyboard shortcuts. Browser-based applications cannot map these shortcuts to other meanings within the application.

- Browsers do not support drag-and-drop items from the operating system directly into the application.

The next few sections explain these limitations in more detail.

Browser sandbox limits application functionality

There are a number of limitations to browser-based applications directly related to the security sandbox of the web browser. Chief among these is the inability to interact with the file system. With the exception of cookies (for HTML-based applications), or shared objects (for Flash-based applications), browser-based applications have no ability to create, read, write, update, or delete information to and from the file system. This can complicate many matters in application development. For example, imagine building an application that tries to synchronize files between a client and server. In a purely browser-based application, it wouldn't be possible to scan a directory of files on the local machine, compare the last changed date with those on the server, and automatically update those that are out-of-date. Using other browser plug-in technologies, such as Java applets or ActiveX controls, some of this becomes possible, although it requires additional plug-ins outside of the normal browser install.

With the use of cookies (or shared objects), it is possible to store some user information locally, although usually that information tends to be a unique identifier (such as the primary key) that maps the user to information stored on the server. If an application needed to work with or without an Internet connection and wanted to store application data, such as an address book, client list, or even user preference data, the size limitation of cookies would be inadequate.

There are dozens of other application use cases that are either extremely difficult or entirely impossible in browser-based applications because of these sandbox restrictions. For years, web developers have worked around these by relying more heavily on the server, or simply excluded these features from their applications.

Browser native behavior intrudes on application controls

You can also run into problems with browser-based applications when the browser's native behaviors intrude on an application's intended behaviors. One of the easiest examples to see is the inability to drag an image from the file system into a browser-based application and have the application react to it. Why isn't this possible? The browser has native behaviors that intercept the image being dragged, and the browser handles it in its own way, which involves replacing the web page (or web application) with the image.

Another frequently requested feature that isn't entirely possible with browser-based applications is the ability to have an application react to the function keys from the user's keyboard. While some keys will work, the browser intercepts others and triggers specific features in the browser. For instance, in a browser, the F1 key opens Help, F5 refreshes the page, F6 gives focus to the address bar, and F11 toggles the browser in and out of kiosk (full-screen) mode. While the function keys are just one example, the browser will natively intercept a number of different key combinations, and react, rather than passing those keystrokes to the application.

Browser applications rarely work while disconnected

Browser applications rarely work while disconnected. A serious limitation of browser-based applications is that it's difficult to create a true occasionally connected client (OCC). Because the browser lacks the ability to interact with the file system, or otherwise save data locally to the client, most browser-based applications rely heavily on the server to store data. A more robust client-side storage mechanism (such as creating files, writing to a local database, and so on) is needed to truly create an OCC.

AIR Breaks Out of the Browser

AIR offers an alternative for web developers. They can use the technologies they know to build an application outside the web browser. AIR applications can escape all the browser's limitations:

- AIR applications have direct access to the file system.
- AIR offers an embedded database, allowing for even greater client-side storage possibilities.
- In AIR applications, with the windowing API, the look and feel of the application can be completely customized or even hidden away, allowing for "background" applications.
- AIR offers a robust API to allow for easy development of occasionally connected applications.
- AIR applications exist outside the browser, so there are no "off-limits" keyboard shortcuts.
- AIR applications can support drag-and-drop of items from the operating system directly into the application.

The remainder of this book explores the features of AIR in much greater detail.

Prerequisites

What does a developer need to know to start building AIR applications? Either HTML and JavaScript, Flash, or Flex. Content written with any of these common everyday web technologies can be easily deployed as desktop applications. However, this book is focused primarily on building AIR applications using Flex content. You will find some information relevant to building AIR applications with HTML/JavaScript scattered throughout the book, but that is not the primary focus.

Outline

Chapter 1, "Building Your First AIR Application," shows how to build a simple AIR application using either HTML or Flex-based content. Chapter 2, "Working with the Time Tracker Application," walks you through downloading the source code and installers for a particular AIR application and allows you to import the code as a Flex Builder project.

The rest of the book explores the dpTimeTracker application and investigates the functionality available in AIR, as it is used in that application.

- **Chapter 1:** Building Your First AIR Application
- **Chapter 2:** Working with the Time Tracker Application
- **Chapter 3:** Interacting with the Clipboard
- **Chapter 4:** Implementing Drag and Drop between the OS and AIR
- **Chapter 5:** Reading and Writing to a SQLite Database
- **Chapter 6:** Interacting with the File System
- **Chapter 7:** Customizing the Look and Feel of an Application
- **Chapter 8:** Working with the Presence API
- **Chapter 9:** Using HTML Content in a Flex/AIR Application
- **Chapter 10:** Understanding the Need for Remote Data
- **Chapter 11:** Communicating with Adobe BlazeDS
- **Chapter 12:** Testing AIR Applications with Fluint

- **Chapter 13:** Deploying AIR Applications
- **Chapter 14:** Understanding AIR Security

Who Is This Book For?

This book is intended for web developers currently using Flex to build RIAs. The materials in this book can offer great insight to web developers wishing to leverage their skills to build desktop applications, however, all the examples are specifically shown and discussed using Flex-based content.

The Project Application

Starting in Chapter 2, "Working with the Time Tracker Application," readers will be directed to download the source code and installer for the dpTimeTracker application. This is an AIR-based application, built using Flex content. dpTimeTracker allows anyone who charges for their work based on number of hours worked. It allows for creation and maintenance of a client list, with each client having one or more projects against which time can be tracked. In the latter chapters of this book, you'll see how this application can be integrated with third-party tools, like Harvest Time Tracker, to export hours into a centralized repository.

Standard Elements in the Book

After downloading the source code in Chapter 2, each subsequent chapter explores a feature of the AIR platform and uses the dpTimeTracker application to reinforce those concepts in a real-world scenario. You'll see some standard conventions throughout the book to help distinguish different elements.

TIP **Alternative ways to perform tasks and suggestions to consider when applying the skills you are learning.**

NOTE **Additional background information to expand your knowledge, and advanced techniques you can explore to further develop your skills.**

CAUTION **Information warning you of situations you might encounter that could cause errors, problems, or unexpected results.**

Boldface text—Words that appear in **boldface** are terms that you must type while working through the steps in the lessons.

Boldface code—Lines of code that appear in **boldface** within code blocks help you easily identify changes in the block that you are to make in a specific step in an exercise.

```
public function set pasteTextCallback( value:Function ):void
{
    pasteTextCallback = value;
}
```

Code in text—`Code` or `keywords` appear slightly different from the rest of the text so you can identify them.

Code blocks—To help you easily identify ActionScript, XML, and HTML code within the book, the code has been styled in a special font that's unique from the rest of the text. Single lines of code that are longer than the margins of the page allow, wrap to the next line. They are designated by an arrow at the beginning of the continuation of a broken line and are indented under the line from which they continue. For example:

```
private function createXLS():Array
    {
    var file:File = File.createTempDirectory().resolvePath(
    ➥ "data-"+dateFormatter.format(new Date())+".xls");
    var fileStream:FileStream = new FileStream();
    fileStream.open(file, FileMode.WRITE);
    fileStream.writeUTFBytes(dgToHTML());
    fileStream.close();
    return new Array(file);
    }
```

Italicized text—Words that appear in *italics* are either for *emphasis* or are *new vocabulary.*

Italics are also used on placeholders, in which the exact entry may change depending on your situation. For example:

```
adt -package SIGNING_OPTIONS output_file_name app_xml [files_and_dirs ... ]
```

Menu commands and keyboard shortcuts—Menu commands are shown with angle brackets between the menu names and commands: Menu > Command > Subcommand. Keyboard shortcuts are shown with a plus sign between the names of keys to indicate that you should press the keys simultaneously; for example, Shift+Tab means that you should press the Shift and Tab keys at the same time.

Appendixes—Appendix A contains instructions on installing the AIR Runtime and AIRSDK. Appendix B provides information on the special considerations when creating and working with AIR 1.1 applications.

Website—All the code referenced in this book is available from a Google-code repository. Instructions for integrating with this are available in Chapter 2.

BUILDING YOUR FIRST AIR APPLICATION

CHAPTER 1

When learning any new technology, it's usually helpful to start with a small Hello World application that uses the technology to show a simple message on the screen. In this chapter, you'll learn how to build your first AIR application, using both HTML and Flex-based content.

How to Build AIR Applications

AIR provides a platform in which web developers can build desktop applications using technologies they already know, such as HTML and JavaScript or Flex and Flash. An important thing to understand about AIR, regardless of whether your application is primarily HTML or SWF-based content, is the application will always consist of at least two files. One will be the main contents (either HTML or SWF), and the other will be an application XML file. Regardless of which type of AIR application you are building, the contents of the XML file will be very similar.

TIP Remember, you can build SWF-based content using either Flex or Flash Studio.

Building a Hello World Application with AIR and Flex

Any Flex application can be built to be deployed to the desktop with AIR. The key difference between a Flex application intended to run in a web browser versus one intended to run on the desktop is the root node of the application. As you probably already know, Flex applications normally start with the `<mx:Application>` tag as a root node. By changing the root node from `<mx:Application>` to `<mx:WindowedApplication>`, the Flex application can now be more readily packaged to run on the desktop within AIR.

NOTE This book is not intended to teach Flex development. If you are interested in learning more about Flex development, we highly recommend the Adobe Press book: *Adobe Flex 3, Training from the Source*.

Following is a simple Flex application that when run displays the text "Hello World" as shown in the figure.

Listing 1

```
<?xml version="1.0" encoding="utf-8"?>
<mx:Application xmlns:mx="http://www.adobe.com/2006/mxml">
    <mx:Label text="Hello World" fontSize="40"/>
</mx:Application>
```

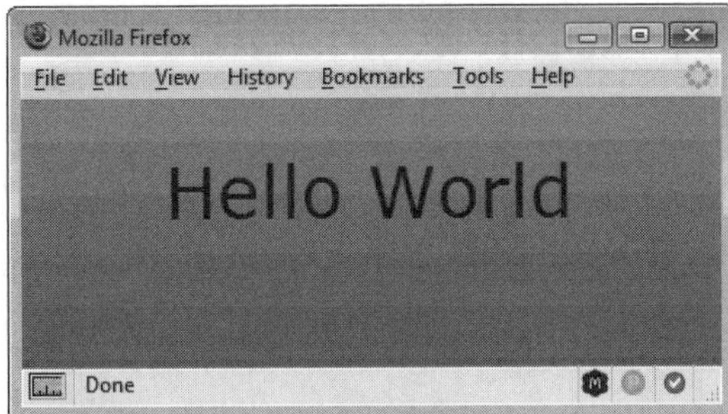

Figure 1: A simple Flex-based Hello World application running in a browser

If this same application used the root node `<mx:WindowedApplication>` instead of `<mx:Application>`, you could then deploy the application to run in the desktop via AIR. The following code shows the AIR version of the Hello World Flex application, and the figure shows the result.

Listing 2

```
<?xml version="1.0" encoding="utf-8"?>
<mx:WindowedApplication xmlns:mx="http://www.adobe.com/2006/mxml">
    <mx:Label text="Hello World" fontSize="40"/>
</mx:WindowedApplication>
```

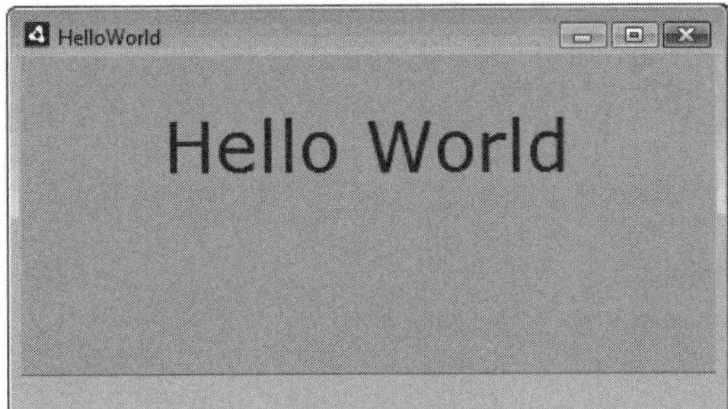

Figure 2: A simple Flex-based Hello World application running in AIR

NOTE If you are using Flex Builder to build Flex applications, you will actually need to create a new AIR project to allow the Flex-enabled application to run in AIR. However, if you are using the command line tools and have properly built the app.xml file, you can easily change between AIR and browser-based Flex content. We will explore the app.xml file later in this chapter.

Building a Hello World Application with AIR and HTML

Just as it is easy to deploy any Flex-based content to AIR, it is also possible to deploy any HTML-based content to AIR. While most of this book will focus on the uses of Flex and AIR, the HTML version of Hello World is included to show the similarities between deploying Flex or HTML content to AIR. Here is the AIR version of the Hello World HTML application.

Listing 3

```
<html>
    <head>
        <title>Hello World HTML</title>
    </head>
    <body>
        <h1 align="center" >Hello World</h1>
    </body>
</html>
```

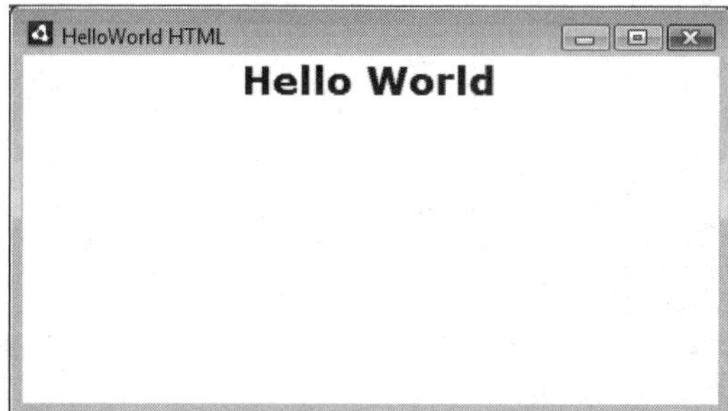

Figure 3: A simple HTML-based Hello World application running in AIR

Describing Your Application with an Application Descriptor

Before content (regardless of whether it is HTML or SWF-based) can run in AIR, the AIR Developer Tool (more commonly referred to by its acronym ADT) needs an application.xml file to specify what to package in the AIR file. At a bare minimum, the application.xml file contains an id for the application, a name of the file to create, a version number for the AIR application, the contents to package, and whether or not the application should start up as visible. The following code shows the bare minimum needed for an application XML file for the previous Flex-based Hello World example shown in Listing 2.

NOTE By convention, the application.xml file is frequently given the same name as the main application file, with -app appended to the end of the file, so for the HelloWorld.swf application, the application XML file would conventionally be called HelloWorld-app.xml.

Listing 4

```
<?xml version="1.0" encoding="utf-8" standalone="no"?>
<application xmlns="http://ns.adobe.com/air/application/1.1">
    <id>net.digitalprimates.airBook.HelloWorld</id>
    <filename>HelloWorld</filename>
    <version>1.0</version>
    <initialWindow>
        <content>HelloWorld.swf</content>
        <visible>true</visible>
    </initialWindow>
</application>
```

Like all good XML files, this app.xml file starts with an XML declaration, followed by the root node, `<application>`. The application tag defines a default namespace that points to the `http://ns.adobe.com/air/application/1.1` URI. The AIR namespace will change with each major release of AIR (but not with minor patches). The last segment of the namespace (1.1 in this example) indicates the runtime version the application requires. Optionally, you can specify a `minimumPatchLevel` attribute on the application node to indicate a minimum version of AIR for this application. If the user is running an older version of the runtime, they will be prompted to update to the required version.

NOTE This book does not cover details on XML, such as XML Namespaces. There are many good books available that cover these, such as the Adobe Press book: *Adobe Flex 3, Training from the Source.*

Next, the id node specifies a unique identifier for this application. It is really important to specify a unique `id` for each application. When a user tries to install an AIR application, the operating system (OS) uses this `id` to determine if the application is already installed. If the OS finds that an application with the same `id` is already installed, it will ask the user if they want to run, re-install, or uninstall the application. As a best practice, use naming conventions similar to those in Java for fully qualified class paths. The previous example uses the reverse of our company's domain (net.digitalprimates instead of digitalprimates.net), followed by a broad classification (airBook), and then the specific name for the application (HelloWorld). Putting these all together gives us a reasonable likelihood of a unique name, `net.digitalprimates.airBook.HelloWorld`, which is not likely to conflict with any other applications.

After the id node, the filename node determines what to call the program file once installed by a user.

NOTE The filename node determines the name of the program file, not of the packaged installer. Later in this chapter, you will see how to tell ADT what to name the installer. It should also be noted that the filename is specified without an extension, and needs to be a syntactically valid filename for your operating system. Frequently, the filename is the same as the name of the main content file.

After the filename node, the version node indicates the version of the application being used. This version helps determine if a user is installing a newer version of the application than they currently have, or prevents them from accidently installing an older version.

After the version node, the initialWindow node specifies the contents and appearance of the application as it starts. The only truly required child node of the initialWindow node is content, which specifies the relative path from the application xml file to the HTML or SWF content the AIR application will package, which further define the application. The following code shows a fully populated application.xml file; the required nodes are in boldface type.

Listing 5

```
<?xml version="1.0" encoding="utf-8" standalone="no"?>
<application xmlns="http://ns.adobe.com/air/application/1.1">
    <!-- The application identifier string, unique to this application.
    Required. -->
    <id>net.digitalprimates.airBook.HelloWorld</id>
    <!-- Used as the filename for the application. Required. -->
```

Listing 5 (continued)

```
<filename>HelloWorld</filename>
<!-- The name that is displayed in the AIR application installer.
    Optional. -->
<name>Hello World!</name>
<!-- An application version designator (such as "v1", "2.5", or "Alpha 1").
    Required. -->
<version>1.0</version>
<!-- Description, displayed in the AIR application installer. Optional. -->
<description>My First AIR Application.  I Hope you enjoy it as much as I
    do.</description>
<!-- Copyright information. Optional -->
<copyright>No Rights Reserved.</copyright>
<!-- Settings for the application's initial window. Required. -->
<initialWindow>
    <!-- The main content file of the application. Can be HTML or SWF.
        Required. -->
    <content>HelloWorld.swf</content>
    <!-- The title of the main window. Optional. -->
    <title>Hello World!!!</title>
    <!-- The type of system chrome to use (either "standard" or "none").
        Optional. Default standard. -->
    <systemChrome>standard</systemChrome>
    <!-- Whether the window is transparent. Only applicable when
        systemChrome is false. Optional. Default false. -->
    <transparent>false</transparent>
    <!-- Whether the window is initially visible. Optional. Default
        false. -->
    <visible>true</visible>
    <!-- Whether the user can minimize the window. Optional. Default
        true. -->
    <minimizable>true</minimizable>
    <!-- Whether the user can maximize the window. Optional. Default
        true. -->
    <maximizable>true</maximizable>
    <!-- Whether the user can resize the window. Optional. Default
    true. -->
    <resizable>true</resizable>
    <!-- The window's initial width. Optional. -->
```

code continues on next page

Listing 5 (continued)

```
        <width>1024</width>
        <!-- The window's initial height. Optional. -->
        <height>768</height>
        <!-- The window's initial x position. Optional. -->
        <x>200</x>
        <!-- The window's initial y position. Optional. -->
        <y>200</y>
        <!-- The window's minimum size, specified as a width/height pair, such
            as "400 200". Optional. -->
        <minSize>800 600</minSize>
        <!-- The window's initial maximum size, specified as a width/height
            pair, such as "1600 1200". Optional. -->
        <maxSize>1280 1024</maxSize>
    </initialWindow>
    <!-- The subpath of the standard default installation location to use.
        Optional. -->
    <installFolder>DP TimeClock</installFolder>
    <!-- The subpath of the Windows Start/Programs menu to use. Optional. -->
    <programMenuFolder>DPTools/Applications</programMenuFolder>
    <!-- The icon the system uses for the application. For at least one
        resolution, specify the path to a PNG file included in the AIR
        package. Optional. -->
    <icon>
    <image16x16>icons/smallIcon.png</image16x16>
    <image32x32>icons/mediumIcon.png</image32x32>
    <image48x48>icons/bigIcon.png</image48x48>
    <image128x128>icons/biggestIcon.png</image128x128>
    </icon>
    <!-- Whether the application handles the update when a user double-clicks
        an update version of the AIR file (true), or the default AIR
        application installer handles the update (false).
        Optional. Default false. -->
    <customUpdateUI>false</customUpdateUI>
    <!-- Whether the application can be launched when the user clicks a link in
        a web browser. Optional. Default false. -->
    <allowBrowserInvocation>true</allowBrowserInvocation>
```

Listing 5 (continued)

```
    <!-- Listing of file types for which the application can register.
        Optional. -->
    <fileTypes>
    <!-- Defines one file type. Optional. -->
    <fileType>
        <!-- The name that the system displays for the registered file type.
            Required. -->
        <name>dpTimeClock</name>
        <!-- The extension to register. Required. -->
        <extension>dpt</extension>
        <!-- The description of the file type. Optional. -->
        <description>A Report File to be used with the dpTimeClock
            application</description>
        <!-- The MIME type. Optional. -->
        <contentType>application/octet-stream</contentType>
            <icon>
                <image16x16>dpt16.png</image16x16>
                <image32x32>dpt32png</image32x32>
                <image48x48>dpt48png</image48x48>
                <image128x128>dpt128.png</image128x128>
            </icon>
        </fileType>
    </fileTypes>
</application>
```

Full descriptions of all these nodes are in Adobe's livedocs at:
http://livedocs.adobe.com/air/1/devappshtml/help.html?content=File_formats_1.html.

Testing Your Application

You can package AIR applications either using the command line tools, which are part of the Free SDK (http://www.adobe.com/products/air/tools/), or with integrated development environments, such as Flex Builder (http://www.adobe.com/go/flexbuilder) for Flex-based content, or Aptana (http://www.aptana.org) for HTML-based content.

Testing your application with the command line tools

Once you have your HTML or SWF-based content ready and assembled in your application.xml file, you can run your application using the AIR Debug Launcher (ADL) before packaging it into an AIR file. ADL is a tool provided as part of the AIR SDK and exists so that you can run AIR applications without having to package them as AIR files or install them first. This can help develop applications efficiently, as it removes the requirements of packaging and installing an application before testing it. This tool is very useful if you are not using a development environment like Flex Builder or Aptana to create your AIR applications.

To run ADL from a command line interface, use the following syntax:

```
adl <appXmlFileName>
```

Assuming you have your HelloWorld project in a c:\AIRProjects directory, your application xml (HelloWorld-app.xml) file in the root of the HelloWorld directory, and have the AIR SDK in c:\AIRSDK, the following command will launch your application.

```
cd c:\AIRProjects
c:\airSDK\bin\adl HelloWorld-app.xml
```

ADL will read the application XML file (indicated as HelloWorld-app.xml in the preceding example), and it will run the application specified in that file using the AIR runtime, without the need to install it first.

Figure 4: Testing the application with ADL

Testing your application from an IDE

If you are fortunate enough to have an IDE at your disposal, the process of building, testing, and debugging becomes much easier. To test your application directly from an Eclipse-based IDE (such as Aptana or Flex Builder), click the Run Button located in the top toolbar. This will launch your application, just as the ADL tool did, as seen in the following figure.

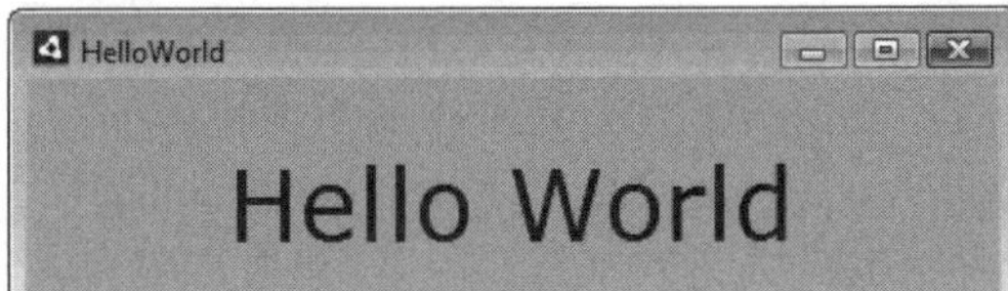

Figure 5: Hello World launched from Flex Builder

Debugging Your Application

Tools are available for debugging your AIR applications, regardless of whether you are testing via ADL or using an IDE. The tools in Flex Builder are by far the most robust for any Flex-based content, including a fully interactive debugger, a memory profiler, console window, and more. Chapter 2, "Working with the Time Tracker Application," explores debugging more fully, when you download a full application and have more application content to explore.

Packaging Your Application for Deployment

Once you are done developing your application and are ready to distribute it to users, you need to package it for distribution. You have options, whether you use command line tools or an IDE to package your application.

Every AIR application must, at a minimum, have an application descriptor file and a main SWF or HTML file. Any other installed application assets must be packaged in the AIR file as well. Additionally, all AIR installer files must be signed using a digital certificate. The AIR installer uses the signature to verify that your application file has not been altered since it was signed. You can choose to use a certificate from a certificate authority, like VeriSign or Thawte, or you can use a self-signed certificate. Certificates from an authority provide users some assurance of your identity as publisher, while a self-signed certificate provides fewer assurances to the user.

Using the AIR Developer Tool (ADT) to Package Your Application

The AIR Developer Tool (ADT) creates application package (AIR) files, which can be easily distributed to end users. It is part of the AIR SDK. In reality, ADT has been implemented as a Java JAR file. Therefore, you can invoke it from the command line, if you already have a Java JRE or JDK installed on your system. It will be easiest to use if you have the path to the Java bin folder available from your system path. Additionally, it eases the process if the path to the ADT.jar file is also set in the `CLASSPATH` variable.

You can use the ADT to both package and sign an AIR file in a single step, using the `--package` command.

```
Adt -package -storetype pkcs12 -keystore airBook.p12 HelloWorld.air
HelloWorld-app.xml
```

NOTE If you want to package and sign the file in two separate steps, you would first create an intermediate file using the `-prepare` command, and then sign with the `-sign` command.

This command asks ADT to create a HelloWorld.air package, based on the information in HelloWorld-app.xml. Additionally, it specifies pkcs12 as the Keystore format (which is native to most Java installations) and indicates the self-signed certificate is the airBook.p12 file.

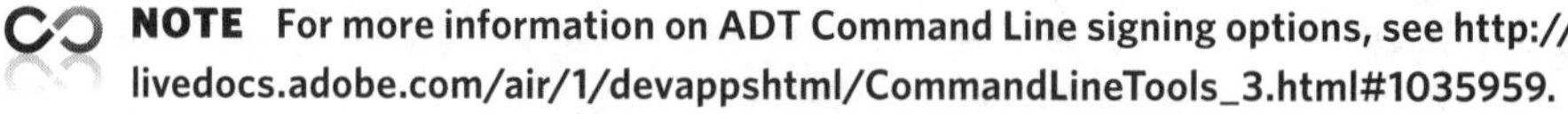

NOTE For more information on ADT Command Line signing options, see http://livedocs.adobe.com/air/1/devappshtml/CommandLineTools_3.html#1035959.

Using Flex Builder to Package Your Application

Flex Builder can also simplify the process of creating a deployable AIR file. To package your application, choose Project > Export Release Build from the top menu. The Export Release Build wizard will launch.

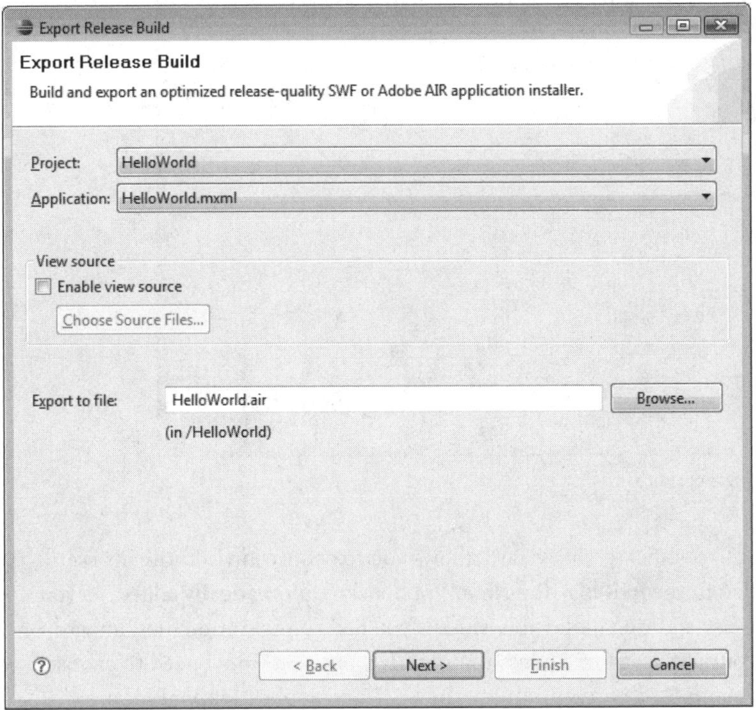

Figure 6: Packaging the AIR file from Flex Builder

After clicking the Next button, a wizard allows you to specify how you want to sign your installer. You can either choose to create a self-signed certificate, or browse to an existing one. If you choose an existing one, you must enter a password to use when creating the certificate.

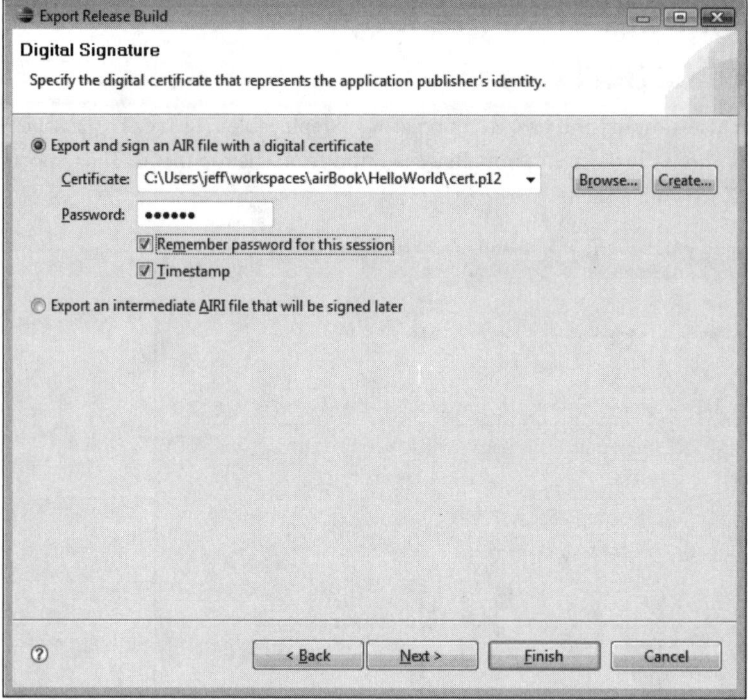

Figure 7: Choosing a certificate

After choosing the certificate, the wizard allows you to choose any additional assets you want included in the AIR file. The HelloWorld.swf is automatically added, so you only need to specify additional files you want. If you had configuration files, images, or any other files your application requires to properly work, you would need to choose them from this menu. At a bare minimum, the SWF and application.xml file are required.

With this bit of knowledge, you can now create, test, and package an AIR application. Double-clicking the resulting AIR file, created either through Flex Builder or ADT, will install the AIR file on the end user's machine.

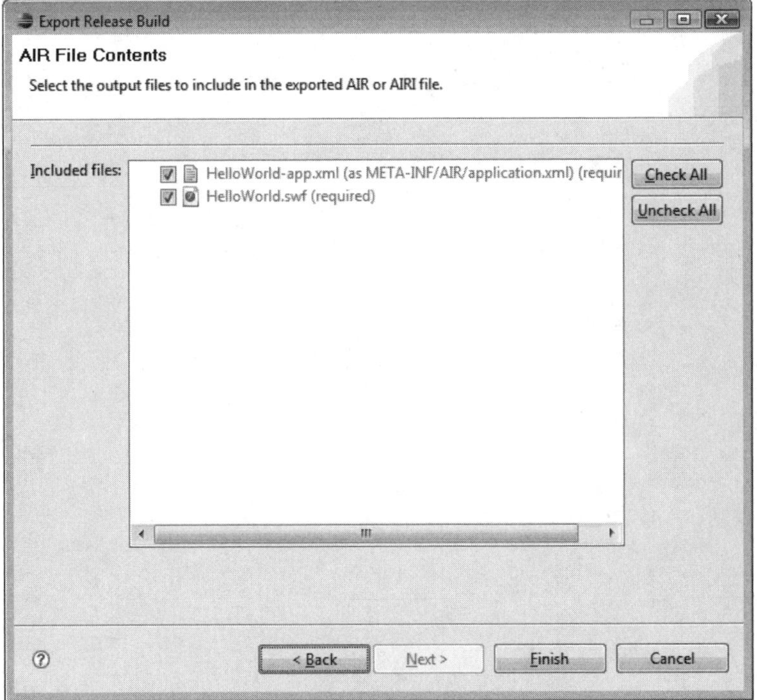

Figure 8: Including additional content in the AIR package

Next Steps

For the remainder of this book, we will be exploring an AIR-based application, dpTimeTracker, which is built primarily in a Flex-based SWF. The examples from this point forward will assume use of Flex Builder, instead of the command line tools. Keep in mind that it is entirely possible to do the same explorations without having Flex Builder, but it will require more work.

The next chapter discusses how to install the dpTimeTracker application, how to download the source code, and will start you on your explorations.

WORKING WITH THE TIME TRACKER APPLICATION

CHAPTER 2

Throughout this book, the capabilities of AIR are explored and demonstrated through an open-source time tracking application known as dpTimeTracker. This chapter instructs you how to download both the source code as well as the installer for the application, how to import the downloaded code into Flex Builder, and how to get started with your explorations of the content.

Getting Started with dpTimeTracker

This application lets a user track the time they spend working on projects for various clients, and allows for numerous ways to enter new clients and projects to be tracked. It can be used to export timesheets for use by third-party invoicing and billing applications.

The following figure shows the dpTimeTracker in action.

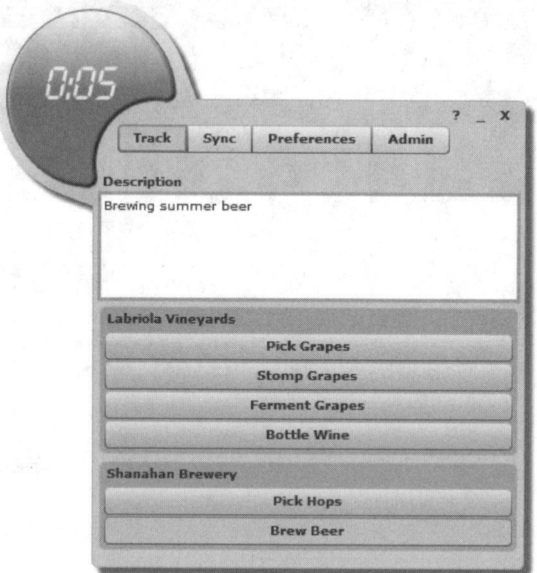

Figure 1: The dpTimeTracker application tracking hours spent on projects for two clients

Downloading the dpTimeTracker Code

This application and its full source are freely available on Google Code. To get the source code for the application, open http://dptimetracker.googlecode.com. On the home page for the project, you will see many links, including one to download the compiled AIR application, and one to download the source. Click the Download Source Code link, and save the file to your desktop (or any other convenient location). The downloaded file is a zip file format of an exported Flex Builder project. If you would like to download and install the application, but not the source code, click the Download Installer link, and step through the instructions that follow.

Importing the Project

Once you have Flex Builder installed and have downloaded the source code, just import the downloaded source into Flex Builder. To import the project, open Flex Builder, and choose File > Import > Flex Project. A screen displays prompting you to specify the archive file (zip file) or Project folder containing the project. Enter the path and file name of the source code zip file you downloaded, and then click Finish. When completed, the project should be fully imported and available to you in Flex Builder.

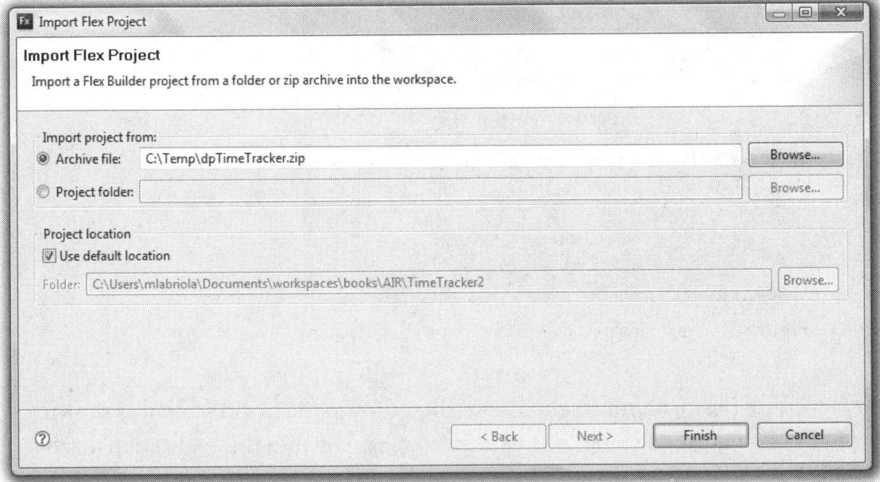

Figure 2: Importing the dpTimeTracker application into Flex Builder

Using the Application

Once you have imported the project, you can run it by clicking the Run Application button in the top toolbar. This will prompt you to log into the application. If this is your first time running it, you won't have a username and password stored, so you will need to create an account. To do this, enter your desired username and password, and click the "Create New User" button. This will transition the screen, adding a second section labeled "Server Login Information."

For now, you can leave the "Remote Password same as Local?" checkbox selected, and complete the process by clicking the Create New User button, as shown in Figure 3. In Chapter 11, "Communicating with Adobe BlazeDS," you will learn that you can build this application to synchronize with a server-based tool, such as Harvest Time Tracking. When integrating with one of the server products, the server login information is used to authenticate against the server. The top username and password will always be used to authenticate the user locally.

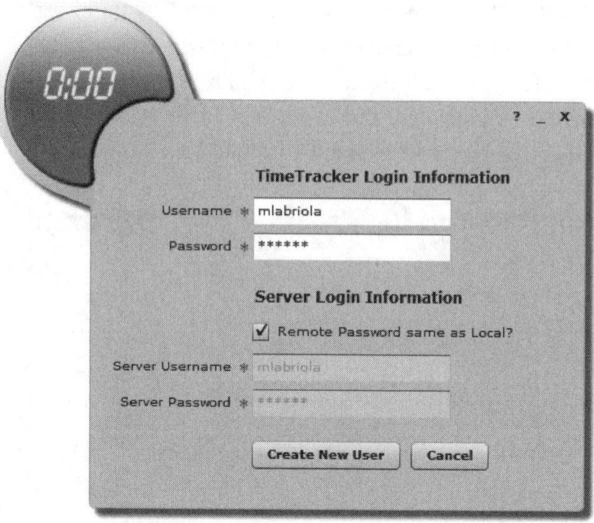

Figure 3: Creating a new user

After you create the login information, you will return to the Login screen, as shown in the following figure. Clicking the Login button logs you into the application for the first time.

Figure 4: Logging into the application

Once you have logged in, you'll see a one-line toolbar, which, at the first login, will just have the top menu bar.

Figure 5: The Main Application toolbar

Before you can start tracking your time, you need to add clients and projects. Click the Admin link in the toolbar, which switches to a view that allows you to create, modify, or delete Clients, Projects, and Categories.

Figure 6: The Administrative screen

With the Clients tab selected, click the Add button. A form to enter a client name and description will appear. Enter a name and description for the client, and then click the Save button.

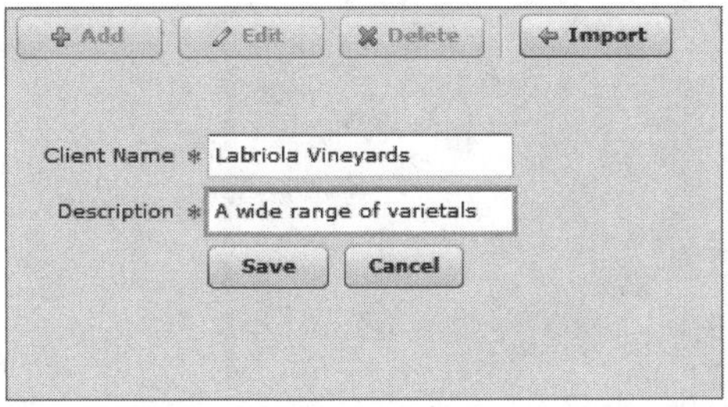

Figure 7: Adding a client

After saving, the entry displays in the Client datagrid. You can change or delete the information by selecting the client row in the datagrid and clicking the Edit or Delete button.

Once you have at least one client, click the Projects tab to start entering project information. In the dpTimeTracker application, time entries are always recorded against a project, rather than a client, allowing you to independently track the time spent on various projects for each client. On the Projects tab, click the Add button to create a new project. The project editing form is a bit more complex than the client editing form, as is shown in Figure 8. It has a combo box to allow selection of the client, and required fields for the name and description of the project. You can use the checkbox to determine if hours entered against this project are billable or not by default. (You can always change the ability to bill individual entries later.) For billable hours, there is also a field to select the default hourly rate for the project. This too can be changed later if needed. Lastly, there is an input to optionally enter a purchase order for the project, if necessary.

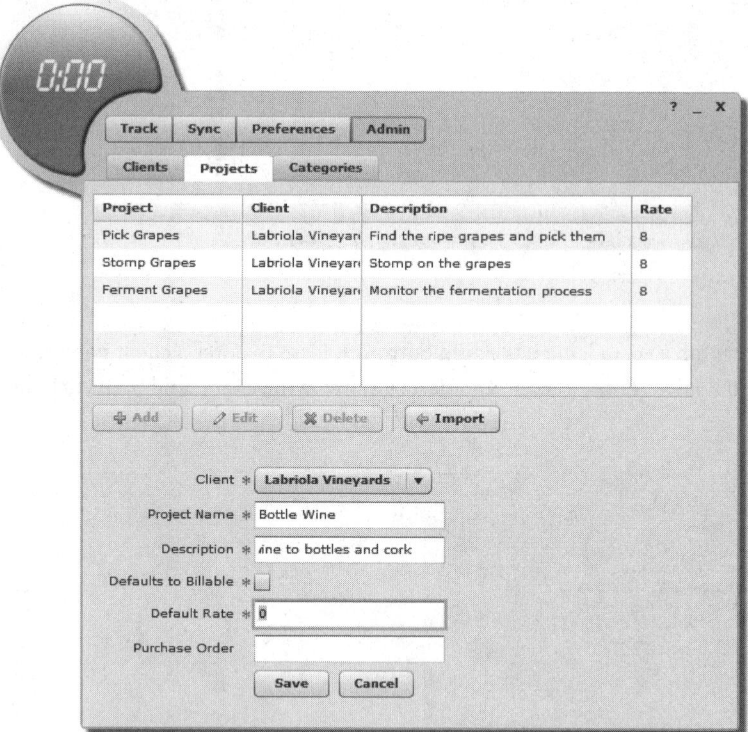

Figure 8: Adding projects

Once you have at least one client and one project entered, you can use the dpTimeTracker to track your time spent on the projects. Click Track in the top menu. You will see a dark gray box with each client listed. When you begin working on a project, start tracking time by clicking the button for the project. When you take a break or finish, click the same button again to stop the counter. If you click another project, time tracking will stop on the first and start on the second.

Figure 9: Tracking time

The application has a few other subtleties. Even though the window doesn't look like a native operating system window, it still can be moved around the screen by clicking the top-left area near the counter and dragging. It also can be minimized to the taskbar by clicking the minimize button in the top-right corner. It also can be closed, just like any other application, by clicking the X in the top-right corner.

Getting Started with the Flex Builder Debugger

One of the benefits of Flex Builder as an IDE for AIR is the ability to run the application in a debugger. With the dpTimeTracker project open, click the Debug button instead of the Play button.

Breakpoints

Usually, developers launch in Debug mode instead of running the application if they have a runtime error or some other unexpected behaviors. If you are running in Debug mode, and the application encounters a runtime error, focus switches over to Flex Builder. You will be able to use the Debug and Variables views to inspect the state of your application at the time of the error. To simulate this, open TimeTracker2.mxml from the src folder of the project, and add `throw new Error("stop!");` to the top of the `setupApplication()` method so that it reads:

```
protected function setupApplication():void {
    throw new Error("stop!");
    var sequence:CommandSequencer = new CommandSequencer();
    sequence.add( new CreateDatabase() );
    sequence.add( new LoadDatabaseData() );
    sequence.execute();
  }
```

Save and run the application in Debug mode, and you will be able to see how Flex Builder is able to intercept any runtime errors.

TIP Running in debug mode requires a debug version of Flash Player. This will be installed by default when you install Flex Builder. If you do not have the debug player installed, please see "About running and debugging applications" in the Flex Builder Help Files.

You can get to the same level of introspecting your application without an error through the use of breakpoints. In Flex Builder, you can add a breakpoint by double-clicking to the left of a line number, or by right-clicking a line number and choosing Toggle Breakpoint, as seen in the following figure. When a breakpoint is added, it will show as a small blue dot to the left of the line number.

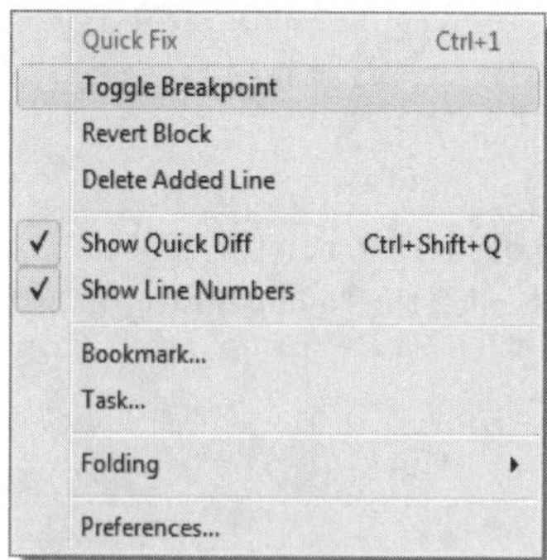

Figure 10: Adding a breakpoint

When running in Debug mode, if the application encounters a line with a breakpoint, it will hand control back to Flex Builder, just as it did when it encountered a runtime error.

Trace Statements

Another useful feature of the debugger is the ability to log messages to a console when running in Debug mode. In Flex-based AIR development, this is done through the use of trace statements. Whenever AIR encounters a `trace` statement while running an application in Debug mode, whatever is passed to the `trace` statement will be output in the Flex Builder Console view. For example:

```
trace("hi there");
```

will output

```
hi there
```

to the Console view. This is also useful for evaluating expressions. For example, open the `AuthenticateCommand` class in the `modules.authentication.commands` package. Add the line `trace("username:"+username +"\npassword:"+password)` to the constructor, as seen in the following text. When you save and run the application in Debug mode, you will see the username and password you typed reflected in the Console view when you log in.

```
public function AuthenticateCommand( username:String, password:String )
{
    trace("username:"+username +"\npassword:"+password);
    super();
    username = username;
    password = password;
}
```

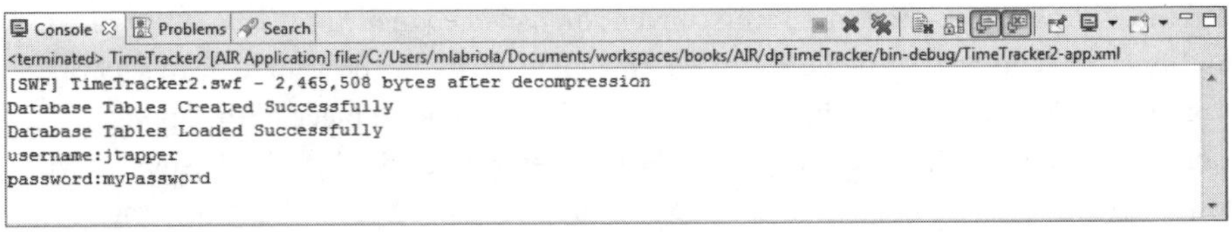

```
Console ☒ | Problems | Search
<terminated> TimeTracker2 [AIR Application] file:/C:/Users/mlabriola/Documents/workspaces/books/AIR/dpTimeTracker/bin-debug/TimeTracker2-app.xml
[SWF] TimeTracker2.swf - 2,465,508 bytes after decompression
Database Tables Created Successfully
Database Tables Loaded Successfully
username:jtapper
password:myPassword
```

Figure 11: Seeing `trace` statements output in the console

Using the combination of breakpoints and trace statements offers a tremendous amount of power to application developers to truly understand what is happening in their applications.

For more about Flex Builder debugger, see see Lesson 25, "Debugging Flex Applications," of *Adobe Flex 3, Training from the Source* by Adobe Press.

Understanding the Application Framework

The dpTimeTracker application was built using an architecture based on a few key design patterns. Chief among these is the Command pattern. The Command pattern exists to allow an application to request functionality that it does not know how to do on its own. For example, the LoginView component can request that a user be authenticated, without having to know how to perform the authentication itself. Each "action" is encapsulated into a Command. Each command is a class, which implements a simple interface, requiring that it (the Command) has a method named `execute`, which takes no arguments and returns nothing. The contents of the `execute` method contain the logic for how a particular command does its task. The beauty of this design is that the contents of a Command (such as the AuthenticateCommand mentioned earlier in this chapter) can completely change, but so long as the new command implements the same interface, the application will not have to change how it works. So, you can replace AuthenticateCommand with AuthenticateAgainstLDAPCommand, which has a completely different authentication mechanism, but the parts of the application using it (such as LoginView.mxml) can just call this new class instead, and keep working.

The dpTimeTracker architecture makes use of commands for interacting with any external data, regardless whether it's stored on a remote server, in the user's file system, in an SQLite database, or anywhere else. Later chapters will explore in more detail these different types of commands (including the `ServiceFactory` that the commands use to find remote data).

This application uses another coding convention called *code behind*. This is less of an architectural choice than a coding standard, which exists to allow for a clean separation of the MXML layout code from the ActionScript for each piece of the application. If you look at LoginView.mxml (in the `modules.authentication` package), you will notice that it looks like a pretty standard MXML component. One thing you might notice is that the root node (which represents the base class of an MXML component) isn't a standard Flex control or container (such as `mx:VBox` or `mx:Form`); instead it's subclassing `Login`. The other thing to notice is that there is no `mx:Script` block in LoginView.mxml, only MXML tags. All the scripting for this component is in the superclass, Login.as, which is an ActionScript class. This is the essence of code behind. All the logic for the component exists in an ActionScript class, and the view extends that class and provides the layout. You might also notice that the `Login` class itself extends the `Form` class, so the `LoginView` component itself acts as if it were using a `Form` as its root node, but has the added benefit of being able to encapsulate its logic in a superclass.

Another design pattern used in the application is the Singleton pattern. The Singleton pattern exists to ensure that only one instance of a particular class is ever instantiated, and provides a global point of access to that instance. In complex multiuser systems, this can be problematic, as you need a means to replicate that single instance across a cluster of servers, but, in RIA development, you can know definitively that your client-side code will only have a single user ever running it, removing many of the pitfalls inherent to Singletons on the server. dpTimeTracker uses Singletons to allow any place in the application to easily get a handle on a particular object that might be needed throughout the application. To do this, it exposes a single, public, static method, called `getInstance()`. This method will return the only instance of the object. If the object hasn't been instantiated yet, when `getInstance` is called, it will first instantiate it, and then return it. In dpTimeTracker, the main usage of a Singleton is in the `AppModel` class (located in the `model` package). `AppModel` is a class that holds all the client-side data. Data elements, such as the array of clients, projects, time entries, and so on, are all stored in the `AppModel`. This provides a single point of access for all of the commonly used data in the application. So, any place you see something like `protected var appModel:AppModel = AppModel.getInstance()`, you know that the class is providing access to the central client data storage area. Take a look at the directory structure of the application. You'll notice the src folder has subdirectories for assets, commands, components, events, helpers, model, modules, services, and net. The application is structured this way to ease development and maintenance, so you can always know that a certain type of class will exist in a specific location in this structure. The following table lists the subdirectories and an explanation of the use of the files.

Directory	Usage
assets	Any files related to the design of the application. You'll find two primary types of assets: graphical files (mostly .png) and CSS style sheets.
commands	Commands encapsulate each action the application can perform. A subdirectory of commands called sql exists to house all the commands specifically related to database actions.
components	Small, reusable pieces of MXML or ActionScript built exclusively for this project.
events	Event subclasses dispatched by the application.
helpers	Functions shared by several classes throughout the system.
model	Repositories for application-level data.

continues on next page

Directory	Usage
modules	Each of the different "screens" in the application is represented as subdirectories of the modules package. Each of these may contain more subdirectories, as the functionality becomes more and more granular. For example, the administration package contains subdirectories for administrating categories, clients, and projects.
net	When including previously written components in an application, they must be placed in a directory that matches the package name of the component. The dpTimeTracker application uses previously written components from Digital Primates and others.
services	This directory contains all the service factories for accessing remote data. These will be explored in detail in Chapter 10, "Understanding the Need for Remote Data."

Next Steps

With a solid understanding of the structure and packages used in the application, you are ready to begin your explorations of AIR.

INTERACTING WITH THE CLIPBOARD

CHAPTER 3

AIR is a very compelling technology, as it allows you to leverage the web application development skills you already possess to build desktop applications. One of the major benefits of desktop applications over a browser-based application is the ability to interact with the local operating system (OS). The ability to leverage the ease of development and compelling capabilities of a Rich Internet Application, combined with the power of desktop integration, allows tremendous opportunities for creating next-generation applications. In this chapter, you will learn how to reap the benefits of AIR and use the clipboard to interact with the OS.

Integrating with the Operating System

There are many integration points between an AIR application and the OS. Each of these points allows more possibilities for the applications you can develop today. The AIR APIs provide a consistent mechanism to interact with the OS, regardless of the host OS.

AIR allows system-level functionality such as:

- Reading and writing to the file system
- Complete interaction with the OS's clipboard
- Native drag-and-drop capabilities
- Integration with standard desktop elements, such as the Mac OS Dock and the Windows System Tray
- And much more

In this chapter, you will explore the OS's integration with AIR through the use of the Clipboard API.

Interacting with the Clipboard

Copying and pasting data to the system's clipboard is a very common interaction for computer users today. Users at all points on the technical spectrum routinely use copy-and-paste actions, whether it is a user copying text into Microsoft Word, copying an HTML block into an email, copying an image into Microsoft PowerPoint, or simply copying files from one directory to another. Use of the clipboard to transfer various types of data is an everyday action.

While the web browser allows end users to copy elements from web pages, the interaction is completely handled by the browser; you as a developer have no control over how data is added to or read from the clipboard. AIR provides a robust API, which allows developers to completely control the use of the clipboard in their applications.

Exploring the Clipboard Class

In AIR, any interaction with the system's clipboard is handled by the `Clipboard` class. To get a reference to the clipboard of the user's OS, you use the static `generalClipboard` property of the Clipboard class. Reading from the clipboard is done via the getData() method, as shown in this simple example.

```
var clip:Clipboard = Clipboard.generalClipboard;
var txt:String = clip.getData(ClipboardFormats.TEXT_FORMAT).toString();
```

Here, a reference to the clipboard is stored in the variable clip, and the text currently stored in the clipboard is retrieved via the getData() method. Notice that getData() takes a clipboard format as an argument. Clipboard formats allow for developers to store a single piece of information in various ways, so that different applications in which it might be used can handle it independently. The next section, "Understanding Clipboard Data Formats," will cover clipboard formats in more detail.

To write to the system's clipboard, you use the setData() method. The example below shows an application in which the user can enter text, and that text can be added to the clipboard.

```
<?xml version="1.0" encoding="utf-8"?>
<mx:WindowedApplication xmlns:mx="http://www.adobe.com/2006/mxml">
    <mx:Script>
    <![CDATA[
        private function doCopyToClipboard( copyText:String ) : void{
            Clipboard.generalClipboard.clear();
            Clipboard.generalClipboard.setData(
            ➥ClipboardFormats.TEXT_FORMAT, copyText );
        }
    ]]>
    </mx:Script>

    <mx:HBox>
        <mx:Label text="Enter text to be copied to the clipboard " />
        <mx:TextInput id="txtCopy" text="Simple String" />
            <mx:Button id="btnCopy"
                label="Copy"
                click="doCopyToClipboard(txtCopy.text)" />
    </mx:HBox>
</mx:WindowedApplication>
```

As you can see, the data is set in the clipboard via the setData() method. This method requires two arguments: the first is the format for the data, and the second is the data itself. In this example, the format ClipboardFormats.TEXT_FORMAT is passed to indicate the clipboard data will be stored as plain text. The clipboard data is the string the user entered.

TIP The clipboard will only store a single element for each format at any given time. As a best practice, you should usually clear the clipboard of any data when you set data in the clipboard to avoid the confusion that might ensue if there is still data lingering in an unrelated data format.

Understanding Clipboard Data Formats

There are times when you might want to add data to the clipboard in several different formats. Imagine an application that allows users to select and copy an image. You may want to set data in several different formats, so depending on where the user chooses to paste, a different piece of data (which can be specifically used by the target) is used. If the user chooses to paste into a graphics program (such as Photoshop), the image data itself can be pasted; however, if they instead choose to paste into a program that can render HTML (such as Microsoft Word), the rich text of the HTML can be rendered, which would in turn download the image. A text format containing metadata about the picture (artist, copyright, dateCreate, title, and so on) could be used if the user were to paste into a text editor such as Notepad.

```
<?xml version="1.0" encoding="utf-8"?>
<mx:WindowedApplication xmlns:mx="http://www.adobe.com/2006/mxml">
    <mx:Script>
        <![CDATA[
            [Bindable]
            private var imageURL:String =
            ➥ "http://farm4.static.flickr.com/3039/2516892122_d244e9cf4d.jpg?v=0";
            private function copyImage():void{
                var clip:Clipboard = Clipboard.generalClipboard;
                var html:String = "<img src='"+imageURL+"'/>"
                var bmpData:BitmapData = Bitmap(img.content).bitmapData;
                var text:String = "Yellow Flowers";
                clip.clear();
                clip.setData(ClipboardFormats.BITMAP_FORMAT, bmpData);
                clip.setData(ClipboardFormats.HTML_FORMAT,html);
                clip.setData(ClipboardFormats.TEXT_FORMAT,text);
```

```
            }
        ]]>
    </mx:Script>
    <mx:Image id="img"
        source="{imageURL}" />
    <mx:Button click="copyImage()" label="Copy Image"/>
</mx:WindowedApplication>
```

If you run this application and click the Copy Image button, you can successfully paste into graphics, HTML, or text applications, and have something useable by each.

Each type of data that can be added to the clipboard is represented by the various clipboard data formats. There are constants in the `ClipboardFormats` class, which specify the five built-in formats. These formats are:

- BITMAP_FORMAT—Specifies that image data is stored on the clipboard.
- FILE_LIST_FORMAT—Specifies that one or more files are stored on the clipboard. For more information on the `File` class, see Chapter 6, "Interacting with the File System."
- URL_FORMAT—Specifies that one or more files are stored on the clipboard by their URLs. This data is passed as ActionScript strings, instead of as instances of the `File` class. The delimiters between the URLs (if there are more than one) is a line break and line feed character (\r\n).
- TEXT_FORMAT—Specifies that plain, unformatted text is stored on the clipboard.
- HTML_FORMAT—Specifies that HTML-formatted text is stored on the clipboard.

Notice that FILE_LIST_FORMAT and URL_FORMAT are two separate mechanisms for passing a list of files, much like HTML_FORMAT and TEXT_FORMAT are both formats for passing textual information. In both cases, the different formats each have their own unique uses when interfacing with outside applications. For example, if you were to write the string `<b>Hello There</b>` to the clipboard in text format and paste it into Word, you would see the text, including the tags; however, if you took the same string and wrote it to the clipboard in HTML format, it would paste as boldfaced text.

Creating Custom Formats

You are not limited to the five formats specified. You can specify your own custom format, which has its own unique meaning to your application. If you were to use the clipboard to copy data from one datagrid in your application to another, you might choose to write that data using a custom format, so that you knew when it was pasted that it was intended to be datagrid data. Be careful to note that custom formats are only readable from within AIR applications and will not be accessible to other applications.

```
<?xml version="1.0" encoding="utf-8"?>
<mx:WindowedApplication xmlns:mx="http://www.adobe.com/2006/mxml"
    layout="horizontal">
    <mx:Script>
    <![CDATA[
        private const DATA_PROVIDER_FORMAT:String = "dataProviderFormat";
        private function doShowClipboardContent() : void{
            listPaste.dataProvider = doPaste();
        }

        private function doCopyToClipboard(copyCustomDataType:Object):void{
            var clip:Clipboard = Clipboard.generalClipboard;
            clip.clear();
            clip.setData(DATA_PROVIDER_FORMAT, copyCustomDataType, true );
        }

        private function doPaste() : Object {
            var clip:Clipboard = Clipboard.generalClipboard;
            if( clip.hasFormat(DATA_PROVIDER_FORMAT ) ){
                return clip.getData( DATA_PROVIDER_FORMAT,
                ➥ ClipboardTransferMode.CLONE_ONLY);
            } else {
                return null;
            }
        }
        ]]>
    </mx:Script>
    <mx:VBox>

        <mx:List id="listCopy" width="100">
```

```
            <mx:dataProvider>
                <mx:String>AK</mx:String>
                <mx:String>AL</mx:String>
                <mx:String>AR</mx:String>
           </mx:dataProvider>
      </mx:List>
      <mx:Button id="btnCopy"
          label="Copy dataprovider to clipboard"
          click="doCopyToClipboard( listCopy.dataProvider )" />
    </mx:VBox>
    <mx:VBox>
        <mx:List id="listPaste"  width="100"/>
            <mx:Button id="btnPaste"
                label="Paste from clipboard"
                click="doShowClipboardContent()" />
    </mx:VBox>
</mx:WindowedApplication>
```

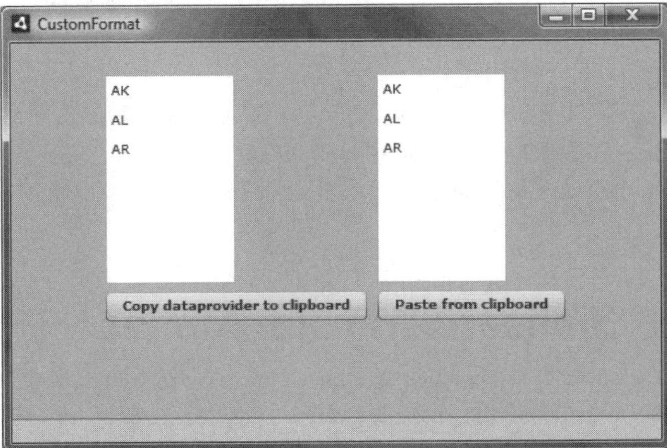

Figure 1: A custom format has been used to copy the dataProvider from one List to the other

To use a custom format, just pass any arbitrary string as the format, instead of using one of the constants from the `ClipboardDataFormat` class. This example uses the string "dataProviderFormat" (a constant named DATA_PROVIDER_FORMAT has been created to avoid misspellings). There is a restriction in that your custom format cannot begin with the string "air:" or "flash:" Adobe suggests using a string that begins with your application `id` as a custom format, but in reality, as long as your custom format doesn't begin with either flash: or air:, you are free to use any string. If you were to create a second AIR application that also looked for a format named `dataProviderFormat`, you could access the same information there as well.

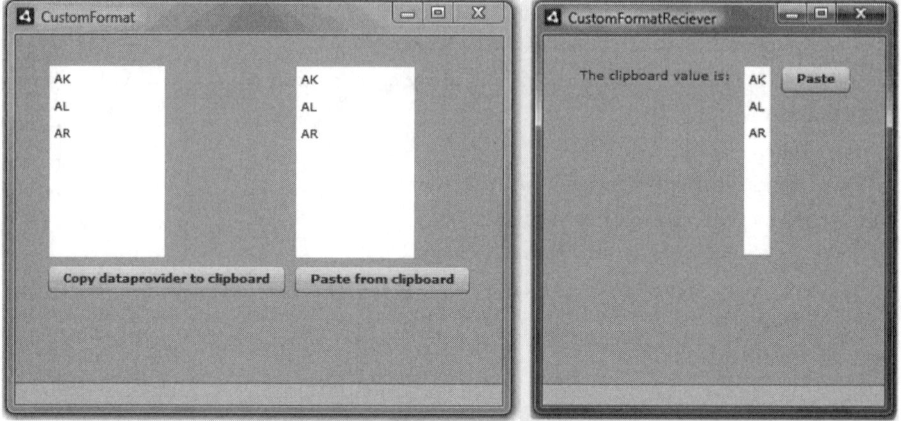

Figure 2: The data in the custom format is pasted into a separate AIR application

If you run the first application, click the "Copy dataprovider to clipboard" button, launch the second application, and click the "Paste from clipboard" button, you can see how a custom format can help to copy and paste data between two separate AIR applications.

Understanding Clipboard Transfer Modes

When data is pasted from the clipboard, it can be pasted by value or by reference. You have probably run across the concepts of "pass by value versus pass by reference" in your previous programming experience, but in case you haven't, it basically describes the two different ways that an object can be assigned to another place. In a "pass by value" situation, an independent copy of the item is made; any change to one of the copies has no impact whatsoever on the other. In a "pass by reference" situation, a new reference is made back to the original object, so that the same object is being referenced from more than one location. If there are any changes to the original, the changes are also made to the copy (since they are not independent, but simply pointers back to the same place). Likewise, when data is pasted from the clipboard, you have some control over whether the pasted data is a new copy or a reference to the original. This is determined by the ClipboardTranserMode. AIR has pre-defined constants that represent the built-in transfer modes that determine whether objects are references or copies.

- ClipboardTransferModes.ORIGINAL_ONLY—Will only paste a reference. If the system is unable to paste a reference, it will paste a null value in its place.
- ClipboardTransferModes.ORIGINAL_PREFERRED—Will attempt to paste a reference. If the system is unable to create a reference, it will paste a copy in its place.
- ClipboardTransferModes.CLONE_ONLY—Will only paste a copy (passing by value). If the system is unable to paste a copy, it will paste a null value in its place.
- ClipboardTransferModes.CLONE_PREFERRED—Will attempt to paste a copy. If the system is unable to create a copy, it will paste a reference in its place.

Understanding Data Serialization

For the AIR runtime to be capable of pasting a copy instead of a reference to an object, the data must be *serializable.* Serialization simply means that the class is capable of being copied. In practice, serialization is the process of converting the properties of a class into a `ByteArray`. When an object is pasted by value, the `ByteArray` containing all the properties of the class are copied into a new instance of the class. The process of pasting the copy in this way is referred to as *deserialization.*

Many of the native Flash and Flex classes are inherently serializable, including all of the primitive data types (such as int, String, Array, and so on) as well as any class that implements the `IExternalizable` interface.

In actuality, some classes that are neither primitives nor implementers of `IExternalizable` can also be serialized. In these cases, copies can only be made of the public variables of the class, as any internal, protected, or private members will be ignored.

This may seem a bit frightening to consider. Remember that the only times you'll need to explicitly implement the `IExternalizable` interface yourself is when you're copying instances of your own custom classes to the clipboard and you need the pasted versions to have more than the public properties. For routine operations such as copying an ArrayCollection of strings from the dataProvider of a DataGrid, there is no need to implement this interface.

The IExternalizable interface enforces that implementing classes have two methods: readExternal() and writeExternal(). Here is a basic skeleton of a simple serializable class.

```
package model.vo{
    import flash.utils.IExternalizable;
    import flash.utils.IDataInput;
    import flash.utils.IDataOutput;

    [Bindable]
    public class SerializablePerson implements IExternalizable {
        public var firstName:String;
        public var empID:uint;

        public function SerializablePerson (){
        }

        public function writeExternal(output:IDataOutput):void{
        }

        public function readExternal(input:IDataInput):void{
        }

    }
}
```

Notice that the writeExternal() method accepts a parameter called output in this example, which is an object that implements IDataOutput. This parameter is actually performing the process of serialization. The output parameter actually writes the data to the ByteArray with the specific data type needed. This example shows two different types of data—a string and an unsigned integer.

```
public function writeExternal(output:IDataOutput):void{
    output.writeUTF( this.firstName );
    output.writeUnsignedInt( this.empID );
}
```

When this object needs to be serialized, the AIR framework implicitly calls writeExternal(), and passes in a ByteArray to which the data will be written. The ByteArray class is an implementer of IDataOutput. When the data is to be deserialized, the readExternal() method of the class is implicitly invoked, and the fully populated ByteArray is passed in.

```
public function readExternal(input:IDataInput):void{
    this.firstName= input.readUTF();
    this.empID = input.readUnsignedInt();
}
```

It is important to note that the order of serialization must exactly match the order of deserialization. Since the data is stored in a ByteArray, the first element added to the array must be the first element read from the array. So, in the previous example, the process would fail if the order in which elements were set in readExternal() did not match the order in which they were written in writeExternal().

One more step must be taken to control the serialization process of a class to register an alias for the class, using the flash.net.registerClassAlias method. This step allows for the class information to be written into the ByteArray with the data. If this step is omitted, the deserialized copy of the data will be a generic instance of the Object class, instead of the specific class that you were copying. Frequently, the registerClassAlias method is called from the constructor. Below, you can see a full example of a class capable of being serialized.

```
package model.vo{
    import flash.utils.IExternalizable;
    import flash.utils.IDataInput;
    import flash.utils.IDataOutput;
    import flash.net.registerClassAlias;

    [Bindable]
    public class SerializablePerson implements IExternalizable {
        public var firstName:String;
        public var empID:uint;

        public function SerializablePerson (){
            registerClassAlias("model.vo.SerializablePerson",SerializablePerson);
        }

        public function writeExternal(output:IDataOutput):void{
            output.writeUTF( this.firstName );
            output.writeUnsignedInt( this.empID);
```

```
        }

        public function readExternal(input:IDataInput):void{
            this.firstName= input.readUTF();
            this.empID = input.readUnsignedInt();
        }

    }
}
```

Deferred Rendering

Another concept available in AIR applications is that of *deferred rendering.* Deferred rendering allows developers to pass a reference to a method to the clipboard instead of actually passing data. When deferred rendering is used, the data is not actually added to the clipboard until the user requests a paste operation. This can be extremely useful when dealing with large sets of data, or data that could be overly taxing on the user's processor in order to copy the information to the clipboard. To accomplish deferred rendering, the `setDataHandler()` method is used instead of `setData()`. The method is passed instead of the actual data; the method is not executed until the user attempts a paste operation. The single drawback to using deferred rendering is that the data will no longer be available after the user closes the AIR application. Because you have control over the application and can react to an event when the application is closed, you can mitigate this disadvantage, if needed. To do this, you can listen for the `flash.events.Event.Exiting` event, and ask the user if they want the data they copied earlier (which wasn't truly copied because it was using deferred rendering) available outside the AIR application. If they do, the data can be copied to the clipboard using the `setData()` method, so it will continue to be available after the AIR application has shut down.

Exploring the dpTimeTracker Use of the Clipboard

To begin tracking time for a project, the TimeTracker needs to know about the clients and projects with which you will be working. The dpTimeTracker application allows you to manually enter this content (as shown in Chapter 2, "Working with the Time Tracker Application"), but this is a time-consuming process. If this data already exists in another application, it would be much more convenient to copy and paste this data in. Likewise, when you need to create an Excel file based on your list of clients, you can simply navigate to the Client tab of the Admin section in dpTimeTracker, select the rows of data you need to copy, and use the Windows standard Ctrl+C to copy that data to the clipboard.

If you haven't done so already, enter a few clients into the TimeTracker (instructions for this are available in the section "Using the Application" in Chapter 2). Once you are logged in and have client data available, browse to the client section of the Admin area. Select the first row of data in the grid, press the Shift key, and then select the last row, selecting all the rows.

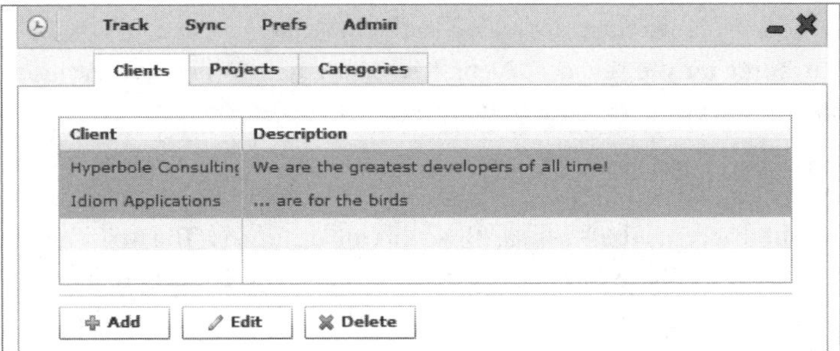

Figure 3: Selecting all the rows of the datagrid

Press Ctrl+C (or Cmd+C on a Mac). This will copy the data associated with that selection to the clipboard. Minimize the application, click your desktop, and paste. You should see a new file appear on the desktop.

Figure 4: The Microsoft Excel file is created when the data is pasted to the desktop

If you have Microsoft Excel installed on your system, open the file, and you will see that all of the data you selected is now available inside the Excel spreadsheet.

	A	B	C	D	E
1	Idiom Applications	... are for the birds			
2	Hyperbole Consulting	We are the greatest developers of all time!			
3					
4					

Figure 5: The contents of the Excel file created by the paste operation

To see how this works, open the ClientAdministrationView.mxml file from the modules/administration/views/client directory. On line 11 of this file, notice that an instance of the `ListToExcelClipboardDragDropHandler` class is instantiated, and its `list` property is bound to `list`, the instance name of the datagrid defined on line 16.

```
<dragDrop:ListToExcelClipboardDragDropHandler list="{list}"/>
```

The `ListToExcelClipboardDragDropHandler` class is based on the `DragExcel` class (written by Christophe Coenraetes) and is where all the magic happens. This class allows you to copy and paste data from a listbase control (which includes DataGrid, Tree, and List, among others) into an Excel spreadsheet. Open that class file from the net/digitalprimates/dragDrop directory to explore how it works.

In the `set list()` method, event listeners are added to the list that is passed in. One of these is specifically listening for the `KeyboardEvent.KEY_DOWN` event. When that event is heard, it is handled by the `keyListener()` method.

```
_list.addEventListener(KeyboardEvent.KEY_DOWN, keyListener);
```

The `keyListener()` method accepts the KeyboardEvent as an argument. The first line inside this method checks to see if the Control key (or Command key) is pressed. If either key is pressed, it uses a switch statement to determine if either the C or V keys are also pressed. If Ctrl+C (or Cmd+C on a Mac) are both pressed, the `copyData()` method is fired. If Ctrl+V (or Cmd+V on a Mac) are both pressed, the `pasteData()` method is called instead.

```
private function keyListener(event:KeyboardEvent):void{
    if(event.ctrlKey || event.commandKey){
        event.preventDefault();
        switch(String.fromCharCode(event.charCode)){
            case "c":
                copyData();
                break;
             case "v":
                pasteData();
                break;
        }
    }
}
```

TIP In Chapter 7, "Customizing the Look and Feel of an Application," you will learn a strategy using menus that will greatly simplify the process of standardizing keyboard shortcuts, such as Copy, Paste, and so on.

The copyData() method clears the clipboard and then sets the data in both HTML and file list formats, using the setDataHandler() method.

```
private function copyData():void {
    Clipboard.generalClipboard.clear();
    Clipboard.generalClipboard.setDataHandler( ClipboardFormats.HTML_FORMAT,
    ➥ dgToHTML );
    Clipboard.generalClipboard.setDataHandler(
    ➥ ClipboardFormats.FILE_LIST_FORMAT, createXLS );
}
```

You should remember that the setDataHandler() method allows for deferred rendering. For the deferred rendering of the HTML format, the dgToHTML() method is used. For deferred rendering of the file list format, the createXLS() method is used. If you examine the dgToHTML() method, you can see that the datagrid's dataProvider is looped over, and a new row is added to an HTML table for each row of data in the dataProvider.

```
private function dgToHTML():String{
    var rows:Array = _list.selectedItems;
    if (!rows || rows.length == 0) {
        return "";
    }
    var html:String = "<table>";
    for (var j:int = 0; j<rows.length; j++){
        var row:Object = rows[j];
        html += "<tr>";
        for (var k:int = 0; k<_list.columnCount; k++){
            var data:Object = DataGridColumn( DataGrid( _list ).columns[k]).
            ➥ itemToLabel( row );
            if (data) {
                html += "<td>" + data + "</td>";
            }
        }
        html += "</tr>";
    }
    html += "</table>";
    return html;
}
```

If you were to copy from that datagrid and paste into an already open Excel file, the HTML format would be used, as Excel natively renders an HTML table as rows and columns in the spreadsheet.

For the creation of an Excel spreadsheet, the createXLS() method is used. Most of the contents of this method handles writing the file to the user's disk, and will be explored in depth in Chapter 6. The important thing to note here is the creation of an Excel file with the use of the dgToExcel() method.

```
var excelFile:ExcelFile = dgToExcel();
```

The dgToExcel() method loops over the datagrid's dataProvider and uses the methods of the as3XLS open source project (available from http://code.google.com/p/as3xls/) to create an actual Microsoft Excel binary file.

```
private function dgToExcel():ExcelFile{
    var xls:ExcelFile = new ExcelFile();
    var rows:Array = _list.selectedItems;
    if (!rows || rows.length == 0){
        return xls;
    }
    /* Set up the Excel sheet and size it to the same number of
        rows and columns as our datagrid*/
    var sheet:Sheet = new Sheet();
    sheet.resize(rows.length, _list.columnCount );
    // Loop over the DataGrid's dataProvider and set each cell
    for(var i:uint = 0; i < sheet.rows; i++) {
        var row:Object = rows[i];
        for(var j:uint = 0; j < sheet.cols; j++) {
            var cellData:Object = DataGridColumn( DataGrid(_list).columns[j] )
            ➥ .itemToLabel( row );
            sheet.setCell(i, j, cellData );
        }
    }
    // Add the sheet to the excel file
    xls.sheets.addItem( sheet );
    return xls;
}
```

Next Steps

This chapter explained how AIR can integrate with the OS and introduced how to interface with the system clipboard to transfer rich information. Now that you are familiar with the clipboard classes, the next chapter will expand on these ideas and show how you can use the same classes to facilitate drag-and-drop operations between the user's OS and an AIR application.

IMPLEMENTING DRAG AND DROP BETWEEN THE OS AND AIR

CHAPTER 4

The previous chapter explored the rich integration that AIR has with the Operating System (OS) clipboard. In this chapter, you will further explore integration possibilities using drag and drop, a technique familiar to most desktop application users. This technique, combined with others you will learn throughout this book, allows you to create AIR applications that have the look and feel of more traditional desktop applications.

The following sections explain the `DragManager` and `NativeDragManager` classes, and include several examples of using each. You will also explore the drag-and-drop operations used within the dpTimeTracker to gain an understanding of how these pieces can be used together in a larger application.

To use drag and drop successfully, you will need familiarity with two main classes, namely `DragManager` and `NativeDragManager`. These classes are responsible for handling all elements dragged within an application. Both are responsible for initiating, accepting, and presenting feedback for drag-and-drop operations, application wide. You will learn about the `DragManager` first to give you an understanding of basic drag-and-drop operations within an application. Then you will explore the `NativeDragManager` to learn about dragging items in and out of the application and interacting with the OS.

Drag and Drop in an Application (DragManager Class)

The `DragManager` is native to the Flex API and handles all the internal drag-and-drop actions in an application, but it has no effect outside of the application window. All Flex components have some level of support for drag-and-drop operations. It is up to the developer to handle the specific user actions (such as mouse down, drag enter, and so on) and properly use the `DragManager` to handle them. The drag-and-drop process has a few important terms and events worth noting. Keep in mind that the `NativeDragManager` also uses similar events and terms with slight variances, which we will discuss in the next section.

- Drag Initiator—The interactive object that begins the drag action and also dispatches the `dragStart` and `dragComplete` events.
- Drag Proxy—The visual representation of the item being dragged that follows your cursor. Usually it is depicted as a faded silhouette of the object, but it can be customized by the user as well. `DragManager` can assign any InteractiveObject to be the proxy.
- Drop Target—A visual object where a dragged item can be dropped. The drop target makes the final decision on whether the type of object being dragged can be dropped at this location.
- `dragEnter`—The event dispatched when an item is dragged over a possible drop target. As you will see, this event is often used with the `DragManager.acceptDrop()` method to grant an object permission to be dropped.
- `dragOver`—The event dispatched repeatedly as the item is dragged over an interactive object.
- `dragExit`—The event dispatched when the dragged item leaves an interactive object.
- `dragDrop`—The event dispatched when the mouse is released over an eligible drop target. The event handler will be able to access the dropped data by using the `event.dragSource` object.

- `dragComplete`—The event dispatched from the drag initiator when the drop is completed. This event allows you to gather feedback on the success of the drop as well as clean up data in the drag initiator.

This first sample shows dragging from a simple list control to another. When initiating a drag between two drag-enabled components (such as List, Tree, and DataGrid, to name a few), it is a simple process to configure the controls. Listing 1 shows the MXML tags for the List control; take note of the `dragEnabled`, `dropEnabled`, and `dragMoveEnabled` attributes.

Listing 1

```
<?xml version="1.0" encoding="utf-8"?>
<mx:WindowedApplication xmlns:mx="http://www.adobe.com/2006/mxml" >
    <mx:List
        id="list1"
        height="50%"
        dragEnabled="true"
        dropEnabled="true"
        dragMoveEnabled="true">
        <mx:dataProvider>
            <mx:String>AIR</mx:String>
            <mx:String>Flex</mx:String>
            <mx:String>Flash</mx:String>
            <mx:String>PhotoShop</mx:String>
            <mx:String>Fireworks</mx:String>
        </mx:dataProvider>
    </mx:List>
    <mx:List
        id="list2"
        height="50%"
        dragEnabled="true"
        dropEnabled="true"
        dragMoveEnabled="true">
        <mx:dataProvider>
            <mx:String>LiveCycle ES</mx:String>
            <mx:String>Blaze DS</mx:String>
            <mx:String>ColdFusion</mx:String>
        </mx:dataProvider>
    </mx:List>
</mx:WindowedApplication>
```

With dragEnabled, dropEnabled, and dragMoveEnabled attributes set to true, the Lists will allow users to move items from one List control to the other by clicking it and dragging it. If you want the user to copy from one to the other, instead of moving, change the dragMoveEnabled attribute from true to false, or remove the attribute entirely (false is the default value). The List will automatically update the drop target's (the destination List's) data provider. Using this technique, you do not have control over the appearance of the item as it is being dragged, or any fine-grained control over the operation. However, using this approach you can very quickly enable basic drag-and-drop operations in an application.

Listing 2 shows dragging from a List to any other type of UI control, in this case, a Label. Much like the List control from the previous example, the dragEnabled and dragMoveEnabled properties remain true on the List. However, the dropEnabled property is no longer needed and has been removed (so it will have the default value of false).

Listing 2

```
<?xml version="1.0" encoding="utf-8"?>
<mx:WindowedApplication xmlns:mx="http://www.adobe.com/2006/mxml">
    <mx:Script>
    <![CDATA[
    import mx.managers.DragManager;
    import mx.events.DragEvent;
    protected function handleDragEnter( event : DragEvent ) : void{
        DragManager.acceptDragDrop( event.target as Label );
    }
    protected function handleDrop ( event : DragEvent ) : void{
        var dropItem:Object = event.dragSource.dataForFormat( "items" );
        dropLbl.text = dropItem.toString();
    }
    ]]>
    </mx:Script>
    <mx:Label id="dropLbl"
        text="Drop on Me"
        dragDrop="handleDrop( event )"
        dragEnter="handleDragEnter( event )"/>

    <mx:List id="list1"
```

Listing 2 (continued)

```
        height="50%"
        dragEnabled="true"
        dragMoveEnabled="true">
        <mx:dataProvider>
            <mx:String>AIR</mx:String>
            <mx:String>Flex</mx:String>
            <mx:String>Flash</mx:String>
            <mx:String>PhotoShop</mx:String>
            <mx:String>Fireworks</mx:String>
        </mx:dataProvider>
    </mx:List>

</mx:WindowedApplication>
```

Unlike the `List` from Listing 1, the `Label` class does not have a `dropEnabled` property (only a few classes, such as `List`, `DataGrid`, and `Tree` do), so for it to accept the drop, the user must create the event handlers to deal with this action. Notice that a `dragEnter` event handler has been added to the Label. This event fires when the user drags a component over the Label. When this happens, the `handleDragEnter()` function will execute.

In the `handleDragEnter()` function, the `DragManager` is instructed to allow the drop on this target. To do this, `handleDragEnter()` calls `DragManager.acceptDragDrop()` and passes the element on which the drop will be allowed (in this case the Label). In more complex examples, a conditional statement would determine if the item being dragged is the proper type and if it is allowed by the current target. In this simple example, all dragged elements are allowed to be dropped.

When dropping an element on the target, the target's `dragDrop` event fires. In this example, the `handleDrop()` function is registered to handle the `dragDrop` event. In the `handleDrop()` function you will change the text displayed in dropLbl, which is the name of your Label control in Listing 2. The `text` property will be set using the data from the drag event.

Internally, `DragManager` keeps all the data being dragged in an instance of the `DragSource` class. This `DragSource` instance contains one or more copies of the data in different formats. For example, the same data could be dragged as text, as an image, or perhaps as HTML. When the dragged item is dropped, the instance of the `DragSource` class containing this data is available via the `dragSource` property of the DragEvent event.

The data inside dragSource is retrieved by using the dataForFormat() function of the dragSource, which accepts a string as an argument. When data is dragged from a drag-enabled List control, it is available in a format named "items." In this case, the data provider contains only a collection of strings, so it can easily be set as the text property of the Label.

In this last example for this section, you will learn to use the DragManager to copy a simple "person" object, created from data in a Label, into a List control without using any of the native drag-and-drop behaviors of the List.

Listing 3

```
<?xml version="1.0" encoding="utf-8"?>
<mx:WindowedApplication xmlns:mx="http://www.adobe.com/2006/mxml">
<mx:Script>
    <![CDATA[
    import mx.collections.ArrayCollection;
    import mx.core.IUIComponent;
    import mx.core.DragSource;
    import mx.managers.DragManager;
    import mx.events.DragEvent;

    private function handleDragBegin( event : MouseEvent ):void {
        var person : Object = new Object();
        person.nameAge = Label(event.currentTarget).text;
        person.comment = "We are dragging " + person.nameAge;
        var dSource : DragSource = new DragSource();
        dSource.addData( person, "people" );
        var label:Label = new Label();
        label.text = person.comment;
        DragManager.doDrag( event.currentTarget as Label, dSource, event,
        ➥ label, 0 , 0, .5);
    }
    private function handleDragEnter( event:DragEvent ):void {
        if ( event.dragSource.hasFormat("people") ) {
            DragManager.acceptDragDrop( IUIComponent(
            ➥ event.currentTarget ) );
            DragManager.showFeedback( DragManager.COPY );
        }
    }
```

Listing 3 (continued)

```
    private function handleDrop( event : DragEvent ):void {
        if(!list1.dataProvider){
            list1.dataProvider = new ArrayCollection();
        }
        list1.dataProvider.addItem( event.dragSource.dataForFormat(
        ➥ "people") );
    }
    ]]>
</mx:Script>
<mx:HBox>
    <mx:Label
        text="Frank, 26"
        mouseDown="handleDragBegin( event )"/>
    <mx:Label
        text="Mike, 33"
        mouseDown="handleDragBegin( event )"/>
    <mx:Label
        text="Jeff, 37"
        mouseDown="handleDragBegin( event )"/>
</mx:HBox>
<mx:List
    id="list1"
    height="50%"
    labelField="nameAge"
    dragEnabled="false"
    dropEnabled="false"
    dragDrop="handleDrop( event )"
    dragEnter="handleDragEnter( event )"/>

</mx:WindowedApplication>
```

The `handleDragBegin()` function is registered to handle the `mouseDown` event on any of the three labels. When a `mouseDown` event occurs on one of these labels, the dragging process begins. Look at the following `handleDragBegin()` function from Listing 3.

```
private function handleDragBegin( event : MouseEvent ):void {
    var person : Object = new Object();
    person.nameAge = Label(event.currentTarget).text;
    person.comment = "We are dragging " + person.nameAge;
```

```
    var dSource : DragSource = new DragSource();
    dSource.addData( person, "people" );
    var label:Label = new Label();
    label.text = person.comment;
    DragManager.doDrag( event.currentTarget as Label, dSource, event,
    ➥ label, 0 , 0, .5);
}
```

In the handleDragBegin() function, several different things need to take place to prepare the drag. First, an object is created and the nameAge property is set to the text of the label that is being dragged. Next, the comment property is set to the string "We are dragging" followed by whatever the text was in the selected label, so it will read "We are dragging Mike, 33," when the middle label is dragged. Next a DragSource instance called dSource is created. As the previous example explained, this is where the data related to the drag operation will be stored.

```
var dSource : DragSource = new DragSource();
dSource.addData( person, "people" );
```

The addData() function on dSource adds the person object. The addData() function requires an argument of type Object and a format of type String. In this case, the person object will be the data and the format will be the string "people".

NOTE "items" was the format for the last drag because it was implicitly created through the use of a drag-enabled List. Now that the DragSource is manually created, its format can be set to any string you think appropriate.

The next piece of this function involves making a drag proxy image that will represent the drag when you're moving your cursor. This step is optional.

```
var label:Label = new Label();
label.text = person.comment;
```

If you decide to create a proxy, you'll need a visual component to represent the dragged data. This example uses a label, with the text "you are dragging" followed by whatever text the dragged label contained.

Now you're ready to start the drag, is done by using the static function DragManager.doDrag().

```
DragManager.doDrag( event.currentTarget as Label, dSource, event, label,0 ,0,.5);
```

Notice that the doDrag() function requires several arguments. The first argument is the dragInitiator—the item that is being dragged; this can usually be obtained by using the event.currentTarget. The second argument is the DragSource; this can simply be set to the dSource instance discussed earlier. The third argument is the mouseEvent that started the drag; this would simply be the event parameter passed into this function.

```
protected function handleDragBegin(event : MouseEvent):void
```

The next four arguments are for the dragImage, xOffset, yOffset, and imageAlpha, and all are optional. These are all related to the proxy that is shown when the label is being dragged around. In this example, the dragImage is the newly created label "you are dragging." The xOffset and yOffset determine where to place the image in relation to your mouse cursor as you are dragging. Lastly, the imageAlpha defines the opacity of the proxy image, with 1 indicating that it should be fully opaque and 0 indicating that it should be completely transparent (to the point of invisibility). The value of .5 offers a half–faded-out label as the proxy.

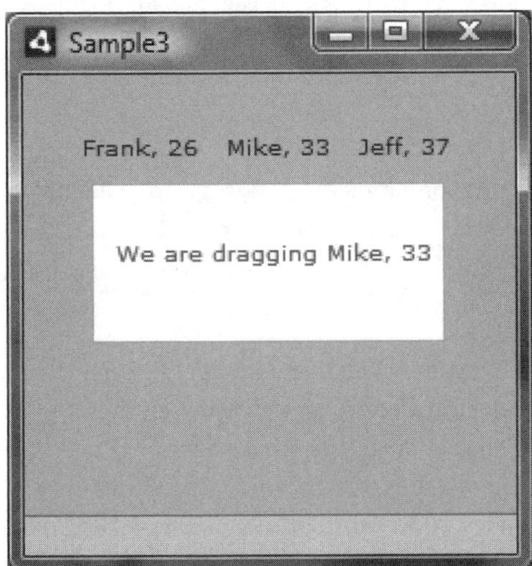

Figure 1: By using a drag proxy, the elements shown during a drag are customized.

That covers the events to begin the drag operations. Next you will explore the events on the drop target, dragEnter and dragDrop. Look at the drop target section of Listing 3 that follows.

```
<mx:List
    id="list1"
    height="50%"
```

```
    labelField="nameAge"
    dragEnabled="false"
    dropEnabled="false"
    dragDrop="handleDrop( event )"
    dragEnter="handleDragEnter( event )"/>
```

Notice that the `dragEnabled` and `dropEnabled` properties are disabled and that event handlers for `dragEnter` and `dragDrop` have been added. The `handleDragEnter()` is the listener function for the `dragEnter` event. This function determines if the item being dragged is allowed to be dropped onto this List. It does so by checking the format (type) of data in the dragSource. If it matches an acceptable format, it will accept the drop.

Listing 4

```
private function handleDragEnter(event:DragEvent):void {
    if ( event.dragSource.hasFormat("people") ) {
        DragManager.acceptDragDrop( IUIComponent( event.currentTarget ) );
        DragManager.showFeedback( Dragmanager.COPY );
    }
}
```

In this case, the conditional statement is looking for data with the format "people". If the `dragSource` has a format (type) of "people", then `DragManager.acceptDrop()` is called and passes the currentTarget (the List) as the drop target. The List will now accept the drop should you release the mouse.

The next statement marks the first of a few divergences between Flex applications running in the web browser and in AIR. When running from a web browser, the `DragManager.showFeedback( feedback : String)` changes the mouse cursor. This technique is often used along with keyboard shortcuts (such as the Ctrl or Shift key) to indicate if the data is to be copied or moved. Flex offers four built-in cursors related to drag operations to show that the item will be moved, copied, linked, or not allowed to be dropped. In this example, passing `DragManager.COPY` to the `showFeedback()` method changes the mouse pointer to a green plus sign, giving you a visual confirmation that the drop is allowed. The four possible cursors are `DragManager.COPY`, `DragManager.MOVE`, `DragManager.LINK`, and `DragManager.NONE`. The following figures shows the possible cursors.

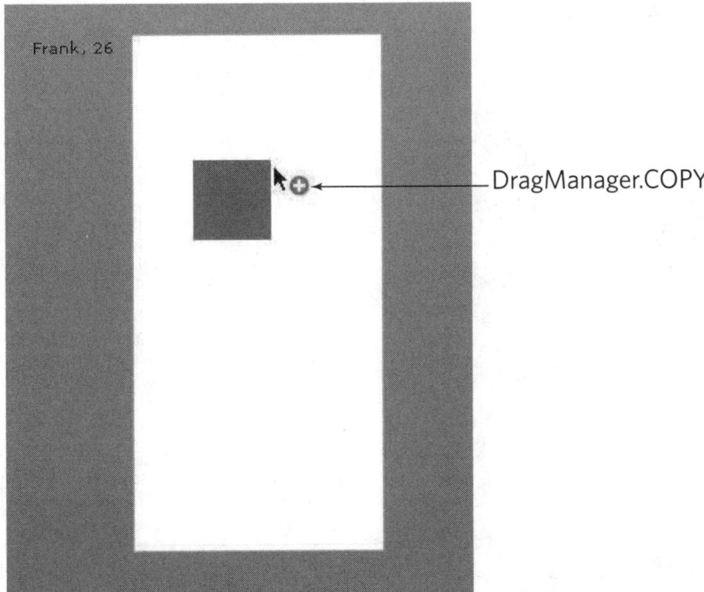

Figure 2: The DragManager.COPY feedback

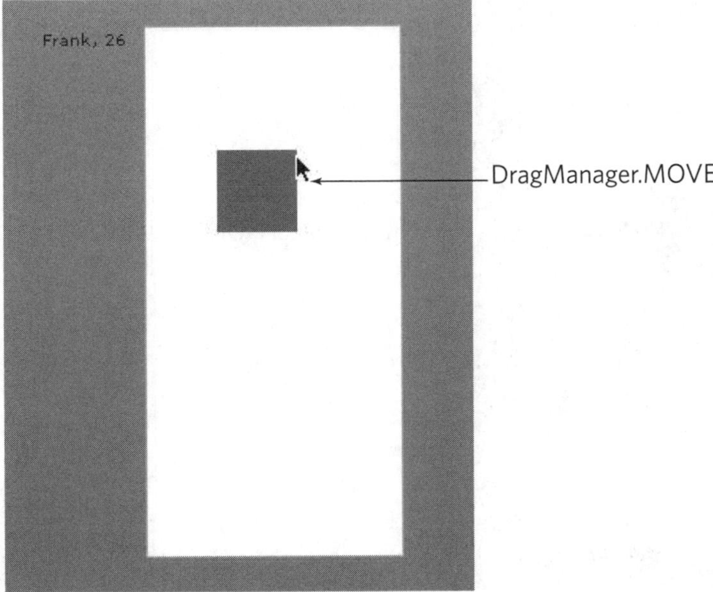

Figure 3: The DragManager.MOVE feedback

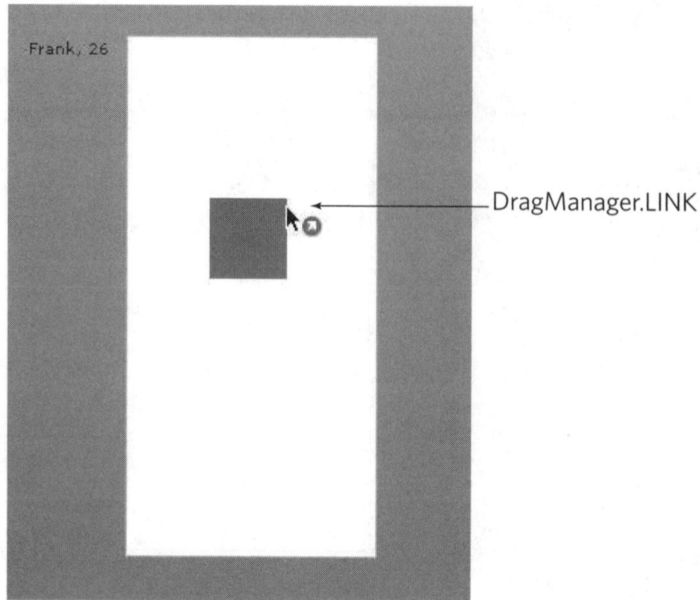

Figure 4: The DragManager.LINK feedback

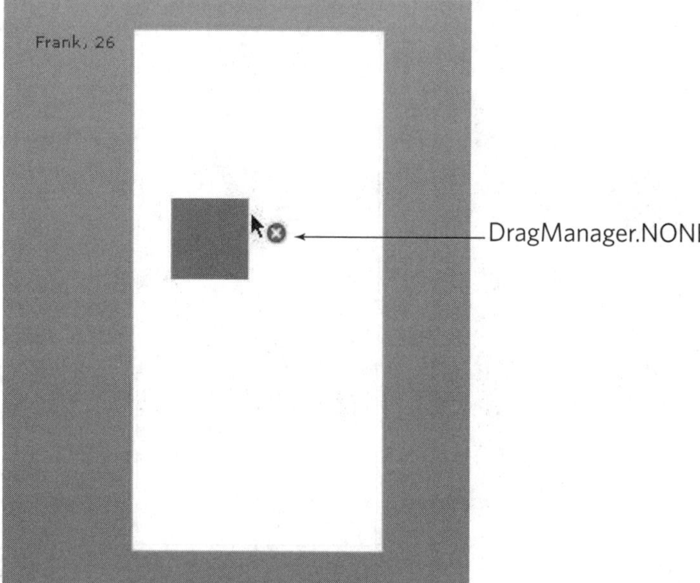

Figure 5: The DragManager.NONE feedback, indicating you are not over an acceptable drop target

Unfortunately, at this time, these feedback options do not work by default in AIR, only in the web browser, due to a difference in the DragManager implementation used in these two environments. This information has been included as it is likely this limitation will disappear in future AIR releases.

NOTE While it is beyond the scope of this book to explain the process, it is possible to choose different implementations of the DragManager to regain this behavior.

The final step to complete the drag-and-drop operation is to handle the drop event using the handleDrop listener function. Listing 4 adds the person object to the dragSource using the "people" format. This object will be copied into the list's dataProvider when the drop operation completes successfully. Using the event.dragSource.dataForFormat("people"), you can retrieve the person object that was created when the mouse was first clicked and moved above the Label. The following function is from Listing 3.

```
private function handleDrop ( event : DragEvent ) : void{
    if(!list1.dataProvider){
        list1.dataProvider = new ArrayCollection();
    }
    list1.dataProvider.addItem( event.dragSource.dataForFormat("people") );
}
```

This function checks if list1's dataProvider exists. If it does not, the function creates a new ArrayCollection and provides it to the dataProvider property of the list. Lastly, it adds the data from the dragged label to the list's dataProvider.

The drag operation is currently making a copy of the data, meaning that you could perform this operation multiple times and have duplicate data in the list. If you are interested in moving the item rather than copying it, you could use the dragComplete event to remove the drag initiator from its parent. The following code sample shows you how to go about removing the dragged label using the dragComplete handler.

```
private function dragCompleteHandler(event:DragEvent):void {
    var draggedLabel:Label = event.dragInitiator as Label;
    var dragParent: Object = draggedLabel.parent;
    if (event.action == DragManager.MOVE)
        dragParent.removeChild( draggedLabel );
}
```

You now have an understanding of how to drag simple objects using the DragManager, using both drag-enabling properties and custom drag functions.

Drag and Drop Between the OS and the Application (NativeDragManager)

When building an AIR application that allows users to drag items to and from the OS, you will need to use the NativeDragManager class, which is responsible for handling drag-and-drop operations with the OS. The NativeDragManager handles the dragged items a bit differently than the DragManager you examined in the last section. It uses the computer's clipboard to pass data between objects, rather than passing the data in a dragSource object. Further, it imposes additional security restrictions as you are moving data in and out of an application. Fortunately, many of the functions and events used by the NativeDragManager are very similar to those in DragManager.

Drag and Drop Items into an AIR Application from the OS

Unlike the component-level drag-and-drop operations we have examined so far in this chapter, there are unknowns when using drag and drop with the OS. For example, when an item is dragged into the application from the OS, the drag initiator is not a Flex UI control and is unknown to AIR. Because the drag initiator is responsible for broadcasting start and complete events, you will not be able to capture a nativeDragStart or nativeDragComplete event.

Similarly, when you are dragging from the application to the OS, you will not receive nativeDragEnter, nativeDragDrop, or nativeDragOver events, however the drag initiator will still dispatch a nativeDragComplete event to indicate the success or failure of the drop.

Listing 5 shows how you can drag an image from the desktop into a box with the application and set the source of an image.

Listing 5

```
<?xml version="1.0" encoding="utf-8"?>
<mx:WindowedApplication xmlns:mx="http://www.adobe.com/2006/mxml">
    <mx:Script>
```

Listing 5 (continued)

```
    <![CDATA[
        protected function handleDragEnter( event:NativeDragEvent ):void{
            if( event.clipboard.hasFormat(
            ➥ ClipboardFormats.FILE_LIST_FORMAT ) ){
                NativeDragManager.acceptDragDrop(
                ➥ event.currentTarget as InteractiveObject );
            }
        }
        protected function handleDrop ( event : NativeDragEvent ) : void{
            var temp : Object = event.clipboard.getData(
            ➥ ClipboardFormats.FILE_LIST_FORMAT );
            var tempImg : File = temp[0] as File;
            img1.source = tempImg.nativePath;
        }

        ]]>
    </mx:Script>
    <mx:Label text="Drag an image into the box below"/>
    <mx:HBox backgroundColor="red"
        nativeDragEnter="handleDragEnter( event )"
        nativeDragDrop="handleDrop( event )"
        width="300" height="300">
        <mx:Image id="img1"
            height="100%"
            width="100%"/>
    </mx:HBox>
</mx:WindowedApplication>
```

When accepting a drop, much like the previous examples with the `DragManager`, you need to add a listener for both the enter and drop events. These events are named `nativeDragEnter` and `nativeDragDrop` when using the NativeDragManager. In this example, the `handleDragEnter()` function handles the `nativeDragEnter` event. The purpose of this method is similar to that of the `dragEnter` handler used in the previous examples with the `DragManager`, but with a few differences.

The major difference is the approach used when checking for the existence of a format. In the `DragManager` examples, the `hasFormat()` method was called on the dragSource object. In this example, the `hasFormat()` method is called on the clipboard.

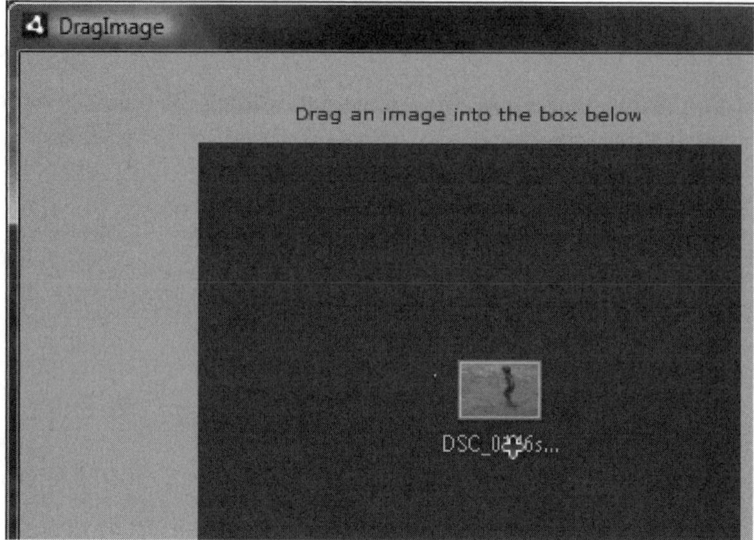

Figure 6: An image dragged into the application from the OS, showing an icon indicating this is a valid drop target

When dragging an image file into the application, `ClipboardFormats.FILE_LIST_FORMAT` will be the format type. This format consists of an array of File objects, each of which contains a `nativePath` property. The `nativePath` property tells you the exact path on your hard drive of the file being dragged.

NOTE For more information on the `File` class and the properties associated with it, please see Chapter 6, "Interacting with the File System."

You accept the drop in the exact same way as `DragManager`, with the `acceptDragDrop()` function of the `NativeDragManager`, passing it the drop target.

You will handle the drop in the `handleDrop()` method in a very similar way. When the drop occurs, you will retrieve the data being dragged. To retrieve this data from the clipboard, you will use the clipboard's `getData()` method, which mirrors the method `dataForFormat()` of the `dragSource()`. You pass the desired format into this method, in this case `ClipboardFormats.FILE_LIST_FORMAT`, and the method returns the data cast as a generic object. When using the `ClipboardFormats.FILE_LIST_FORMAT` format specifically, the data returned from the clipboard is actually an array of File objects. In this example, you only care about the first object in the array and set the source of `img1` (a Flex Image instance) to the `nativePath` of the image dragged into the application.

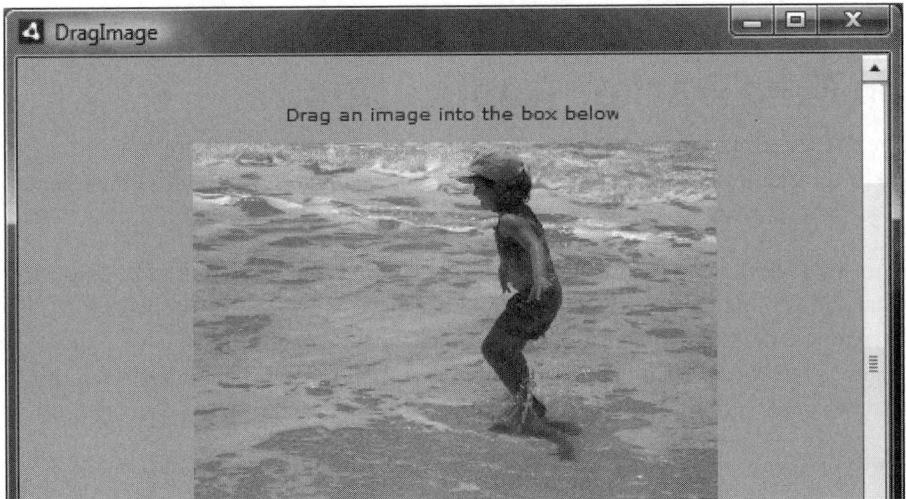

Figure 7: An image dropped in an application shows a full-size version.

The NativeDragManager handles incoming and outgoing drag-and-drop operations by using the system clipboard. As explained in the previous chapter, the clipboard is able to handle several different format types such as Bitmaps, Files, Text, URL strings, and Serialized Objects.

There are security measures that protect data stored on the clipboard due to a dragging operation. Dragged data is only allowed to be retrieved from within the NativeDragEvent handlers. This helps protect your sensitive data from being accessed in unexpected ways. A simple example of this can be seen by placing a dragOver event listener on any component in your application.

Listing 6

```
protected function handleDragOver( event:DragEvent ):void {
    var temp : Object = Clipboard.generalClipboard.getData(
    ➥ ClipboardFormats.FILE_LIST_FORMAT );
    //temp returns null even though it has data
}
```

This function is not a NativeDragEvent handler, so the attempt to access the Clipboard manually will return null and not the data you intended.

Drag Items into the dpTimeTracker Application

The dpTimeTracker application uses the techniques you've learned this chapter to exchange data with the OS. The application allows you to drag a CSV file to the Clients page as an alternative to manually typing in new client entries.

Launch the dpTimeTracker application and log in using your username and password. Click the Admin link and navigate to the Clients page. The Client Admin page will allow you to drag any file with a .csv extension onto the datagrid. The import code will assume that the first column is the client name and the second column is the description. A sample CSV file is included in the assets directory of the dpTimeTracker project.

Much like the clipboard code in the previous chapter, most of the code that handles this drag-and-drop technique exists in the `ListToExcelClipboardDragDropHandler` class in the net/digitalprimates/dragDrop directory.

When the file is dragged into the DataGrid, a `nativeDragEnter` event is broadcast. The following code shows the `dragEnter` handler that responds to this event.

Listing 7

```
private function dragEnter( event:NativeDragEvent ):void {
        if( event.clipboard.hasFormat( ClipboardFormats.FILE_LIST_FORMAT ) ){
            var fileList:Array =
            ➥ event.clipboard.getData(
            ➥ ClipboardFormats.FILE_LIST_FORMAT ) as Array;
            var csvFile:File = fileList[0] as File;

            if ( csvFile.extension == 'csv' ) {
                NativeDragManager.acceptDragDrop(
                ➥ event.currentTarget as InteractiveObject );
             }
        }
}
```

Before the drop is accepted, the handler ensures that the clipboard has a format of FILE_LIST_FORMAT. It then further inspects the data in this format to ensure that the file has a .csv extension. If these conditions are met, the `acceptDragDrop()` method is called, passing the datagrid as the target.

If the user releases the mouse button over this datagrid, a nativeDragDrop event is broadcast and handled by the doDragDrop() method.

This method uses the getData() method from the event.clipboard object to retrieve the file list. It then uses the File API to read data from that file into the AIR application. Once this data has been read, it parses the data, converting it into an object with rows and columns. A confirmation screen is then displayed, allowing you to import this data into your AIR application, if it is correct.

Drag Items from an AIR Application to the OS

When initiating a doDrag() using NativeDragManager, you must pass the method a dragInitiator and a clipboard object. You can also optionally pass a BitmapData object for the proxy, an offset for the proxy from the cursor position, and finally a NativeDragOptions object.

The dragInitiator serves the same role it did in the DragManager class, which is a reference to the component that is beginning the drag action. The second argument is the clipboard (DragManager uses dragSource instead) to store the data along with format information for translation to the OS, another control, or another application.

The optional arguments vary more significantly from the DragManager class. The first is the dragImage, which accepts a BitmapData instead of an IFlexDisplayObject. The second is the offset, which is a Point object that contains an *x*- and *y*-coordinate, instead of passing these as discrete properties. Finally, there is the NativeDragOptions object, which is made up of three properties (allowCopy:Boolean, allowLink:Boolean, and allowMove:Boolean) that determine which actions can be performed on a drop. If NativeDragOptions is null, then by default all actions are allowed.

Next, you will see how to drag items from your application to the desktop. This example allows you to drag an image from the AIR application to the desktop.

Listing 8

```
<?xml version="1.0" encoding="utf-8"?>
<mx:WindowedApplication xmlns:mx="http://www.adobe.com/2006/mxml" >
<mx:Label text="Drag this image to your desktop"/>
    <mx:Script>
```

code continues on next page

Listing 8 (continued)

```
    <![CDATA[
        import mx.controls.Alert;


        protected function handleDragBegin( event : MouseEvent ):void {
            var imageFile:File = new File();
            imageFile.nativePath = img1.source.toString();
            var fileArray : Array = new Array();
            fileArray.push( imageFile );
            var clip : Clipboard = new Clipboard();
            clip.setData(ClipboardFormats.FILE_LIST_FORMAT,fileArray);
            var dragOptions : NativeDragOptions = new
            ➥NativeDragOptions();
            dragOptions.allowCopy = true;
            dragOptions.allowLink = true;
            dragOptions.allowMove = false;

            NativeDragManager.doDrag( event.currentTarget as
            ➥InteractiveObject, clip, null, null, dragOptions );
        }
        protected function handleDragComplete(event:NativeDragEvent):void {
            var x : String = event.dropAction;
            Alert.show("The Drop Action was " + x );
        }
    ]]>
    </mx:Script>
    <mx:HBox backgroundColor="red"
        width="300" height="300">
        <mx:Image id="img1"
            source="c:\images\mypic.jpg"
            mouseDown="handleDragBegin( event )"
            nativeDragComplete="handleDragComplete( event )"/>
    </mx:HBox>

</mx:WindowedApplication>
```

NOTE If you wish to run the code in Listing 8, substitute your own image for c:\images\mypics1.jpg in the Image tag. This image must be physically located on your computer.

You will notice two event handlers on img1: one for the mouseDown event and the other for nativeDragComplete. Similar to the DragManager examples earlier in this chapter, a native drag operation often begins with a mouseDown event. In this case, the handleDragBegin() is called, starting the drag process. The following handleDragBegin() method is from Listing 8.

```
protected function handleDragBegin( event : MouseEvent ):void {
    var imageFile:File = new File();
    imageFile.nativePath = img1.source.toString();

    var fileArray : Array = new Array();
    fileArray.push( imageFile );

    var clip : Clipboard = new Clipboard();
    clip.setData(ClipboardFormats.FILE_LIST_FORMAT,fileArray);

    var dragOptions : NativeDragOptions = new
    ➥NativeDragOptions();
    dragOptions.allowCopy = true;
    dragOptions.allowLink = true;
    dragOptions.allowMove = false;

    NativeDragManager.doDrag( event.currentTarget as
    ➥InteractiveObject, clip, null, null, dragOptions );
}
```

As you learned earlier, moving files between the OS and your AIR application is usually accomplished using a format named ClipboardFormats.FILE_LIST_FORMAT, which is an array of File objects. In handleDragBegin(), you create an imageFile of type File and set its path to the source path of the image instance in your application. Next, you create an array and push the File instance into the array.

```
var fileArray : Array = new Array();
fileArray.push( imageFile );
```

A Clipboard object is instantiated, which is used in place of DragSource in native drag-and-drop operations. Using the setData() function, you set the ClipboardFormat and the data that you wish to drag. ClipboardFormat.FILE_LIST_FORMAT is the format for a group of Files.

You may also choose to use setDataHandler() instead of setData(). When using the setData() method, the actual data is passed into the method. With setDataHandler(), you can specify a function that will produce the requisite data for the given format when the drag-and-drop operation is complete. You will see a further demonstration on this in the dpTimeTracker application in the next section.

```
clip.setData( ClipboardFormats.FILE_LIST_FORMAT, fileArray );
```

Next, the NativeDragOptions are set. This step is optional, as AIR provides defaults, but it is suggested for more granular control over the allowable drag actions. If you choose to specify the options, you will set the `allowCopy`, `allowLink`, and `allowMove` properties to either `true` or `false`.

```
var dragOptions : NativeDragOptions = new NativeDragOptions();
dragOptions.allowCopy = true;
dragOptions.allowLink = true;
dragOptions.allowMove = false;
```

Setting these drag options does not actually prevent you from moving, copying, or linking, but enables or disables the feedback indicators on your mouse and prevents the incorrect `dropAction` from being set when the drag is completed. We cover this in more detail later in the section.

Next, you call the `NativeDragManager.doDrag()` function to start the drag operation providing the required arguments.

```
NativeDragManager.doDrag( event.currentTarget as InteractiveObject, clip,
➥ null, null, dragOptions );
```

The `NativeDragManager.doDrag()` function consists of five arguments. The first argument is the drag initiator and in this case is `img1` (the Image component). Next is the clipboard object containing the data to be transported during the drag.

The next two arguments deal with the appearance of the item as it is being dragged. First is the `dragImage`, which must be of type BitmapData, and second is the offset from the cursor, which is of type Point. Those two arguments are left null in this example and are only required if you wish to display an image proxy and change its alignment on the cursor.

The last argument is the NativeDragOptions object. The user is now free to drag the image outside of the application and drop it in the native file system.

When the drop operation is complete, a `nativeDragComplete` event dispatches from the dragInitiator (the image).

```
<mx:Image
    id="img1"
    height="100"
```

```
    width="100"
    mouseDown="handleMouseDown( event )"
    nativeDragComplete="handleDragComplete( event )"/>

protected function handleDragComplete( event : NativeDragEvent ) : void {
    var x : String = event.dropAction;
    Alert.show("The Drop Action was " + x );
}
```

Using information provided in `event.dropAction`, you will be able to identify the exact action that took place when the drag was released. The `dropAction` will indicate whether or not the drop was successful. If the `dropAction` is equal to `NativeDragActions.NONE`, then the drop was either not accepted by the OS or the drop was released over something that was not prepared to accept it.

This is where setting the `NativeDragOptions` also becomes important. It provides a suggestion on the type of drop operation your code can handle. Then, depending on the `dropAction`, you will need to determine the appropriate action to take with the source data. In other words, if the `dropAction` is equal to "move", then the original source data should be removed, whereas if it was equal to "copy", then the source data will likely remain. If you are not prepared, or cannot delete that piece of source data, then you should also not allow move as a possibility in the drag options.

Drag Items into the OS

If you examine the code for the dpTimeTracker application, you will see that it uses a technique similar to the one described in the previous section. Examine the `ListToExcelClipboardDragDropHandler` class in the net/digitalprimates/dragDrop directory. The function `startDragging()` is called in response to the `DRAG_START` event.

Listing 9

```
private function startDragging(event:MouseEvent):void
{
    if (!event.buttonDown)
    {
        return;
    }
    var options:NativeDragOptions = new NativeDragOptions();
    options.allowCopy = true;
```

code continues on next page

Listing 9 (continued)

```
    options.allowLink = true;
    options.allowMove = false;

    var clipboard:Clipboard = new Clipboard();
    clipboard.setDataHandler(ClipboardFormats.HTML_FORMAT, dgToHTML );
    clipboard.setDataHandler(ClipboardFormats.FILE_LIST_FORMAT, createXLS );
    NativeDragManager.doDrag(_list, clipboard, dragIcon, null, options);
}
```

The `NativeDragOptions` is set to `allowCopy = true`, `allowLink = true`, and `allowMove = false`. Next a new clipboard is created, and two formats are added using the `clipboard.setDataHandler` method: `ClipboardFormats.HTML_FORMAT` and `ClipboardFormats.FILE_LIST_FORMAT`, indicating that we can provide either an HTML-based representation of our data or a file list. The `setDataHandler()` method defers creation of the dragged data until it is dropped successfully. This can become very important if the operation to produce this data is processor- or memory-intensive.

For `ClipboardFormats.TEXT_FORMAT`, the `dgToHTML()` function grabs the selected rows in the datagrid and returns a String formatted into an HTML table using `<table>`, `<tr>`, (table row), and `<td>` (table data) tags.

The `ClipboardFormats.FILE_LIST_FORMAT` has the function `createXLS()` assigned to it. This function will open a file stream and actually create a properly formatted Excel file with the word *data-* followed by the current date. Both `dgToHTML()` and `createXLS()` are in the same class as the `startDragging()` function.

NOTE The Excel file is created with the help of as3xmls, an open source Google Code project with source code available at http://code.google.com/p/as3xls/.

Listing 10

```
private function createXLS():Array {
    var file:File = File.createTempDirectory().resolvePath(
    ➥ "data-"+dateFormatter.format(new Date())+".xls");
    var excelFile:ExcelFile = dgToExcel();
    var fileStream:FileStream = new FileStream();
    fileStream.open(file, FileMode.WRITE);
    fileStream.writeBytes( excelFile.saveToByteArray() );
```

Listing 10 (continued)

```
    fileStream.close();
    return new Array(file);
}
private function dgToExcel():ExcelFile{
    var xls:ExcelFile = new ExcelFile();

    var rows:Array = _list.selectedItems;
    if (!rows || rows.length == 0)
    {
        return xls;
    }

    // Set up the Excel sheet and size it to the same number of rows and
    // columns as our datagrid
    var sheet:Sheet = new Sheet();
    sheet.resize(rows.length, _list.columnCount );

    // Loop over the DataGrid's dataprovider and set each cell
    for(var i:uint = 0; i < sheet.rows; i++) {
        var row:Object = rows[i];

        for(var j:uint = 0; j < sheet.cols; j++) {
            var cellData:Object = DataGridColumn(
            ➥ DataGrid(_list).columns[j] ).itemToLabel( row );
            sheet.setCell(i, j, cellData );
        }
    }

    // Add the sheet to the Excel file
    xls.sheets.addItem( sheet );

    return xls;
}
```

The ClipboardFormats.FILE_LIST_FORMAT requires that the data be formatted into objects of type File and that each File be stored inside an array. That is the function of the createXLS() function. It will be called only if the drop operation occurs, as it is assigned as the data handler function for ClipboardFormats.FILE_LIST_FORMAT.

Listing 11

```
private function dgToHTML():String {
    var rows:Array = _list.selectedItems;
    if (!rows || rows.length == 0)
    {
        return "";
    }
    var html:String = "<table>";
    for (var j:int = 0; j<rows.length; j++)
    {
        var row:Object = rows[j];
        html += "<tr>";
        for (var k:int = 0; k<_list.columnCount; k++)
        {
            var data:Object = DataGridColumn(
            ➥ DataGrid(_list).columns[k] ).itemToLabel( row );
            if (data)
            {
                html += "<td>" + data + "</td>";
            }
        }
        html += "</tr>";
    }
    html += "</table>";
    return html;
}
```

The `ClipboardFormats.HTML_FORMAT` requires that the data be formatted into a String. The `dgToHTML()` function formats the data grid information into HTML style in a String variable. By using the HTML tags `<table>`, `<tr>`, and `<td>`, the data can be formatted in such a way that when dropped onto a spreadsheet application it will populate the correct rows and columns. The `<tr>` tags are responsible for keeping track of the current row, and the `<td>` tag indicates that the data be displayed in that row.

Next Steps

At this point, you have a solid understanding of the roles `DragManager` and `NativeDragManager` play in improving user application experience. Using all the examples and the dpTimeTracker application, you have enough knowledge and reference material to design your own drag-enabled applications and components with desktop drag-and-drop functionality.

READING AND WRITING TO A SQLITE DATABASE

CHAPTER 5

Another compelling feature of AIR is local embedded database support provided by SQLite. Using this support, developers can persist data locally on the end user's machine, allowing functionality far beyond what is possible for applications running in a web browser environment.

A few common uses for this local database support include caching application data that would normally be downloaded on application startup, creating occasionally connected clients that exchange data with the server only when Internet access is available, or creating an application that is intended to run entirely locally, without a server for storage.

This chapter assumes familiarity with SQL (Structured Query Language) and uses many terms and concepts associated with databases. Neither this chapter nor the book in its entirety is large enough to cover these concepts at any significant level of detail. If you are unfamiliar with any of the database or SQL terms, there are thousands of great SQL tutorials online and hundreds of books dedicated to exploring these topics.

Introducing SQLite

SQLite is a cross-platform and public domain software library that implements a SQL database engine. It is self-contained, server-less, and widely deployed on many consumer electronic devices. It does not require setup or installation and simply creates a file on the end user's system for each database defined. The database file created by SQLite is also cross-platform and can be copied between varying operating systems and architectures. Its cross-platform nature, economical size, and file-system–based storage likely lead to Adobe's decision that SQLite would be the database distributed with AIR.

SQLite Features

SQLite supports the majority of the features defined in SQL-92, the third revision to the SQL database query language standard, making it relatively easy to use for any developer with a database background.

NOTE A list of the standard SQL features missing from SQLite can be found at www.sqlite.org/omitted.html.

It allows the developer to create multiple databases, which simultaneously can participate in querying. A database can be up to a terabyte in size with up to gigabyte-sized strings, making it a practical choice for even data-intense applications. SQLite supports serializable transactions that are atomic, consistent, isolated, and durable even in the event of a mid-transaction computer or program crash.

SQLite also defines a few extensions to the SQL-92 standard, a few of which will be discussed in this chapter. For a complete list of these additions, please refer to the SQLite site at www.sqlite.org/.

Data Types

Most database engines require the developer to define a series of columns, each with a specific data type. These columns collectively define the table where data is stored. SQLite instead uses a technique called *manifest typing*, where the value of the data to be stored defines the type, not the column definition.

To illustrate this concept, consider a traditional database table consisting of three columns, with a single row of data.

ID (Integer)	Name (Character)	Age (Real)
1	Bob	30.5

Figure 1: Traditional database table

The data in each row is expected to conform to the data type of the columns, in this case integer numbers, characters, and real numbers, respectively. Attempting to add the word *unknown* to the Age column would result in an error.

However, with manifest typing, the column data type (or type affinity) is just a suggestion or recommendation. The real type is attached to the value. To a database engine using manifest typing, the following is perfectly legal and does not cause an error.

ID (Integer)	Name (Character)	Age (Real)
1	Bob	30.5
2	12/21/07	Who cares?

Figure 2: Manifest typing database table

The practical implication of this is that any piece of data can be inserted into any column regardless of its affinity. This can be interesting and scary at the same time, however, it is important to understand that the database will not throw errors and will succeed at inserting "Who cares?" into a column designed to hold real numbers.

When inserting text data into a row, the database will make an attempt to convert this data to the appropriate affinity. If it succeeds, it will be stored as a numeric value else it will remain as a text value. No attempt is made to convert null and Blob (Binary Large Object) values; they are just stored.

Any column in SQLite can be defined with one of the following type affinities:

- INTEGER—Signed integer value stored in 1 to 8 bytes depending on magnitude
- REAL—Floating point value stored as an 8-byte IEEE floating point number
- TEXT—Text string value stored as UTF-8, UTF-16-BE, or UTF-16-LE depending on the database encoding
- NUMERIC—Data stored as an INTEGER, REAL, or TEXT depending on the success of conversion attempts
- NONE—No preference

Limitations

There are some limitations when working with SQLite, most of which can be found at www.sqlite.org/limits.html, however, a few of the most important items are explained here as they relate to AIR.

SQLite databases are stored as files on the file system. Therefore, any application that has the ability to open that file can view and modify its contents. This means that the only security present on a SQLite database file is the security provided by your operating system. This means that caution must be taken when storing any type of sensitive data in a SQLite database. It cannot be considered a secure method of storage.

SQLite locks the entire database file during read/write operations, meaning that a read from any table prevents any process from writing to any other part of the database. Further, a write to any part of the database blocks the reading of any data from the database.

The ability to alter an existing SQLite database is limited to renaming tables or adding columns to existing tables. The added column becomes the new last column and may not have a PRIMARY KEY or UNIQUE constraint. It also may not have a time-specific–sensitive default value. You may not remove a column or alter a column in any other way.

If you alter a database schema after you begin adding data, the database performance will be reduced due to the way SQLite stores database definition and data. This can be rectified by compacting the database; however, this can be a time-intensive process if your database is large.

You should not store a SQLite database on a network drive and attempt to access it from multiple AIR applications. The SQLite database is not intended to act as a multi-client database, and network file system locking can be unpredictable with SQLite.

While a variety of administrative tools exist for SQLite databases, most do not correctly support the UTF-8 and UTF-16 capabilities of SQLite. It can therefore be difficult to work with a local SQLite database in languages using extended character sets.

Accessing SQLite from AIR

Earlier in this chapter, it was noted that SQLite databases are stored as files on the user's file system and that there is no practical limit to the number of databases that can be created. AIR does not enforce any particular pattern for using these databases, meaning every application you create could share a single database or each could define its own. All users of any particular application could also share a single database, or each user could have their own. These decisions are left up to you as the developer.

To work with a SQLite database from AIR, you must first open it, then issue commands to create tables, insert or query data, and finally close it. AIR provides an API to work with the SQLite database using patterns already familiar to ActionScript and JavaScript developers.

Communicating Synchronously or Asynchronously

The SQLite API provided with AIR allows you to communicate synchronously or asynchronously with the database. Synchronous communication is the method familiar to most developers. If you call a method named `abs()` on an object, you expect that method to execute, do whatever work is required, and when it returns, the next line of your code can access whatever result was created by this method. The `trace` statement below will display the correct result on the console because this code is executing synchronously.

```
var absoluteValue:Number = Math.abs( -5 );
trace( absoluteValue );
```

Synchronous access to the SQLite database is the least complicated method of accessing the SQLite database. It requires the least amount of code and is extremely easy to read and understand. Unfortunately, using synchronous SQL operations can reduce the perceived performance of your application. The application will be unable to respond to user gestures, such as mouse clicks, while processing any database request. If your SQL commands take a long time to execute, the application can seem to stall and quickly become a poor experience for the end user.

The following diagram explains what a series of calls to the database might look like if using synchronous mode:

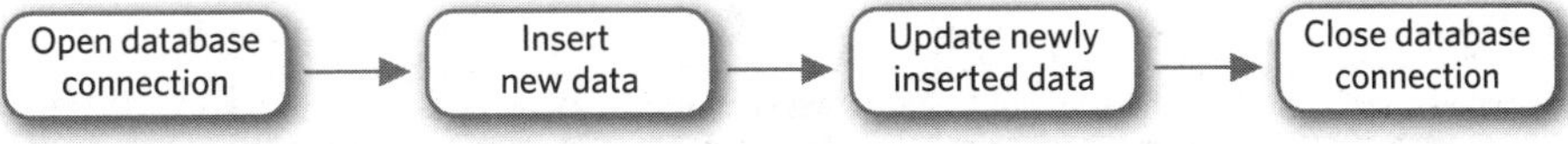

Figure 3: Synchronous database calls

Developers approaching AIR with a Flex background should not be strangers to asynchronicity. Every interaction with a remote server or even setting a property on a

UIComponent is inherently asynchronous. The Flex pseudo-code below would fail to provide the correct result:

```
var myService:HTTPService();
myService.send();
trace( myService.lastResult );
```

When the send() method of the myService object executes, Flex initiates a request for data from a remote server. However, it takes some indeterminate period of time before that server responds and the results are available. In this example, the code is not waiting for the results to arrive, but rather just attempting to trace them immediately. This will not provide correct data.

To correct this problem, you would wait for a result event to occur. When that event occurs, you can be sure the result has arrived and is ready to display as the following Flex pseudo-code shows:

```
var myService:HTTPService();
myService.addEventListener( ResultEvent.RESULT, handleResult );
myService.send();

function handleResult( event:ResultEvent ):void {
    trace( myService.lastResult );
}
```

This use of events in remote services mirrors the idea behind asynchronous communication with SQLite from AIR. The following diagram explains what a series of calls to the database might look like if using asynchronous mode:

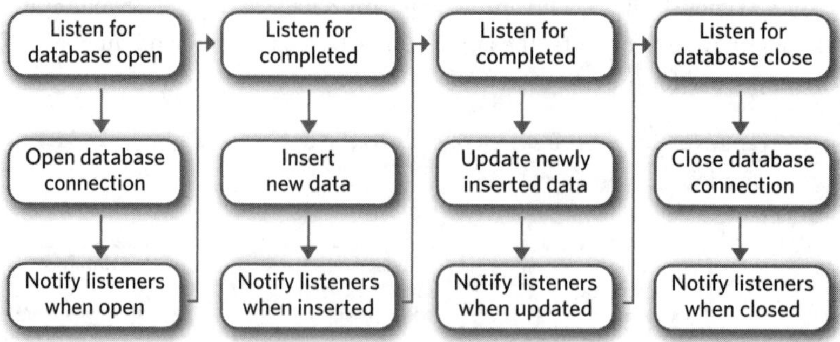

Figure 4: Asynchronous database calls

Obviously using the asynchronous method is more complicated than the synchronous method for handling these types of transactions; however, it allows your application to continue to respond to user gestures and process other forms of data while it is waiting for responses from SQLite. The dpTimeTracker application code uses the asynchronous method.

The decision to use either synchronous or asynchronous operations with SQLite is made when the database opens. You cannot mix and match synchronous and asynchronous operations against a single database. The next section shows how to specify whether a database should open synchronously or asynchronously.

Opening and Creating a SQLite Database

Before executing SQL commands against a SQLite database, the database must be open, and before a database can be opened, it must exist. The AIR SQLite API handles both of these operations in a single statement, allowing you to create any database that does not exist when you try to open it.

Opening a SQLite database requires the use of the `SQLConnection` class.

```
import flash.data.SQLConnection;
var conn:SQLConnection = new SQLConnection();
```

This code creates a new instance of the `SQLConnection` class that can be used to open a SQLite database, examine the database schema, and perform commit and rollback transactions, which you will learn in detail later in this chapter.

Next, you will use a `SQLConnection` object to open a database. The syntax used for this operation will vary if you wish to open it synchronously or asynchronously. The signature for each of these methods follows:

```
conn.open(reference:Object = null, openMode:String = "create",
➥ autoCompact:Boolean = false, pageSize:int = 1024):void

conn.openAsync(reference:Object = null, openMode:String = "create",
➥ responder:Responder = null, autoCompact:Boolean = false,
➥ pageSize:int = 1024):void
```

The `open()` method of a `SQLConnection` object opens a database synchronously, whereas the `openAsync()` method opens a database asynchronously.

In both cases, the first parameter of the method is a reference to the database file that you wish to open. This argument can either be null, which creates a temporary in-memory database, or an instance of the `flash.filesystem.File` class.

NOTE Chapter 6, "Interacting with the File System," covers the *`flash.filesystem.File`* in detail.

The next argument is the `openMode`. This argument defines how to open the database. The valid options for this argument are constants of the `SQLMode` class. You can pass any of the following values to this argument:

- SQLMode.READ—Open the database in read-only mode. When opening in asynchronous mode, if the database does not exist, an error event will dispatch. When opening in synchronous mode, if the database does not exist, an error is thrown.
- SQLMode.UPDATE—Open the database in update mode. When opening in asynchronous mode, if the database does not exist, an error event will dispatch. When opening in synchronous mode, if the database does not exist, an error is thrown.
- SQLMode.CREATE—Open the database in update mode. If the database does not exist, create it.

The `openMode` argument is ignored when using an in-memory database.

The `openAsync()` method contains one extra argument the `open()` method does not have—a Responder. This argument accepts an instance of the `flash.net.Responder` class. Upon success or failure of the open operation, the SQLConnection instance will call either the result or status method of the Responder instance.

NOTE Unfortunately, responders with the AIR SQL support are implemented in a different way than asynchronous responders with the RPC classes in Flex. Here you need to pass an instance of the *flash.net.Responder* class, which is used as a set of callbacks. With the RPC classes such as HttpService, you add a responder (which is an object that implements the IResponder interface) to the returned token. We will provide a strategy for working around these differences later in this chapter.

The next argument is `autoCompact`, which is a Boolean value indicating whether the database should automatically attempt to reclaim unused space. This argument only applies when creating a new database or when opening a database that does not have tables. This argument is ignored at all other times. Setting this property to `true` can decrease database performance as it constantly attempts to reclaim this space during transactions. It is advisable to leave this argument set to `false` and manually compact the database later, a topic you will learn about later in this chapter.

The final argument is the `pageSize`, which is another argument only valid on a new database or one without tables. A thorough discussion of page size is beyond the scope of this book, and it is advisable to leave it set to the default value.

The following code snippets show examples of opening an in-memory database in synchronous and asynchronous modes.

Synchronous:

```
import flash.data.SQLConnection;

function setUp():void {
    var conn:SQLConnection = new SQLConnection();

    try {
        conn.open();
    }
    catch (error:SQLError) {
        trace("Error:" error.message + ' ' + error.details);
    }
}
```

Asynchronous:

```
import flash.data.SQLConnection;
import flash.events.SQLErrorEvent;
import flash.events.SQLEvent;

function setUp():void {
    var conn:SQLConnection = new SQLConnection();
    conn.addEventListener(SQLEvent.OPEN, openHandler);
    conn.addEventListener(SQLErrorEvent.ERROR, errorHandler);

    conn.openAsync();
}

function openHandler(event:SQLEvent):void {
    trace("database created");
}

function errorHandler(event:SQLErrorEvent):void {
    trace("Error:" event.error.message + ' ' + event.error.details);
}
```

One of the most important things to notice about the differences between these two examples is the method of error handling. When using the asynchronous method of database access, error events are dispatched and handlers are used to deal with these issues. When using synchronous methods, try/catch blocks are required to capture and deal with errors.

Using responders instead of events

Earlier, it was mentioned that you could use responders as opposed to events with asynchronous SQL support in AIR, which is a technique the dpTimeTracker uses constantly. The following code shows the same example using a responder methodology:

```
import flash.data.SQLConnection;
import flash.data.SQLMode;
import flash.events.SQLEvent;
import flash.errors.SQLError;
import flash.filesystem.File;

function setUp():void {
    var conn:SQLConnection = new SQLConnection();

    var dbFile:File =
    ➥ File.applicationStorageDirectory.resolvePath("myData1.db");
    var responder:Responder = new Responder( resultHandler, statusHandler );

    conn.openAsync(dbFile, SQLMode.READ, responder );

    function resultHandler(event:SQLEvent):void {
        trace("database created");
    }

    function statusHandler(error:SQLError):void {
        trace("Error:" error.message + ' ' + error.details);
    }
}
```

This code does not register event listeners for events on the `SQLConnection` instance but rather creates a new `Responder` instance referencing two methods, `resultHandler()` and `statusHandler()` as the result and status functions. The new instance is then passed to the `openAsync()` method, causing the API to call either the result or status handler when a result or error occurs.

The result handler for openAsync() has the same signature whether used as an event listener or a responder (it always takes an event object of type SQLEvent), however the status handler signature is different.

When using events, the error handler takes a single argument of type SQLErrorEvent.

```
function errorHandler(event:SQLErrorEvent):void;
```

When used as a responder, the responder takes a single argument of type SQLError.

```
function statusHandler(error:SQLError):void;
```

The responder support reduces the effort to integrate the SQL support into several commonly used Flex frameworks. However, there is one important item to note. Each type of SQL operation that you will explore in this chapter broadcasts a different type of event when it succeeds. It also sends a different type of data to the result or status handlers if using a responder. In this case, statusHandler() receives a SQLError and the resultHandler() receives a SQLEvent, but this will not always be the case. Be sure to pay attention to these differences if using responders.

Executing SQL Statements

Once a database connection is open, you can execute SQL statements against it and retrieve results. The method by which you retrieve results varies based on your decision to open the connection asynchronously or synchronously, and parameters passed to the SQL API during query execution.

In both cases, the basic procedure to send a SQL statement to SQLite remains constant.

1. Create a new instance of the SQLStatement class.
2. Set the sqlConnection property of the SQLStatement instance to a SQLConnection instance opened either synchronously or asynchronously.
3. Assign the text property of the SQLStatement instance to the actual text of the SQL query.
4. Call the execute() method of the SQLStatement instance, with two optional arguments. The first is a limit on the number of rows to fetch from the database at one time. The second is a responder to call when the execute() method completes.

For the purpose of these example snippets, assume you have two open SQLConnection instances, one named syncConnection and one named asyncConnection.

Synchronous:

```
import flash.data.SQLStatement;

function setUp():void {
    var syncSelect:SQLStatement = new SQLStatement();
    syncSelect.sqlConnection = syncConnection;
    syncSelect.text = "SELECT * FROM sqlite_master";

    try {
        syncSelect.execute();
        var syncResult:SQLResult = syncSelect.getResult();
        /* The syncResult contains an array of results, which
        are generic objects in this example */
    }
    catch (error:SQLError) {
        trace("Error:" error.message + ' ' + error.details);
    }
}
```

Asynchronous with Events:

```
import flash.data.SQLStatement;
import flash.events.SQLErrorEvent;
import flash.events.SQLEvent;

var asyncSelect:SQLStatement = new SQLStatement();

function setUp():void {
    asyncSelect.sqlConnection = asyncConnection;
    asyncSelect.text = "SELECT * FROM sqlite_master";

    asyncSelect.addEventListener(SQLEvent.RESULT, resultHandler);
    asyncSelect.addEventListener(SQLErrorEvent.ERROR, errorHandler);

    asyncSelect.execute();
}
```

```
function resultHandler(event:SQLEvent):void {
    var asyncResult:SQLResult = asyncSelect.getResult();
}

function errorHandler(event:SQLErrorEvent):void {
    trace("Error:" event.error.message + ' ' + event.error.details);
}
```

Asynchronous with Responder:

```
import flash.data.SQLStatement;
import flash.data.SQLResult;
import flash.errors.SQLError;
import flash.net.Responder;

var responderSelect:SQLStatement = new SQLStatement();

function setUp():void {
    responderSelect.sqlConnection = asyncConnection;
    responderSelect.text = "SELECT * FROM sqlite_master";

    var responder:Responder = new Responder(resultHandler, errorHandler);

    responderSelect.execute( -1, responder );
}

function resultHandler(result:SQLResult):void {
    var asyncResultArray:Array = result.data;
}

function errorHandler(error:SQLError):void {
    trace("Error:" error.message + ' ' + error.details);
}
```

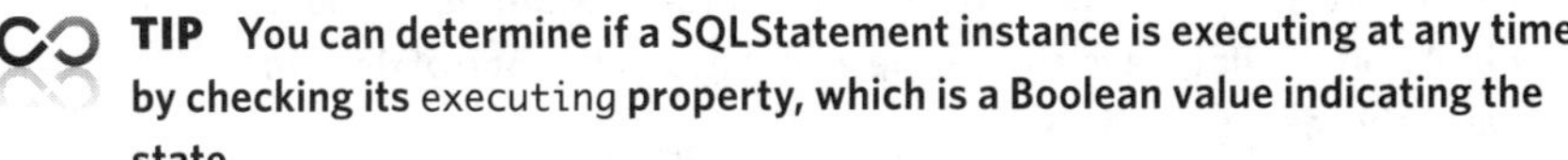

TIP **You can determine if a SQLStatement instance is executing at any time by checking its** `executing` **property, which is a Boolean value indicating the state.**

Retrieving results

You can gather the results of both the synchronous and asynchronous (when using events) operation by calling the `getResult()` method on the `SQLStatement` instance. However, when using a responder, the results are passed via the `data` property of the `SQLResult` argument to the result method.

The behavior of the `getResult()` method is unfortunately a little more complex than it initially seems in these examples. The `getResult()` method is actually a queue operation.

When you call the `execute()` method of the `SQLStatement` instance, the optional first argument is the maximum number of rows to return at one time. If you pass the value of –1 to this argument, all the rows in the result are returned at once. However, if you pass a positive integer value (n), and the total number of rows in the result is greater than this number, only the first (n) records are returned.

The `SQLStatement` also has a `next()` method, which follows the same signature as the `execute()` method. It allows you to fetch the next (n) rows from the database. Every time a record set returns from the database, it is added to a queue. The `getResult()` method removes one of these `SQLResult` objects from the queue each time it is called and returns the object. Each `SQLResult` object has a property named `complete`, which indicates if this particular `SQLResult` contains the final remaining data.

Due to the internals of this methodology of returning data, the API only knows that it has returned all rows once it has moved beyond the end of the dataset. This means that if you instruct the API to retrieve 10 rows and there are only 10 rows, the first `SQLResult` object will not indicate that it is complete. After calling the `next()` method, the subsequent `SQLResult` object will be marked complete, as it has now attempted to return more rows and realized that the dataset is complete.

Finally, you can cancel retrieving more information at any time by calling the `cancel()` method of either the `SQLStatement` instance or the `SQLConnection` instance.

TIP The examples in this section select data from the sqlite_master table of a SQLite database. The sqlite_master table contains information about all other tables in the database and can be a very useful method of determining if a given table exists.

If you choose to use asynchronous responders, an instance of the `SQLResult` class is passed to the result method and an instance of the `SQLError` class is passed to the status method. The AIR SDK effectively calls the `getResult()` method for you and passes that result to the result method.

Queuing SQL statements

Instances of the `SQLConnection` class maintain an internal queue of executing `SQLStatement` instances. If you are using asynchronous mode, you can create multiple instances of the `SQLStatement` class and call their `execute()` methods sequentially, without waiting for results to return. As soon as the first operation completes, the next will immediately be called in the background.

While this is a wonderful technique for executing multiple queries sequentially, there is one limitation. Once a `SQLStatement` instance is executing, you can no longer change the text of the SQL statement in any way. This means that this technique cannot be used if there are dependencies between statements, such as if the first statement returns a value that is used to construct the SQL statement for the second statement.

Closing a Database Connection

When you are finished using a database connection, you should close it. You can manually close it by calling the `close()` method of the `SQLConnection` instance. The `close()` method has the following signature:

```
public function close(responder:Responder = null):void
```

You can explicitly call the `close()` method, however, the runtime will also call `close()` implicitly if the `SQLConnection` instance is garbage collected during normal program execution or when the application terminates.

The following code shows manually closing a database:

```
import flash.data.SQLConnection;

var conn:SQLConnection = new SQLConnection();

...

conn.close();
```

Opening and closing a database connection can be a relatively expensive operation in regards to processing time. Therefore, Adobe advocates reusing a single `SQLConnection` instance and not opening or closing the database each time you need it.

You will notice in the dpTimeTracker application that the database is opened and closed continually. Either of these two approaches will work. It is simply cleaner and easier to demonstrate if you open and close the database each time you need it.

Creating a Database and Tables

As discussed earlier, a database is created whenever you issue an open command with the openMode set to SQLMode.CREATE, which is the default value. For simplicity, the previous examples used in-memory databases, but it is now time to address more permanent storage on the file system, as well as creating tables to store data inside the database.

The first parameter in the open() or openAsync() method of SQLConnection instance is a reference to the database location on the file system. This argument expects an instance of the flash.filesystem.File class, which you will explore thoroughly in the next chapter. For your immediate needs, your database file reference will always be created as demonstrated in the following code snippet:

```
import flash.filesystem.File;
var dbFile:File = File.applicationStorageDirectory.resolvePath("myData.db");
```

This statement simply creates a new file object based on the application's private storage directory, which will also be explained in the next chapter, and the file name myData.db. This reference can then be passed to the open() or openAsync() method of SQLConnection instance to create a new database as the following snippet demonstrates:

```
import flash.data.SQLConnection;
import flash.data.SQLMode;
import flash.events.SQLErrorEvent;
import flash.events.SQLEvent;
import flash.filesystem.File;

function setUp():void {
    var conn:SQLConnection = new SQLConnection();
    var dbFile:File =
    ➥ File.applicationStorageDirectory.resolvePath("myData.db");

    conn.openAsync(dbFile, SQLMode.CREATE);
}

function openHandler(event:SQLEvent):void {
    trace("database created");
}

function errorHandler(event:SQLErrorEvent):void {
    trace("Error:" event.error.message + ' ' + event.error.details);
}
```

Once the database has been created, you are free to create tables to store your data, which you will do using an administrative tool or SQL commands.

Creating a table

Now that your database exists, you are free to administrate it using SQL commands or any number of commonly available SQLite administration tools. Some of these tools are open source; others are shareware or can be purchased commercially. Because each of these administrative methods has its own capabilities and method of use, you will just learn the SQL-based approach here, which you can always use.

The full SQL syntax for creating and dropping (deleting) tables is well documented online in thousands of locations. Rather than attempt to present this information here, let's simply review the basics of a create statement in the dpTimeTracker application.

NOTE The full SQL language reference as understood by SQLite is available online at www.sqlite.org/lang.html.

The following code is from the `commands.sql.clients.CreateClientTable` class in the dpTimeTracker application. It demonstrates creating the Client table.

```
var sqlText:String =
    "CREATE TABLE IF NOT EXISTS Client (" +
    "    clientID TEXT PRIMARY KEY NOT NULL, " +
    "    remoteID TEXT, " +
    "    name TEXT, " +
    "    description TEXT, " +
    "    display INTEGER, " +
    "    deleted INTEGER " +
    ")";

var statement:SQLStatement = new SQLStatement();
statement.sqlConnection = connection;
statement.text = sqlText;
statement.execute( -1, this );
```

This code snippet is for an asynchronous SQL operation and behaves identically to the examples in the section "Executing SQL Statements" earlier in this chapter.

First, a string is created for the SQL statement to be executed. In this case, the SQL statement is a CREATE TABLE statement. The CREATE TABLE syntax can be incredibly complicated if all options are used. In this case, the code reads: Create a table named

Client, if it does not already exist in this database. Add six columns to the Client table. The first, `clientID`, will hold string data and will contain values that uniquely identify each client. The `remoteID`, `name`, and `description` will also contain string data. Finally, the `display` and `deleted` columns will hold integer values.

TIP Later in this chapter you will learn about the `itemClass` property of the `SQLStatement` class, which allows you to map each row of a returned data set directly to an ActionScript object. It is absolutely crucial that the capitalization of the fields in your CREATE TABLE statement match the object you eventually wish to populate. Despite claiming case-insensitivity, the capitalization of your fields does count in this particular situation.

A new `SQLStatement` instance is created and the `sqlConnection` and `text` properties are set. Once again, these properties cannot be modified after the `SQLStatement` instance begins executing.

Finally, the `execute()` method is called. By specifying a –1 for the first argument of the method, you are indicating that you would like to receive all results that may be generated. The second argument of the `execute()` method is a reference to the object containing this code. In the dpTimeTracker application, this code is in a command, which is just a class that implements a design pattern called the *command pattern*. The SQL command in the dpTimeTracker extends the `flash.net.Responder` class and therefore is a `Responder`.

Altering and dropping tables

After creating tables, you are free to begin populating them with data. While careful planning of table structure will always be the best route, occasionally you will need to add an additional column to a table. SQLite will let you rename a table or add a new column to an existing table, provided that the new column meets specific requirements as defined in the SQLite standard.

NOTE A full definition of these requirements can be found at www.sqlite.org/lang_altertable.html.

The following code renames a database table:

```
var sqlText:String =
    "ALTER TABLE MyClient " +
    "    RENAME TO Client ";

var statement:SQLStatement = new SQLStatement();
```

```
statement.sqlConnection = connection;
statement.text = sqlText;
statement.execute();
```

And this code shows adding a column to the Client table:

```
var sqlText:String =
    "ALTER TABLE Client " +
    "    ADD otherID TEXT";

var statement:SQLStatement = new SQLStatement();
statement.sqlConnection = connection;
statement.text = sqlText;
statement.execute();
```

You will be unable to perform more complicated operations than table renaming or column additions on SQLite. To handle these other situations, you will need to drop and recreate your table. If the data in the table to be modified is unimportant, then this operation is quite easily accomplished. If the data in the table is important, then the strategy generally followed is:

1. Rename the existing table to a different name.
2. Create a new table with the original name and the required modifications.
3. Select the data from the renamed table and insert it into the modified table.
4. Drop the renamed table.

The following code demonstrates dropping a table that already exists in the database:

```
var sqlText:String =
    "DROP TABLE Client";

var statement:SQLStatement = new SQLStatement();
statement.sqlConnection = connection;
statement.text = sqlText;
statement.execute();
```

Compacting a table

Compacting a database causes it to attempt to reclaim unused space. The process of compacting a database can be time intensive if the database is large. However, due to the way database information and data are stored in a SQLite database, the database should be compacted after the database is altered in any way.

This includes the altering operations previously discussed or even adding a new table after data has already been entered into the database. Compacting a database is a simple process in the SQL API. The `SQLConnection` class defines a method called `compact()`, which takes a single optional argument—a responder to use in asynchronous mode.

For the purpose of this example snippet, assume you have an open `SQLConnection` instance named `asyncConnection`.

```
import flash.events.SQLErrorEvent;
import flash.events.SQLEvent;

function setUp():void {
    asyncConnection.addEventListener(SQLEvent.COMPACT, resultHandler);
    asyncConnection.addEventListener(SQLErrorEvent.ERROR, errorHandler);

    asyncConnection.compact();
}

function resultHandler(event:SQLEvent):void {
    trace("compact success");
}

function errorHandler(event:SQLErrorEvent):void {
    trace("Error:" event.error.message + ' ' + event.error.details);
}
```

When used asynchronously with responders, an instance of the `SQLEvent` class is passed to the result method and an instance of the `SQLError` class is passed to the status method.

Viewing the database schema

The AIR SQL API also provides a method for retrieving the database schema, which provides information about the tables, columns, triggers, indices, and views. To retrieve this information, invoke the `loadSchema()` method of the `SQLConnection` instance. The `loadSchema()` method has five optional arguments:

```
public function loadSchema(type:Class = null, name:String = null,
➥ database:String = "main", includeColumnSchema:Boolean = true,
➥ responder:Responder = null):void
```

The first argument is type. It limits the scope of the information queried and returned. The default value is null, which means all information should be returned. Optionally, you can pass one of the following class references:

- SQLTableSchema
- SQLTriggerSchema
- SQLIndexSchema
- SQLViewSchema

It is not possible to pass a combination of classes. You must either choose a single class reference from this list for filtering or retrieve the entire schema.

The next argument is name, which works in combination with type to determine the information returned. The following table explains how these two arguments interact.

Type/Name	Null	Table Name	Index Name	View Name	Trigger Name
Null	All Objects	Error	Error	Error	Error
SQLIndexSchema	All Indices	All Indices on Table	The Specified Index	Error	Error
SQLTableSchema	All Tables	The Specified Table	Error	Error	Error
SQLViewSchema	All Triggers	Triggers Associated with Table	Error	Triggers Associated with View	The Specified Trigger
SQLTriggerSchema	All Views	Error	Error	The Specified View	Error

Table 1: Information returned for the type and name arguments combination for the loadSchema() method

The next argument is the database name. Later in this chapter, you will briefly examine the ability to interact with more than one database in a single SQLConnection instance. This argument allows you to specify which database schema you would like to view. By default, it opens the database named main.

The next argument is includeColumnSchema, which determines whether the schema information for each column in a table or view is included or omitted. The default value of true causes this information to be included.

The final argument is a reference to a responder. Like the other responder examples you have reviewed so far, this allows you to use a result and status callback method to handle these events as opposed to events or synchronous mode. In this case, the type of object passed to the result method is a `flash.data.SQLSchemaResult` instance, and the fault method is a `flash.errors.SQLError` instance.

This operation returns the schema via a method named `getSchemaResult()` on the `SQLConnection` instance. This method parallels the operation and functionality of the `getResult()` method of the `SQLStatement` instance, which was discussed earlier in "Retrieving results."

For the purpose of the next example, assume you have an open `SQLConnection` instance named `asyncConnection`.

```
import flash.events.SQLErrorEvent;
import flash.events.SQLEvent;

function setUp():void {
    asyncConnection.addEventListener(SQLEvent.SCHEMA, resultHandler);
    asyncConnection.addEventListener(SQLErrorEvent.ERROR, errorHandler);

    asyncConnection.loadSchema();
}

function resultHandler(event:SQLEvent):void {
    var mySchema:SQLSchemaResult = asyncConnection.getSchemaResult();
}

function errorHandler(event:SQLErrorEvent):void {
    trace("Error:" event.error.message + ' ' + event.error.details);
}
```

The returned instance type of the `getSchemaResult()` method is a `SQLSchemaResult` instance, which contains arrays named `indices`, `tables`, `triggers`, and `views`. The result of the dpTimeTracker database `loadSchema()` method is shown in the following figure.

```
mySchema = flash.data.SQLSchemaResult (@1b9a241)
  indices = Array (@1c77971)
    length = 0
  tables = Array (@1c779e1)
    [0] = flash.data.SQLTableSchema (@1c18129)
      [inherited] =
        database = "main"
        name = "Client"
        sql = "CREATE TABLE Client (    clientID TEXT PRIMARY KEY NOT NULL,
      columns = Array (@1c778c9)
        [0] = flash.data.SQLColumnSchema (@1c17161)
          allowNull = false
          autoIncrement = false
          dataType = "TEXT"
          defaultCollationType = "binary"
          name = "clientID"
          primaryKey = true
        [1] = flash.data.SQLColumnSchema (@1c17071)
        [2] = flash.data.SQLColumnSchema (@1c17ca1)
        [3] = flash.data.SQLColumnSchema (@1c17be1)
        [4] = flash.data.SQLColumnSchema (@1c17c11)
        [5] = flash.data.SQLColumnSchema (@1c17341)
        length = 6
    [1] = flash.data.SQLTableSchema (@1c181f1)
      [inherited] =
      columns = Array (@1c77891)
    [2] = flash.data.SQLTableSchema (@1c18df9)
    [3] = flash.data.SQLTableSchema (@1c182b9)
    [4] = flash.data.SQLTableSchema (@1c18101)
    length = 5
  triggers = Array (@1c77901)
  views = Array (@1c779a9)
```

Figure 5: The `SQLSchemaResult` instance returned when calling `loadSchema()` on the dpTimeTracker database.

When used asynchronously with responders, an instance of the `SQLSchemaResult` class is passed to the result method, and an instance of the `SQLError` class is passed to the status method.

Selecting Data from Your Database

You retrieve data from your database using SQL Select statements. As is the case for the CREATE TABLE statement, there are many books written on methods and approaches for selecting data from your database. Therefore, you will learn useful information regarding using AIR and SQLite select statements together in this section, but the full syntax of using SELECT statements will be left for entire books on the subject.

The following code demonstrates selecting fields from the Clients table of the dpTimeTracker application asynchronously using events. For the purpose of this example, assume you have an open `SQLConnection` instance named `asyncConnection`.

Listing 1

```
import flash.data.SQLStatement;
import flash.events.SQLErrorEvent;
import flash.events.SQLEvent;

var asyncSelect:SQLStatement = new SQLStatement();

function setUp():void {
    var sqlText:String =
    "SELECT clientID, remoteID, name, description, display " +
    "FROM Client " +
    "WHERE deleted <> 1";

    asyncSelect.sqlConnection = asyncConnection;
    asyncSelect.text = sqlText;

    asyncSelect.addEventListener(SQLEvent.RESULT, resultHandler);
    asyncSelect.addEventListener(SQLErrorEvent.ERROR, errorHandler);

    asyncSelect.execute();
}

function resultHandler(event:SQLEvent):void {
    var asyncResult:SQLResult = asyncSelect.getResult();
}

function errorHandler(event:SQLErrorEvent):void {
    trace("Error:" event.error.message + ' ' + event.error.details);
}
```

In the code above, a SQL SELECT statement is created by concatenating a string. The statement asks the database to return the `clientID`, `remoteID`, `name`, `description`, and `display` columns from each row of the Client table where the value 1 is not in its deleted column.

A new `SQLStatement` instance is created and provided the connection information and text of the SQL SELECT statement. Two listeners are added to the `SQLStatement` instance for `SQLEvent.RESULT` and `SQLErrorEvent.ERROR`.

The execute() method is then called without parameters. As you learned in the previous sections, this means that the database will return all applicable results at once.

When the statement returns data successfully, the getResult() method is called and the result assigned to the asyncResult variable. The raw data returned from this method can be accessed via the asyncResult.data property and is shown in the following figure.

```
asyncResult = flash.data.SQLResult (@abb5d91)
    complete = true
    data = Array (@aaa8709)
        [0] = Object (@aaaaee9)
            clientID = "1F9C2202-88D1-822C-B11F-9D2B29487F43"
            description = "This is the first test client"
            display = 1
            name = "First Client"
            remoteID = ""
        [1] = Object (@aaaae99)
            clientID = "D9CCA5D5-2532-EE0E-1398-9D2B4D3EEBFF"
            description = "This is the second test client"
            display = 1
            name = "Second Client"
            remoteID = ""
        length = 2
    lastInsertRowID = 0
    rowsAffected = 0
```

Figure 6: Data returned by the getResult() method

Each row returned from the database becomes a generic object that can be accessed by index in the array called data. Therefore, you can access the clientID column of the second row of returned data via the following syntax asyncResult.data[1].clientID.

If you choose to use asynchronous responders, an instance of the SQLResult class is passed to the result method and an instance of the SQLError class is passed to the status method. The AIR SDK effectively calls the getResult() method for you and passes that result to the result method.

Using itemClass

By default, AIR creates instances of generic objects for each row of data returned from a database. However, it is possible to have AIR create instances of a specific class instead. This is accomplished via the itemClass property of the SQLStatement class.

The itemClass property can be assigned a class reference to a value object class that exists in your project. For AIR to correctly map the returning data to the value object, the value object's constructor must not take any parameters. Further, the capitalization of the properties in the value object must match the capitalization of the column names used when you created the table. If there is a mismatch in capitalization or if a property does not exist in your value object that is returned from the server, it is considered an error.

When used correctly, this is a very powerful feature allowing strong typing of data when programming AIR. For the purpose of this example snippet, assume you have an open `SQLConnection` instance named `asyncConnection`. You will now tell the SQL SDK to use the `model.dbBeans.Client` class instead of a generic object for each row of returning data.

Listing 2

```
import flash.data.SQLStatement;
import flash.events.SQLErrorEvent;
import flash.events.SQLEvent;
import model.dbBeans.Client;

var asyncSelect:SQLStatement = new SQLStatement();

function setUp():void {
    var sqlText:String =
        "SELECT clientID, remoteID, name, description, display " +
        "FROM Client " +
        "WHERE deleted <> 1";

    asyncSelect.sqlConnection = asyncConnection;
    asyncSelect.itemClass = Client;
    asyncSelect.text = sqlText;

    asyncSelect.addEventListener(SQLEvent.RESULT, resultHandler);
    asyncSelect.addEventListener(SQLErrorEvent.ERROR, errorHandler);

    asyncSelect.execute();
}

function resultHandler(event:SQLEvent):void {
    var asyncResult:SQLResult = asyncSelect.getResult();
}

function errorHandler(event:SQLErrorEvent):void {
    trace("Error:" event.error.message + ' ' + event.error.details);
}
```

This example differs from Listing 1 by two lines. The first is the import of the `model.dbBeans.Client` class. The second is the assignment of that class to the `itemClass` property of the `SQLStatement` instance. The following figure shows the resulting data.

```
asyncResult = flash.data.SQLResult (@ace0851)
    complete = true
    data = Array (@abb6d99)
        [0] = model.dbBeans.Client (@abb6b69)
            clientID = "1F9C2202-88D1-822C-B11F-9D2B29487F43"
            deleted = 0
            description = "This is the first test client"
            display = 1
            name = "First Client"
            remoteID = ""
        [1] = model.dbBeans.Client (@abb6469)
        length = 2
    lastInsertRowID = 0
    rowsAffected = 0
```

Figure 7: Data returned by the `getResult()` method when using an `itemClass` property

Unlike the previous example, each of the objects in the `data` array is now of type `model.dbBeans.Client` and not a generic object. This is the result of a successful mapping of the returned rows to the specified `itemClass`.

Selecting from multiple databases

So far in this chapter, you have always used a single `SQLConnection` instance to connect to a single database. This is not abnormal, but there are times that you may want to have your SELECT statement return results that include information from more than one table.

If this situation occurs, AIR provides the ability to attach up to 10 additional SQLite databases. The process of attaching an additional database allows it to be referenced inside your SQL statements.

Additional databases are attached by calling the `attach()` method of your `SQLConnection` instance. The attach method has the following signature:

```
public function attach(name:String, reference:Object = null,
➥ responder:Responder = null):void
```

The first argument defines an alias for the new database to use in SQL statements. By default, the database name of your SQLite database when calling `open()` or `openAsync()` is main, so you may not use the names *main* or *temp,* which are reserved words, for the alias of this new database.

The second argument is a reference, which must be an instance of type `flash.filesystem.File`. This argument works exactly as the reference argument to the `open()` or `openAsync()` method. Additionally, it uses the information provided by either of these methods to determine what to do if the additional database does not exist.

If SQLMode.CREATE was specified when opening the initial connection, then the additional database will be created if it does not already exist. If either of the other options (READ or UPDATE) were specified, an error is thrown, an event is broadcast, or the status method is called dependent upon your choice of synchronous or asynchronous and decision to use events or responders.

If the additional database attaches successfully, the SQLConnection instance will broadcast a SQLEvent.ATTACH. It will broadcast a SQLErrorEvent.ERROR if the attach is unsuccessful. If you are using asynchronous responders, an instance of the `SQLEvent` class is passed to the result method and an instance of the `SQLError` class is passed to the status method.

For the purpose of this example, assume you have an open `SQLConnection` instance named `asyncConnection`.

```
import flash.events.SQLErrorEvent;
import flash.events.SQLEvent;
import flash.filesystem.File;

function setUp():void {
    asyncConnection.addEventListener(SQLEvent.ATTACH, successHandler);
    asyncConnection.addEventListener(SQLErrorEvent.ERROR, errorHandler);

    var dbFile2:File =
    ➥ File.applicationStorageDirectory.resolvePath("myData2.db");

    asyncConnection.attach( 'second', dbFile2 );
}

function successHandler(event:SQLEvent):void {
    trace("attach success");
}

function errorHandler(event:SQLErrorEvent):void {
    trace("Error:" event.error.message + ' ' + event.error.details);
}
```

In this example, you must wait until the SQLEvent.ATTACH event is broadcast before using the additional table now with the alias second. Once this event does occur, you can begin to use tables in this database. In your SQL statements, you must use the alias when attaching to the database. For example:

```
SELECT Client.clientID, Client.name, Contact.firstName
FROM main.Client, second.Contact
WHERE Client.deleted <> 1 AND Client.clientID = Contact.clientID
```

This SQL statement asks for the clientID and name columns from the Client table and the firstName column from the Contact table for each row in the combination of the Client and Contact tables created when the clientID from the Client table is matched to the clientID of the Contact table, but restricted to rows where the deleted field in the Client table is not equal to 1. In this case, the Client table resides in the database that was initially opened, but the Contact table resides in the second, the database attached later.

TIP The SQLite libraries will actually perform better if you always specify the full database and table name as opposed to just the table. Even when there is only one database attached, the libraries still perform an extra step to search for the correct table when the full name is not present.

Inserting Data into Your Database

You use SQL insert statements to insert data into your database. As is the case for the SELECT statement, there is more information on this topic than can be addressed in this chapter or book. Therefore, you will learn useful information regarding using AIR and SQLite insert statements together in this section, but the full syntax of using INSERT statements will be left for books on SQL.

The INSERT statement takes the following basic form:

```
INSERT INTO [database-name.]table-name [(column-list)]
VALUES (value-list)
```

The items in square brackets are optional. For example, to insert data into the Client table, the insert statement might look like this:

```
INSERT INTO Client ( clientID, remoteID, name, description, display, deleted )
VALUES ( '123', '', 'New client', 'New Client Description', 1, 0 )
```

As you learned in the previous section, the default table name of your database is main, so this syntax is also valid.

```
INSERT INTO main.Client ( clientID, remoteID, name, description, display,
deleted)
VALUES ( '123', '', 'New client', 'New Client Description', 1, 0 )
```

The following code demonstrates inserting data into the Clients table of the dpTimeTracker application asynchronously using events. For the purpose of this example, assume you have an open `SQLConnection` instance named `asyncConnection`.

```
import flash.data.SQLStatement;
import flash.events.SQLErrorEvent;
import flash.events.SQLEvent;

var asyncSelect:SQLStatement = new SQLStatement();

function setUp():void {
    var sqlText:String =
    "INSERT INTO main.Client ( clientID, remoteID, name,
    ➥description, display, deleted) VALUES (
    ➥'123', '', 'New client', 'New Client Description', 1, 0 )";

    asyncSelect.sqlConnection = asyncConnection;
    asyncSelect.text = sqlText;

    asyncSelect.addEventListener(SQLEvent.RESULT, resultHandler);
    asyncSelect.addEventListener(SQLErrorEvent.ERROR, errorHandler);

    asyncSelect.execute();
}

function resultHandler(event:SQLEvent):void {
    trace("Insert Success");
}

function errorHandler(event:SQLErrorEvent):void {
    trace("Error:" event.error.message + ' ' + event.error.details);
}
```

It is unlikely that you would insert this particular row of data into a table more than once. In practice, you are usually inserting data gathered from the user interface or from other sources, which means the SQL INSERT statement needs to be dynamic.

Using parameters

Parameters are a method of making your SQL statements dynamic. When you define a SQL statement, you simply define placeholders for values that will be added dynamically later. These placeholders are then assigned values just before the statement executes. In addition to making your code more readable and reusable, this technique drastically reduces the chance that you will make a typo when adding all the single quotes and other syntax involved in constructing a SQL statement. It also decreases the possibility of a SQL injection attack, where a user intentionally types a SQL statement into a text field, which your code graciously accepts and passes along to the database. Finally, it provides the only method to support explicit typing of data to be stored in a column.

There are two methods of using parameters with SQL statements: unnamed and named. To demonstrate these techniques, consider the following SQL statement. It retrieves the properties from a client object and constructs a SQL statement using string concatenation.

For the purpose of all of the following examples, assume you have an open `SQLConnection` instance named `asyncConnection`.

```
var sqlText:String =
"INSERT INTO Client (clientID, remoteID, name, description, display, deleted) " +
"VALUES ( '" + client.clientID + "'," +
"'" + client.remoteID + "'," +
"'" + client.name + "'," +
"'" + client.description  + "'," +
client.display  + "," +
client.deleted  + ")";

var asyncSelect:SQLStatement = new SQLStatement();
asyncSelect.sqlConnection = asyncConnection;
asyncSelect.text = sqlText;

asyncSelect.execute();
```

This statement is difficult to maintain and read. Further, it is prone to failure. If you enter the name "O'Leary" for the Client's name value, this SQL statement will fail to execute. The apostrophe in "O'Leary" will confuse the SQL statement and cause an error.

You can rewrite this same statement using unnamed parameters. In this case, the portions of the statement that are dynamic are replaced with a question mark. The statement will then read as follows:

```
var sqlText:String =
"INSERT INTO Client (clientID, remoteID, name, description, display, deleted) " +
"VALUES ( ?, ?, ?, ?, ?, ? )";

var asyncSelect:SQLStatement = new SQLStatement();
asyncSelect.sqlConnection = asyncConnection;
asyncSelect.text = sqlText;

asyncSelect.parameters[0] = client.clientID;
asyncSelect.parameters[1] = client.remoteID;
asyncSelect.parameters[2] = client.name;
asyncSelect.parameters[3] = client.description;
asyncSelect.parameters[4] = client.display;
asyncSelect.parameters[5] = client.deleted;

asyncSelect.execute();
```

Using the unnamed syntax, the final values are elements of an array for the `SQLStatement` instance.

You can also rewrite this same statement using named parameters. Named parameters require that you replace each piece of dynamic information with a colon (or @ as an alternate syntax) followed by a label:

```
var sqlText:String =
"INSERT INTO Client (clientID, remoteID, name, description, display, deleted) " +
"VALUES ( :clientID, :remoteID, :name, :description, :display, :deleted )";

var asyncSelect:SQLStatement = new SQLStatement();
asyncSelect.sqlConnection = asyncConnection;
```

```
asyncSelect.text = sqlText;

asyncSelect.parameters[ ":clientID" ] = client.clientID;
asyncSelect.parameters[ ":remoteID" ] = client.remoteID;
asyncSelect.parameters[ ":name" ] = client.name;
asyncSelect.parameters[ ":description" ] = client.description;
asyncSelect.parameters[ ":display" ] = client.display;
asyncSelect.parameters[ ":deleted" ] = client.deleted;

asyncSelect.execute();
```

This final method is the best option for both easy-to-read and self-documenting code. Further, it offers the best solution for easy integration with value objects, as you will see in the dpTimeTracker code.

NOTE When you call the `execute()` **method of a SQLStatement instance, the runtime goes through a series of steps to compile the statement. If the same statement is later re-executed without modifying its** `text` **property, this compilation step is not required. This means that the statement will execute more quickly the second time. Changing dynamic parameters through this technique does not force the statement to recompile.**

Retrieving a database created primary key

SQLite provides the option to auto-generate unique values for a primary key column in your tables. This can be a convenient way to auto-generate new unique identifiers without writing this logic into the client application.

Any column declared as an INTEGER PRIMARY KEY when creating a table in SQLite will automatically be assigned a new key if you do not attempt to insert your own value.

For example, a table created using the following CREATE TABLE statement:

```
CREATE TABLE myProject (
projectID INTEGER PRIMARY KEY,
name TEXT )
```

will auto-increment the projectID field if your insert statement follows this format:

```
INSERT INTO myProject (name) VALUES ( 'project name' );
```

Unfortunately, using this methodology, the database creates the new primary key. This is problematic should you need this value for another insert statement or for some future manipulation. The SQL API in AIR solves this problem by providing a property named `lastInsertRowID` in the `SQLResult` object. After an insert, this value contains the newly inserted key. To use this method properly, you must keep several things in mind:

This property is intended to work with integer primary keys. If your primary key is not an integer or is a composite of multiple columns, the `lastInsertRowID` in the `SQLResult` object will contain a row identifier, which is a value the database internally uses to identify rows.

This property always contains the identifier of the most recently inserted row. This can be confusing if your transaction inserts more than one row, or if you have a mechanism (such as database triggers) to insert additional data on an insert.

The following code demonstrates retrieving the primary key using the previous table definition. For the purpose of this example, assume you have an open `SQLConnection` instance named `asyncConnection`.

```
import flash.data.SQLStatement;
import flash.events.SQLErrorEvent;
import flash.events.SQLEvent;

var asyncSelect:SQLStatement = new SQLStatement();

function setUp():void {
    var sqlText:String =
    ➥"INSERT INTO myProject (name) VALUES ( 'project name' )";

    asyncSelect.sqlConnection = asyncConnection;
    asyncSelect.text = sqlText;

    asyncSelect.addEventListener(SQLEvent.RESULT, resultHandler);
    asyncSelect.addEventListener(SQLErrorEvent.ERROR, errorHandler);

    asyncSelect.execute();
}

function resultHandler(event:SQLEvent):void {
    var result:SQLResult = asyncSelect.getResult();
    var primaryKey:Number = result.lastInsertRowID;
```

```
}

function errorHandler(event:SQLErrorEvent):void {
    trace("Error:" event.error.message + ' ' + event.error.details);
}
```

After the `getResult()` method returns the result, the primary key is available using the `lastInsertRowID` property.

Updating and Deleting Data

You can update and delete data in your database using SQL UPDATE and DELETE statements. The UPDATE and DELETE statements are used identically to all of the other SQL statements in this chapter. You define the SQL text, create a `SQLStatement` instance, assign it a connection and the text, and finally execute the statement.

The UPDATE statement takes the following basic form:

UPDATE [database-name .]table-name

SET assignment [, assignment]*

[WHERE expr]

The DELETE statement takes the following basic form:

DELETE FROM [database-name .] table-name

[WHERE expr]

The following code demonstrates updating and deleting data from the Clients table. For the purpose of this example, assume you have an open `SQLConnection` instance named `asyncConnection`.

Update:

```
public function setUp():void {
    var sqlText:String =
    "UPDATE Client " +
    "SET name=:name " +
    "WHERE clientID = :clientID";

    var asyncSelect:SQLStatement = new SQLStatement();
    asyncSelect.sqlConnection = asyncConnection;
```

code continues on next page

```
    asyncSelect.text = sqlText;

    asyncSelect.parameters[ ":clientID" ] = client.clientID;
    asyncSelect.parameters[ ":name" ] = client.name;

    asyncSelect.execute();
}
```

Delete:

```
function setUp():void {
    var sqlText:String =
    "DELETE FROM Client " +
    "WHERE clientID = :clientID";

    var asyncSelect:SQLStatement = new SQLStatement();
    asyncSelect.sqlConnection = asyncConnection;
    asyncSelect.text = sqlText;

    asyncSelect.parameters[ ":clientID" ] = client.clientID;

    asyncSelect.execute();
}
```

Using Transactions

SQL statements sent to the SQLite database each constitute their own implicit transaction, ending when the transaction completes successfully or fails. There are times when multiple statements need to be considered part of the same transaction so that they all succeed collectively, or, if one fails, you can undo them as a group. Undoing a group of transactions is called a *rollback,* whereas making several proposed database changes permanent is called *committing.*

Transactions are very useful for ensuring data integrity. Imagine you have a database with two tables. The first table, named Client, has a value called `clientID`. The second table, Project, keeps a copy of that `clientID` to relate the two tables. If the `clientID` were to be updated in the Client table without updating those same references in the Project table, the client and projects would no longer be correctly associated. It is therefore critical that, once the process of updating the `clientID` has begun, all of the changes either collectively succeed or all of the changes are reverted, leaving your database in its original state.

Transactions also lock the database that is being updated to ensure that other portions of your application, or even other AIR applications running on the same machine, cannot make an unexpected change to this data during the transaction.

Using AIR, an explicit transaction begins by calling the `begin()` method of the `SQLConnection` instance. The `begin()` method has the following signature:

```
public function begin(option:String = null, responder:Responder = null):void;
```

The first argument, `option`, defines the method SQLite will use to lock the database during this transaction. There are three options:

- `SQLTransactionLockType.DEFERRED`—the database will not be locked until the first time that you attempt to read or write data to the database.
- `SQLTransactionLockType.EXCLUSIVE`—the database will be locked as soon as possible. Other connections can neither read nor write from this database until the transaction is complete.
- `SQLTransactionLockType.IMMEDIATE`—the database will be locked as soon as possible. Other connections will be allowed to read, but not write, to the database.

If you do not provide this argument, `SQLTransactionLockType.DEFERRED` is the default.

The next argument is a responder, which will be called if the operation succeeds or fails. When using responders, an instance of the `SQLEvent` class is passed to the result method and an instance of the `SQLError` class is passed to the status method. If a responder is not defined, the `SQLConnection` instance will broadcast a `SQLEvent.BEGIN` event on success and a `SQLErrorEvent.ERROR` on failure.

In synchronous mode, you may begin executing `SQLStatements` immediately after the `begin()` method is called.

In asynchronous mode, you must wait until the `SQLEvent.BEGIN` is broadcast or the result responder is called before continuing. At that time, you simply execute SQL statements as you learned previously in this chapter. If any SQL statement has a dependency on a value returned from a previous statement, you must wait for it to succeed (either broadcast a `SQLEvent.RESULT` or call the result method of your responder) before continuing.

When you are finished executing SQL statements, you call the `commit()` method of the `SQLConnection` instance to make the changes permanent. The `commit()` method has the following signature:

```
public function commit(responder:Responder = null):void
```

The only argument is a responder, which will be called if the operation succeeds or fails. When using responders, an instance of the `SQLEvent` class is passed to the result method and an instance of the `SQLError` class is passed to the status method. If a responder is not defined, the `SQLConnection` instance will broadcast a `SQLEvent.COMMIT` event on success and a `SQLErrorEvent.ERROR` on failure.

If at any point in time one of your SQL statements fails to execute correctly, you will instruct the SQLConnection instance to rollback all of the individual statements that have executed in this transaction by calling the `rollback()` method.

```
public function rollback(responder:Responder = null):void
```

The only argument is a responder that will be called if the operation succeeds or fails. When using responders, an instance of the `SQLEvent` class is passed to the result method and an instance of the `SQLError` class is passed to the status method. If a responder is not defined, the `SQLConnection` instance will broadcast a `SQLEvent.ROLLBACK` event on success and a `SQLErrorEvent.ERROR` on failure.

For the purpose of these examples, assume you have two open `SQLConnection` instances, one named `syncConnection` and one named `asyncConnection`. The code attempts to insert two different clients into the Client table with the same `clientID`. Earlier when the Client table was defined, it was indicated that this column must contain unique identifiers. Therefore, the second statement will cause an error. When this occurs, both transactions will be rolled back in the database.

Synchronous:

```
import flash.data.SQLStatement;

function setUp():void {
    var syncSelect1:SQLStatement = new SQLStatement();
    syncSelect1.sqlConnection = syncConnection;
    syncSelect1.text =
    "INSERT INTO Client ( clientID, remoteID, name, description,
    ➥ display, deleted) VALUES ( '123', '',
    ➥ 'Client 1', 'Client 1 Description', 1, 0 )";

    var syncSelect2:SQLStatement = new SQLStatement();
    syncSelect2.sqlConnection = syncConnection;
    syncSelect2.text =
```

```
    ➥"INSERT INTO Client ( clientID, remoteID, name, description,
    ➥display, deleted) VALUES ( '123', '',
    ➥'Client 2', 'Client 2 Description', 1, 0 )";

    try {
        syncConnection.begin();
        syncSelect1.execute();
        syncSelect2.execute();
        syncConnection.commit();
    }
    catch (error:SQLError) {
        syncConnection.rollback();
    }
    finally {
        syncConnection.close();
    }
}
```

Asynchronous with Events:

```
import flash.data.SQLStatement;
import flash.events.SQLErrorEvent;
import flash.events.SQLEvent;

private var asyncSelect1:SQLStatement = new SQLStatement();
private var asyncSelect2:SQLStatement = new SQLStatement();

function setUp():void {
    asyncConnection.addEventListener(SQLEvent.COMMIT, commitHandler);
    asyncConnection.addEventListener(SQLEvent.ROLLBACK, rollbackHandler);
    asyncConnection.addEventListener(SQLErrorEvent.ERROR,
    ➥connectionErrorHandler );

    asyncSelect1.sqlConnection = asyncConnection;
    asyncSelect1.text =
    "INSERT INTO Client ( clientID, remoteID, name, description,
    ➥display, deleted) VALUES ( '123', '', 'Client 1',
    ➥'Client 1 Description', 1, 0 )";
```

code continues on next page

```
        asyncSelect1.addEventListener(SQLEvent.RESULT, resultHandler1);
        asyncSelect1.addEventListener(SQLErrorEvent.ERROR, errorHandler);
        asyncSelect1.execute();


        asyncSelect2.sqlConnection = asyncConnection;
        asyncSelect2.text =
        "INSERT INTO Client ( clientID, remoteID, name, description, display,
        ➥ deleted) VALUES ( '123', '', 'Client 2',
        ➥ 'Client 2 Description', 1, 0 )";

        asyncSelect2.addEventListener(SQLEvent.RESULT, resultHandler2);
        asyncSelect2.addEventListener(SQLErrorEvent.ERROR, errorHandler);
    }

    function resultHandler1(event:SQLEvent):void {
        asyncSelect2.execute();
    }

    function resultHandler2(event:SQLEvent):void {
        asyncConnection.commit();
    }

    function commitHandler(event:SQLEvent):void {
        asyncConnection.close();
    }

    function rollbackHandler(event:SQLEvent):void {
        asyncConnection.close();
    }

    function errorHandler(event:SQLErrorEvent):void {
        asyncConnection.rollback();
    }

    function connectionErrorHandler(event:SQLErrorEvent):void {
        //something very bad happened
        asyncConnection.close();
    }
```

Asynchronous with Responder:

```
import flash.data.SQLStatement;
import flash.data.SQLResult;
import flash.errors.SQLError;
import flash.net.Responder;

var asyncSelect1:SQLStatement = new SQLStatement();
var asyncSelect2:SQLStatement = new SQLStatement();

function setUp():void {
    var as1Responder:Responder = new Responder(resultHandler1, errorHandler);
    var as2Responder:Responder = new Responder(resultHandler2, errorHandler);
    var rollbackResponder:Responder = new Responder(rollbackHandler,
    ➥connectionErrorHandler );
    var commitResponder:Responder = new Responder(commitHandler,
    ➥connectionErrorHandler );

    asyncSelect1.sqlConnection = asyncConnection;
    asyncSelect1.text =
    ➥"INSERT INTO Client ( clientID, remoteID, name, description,
    ➥display, deleted) VALUES ( '123', '', 'Client 1', 'Client 1 Description',
    ➥1, 0 )";

    asyncSelect1.execute( -1, as1Responder );

    asyncSelect2.sqlConnection = asyncConnection;
    asyncSelect2.text =
    ➥"INSERT INTO Client ( clientID, remoteID, name, description,
    ➥display, deleted) VALUES ( '123', '', 'Client 2',
    ➥'Client 2 Description', 1, 0 )";
}

function resultHandler1(event:SQLEvent):void {
    asyncSelect2.execute( -1, as2Responder );
}

function resultHandler2(event:SQLEvent):void {
    asyncConnection.commit(commitResponder );
}
```

code continues on next page

```
function commitHandler(event:SQLEvent):void {
    asyncConnection.close();
}

function rollbackHandler(event:SQLEvent):void {
    asyncConnection.close();
}

function errorHandler(event:SQLError):void {
    asyncConnection.rollback( rollbackResponder );
}

function connectionErrorHandler(event:SQLError):void {
    //something very bad happened
    asyncConnection.close();
}
```

As you can see, the asynchronous code can become quite a bit longer and more intricate than the synchronous code when examining more than the simplest case. Later in this chapter, you will review how the dpTimeTracker application deals with that complexity.

One additional benefit of using the grouped transaction method is that results are written to permanent storage only after the `commit()` method is called. This results in significantly increased performance by removing the need to perform these extra writes to permanent storage.

Optimizing Database Performance

This section discusses methods to make the database access from within Adobe AIR perform better, reducing the amount of time users spend waiting for data to arrive. However, it is toward the end of this chapter for a reason. Unless you have a very large database with many transactions occurring frequently, the recommendations here are going to make a very minimal impact in the overall performance of your application.

As a general rule, optimization is important, but many developers spend time optimizing the wrong areas and aspects of their application and receive minimal benefits for their efforts. It is therefore generally advisable to identify a performance problem before dwelling too heavily on the following items. Truthfully, the dpTimeTracker flagrantly ignores some of these suggestions, and still manages to be a functional and useful experience for the user.

NOTE Some of the topics in this section refer to more advanced database concepts that have not been covered. For a full discussion of these techniques and the methods available, please refer to the SQLite documentation available online at www.sqlite.org/.

Using Analyze

The `SQLConnection` instance has a method named `analyze()`, which gathers information about database indices and stores this data for latter use by the database's query optimizer. The query optimizer is responsible for determining which indices to use when executing a particular query.

While the database engine will always use available indices when querying, calling `analyze()` stores additional information that can be used to choose the most efficient index when multiple choices are available. This stored information is not automatically updated when new data is entered or modified in the database. Therefore, it is advisable to call `analyze()` after any significant changes to the data.

The analyze method has the following signature:

```
public function analyze(resourceName:String = null,
                        responder:Responder = null):void;
```

The first argument is the `resourceName`, which is the name of the database or table to be analyzed. Whenever possible, provide this argument as a fully qualified table name, such as main.Clients, to prevent ambiguity, especially when multiple databases are attached. When `null` is provided for this argument, the entire database, and any attached databases, are analyzed.

The second argument is a responder, which will be called if the operation succeeds or fails. When using responders, an instance of the `SQLEvent` class is passed to the result method and an instance of the `SQLError` class is passed to the status method. If a responder is not defined, the `SQLConnection` instance will broadcast a `SQLEvent.ANALYZE` event on success and a `SQLErrorEvent.ERROR` event on failure.

The information created by the `analyze()` method consumes space inside the database. If you wish to reclaim that space, you may do so by calling the `deanalyze()` method. It has the following signature:

```
public function deanalyze(responder:Responder = null):void;
```

The only argument is a responder, which will be called if the operation succeeds or fails. When using responders, an instance of the `SQLEvent` class is passed to the result method and an instance of the SQLError class is passed to the status method. If a responder is not defined, the SQLConnection instance will broadcast a SQLEvent.DEANALYZE event on success and a SQLErrorEvent.ERROR event on failure.

Optimizing SQLStatement

Before SQLStatement instances can execute against the database, they need to be complied after setting their text property. Setting up a single SQLStatement instance for each type of database transaction and reusing those statements with dynamic parameters will increase performance significantly. One of the worst things you can do for performance is to recreate a needed SQLStatement at the function level each time it is required.

Further, explicitly specifying the column names in your SELECT and INSERT statements, as opposed to using wildcards, reduces some overhead when executing statements. Finally, if the dataset returned from a query is very large, avoid retrieving it all at once. Instead consider paging through this data using the next() method.

Understanding Database Access in the dpTimeTracker Application

This chapter covers a significant number of features of the AIR SQL support individually. However, applications rarely use these features in this way. It is far more likely that your application will connect to a database, issue dozens of different SQL commands, retrieve results, and update other views with this new data.

It is also very likely that dependencies will exist between many of these operations. For example, on startup, the application ensures that the database tables exist and only attempts to query them after this operation. Attempting to load data before the tables exist is nonsensical and would result in an error.

When these types of problems occur multiple times, especially across multiple applications, it makes sense to factor the solution out of the original code and into a more generic form that can be reused. This is the essence of the framework in the dpTimeTracker project. The word *framework* is used loosely with respect to the items discussed in this and other lessons. Truthfully, this framework is little more than a collection of design patterns and supporting code.

As discussed in Chapter 2, "Working with the Time Tracker Application," the most important of these design patterns is the Command pattern. To briefly review, a command is an object that wraps the functionality of a complex operation and implements a specific interface. The only enforced requirement is that the object must have an `execute()` method and an `asyncToken` property. This allows the developer to use commands as pluggable classes that handle behavior without the need to understand the internals.

The Command pattern is extremely useful and is used widely in this application, but not everywhere. The command is particularly adept at handling "fire and forget" scenarios, where an action is begun but the function from which the command was invoked does not need to wait or be notified of the result. An example of this might be logging, where a message needs to be logged to some repository, but the application does not need to receive a status once this entry is complete. An extension of this concept is an asynchronous transaction. In this application, commands are used exclusively anywhere asynchronicity is required. This allows the code required to handle results and faults from an asynchronous operation to be organized in the same location as the asynchronous execution, which is a great benefit in a large application. You will see many examples of this concept in the coming pages.

For those of you familiar with the Cairngorm micro-architecture, the commands used in this application are similar but have a few important differences. Most notably, the commands used here do not accept any parameters in the `execute()` method. Instead, parameters are passed into the constructor of the command when it is created. Further, the commands are called directly by the developer and do not pass through a front-controller first.

One more critical component to understand when using this framework is asynchronous tokens (or just asyncTokens). AsyncTokens are a method Flex uses to handle asynchronous server calls in many of their classes. Every time you ask an `HTTPService` or `RemoteObject` class to gather data from the server, it returns an asyncToken. You can call a special method on this token called `addResponder()` and pass it an object that implements the `IResponder` interface, which just guarantees there will be a result and fault method available to be called in the event of a result or fault.

This consistent methodology allowed developers to create frameworks that abstracted the details of the service away from the code responsible for displaying the user interface. The result was that the user interface code could remain identical, even if the method of retrieving data changed drastically.

This same logic should apply for database access. This application uses a local SQLite database, but you should be able to change it to use a remote database accessed via a different protocol and never change a line of the user interface code. Unfortunately, the AIR DSK does not use asyncTokens for asynchronous SQL operations, but rather events or direct callbacks through a pseudo-responder. Therefore, one of the key functions of the `SQLCommand` class is adapting AIR's methodology for asynchronous access to be consistent with other classes in the Flex framework and re-establishing the consistency across service types.

We are not advocating the use of this framework over any other. This is simply a solution among many for dealing with these more complex problems. In general, you should use the methodology that makes the most sense for your project and situation. All of the ideas presented herein can be applied to any architecture of your choosing.

Using the SQL Command

Central to this application is the use of SQL commands, which are merely commands that execute a SQL statement and contain logic to handle the result or fault. As a convenience, the framework provides a class named `SQLCommand`, which contains much of the logic required to make AIR SQL statements work well with the Command pattern.

As a first example, let's review the `commands.sql.clients.LoadClientsFromDB` class line by line to examine its syntax and functionality. Line numbers have been added to the code to make referencing specific areas easier in the description text.

Listing 3

```
 1 package commands.sql.clients
 2 {
 3      import flash.data.SQLConnection;
 4      import flash.data.SQLResult;
 5      import flash.data.SQLStatement;
 6
 7      import helpers.DBObjectHelper;
 8
 9      import model.AppModel;
10      import model.beans.Client;
11
12      import mx.collections.ArrayCollection;
13
14      import net.digitalprimates.framework.command.SQLCommand;
15
16      public class LoadClientsFromDB extends SQLCommand
17      {
18          protected var appModel:AppModel = AppModel.getInstance();
```

Listing 3 (continued)

```
19
20         private var statement:SQLStatement;
21         private static const sqlText:String =
22             "SELECT clientID, remoteID, name, description, display " +
23             "FROM Client " +
24             "WHERE deleted <> 1";
25
26         override public function execute():void {
27             statement.execute( -1, this );
28             super.execute();
29         }
30
31         override public function result(data:Object):void {
32             var asyncResult:SQLResult = data as SQLResult;
33             appModel.dbClients = new ArrayCollection(asyncResult.data);
34             appModel.dbClients.filterFunction =
               ➥ DBObjectHelper.filterDeleted;
35             super.result( data );
36         }
37
38         public function LoadClientsFromDB( connection:SQLConnection ) {
39             super(connection);
40             statement = new SQLStatement();
41             statement.sqlConnection = connection;
42             statement.text = sqlText;
43             statement.itemClass = Client;
44         }
45     }
46 }
```

Lines 1–15 define the package and import several classes, some defined by the AIR SDK and others by this project or the framework.

Line 16 defines a new class named `LoadClientsFromDB`, which extends `SQLCommand`. This class can be found in the framework code and simply provides some convenience methods for working with the AIR SQL support. The `SQLCommand` class inherits from `flash.net.Responder` and implements the `ICommand` interface.

Line 18 retrieves a new reference to the AppModel instance. The application model is a Singleton and was discussed briefly in Chapter 2. All of the classes in this application share a single application model.

Line 20 defines a SQLStatement that will be used in this command.

Lines 21–24 define the text of the SQL statement that will be used by this command as a private static const. The static keyword informs Flex that this variable is defined on the class, not the instance. This means you will always have just one copy of this string in memory, regardless if you call this command once or thousands of times. The const keyword reinforces the idea that this text will not be changed. Any dynamic properties will be set through the use of the SQL statement parameters.

Lines 26–29 define the execute() method for this particular command. This class inherits from SQLCommand and already has a default implementation of execute(). To change this behavior, you use the override keyword. First, the execute() method of the SQLStatement is called. This method is passed two arguments. The first is -1, meaning that any results from this command should all be returned at one time. The second argument is a reference to the object executing this code.

The second argument of a SQLStatement instance's execute() method requires a Responder. This command, LoadClientsFromDB, extends from SQLCommand, which extends from flash.net.Responder. Therefore, this class is a Responder and satisfies the requirement of the second argument. The SQLCommand class defines a default result and fault method that can be overridden to provide any specific functionality required on the success or failure of this SQL statement's execution.

The final statement in the execute() method is to call the execute() method super class.

Lines 31–36 override the default behavior of the result() method. When the statement succeeds, the result() method is called and a SQLResult object is passed as the only argument. This argument is immediately cast as a SQLResult and assigned to the variable asyncResult. Next, an ArrayCollection is constructed based on the array of results in the data property of the asyncResult. This collection is assigned to the clients property of the application model.

A filter function is then assigned to the collection, which will prevent items marked as deleted from appearing in the collection. The SQL query in this class already eliminates deleted items before returning results. However, if a user marks one of these client records as deleted during this session, the filter function will cause the row to immediately disappear from view without re-executing this entire query.

As the final statement of this method, the super class is called and passed the data object. The super class performs some additional functions, allowing this class to participate in sequencing and use other types of callbacks. These concepts will be demonstrated shortly.

Lines 38–44 are the constructor for this class. The constructor takes a single argument, which is the SQLConnection instance to use when executing this command. First the super class is called, passing this connection instance. Next, a new SQLStatement instance is created, using the connection and the static sqlText defined in this class. Finally, the itemClass property is passed a reference to the Client class, indicating that each row returned from this query should be made into a Client instance.

Executing the command

Assuming you have an open SQLConnection instance named asyncConnection, this command can be executed using either of the following methods:

```
var loadClients:LoadClientsFromDB = new LoadClientsFromDB( asyncConnection );

loadClients.execute();
```

or

```
new LoadClientsFromDB( asyncConnection ).execute();
```

Without the need to understand how the clients are loaded from the database, the user simply executes this command. When the execution is complete, the client information will exist in the clients property of the application model.

Using callbacks

There are times when the object that invokes the command's execute() method needs to be notified of a result or fault. The SQLCommand handles this task through the use of callbacks, which are virtually identical to the way the AIR SQL support uses responders.

The SQLCommand provides a method named setCallbacks(), with the following signature:

```
public function setCallbacks(resultCallback_:Function = null,
➥ faultCallback_:Function = null):SQLCommand;
```

The method accepts two arguments, a result method to be called on success and a fault method to be called if the operation fails. The method returns a reference to the SQLCommand, allowing the chaining of these function calls. For example:

```
var loadClients:LoadClientsFromDB = new LoadClientsFromDB( asyncConnection );

loadClients.setCallbacks( myResultFunc, myFaultFunc ).execute();
```

Sequencing SQL Commands

Some of the earlier code samples demonstrated chaining together multiple asynchronous statements. Each statement waited for the successful completion of the previous statement before executing. The code for this type of operation can become unwieldy as each statement needs its own result and fault handler. It is further complicated when you use manual transactions with the begin() and commit() methods. The dpTimeTracker application uses a methodology referred to as command sequencing to handle the complexity of these operations in a much more manageable fashion.

Command sequencing involves adding a series of commands to a sequence, then executing the sequence. The sequence begins at the first command, executes it, and proceeds if the command succeeds. The sequence stops if the command fails. Note that this is different from the SQLConnection instance's queuing capabilities. A SQLConnection instance will queue statements and execute them in order, however, the next statement is always executed, regardless of the success of the previous one.

The first example that follows is just a snippet from the commands.CreateDatabase class and shows the creation of the sequence:

```
sqlConnection = new SQLConnection();

var sequence:CommandSequencer = new CommandSequencer();
sequence.add( new OpenDatabase( sqlConnection ) );
sequence.add( new CreateClientTable( sqlConnection ) );
sequence.add( new CreateProjectTable( sqlConnection ) );
sequence.add( new CreateUserTable( sqlConnection ) );
sequence.add( new CreateCategoryTable( sqlConnection ) );
sequence.add( new CreateTimeEntryTable( sqlConnection ) );
sequence.add( new CloseDatabase( sqlConnection ) );
```

This code creates a new SQLConnection instance named sqlConnection and a new CommandSequencer named sequence. Next, it creates instances of each command to be executed in this sequence, passing the sqlConnection as an argument to the constructor. Each of these commands is added to the sequence via the `add()` method of the `CommandSequencer` instance.

This sequence opens the database connection; creates the client, project, user, category, and timeEntry tables, waiting for each to succeed before proceeding to the next; and finally closes the database connection. All of these steps are performed asynchronously, allowing the client to still respond to user input. Using the sequencer allows the code for long chains of asynchronous operations to be written in a much more maintainable fashion.

This goes against the advice issued earlier in the lesson, which states that keeping a single database connection open and reusing it throughout the application will increase performance. This still holds true. If you are performing many transactions and the speed of opening and closing the database each time is a barrier, then cache the `SQLConnection` instance. However, in this application and many others, the database access is infrequent. Opening and closing the database each time is a paradigm familiar to developers in many other environments, and the `OpenDatabase` and `CloseDatabase` commands provide a simple way to integrate this function into a sequence.

Sequences either succeed or fail as a whole, meaning there is a convenient place to test for success or failure and react as needed. The next example shows the entire `commands.CreateDatabase` class. Line numbers have been added to the code to make referencing specific areas easier in the description text.

Listing 4

```
package commands
{
    import commands.sql.CloseDatabase;
    import commands.sql.OpenDatabase;
    import commands.sql.category.CreateCategoryTable;
    import commands.sql.clients.CreateClientTable;
    import commands.sql.project.CreateProjectTable;
    import commands.sql.timeEntry.CreateTimeEntryTable;
    import commands.sql.users.CreateUserTable;

    import flash.data.SQLConnection;

    import net.digitalprimates.framework.command.CommandAdapter;
    import net.digitalprimates.framework.command.CommandSequencer;

    public class CreateDatabase extends CommandAdapter {
        private var sqlConnection:SQLConnection;
```

code continues on next page

Listing 4 (continued)

```

        override public function execute():void {
            sqlConnection = new SQLConnection();

            var sequence:CommandSequencer = new CommandSequencer();
            sequence.add( new OpenDatabase( sqlConnection ) );
            sequence.add( new CreateClientTable( sqlConnection ) );
            sequence.add( new CreateProjectTable( sqlConnection ) );
            sequence.add( new CreateUserTable( sqlConnection ) );
            sequence.add( new CreateCategoryTable( sqlConnection ) );
            sequence.add( new CreateTimeEntryTable( sqlConnection ) );
            sequence.add( new CloseDatabase( sqlConnection ) );
            asyncToken = sequence.asyncToken;
            asyncToken.addResponder( this );
            sequence.execute();
        }

        override public function result(data:Object):void {
            trace("Database Tables Created Sucessfully");
            super.result( data );
        }

        override public function fault( info:Object ):void {
            trace("Failed to create Database Tables");
            var closeDB:CloseDatabase = new CloseDatabase(
            ➥ sqlConnection )
            closeDB.execute();
            super.fault( info );
        }
    }
}
```

This command is very similar to Listing 3 that you reviewed in detail, but there are some important differences. First, this command extends `CommandAdapter` as opposed to `SQLCommand`. The `SQLCommand` class provides convenience methods and logic when executing SQL statements. This class is simply executing other commands in a sequence. These commands may have to deal with the nuances of SQL statements, but the nature of the command pattern hides this detail from us. `CommandAdapter` provides the basis for most generic commands in this system.

Line 17 creates a reference named sqlConnection of type SQLConnection.

In the execute() method beginning on line 19, the sqlConnection reference is instantiated. The sequence is then created as explained in the previous example. Two more steps are required to deal with asynchronicity before the execute() method of the sequence is finally called.

The first step is assigning the asyncToken property of the commands.CreateDatabase instance to the asyncToken provided by the CommandSequencer. As mentioned previously, the asynchronous tokens are used to keep track of asynchronous operations. In this case, the code simply states that the asyncToken within the CreateDatabase class is provided by the sequence.

The next step is to add this command as a responder to the asyncToken. This causes the result and fault methods in this class to be called when a result or fault happens during the asynchronous operation represented by the token. This provides a convenient place to know if the entire sequence succeeds or fails.

Finally, the execute() method is called, starting the sequence.

Lines 35–38 define an overridden handler for the sequence result. It simply traces a statement to the console and calls the result handler of the super class. This handle will only execute if all of the steps in the sequence succeed.

Lines 40–45 define an overridden fault handler. Should any part of the sequence fail, the sequence will immediately abort and the fault handler will be called. The fault handler closes the database connection and calls the super class. Ideally, this would also be a great place to determine how to notify the user of the failure.

Inserting and Updating Using SQL Commands

Earlier in this chapter, you learned about using parameters as a best practice for dealing with dynamic SQL statements. The dpTimeTracker application makes use of parameters, specifically named parameters, for all dynamic SQL statements. It also uses the itemClass argument for all returned data to treat returned rows as typed objects.

When inserting a new record or updating an existing record, the commands to perform these operations accept a typed object and internally decide if an insert or update is required. To make the process of using named parameters easier, we use a static method of the DBObjectHelper class named setNamedParameters(), which has the following signature:

```
static public function setNamedParameters( sqlStatement:SQLStatement,
valueObject:Object, delimiter:String=":" ):SQLStatement;
```

This method parses the SQL text provided to the `sqlStatement` instance and inspects the provided `valueObject` argument to find matching parameter names. If a matching field is found, an entry is made in the `sqlStatement` instance's parameters object for this field.

The next example shows the entire `commands.sql.clients.SaveClientToDB` class. Line numbers have been added to the code to make referencing specific areas easier in the description text.

Listing 5

```
package commands.sql.clients {
    import flash.data.SQLConnection;
    import flash.data.SQLStatement;

    import helpers.DBObjectHelper;

    import model.beans.Client;

    import mx.utils.UIDUtil;

    import net.digitalprimates.framework.command.SQLCommand;

    public class SaveClientToDB extends SQLCommand {
        protected var client:Client;
        private var updateStatement:SQLStatement;
        private var insertStatement:SQLStatement;

        private static const updateSqlText:String =
            "UPDATE Client SET" +
            "    remoteID = :remoteID," +
            "    name = :name," +
            "    description = :description," +
            "    display = :display," +
            "    deleted = :deleted" +
            "    WHERE clientID = :clientID";

        private static const insertSqlText:String =
```

Listing 5 (continued)

```
            "INSERT INTO Client ( clientID, remoteID, name,
            ➥description, display, deleted ) " +
            "VALUES ( :clientID, :remoteID, :name, :description,
            ➥:display, :deleted )";

        override public function execute():void {
            //Decide if we need to do an add or update/delete
            if ( client.clientID ) {
                //We have an ID, this is an update/delete
                DBObjectHelper.setNamedParameters(
                ➥updateStatement, client );
                updateStatement.execute( -1, this );
            } else {
                //Set the clientID
                client.clientID = UIDUtil.createUID();
                DBObjectHelper.setNamedParameters(
                ➥insertStatement, client );
                insertStatement.execute( -1, this );
            }

            super.execute();
        }

        public function SaveClientToDB(connection:SQLConnection,
        ➥client:Client ) {
            super(connection);

            this.client = client;

            updateStatement = new SQLStatement();
            updateStatement.sqlConnection = connection;
            updateStatement.text = updateSqlText;

            insertStatement = new SQLStatement();
            insertStatement.sqlConnection = connection;
            insertStatement.text = insertSqlText;
        }
    }
}
```

This command is very similar to Listing 4 that you reviewed in detail, but there are some important differences. First, the constructor of this class accepts both a `SQLConnection` instance and a `Client` object. Second, this class defines two `SQLStatement` instances, an `insertStatement` and an `updateStatement`, and two constants to contain the associated SQL text.

Line 31 begins the `execute()` statement. It examines the instance of the `Client` object provided in the constructor. If the object has a `clientID`, the code assumes this object was retrieved from the database and will therefore issue an update statement to capture any changes. If the object does not have a `clientID`, the code will issue an insert statement to store this object in the database.

When inserting, the code creates a new `clientID` for the client object using the `UIDUtil.createUID()` method provided by Flex. This `id` could be created using any method you choose, including allowing the database to create the new `id` on your behalf.

Next, for both the insert and update, the `DBObjectHelper.setNamedParameters()` method is called and passed the `SQLStatement` instance and the `Client` object. This method examines the `sqlText` property of the `SQLStatement` instance and looks for matching properties in the `Client` object. When complete, the `parameters` property of the `SQLStatement` instance will contain the names and values required to fulfill the requirements set up in the SQL text.

Finally, the `execute()` method is called on the appropriate `SQLStatement` instance, passing a `-1` for the first argument and a reference to the command as the `Responder` property.

The commands dealing with SQL exist mainly in and below the `commands.sql` directory. While the major types of commands needed for working with SQL have been represented in this chapter, reviewing the remainder of this code in detail may provide additional insight when encountering AIR/SQL issues in the future.

Next Steps

At the foundation of most applications is a method to store persistent data. The techniques and APIs presented in this chapter provide a great starting point to develop rich desktop applications.

In the next chapter you will apply your new understanding of the synchronous and asynchronous concepts to the file system using the AIR file API. The combination of storage provided by the SQLite database and the File APIs will open up interesting new possibilities never before available to Flash/Flex and HTML developers.

INTERACTING WITH THE FILE SYSTEM

CHAPTER 6

For web developers, the end user's file system has always been off limits; however, desktop application developers have been able to work with the local file system for years. In fact, file system access is the foundation of many desktop applications, allowing for interactions such as reading and writing of property files and saving application state, to storing and accessing the actual data for the application.

AIR provides a set of synchronous and asynchronous APIs that facilitate interacting with the file system on a user's local machine. While it may seem daunting if you haven't done it before, reading a local file isn't much different than pulling a file from a remote server.

Understanding File Classes

There are a few key classes that are core to understanding how to interact with the file system. This chapter covers these classes and the different ways they are used together to access and manipulate files on a user's local hard drive.

The AIR classes that work with the file system are all members of the `flash.fileSystem` package. They are the `File`, `FileStream`, and `FileMode` classes. The two event classes are `mx.event.FileEvent` and `flash.events.FileIOErrorEvent`.

Referencing the File Location

The `File` class is used as a reference to a file or directory on the user's machine. This is not limited to only the files or directories that already exist. It will also be used when creating a new file. It is safe to think of an instance of the `File` class as a reference to the location of a file, as opposed to the actual file contents.

Interacting with the File Contents

The `File` class represents the location of a file, and the `flash.fileSystem.FileStream` class interacts with the contents of a file. The `FileStream` class allows you to read or write (known as streaming the data) into or out of your AIR application. This class provides the mechanism to perform read and write operations either piecemeal or all at once.

Specifying File Actions

When interacting with a file, it's important that the file be appropriately locked to ensure data integrity and prevent file corruption. These file locks behave similarly to a table lock in a database. For instance, if two operations were trying to update the same file at the same time, that file could end up with corrupt data. By using file locks appropriately, you can guarantee that each update happens safely.

When working with files, the AIR runtime needs to know what kind of lock to place on the file before any actions can be performed on the file. The `flash.fileSystem.FileMode` class provides a series of constants that are used by the `FileStream` class to determine how to lock a file. The four modes of file access are READ, WRITE, APPEND, or UPDATE.

Accessing Files Synchronously or Asynchronously

In Chapter 5, "Reading and Writing to a SQLite Database," you learned how transactions with the SQLite database can be done in either a synchronous or asynchronous manner. These same options exist for interacting with the file system. AIR, by its nature, is a single-threaded runtime, meaning that it needs to finish its current task before beginning the next one. For this reason, reading or writing large files can greatly degrade your application's performance. However, it is not uncommon for an application to need to interact with large files, such as an XML file containing the products in a catalog or a lookup list containing states and countries. Every time you read or write to a large file synchronously, the application suffers in performance. To help solve these problems, you are not limited to synchronous file access; these operations can also be done asynchronously.

To account for both of these use cases, the AIR framework provides for both asynchronous and synchronous file access. Asynchronous file access uses a system of events and event listeners during the manipulation of the files and file system. Asynchronous file access works like asynchronous data access, which the previous chapter discussed. When you run a file command, AIR will trigger an internal process to perform the requested action and then return control back to your AIR application immediately. Because AIR quickly returns control to the application, the end user experience does not freeze and appears to be working as it should, allowing the user to continue interacting with the application. When the action is complete, the appropriate data is returned to the application through an event. The File API will dispatch events when it is done, successfully or not. If you register any event listeners for those events, they will be triggered. An event-driven architecture like this can be extremely useful. For instance, imagine that your application needs to write a few thousand small files (for example, individual mail messages) or copy everything in one folder to another. Doing this operation synchronously prevents the user from having any interactions until it is all complete, which can take several seconds. By doing this asynchronously, the application will know when the task starts, can perform periodic status checks, and will know when it ends, all while the user can be performing other actions.

For most situations, using the asynchronous file operations is the proper choice. However, there are situations in which synchronous access is the better choice. For example, if your application needs to read configuration data on startup, you don't want the user to interact with the application until all the settings for the application have been loaded. This is a classic case in which synchronous file access is preferable. This allows the application to stop any interactions until the file is opened and read, and its properties are properly set. Another reason developers sometimes choose to use synchronous instead of asynchronous file operations is the ease of coding. Synchronous file access is direct and can be easier to write. When you need simple tasks such as reading or writing a small file or a quick delete, it's just easier to write the synchronous file access calls.

Accessing File System Information

AIR is a runtime that is built to operate identically on all supported OSs. When dealing with the file system of the various OSs, there are certain properties that you will need to know to allow your application to work properly on all the supported OSs. For instance, file path separators in between directories differ among OSs. Some OSs use a forward slash (/), while others use a backslash (\ ). To write a cross-platform application, you need to use the proper path separator for the OS on which the application is running. If you always code your application using either the forward slash or backslash, it will not work on an OS that uses the other separator. Specifying the proper path separator allows you to create a path that is valid on any platform. There are several system properties that you can access with static properties of the File object, such as `File.documentsDirectory` and `File.separator`, `File.lineEnding`, `File.systemCharset`, and `File.desktopDirectory`.

Before you can start working with the contents of a file, you need to find the file first. The file system APIs in AIR support a number of different methods to find a file. This support is provided two ways. The first way is various properties to help you define the path correctly on the user's machine. The second way is by allowing for several different methods to reference a particular file or directory. For example, with AIR you can define the location of a file or directory as a hard-coded path, a relative path, or a URL path. All of these are valid ways to access files.

Specifying Paths

When learning how file access works, the first things you need to understand are the differences between OSs. At the lowest level, the first things to learn are the differences in how paths are defined, specifically the file separator character.

With traditional web applications when you call remote servers, all paths use the forward slash (/) character. However, this is not the case with local file access. Both Linux and Mac OS use the forward slash between folders in a file path, but Windows uses the backslash (\ ) character to determine the folder separators. To make matters worse, the backslash character is used as an escape key in strings in several languages, including ActionScript. The following table describes the use of the backslash in combination with another character:

Character Combination	Meaning
\t	tab
\r	carriage return
\n	line feed

Given this multiple use of the backslash character, the confusion is easy. Consider this ActionScript example:

```
public var myFile:File = new File("c:\temp\preferences.xml");
```

This example will actually be interpreted as

```
public var myFile:File = new File("c:      emp\preferences.xml");
```

This happens because the \t, which is found in the string, is replaced with a tab character, creating an invalid path. To reference an actual backslash in a string, you need to use a double backslash (\\ ), which is actually escaping the first "\" character, like this:

```
public var myFile:File = new File("c:\\temp\\preferences.xml");
```

A major feature of AIR is to be able to deploy on Windows, Mac, or Linux desktops with one code base. The right way to do this is to use the system property `File.separator` instead of a hard-coded slash character between folders, such as:

```
public var file:File= File.documentsDirectory.resolvePath("photos"
➥ +File.separator +"christmas 2007" +File.separator +"thumbnails");
```

Using the `File.separator` property, the application will be able to find the Christmas 2007 photos file in the user's Documents directory, regardless whether it's in C:\documents and settings\your username\documents\photos\christmas2007\thumbnails/Mac HD/Documents/photos/christmas2007/thumbnails, or any other supported combination.

NOTE Windows can actually support both the "/" and "\" path separators. So you can cheat by always using the "/" separator, such as c:/temp/foo, but use of `File.separator` is considered to be a best practice.

Determining the OS-Specific Line Ending

The `File.lineEnding` property will tell you what the default new line character is for the files you may be opening. On some OSs, such as the Mac OS, this is the line-feed character (represented in code by \n). However, in Windows this is represented by two characters: the carriage return followed by the line-feed character (\r\n). Rather than trying to hard-code for one OS, you can always code safely using the `File.lineEnding` value.

Specifying File Paths as URLs

File locations can be resolved by defining the absolute path to the file or directory using file path or URL syntax. You can also use relative paths with either syntax. One thing to keep in mind is that with an AIR application, a relative path is relative to the application's installation directory.

If you want to use the URL syntax to specify a file path, AIR provides you with three special URL prefixes to help you find the files you are looking for. These three prefixes are file://, app:/, and app-storage:/.

NOTE Since users can be allowed to select any installation folder they want, the only way to know where the application is installed is by using app:/.

The first URL schema is file://. This URL prefix provides an absolute path to a file. The file:// syntax for a URL operates as a universal path description recognized by many different languages, including JavaScript. If you need to store a path in a database that may be queried from different languages, the file:// syntax will allow other applications to open and access the same file.

The next two code lines show the different approaches to using an absolute file path. There is no real reason you would choose one over the other, but there are times when you will encounter file paths that are specified as URLs with the file:// syntax, such as when dealing with files passed across the clipboard using the `ClipboardFormats.URL_FORMAT`, which was discussed in Chapter 3, "Interacting with the Clipboard." The important thing to note is that regardless which form is used to specify the file path, you will be able to work with it easily.

```
c:\\My Documents\\photos
file://c:\\My Documents\\photos
```

The next URL shortcut syntax that AIR provides is app:/. This is a shortcut that references the location where the AIR application is installed. This will always reference the directory where your application descriptor file is located.

NOTE For security reasons, you cannot write, create, or delete files or directories that are accessed through the "app:/" URL. The application storage directory syntax explained next will avoid this restriction. A third shortcut available is app-storage:/. Every AIR application has a special storage directory created when the application is installed. This folder is the proper place to store application specific files, such as preferences or configuration files. In default installations of Mac OS, the app-storage:/ shortcut refers to a subdirectory of the /users/*yourUserName*/Library/Preferences path. In default installations of Windows XP, this path resolves to an application specific subdirectory of C:\Documents and Settings*yourUserName*\Application Data. In Windows Vista, this defaults to an application specific subdirectory of c:\Users\yourUserName\AppData\Roaming. By using this special URL prefix, AIR is able to resolve the path and find files regardless where they are located.

Using Special Directories

Just like the URL schemas, there are also a number of special directories defined by AIR for referencing user- or application-specific directories. By starting with one of these special directories, you can work with relative paths throughout your application, making it easier for the application to find the files it needs. To do this, you just need to let AIR convert your relative path into an absolute path with the `resolvePath()` method.

When you use the `resolvePath()` method, you are telling AIR to start from a particular directory and find the file in relation to that initial location.

These special directories are also useful when you are looking for user resources. For instance, many Windows users store their photos under My Documents. However Windows allows for the My Documents folder location to be changed on each individual machine.

Working with the special directories and relative paths is a good practice, as it protects your application from people (or corporate security procedures) that move and rename their directories. This also helps to avoid issues across disparate OSs.

Interacting with the user directory

Each OS is structured around the concept of a user. Since OSs are built to allow for one machine to support multiple users, each user has their own directory (sometimes referred to as the *home directory*). Once a user is logged into their OS, the OS inherently knows the user's directory, and therefore AIR has access to it. To access a user's directory, you can use the static `File.userDirectory` property.

Using the User's documents directory

The `documentsDirectory` static property of the `File` class allows access to the user's Documents directory, regardless of their OS or the customizations they may have made to it.

So, to find a pictures subdirectory of a user's Documents directory, you could specify:

```
var myFile:File = File.documentsDirectory.resolvePath(File.fileSeparator+
"pictures");
```

On a Windows Vista machine, with a user named mnimer, this could resolve the same as:

```
var myFile:File = new File("c:\\users\\mnimer\\Documents\Pictures");
```

TIP Never assume the location of an application on a user's machine. The OS allows them to change the default paths, and it's common to find these paths altered. This is especially on corporate networks, where the user's directory is usually on an external file server, which can be more easily backed up.

Working with the user's desktop directory

The `File` class provides access to the user's desktop directory with the static property `File.desktopDirectory`. Much like the Documents directory, there are defaults that can be assumed in many cases as to where the user's desktop directory will be located for a given OS. But, since an OS allows for users to change these default locations, and the locations are different between different OSs, it is always best to use the static `desktopDirectory` property.

Working with the application directory

The `File` class has a static property `applicationDirectory`, which is a reference to the directory where the end user chose to install your application. This resolves to exactly the same directory as the app:/ URL shortcut, but allows for access using the `File` API, instead of URL syntax.

Referencing the application's storage directory

Much like the URL syntax provides app-storage:/, the `File` class provides a static property `File.applicationStorageDirectory`. This resolves to exactly the same directory as the app-storage:/ URL shortcut, but allows for access using the `File` API, instead of URL syntax. This folder is likely to have the right permissions to allow reading and writing of files from either AIR or from other applications.

Using Error Handling

There are two best practices to keep in mind when working with file APIs. The first is to always wrap your file access code inside a `try/catch` block. The second is to always move the logic that closes the connection and releases any locks on a file into a `finally` command. Closing the connection to the `FileStream` instance in the `finally` clause guarantees that the connection to the file will close correctly even if an error occurs. Neglecting to close the connection can cause locking and corruption issues with that file.

```
private function readFile(myFile:File):void{
    //First create the reference and define the variables.
    var fileStream:FileStream;
    var str:String;
    try{
        // inside the try/catch, open the file and read the bytes
        fileStream = new FileStream();
        fileStream.open( myFile, FileMode.READ );
        str = fileStream.readMultiByte(myFile.size, File.systemCharset);
        trace("contents: " +str);
    }catch(err:Error){
    // do your exception handling here
       Alert.show("There was an error reading the file");
    }finally {
        // close the fileStream
        fileStream.close();
        trace("close file");
    }
}
```

Working with Directories

The core of file access in AIR is the File object. Although the name implies that it is a reference to a file, OSs do not draw a distinction between a file and a directory. You can also use the `File` class to reference a directory within the user's file system in AIR. If you're familiar with the FileReference object in the standard Flash Player, you will want to know that the AIR File object extends the FileReference object from Flash Player. In addition, it builds upon the existing file logic in Flash Player and adds the local file access functionality needed by Adobe AIR.

Actions

Working with files and directories is a simple two-step process of defining the directory and location you wish to reference, and then calling the right methods. Remember that the instance of the `File` class is a reference to a location, so the first step is to create a File object and define the path with either a hard-coded path or with the `File.resolvePath()` method.

```
var myPhotosDirectory:File =
➥ File.userDirectory.resolvePath("Pictures/airPictures ");
```

Next, call the method for the action you need, such as:

```
myPhotosDirectory.createDirectory();
```

or

```
myPhotosDirectory.deleteDirectory(true);
```

Calling the `createDirectory()` or `deleteDirectory()` methods will throw an error if not successful, so you will want to put the calls inside a try/catch block to catch the error correctly. The following example shows these concepts put together along with the best practice of using a try/catch block.

```
var myPhotosDirectory:File = File.userDirectory.resolvePath("Pictures\\
➥ airPictures");
try    {
    myPhotosDirectory.createDirectory()
}catch( err:Error ){
    trace("can not create directory");
}

try    {
    myPhotosDirectory.deleteDirectory(true)
}catch( err:Error ){
    trace("can not delete directory");
}
```

There are four directory actions that AIR will allow you to do: browse them, create them, delete them, and list their contents. These actions are covered by the following methods in the File object.

Browsing the directories

Earlier in this chapter, you learned how to create a reference to a folder in your application using the `File` class. There will be times when you need to have the user select a folder. To achieve this, you can use the `browseForDirectory()` method of the `File` class.

The `browseForDirectory()` method works a little differently than all the other `File` functions in that a user interface launches, allowing the user to browse their system for the directory. This `browseForDirectory()` method uses two events: the `cancel` event and the `select` event. By listening for these two events, you will know if the folder browser was closed because the user canceled the operation, or if they successfully selected a folder.

```
<?xml version="1.0" encoding="utf-8"?>
<mx:WindowedApplication xmlns:mx="http://www.adobe.com/2006/mxml">

    <mx:Script>

        public var file:File = new File();

        public function openBrowser():void{
            file.addEventListener(Event.SELECT, directorySelectedHandler);
            file.addEventListener(Event.CANCEL, directoryCanceledHandler);
            file.browseForDirectory("Please select the correct directory");
        }
        private function directorySelectedHandler(event:Event):void{
            //todo: run the code to list the items in the selected directory.
            trace("directory selected");
        }

        private function directoryCanceledHandler(event:Event):void{
            trace("The user canceled the browse, do nothing");
        }

    </mx:Script>
    <mx:Button label="browse"
        click="openBrowser();"/>

</mx:WindowedApplication>
```

This example presents the user with a button labeled *browse.* When the user clicks that button, the OS native file browse window will launch, prompting the user to choose a folder. Should the user click the Cancel button or the Close button from the top of the browse window, the browse window will close and the `directoryCanceledHandler` will fire. Should the user choose a file and click OK, the browse window will close and the `directorySelectHandler()` method will fire.

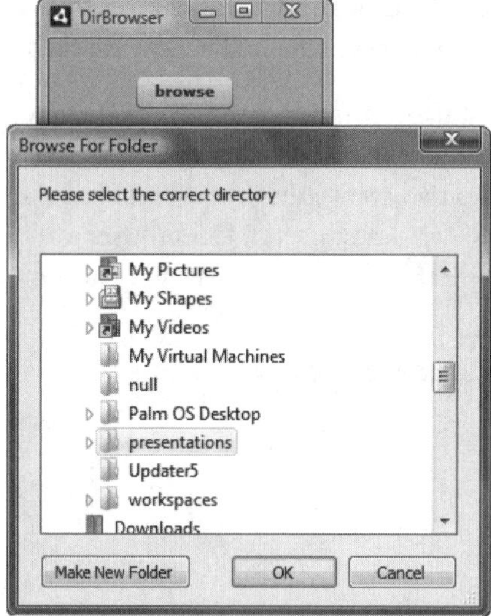

Figure 1: The `browseForDirectory()` method opens an OS native browse window

Creating a directory

There are two methods for creating directories in Adobe AIR: the `createDirectory()` and `createTempDirectory()` methods. If you are using the `createDirectory()` method, you can control the name and location of the new directory. If using the `createTempDirectory()` method, AIR will create the new directory with a unique name in the user's temp folder and return a reference to that new directory. Because the `createDirectory()` method requires you to predefine the reference, it doesn't return any value.

It is useful to use the `createTempDirectory()` method if you need to create a simple directory to store things, such as to store cache files or images during an operation, or if you need a temporary storage location between operations.

If you are attempting to use the `createDirectory()` method and AIR is unable to create it, an `IOError` will be thrown, once again demonstrating why you should always use the try/catch blocks on operations with the potential to fail.

```
<?xml version="1.0" encoding="utf-8"?>
<mx:WindowedApplication xmlns:mx="http://www.adobe.com/2006/mxml">
    <mx:Script>
        <![CDATA[
        import mx.controls.Alert;
        public var myNewDirectory:File;
        public function clickHandler(event:Event):void{
            try{
                myNewDirectory  = File.desktopDirectory.resolvePath(
                ➥ "newDirectory");
            myNewDirectory.createDirectory();
                }catch( err:IOError ){
                Alert.show("Error, could not create directory");
            }
        }
        ]]>
    </mx:Script>
    <mx:Button label="create folder" click="clickHandler(event)"/>
</mx:WindowedApplication>
```

Again, notice the use of the try/catch block, to avoid any errors that might be encountered in the process of creating the directory. Understandably, creating a temp directory is a little simpler.

```
<?xml version="1.0" encoding="utf-8"?>
<mx:WindowedApplication xmlns:mx="http://www.adobe.com/2006/mxml">
    <mx:Script>
        <![CDATA[
        import mx.controls.Alert;

        public var myNewDirectory:File;

        public function clickHandler(event:Event):void{
            try{
                myNewDirectory = File.createTempDirectory();
                trace(myNewDirectory.nativePath);
            }catch( err:IOError ){
                Alert.show("Error, could not create directory");
            }
        }
        ]]>
```

```
    </mx:Script>
    <mx:Button label="create folder" click="clickHandler(event)"/>
</mx:WindowedApplication>
```

This time, as the user clicks the button, a temp directory is created. If you run this in debug mode through FlexBuilder, you can see the full path to the new directory shown in the Console window.

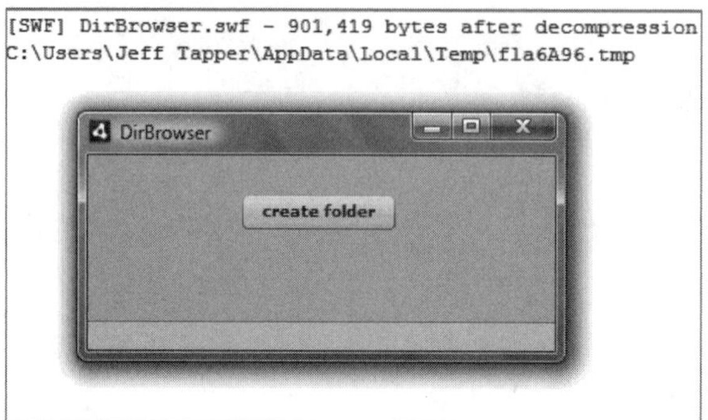

Figure 2: Clicking the button creates a new directory on the user's machine.

Deleting a directory

AIR also offers two ways to delete a directory. You can do a hard delete with the `deleteDirectory()` or `deleteDirectoryAsync()` method, or you can delete items by moving them to the user's trash with the `moveToTrash()` or `moveToTrashAsync()` methods. Moving items to trash is the safer way because users can easily restore the files and folders if needed. If your application creates a directory to temporarily store sensitive information, you should probably remove it using one of the delete directory methods so that the information cannot be compromised by someone retrieving it from the trash. Normally, you will want to delete directories using the move to trash methods, which can allow the user to later retrieve them if necessary.

When deleting a directory, AIR can delete just a directory or a directory and everything in it. Deleting just the directory will work only if the directory is empty. You can simplify the process and bypass this restriction by choosing to delete the directory and its contents, but be careful not to delete more than you expected. To determine if the delete directory methods will also delete the contents of the directory, an optional Boolean argument can be passed to the method, indicating if the contents should also be deleted. By default, the method assumes you do not want to delete the contents. If you want to delete the contents, pass the argument true to the method. The move to trash operations do not accept this Boolean argument; it will always move the folders contents to the trash along with the folder itself. Regardless which of these operations you are using, AIR will throw an IOError if it is unable to delete the folder for any reason, once again demonstrating why you'll always want to put your delete code in a try/catch block, allowing you to determine if the directory was deleted successfully.

<table>
<tr><th>Operation</th><th>Code</th></tr>
<tr><td>Delete</td><td><pre>try{
    var myPhotosDirectory:File =
    ➥ File.userDirectory.resolvePath(
    ➥ "Pictures\\airPictures");
    myPhotosDirectory.deleteDirectory(
    ➥ true);
}catch(err:IOError){
    trace("Unable to delete directory");

}</pre></td></tr>
<tr><td>Move To Trash</td><td><pre>try{
    var myPhotosDirectory:File =
    ➥ File.userDirectory.resolvePath(
    ➥ "Pictures\\airPictures");
    myPhotosDirectory.moveToTrash(
    ➥ true);
}catch(err:IOError){
    trace("Unable to delete directory");
}</pre></td></tr>
</table>

Both deleteDirectory() and moveToTrash() have an asynchronous version that behaves similarly (albeit asynchronous, instead of synchronous). If you are deleting folders with lots of children, the asynchronous operation is a better bet, as the application will not lock up while the OS is performing the delete. Both of these asynchronous methods will dispatch a complete event if the operation is completed successfully.

```
private function createThenDeleteAsynch():void{
    try{
        var file:File = File.userDirectory.resolvePath(
        ➥ "Pictures\\airPictures");
        file.createDirectory();
```

```
        file.addEventListener("complete", deleteCompleteHandler);
        file.deleteDirectoryAsync(true);
    }catch( err:IOError ){
        trace("Unable to delete directory");
    }
}
private function deleteCompleteHandler(event:Event):void{
    trace("delete complete");
}
```

Listing contents of a directory

Frequently, when working with a file system, you will need to generate a list of the files in a directory. To help with this task, the `File` class has a `getDirectoryListing()` method. This method takes no arguments, and returns an array of files in the directory. If you are planning on working with lots of files in a folder or want to be safe because you don't know just how many files you will be working with, AIR provides you with an asynchronous version of the list method called `getDirectoryListingAsync()`. In general, you should use the asynchronous method; it does require a little more code, but it prevents the application from appearing to be frozen while the list method is executing.

Once you have retrieved the array of items in the directory, it's a pretty easy task to loop over the list. If you want to also list the contents of all the subdirectories as well, you can add this recursive logic pretty easily by looping over the results and checking if each item is either a file or a subfolder.

```
private function showFilesInDir(dir:File):void{
    var fileList:Array = dir.getDirectoryListing();
    for each( var file:File in fileList ){
        if( !file.isDirectory ){
        trace( file.name );
        }
    }
}
```

Here is the same method written using the `getDirectoryListingAsync()` method instead.

```
private function showFilesInDir(dir:File):void{
    dir.addEventListener(FileListEvent.DIRECTORY_LISTING, listDirectoryHandler);
    dir.getDirectoryListingAsync();
}
```

```
public function listDirectoryHandler(event:FileListEvent):void
{
    var fileList:Array = event.files;
        for each( var file:File in event.files ){
            if( !file.isDirectory ){
                trace( file.name );
            }
        }
}
```

Both the getDirectoryListing() and getDirectoryListingAsync() functions will return any files or folders found in the directory. Next is an example that will build an array of all the files that can be found in a specific folder or in any subfolder. If it finds a subfolder, it will automatically go into that folder, list the contents, and repeat.

```
// create a class level property that the listDir method can reference
private var files:Array = new Array();

// a start method to set the root folder.
public function findAllFiles():Array{
    // set the path
    var photosDir:File = File.documentsDirectory.resolvePath("photos");
    listDir(photosDir, true);
    return files;
}

// a 2nd method used to recursively walk the tree.
private function listDir(dir:File, recurse:Boolean=true):void{
    var fileList:Array = dir.getDirectoryListing();
    for each( var file:File in fileList ){
        if( file.isDirectory && recurse ){
            listDir(file, true);
        }else{
            files.push(file);
        }
    }
}
```

This example has two methods, one to start the process and a second function to do the recursive calls. In the end, you will end up with one large, flat array of files to display in your application.

Now that you have your list of files, it's very easy to add some conditional logic in the second `listDir()` function to filter out the items you may or may not want.

For instance, if you only wanted an array of PNG files, it's a simple matter of checking the file extension in the loop like this:

```
if( file.extension == "png"){
    files.push(file)
}
```

NOTE You can also use the built-in `filterFunction` property of the `ArrayCollection` class to filter the array. For examples of this, please see Chapter 6, "Using Remote XML Data with Controls," in *Adobe Flex 3, Training from the Source* by Adobe Press.

File and Directory Events

Because the `File` class provides references to both files and directories, it has a unified set of events, which will work equally well for both. Some of these events are:

- **`cancel`**—The `cancel` event is broadcast when a user clicks Cancel and closes the OS browse window. This is not thrown when the code calls the `cancel()` function.
- **`complete`**—The `complete` event is the standard event that dispatches when one of the asynchronous methods completes its task.
- **`directoryListing`**—The `getDirectoryListingAsync()` method is the only exception to the use of the complete event. When this method completes, the event broadcast is a `directoryListing` event, rather than a `complete` event.
- **`progress`**—The `progress` event is thrown periodically while an asynchronous method is running. It provides updates on the status of the work in progress so you can provide the user with a good experience.
- **`securityError`**—The `securityError` event dispatches if your application attempts to invoke a function on a directory or file for which it doesn't have permissions, based on the OS security settings.

- `select`—When a user browses for a file or directory using the file browser, the `select` event dispatches when a user makes a selection.
- `selectMultiple`—When a user browses for files or directories using the file browser, the `selectMultiple` event is dispatched when a user selects more than one item.

Using the FileStream Class

Now you have learned that the File object works similarly for both files and directories. AIR provides access to a basic set of properties, provided by the OS, for every file such as the name, type, size, date created, native location, and more. These properties can help you sort and filter the files as your application requires. The key difference between a file and a directory is its contents. While a directory can contain other files and directories, a file will always contain an array of bytes representing data.

To begin working with the contents of files, AIR works in conjunction with the OS when accessing and manipulating files. In order for AIR to work with a file, you will need to use the `FileStream` class, which contains the methods that let you work with and manipulate the contents of a file.

Understanding file modes

As you open a `fileStream` instance to a file, your application needs to tell the OS how it is interacting with the file, so that the OS can lock the file appropriately. The four ways (or modes) are READ, WRITE, APPEND, and UPDATE. By using these locks, the OS is able to guarantee that you can't do the wrong thing. For instance, you can't accidently overwrite the contents of a file if you open it for a READ action. Think of READ as a read-only lock on the file.

Reading a file

The FileMode.READ constant is the mode you will use when you want to open a file to read its contents into your application. You can read a file all at once or in sections, which is covered in the next section.

```
private function traceFile(myFile:File):void{
    var fileStream:FileStream;
    var str:String;
    try{
        // inside the try/catch, open the file and read the bytes
```

```
        fileStream = new FileStream();
        fileStream.open( myFile, FileMode.READ );
        str = fileStream.readMultiByte(myFile.size, File.systemCharset);
        trace("contents: " +str);

    }catch(err:Error){
        // do your exception handling here
    }finally {
       // close the fileStream
       fileStream.close();
    }
}
```

This example shows a method, traceFile(), into which a file reference is passed. A fileStream instance is created and is used to open the passed in file in READ mode. While the application has a READ lock on the file, no other OS resource will be allowed to write to the file until the READ is complete. Notice the try/catch block at the end, so that the fileStream is always closed, regardless whether or not the file is read successfully.

While this example shows the readMultiByte() method, there are actually two categories of read methods available in the FileStream class: methods that read one byte at a time and methods that read multiple bytes at a time. The methods that read in a single byte at a time will read the next byte in a file based on the current position property of the fileStream. After each successful byte read, the position marker will automatically be advanced by one. If you happen to know the size of the data you need to read in, you can speed things up with the multiple byte methods instead.

The reason there are so many methods for reading a single byte is to allow you to read that byte as a strongly typed object. Because ActionScript is a strongly typed language, and many binary file types store strongly typed data, it is preferable to read the byte in to the proper data type. So with all of these different read methods, you are able to get a value of a certain data type and assign it to a local ActionScript property without any runtime errors.

Single-byte read methods:

- readBoolean
- readByte
- readDouble
- readFloat
- readInt
- readShort
- readUTF
- readUnsignedByte
- readUnsignedInt
- readUnsignedShort
- readUTF
- readUTFBytes

Multibyte read methods:

- readBytes
- readMultiByte
- readObject

Reading in ID3v1 data from an MP3

The ID3v1 metadata is located at the end of an MP3 file, in the last 128 bytes of information. By storing it at the end of the file, any MP3 player that did not know about this data would still be able to play the song (it would just ignore the data at the end).

One piece of metadata available in an MP3 file is called the ID3v1 tag. This metadata contains 6 fields: four 30-byte fields for song title, album title, artist name, and a comment; one 4-byte year field; and one 1-byte genre code.

However, because this data is at the end of an MP3 file, you need to read in the whole file so you can access the last 128 bytes to get the ID3 metadata values.

Since the ID3 specification defines the location and size of the data stored in the MP3 metadata, we don't need to walk through the data one character at a time. Instead you can use the multi-byte methods to get the value of the six fields of data.

```
private function readID3(mp3:File):void{
    var mp3Stream:FileStream = new FileStream();
    mp3Stream.open(mp3, FileMode.READ);
    mp3Stream.position = mp3.size - 128;
    var songTitle:String = mp3Stream.readMultiByte(30, File.systemCharset);
    var artistTitle:String = mp3Stream.readMultiByte(30, File.systemCharset);
    var artistName:String = mp3Stream.readMultiByte(30, File.systemCharset);
    var comments:String = mp3Stream.readMultiByte(30, File.systemCharset);
    var year:String = mp3Stream.readMultiByte(4, File.systemCharset);
    // read the single byte in the last field.
    var genre:String = mp3Stream.readByte().toString(10);
}
```

First, this method creates a `fileStream` instance, which it uses to open the file in READ mode. Next, it sets the position of the stream to be 128 characters from the end. Because this stream was opened synchronously, the application won't proceed to this line until the entire file has been read in. Lastly, the value of the standard six fields of data are read and stored in local variables.

Writing a file

The FileMode.WRITE mode is used when you are creating a new file or trying to overwrite the contents of an existing file. If the file you are writing to already exists and has contents, its contents will be replaced with the contents placed there by the `fileStream`. If the file doesn't exist, it will be created.

Remember, the File object is a reference to a file, not the actual file itself. So, it can be a reference to an existing file or a reference to the file that will be created when the process is complete.

The simplest way to write a file is with a prebuilt string in one method call. Much like the use of `readMultiBytes()` for reading in a whole file at once, you can use `writeBytes()` or `writeUTFBytes()` to fully populate a file, such as:

```
private function writePrefsToFile(myFile:File):void{
    //First create the reference and define the variables.
    var fileStream:FileStream;
    var str:String;
    try{
        // inside the try/catch, open the file and read the bytes
        fileStream = new FileStream();
        fileStream.open( myFile, FileMode.WRITE );

        var fileContents:String = "<preferences>none</preferences>";
        fileStream.writeBytes(fileContents, File.systemCharset);
    }catch(err:Error){
        // do your exception handling here
        trace(err.toString());
    }finally {
        // close the fileStream
        fileStream.close();
    }
}
```

Structurally, this method is very similar to the one that read a file. A file reference is passed in, and a `fileStream` is created and opened on the referenced file. This time, the stream is opened using the FileMode.WRITE mode. Next, a string is built, and written to the file using the `writeMultiByte()` method of the `fileStream`. Then, the `fileStream` is closed in a `finally` block.

Much like the read methods have multiple methods to read a single byte in a specific data type, there are corresponding methods for writing the data back into a binary file.

Single-byte write methods:

- writeBoolean
- writeByte
- writeDouble
- writeFloat
- writeInt
- writeShort
- writeUnsignedInt
- writeUTF
- writeUTFBytes

Multibyte write methods:

- writeBytes
- writeMultiByte
- writeObject

These too can be used to write strongly typed data into a file.

Appending data to the end of a file

FileMode.APPEND mode is useful if you are building up a file a little at a time. An application's log file is a classic example of this. By building a file incrementally, instead of in one large write, it can also help with performance. If you were to open a file, read its entire contents, add onto the contents of the file, and write it back to disk, each subsequent write operation would take longer than the previous one. Rather than rewrite the whole file each time, it makes more sense to append new content onto the existing file; this is what the APPEND file mode will do.

For example, to add a new line to a file, you would do this:

```
private function addLineToFile(file:File,fileContents:String):void{
    var fileStream:FileStream;
    try{
        fileStream = new FileStream();
        fileStream.open( file, FileMode.APPEND );
        fileStream.writeMultiByte(fileContents, File.systemCharset);
    }catch(err:Error){
        // do your exception handling here
       trace(err.toString());
    }finally {
        // close the fileStream
       fileStream.close();
    }
}
```

Syntactically, this looks just like writing a file, except for the FileMode that is used. This minor difference guarantees that the new content will be added to the end of the file, rather than replacing the contents of the file.

Reading and writing to a file

The `FileMode.UPDATE` constant is used when you need to both read and write to the same file, such as if you were trying to replace a specific section within a file instead of either adding to the end of a file, or replacing the whole file. The concepts behind this are similar to the append mode except that the content you add can be at any location within the file.

When you are using the update mode, you need to specify the position you want to update. This can be done in two separate ways: either by specifying the `position` property of the FileStream object or by using the `writeBytes()` method of the `fileStream`, which lets you specify the exact position to write the data.

```
private function replaceFileContents(myFile:File, position:int,
➥ newStr:String):void{
    var fileStream:FileStream;
    try{
        // inside the try/catch, open the file and read the bytes
        fileStream = new FileStream();
        fileStream.open( myFile, FileMode.UPDATE );
        if(fileStream.bytesAvailable > position){
        fileStream.position = position;
    }
        fileStream.writeMultiByte(newStr, File.systemCharset);
    }catch(err:Error){
        // do your exception handling here
        trace(err.toString());
    }finally {
        // close the fileStream
        fileStream.close();
    }
}
```

In this example, the `newStr` argument, that is passed into the function, is inserted into the file, at the position specified. The FileStream object works through a file by maintaining reference to a position marker. When you first open a file, the `position` property starts at 0. AIR will automatically advance this `position` property as you read or write any of the bytes in the file, allowing you to walk through the file. As you can see in this example, you can also set this `position` property directly to jump ahead to any section of the file. However, if you are jumping to the position, be sure to use the `bytesAvailable` property to confirm that the byte you will read next exists, as is shown with the conditional statement in the example code.

When you access a file using one of the standard synchronous methods, the data is available right away. However, when you are using the asynchronous methods, it is important to ensure that the data you want to read has successfully been read into memory before you try to access that portion of a file in an event handler.

While the `FileStream` class is reading data from a file, the contents are stored in a buffer. As the buffer is updated, the `bytesAvailable` property is updated to reflect the amount currently available. By checking this property, you can see if the data you need has been loaded before actually calling the read method on it. If you wanted to replace a section of a file, rather than just inserting at a particular location, the `writeBytes()` method allows you to specify the new content and a starting and ending location where it will be written.

Internally, AIR treats files like a large array of characters, or more specifically an array of bytes. Because the file contents can be treated as an array, it allows you to access specific sections of the file contents easily.

Of course, this assumes that you know which part of a file you need to change. Frequently, you will perform this operation when working with a predefined file specification such as the ID3v1 spec for MP3 files.

Exploring the File Class Further

So far, you have learned that a file object is a reference to a file location, and the `FileStream` class has the actual methods you will use to manipulate the contents of a file. But the `File` class also can do a few other things for you. These other tasks are there to help you manipulate and work with files. These other tasks are Browse, Delete, Copy, Move, and Rename.

Browsing Files

Earlier, you learned how to use the directory and file browser to allow the user to choose items from the file system. These are usually used to allow operations such as allowing the user to open a file (or multiple files), or to save a file by selecting the location for a save.

By default, the file browser will show all files in a particular directory. Frequently, you will want to limit this list to include only files of a certain type. For instance, when opening a user's browse dialog to open a file, you will almost always want to limit the type of files that a user can select. This filtering is done by using the `FileFilter` class. The `File` instance allows you to specify a file filter, which will be used to show only specific file types when browsing the file system.

When you are creating your `FileFilter`, you need to pass two arguments. The first is a clear text description for the filter. This is the name that appears in the drop-down list of file types when the dialog opens. The second argument is a comma-separated list of file patterns that are allowed with this filter.

NOTE There is a third, optional argument you can provide to the `FileFilter` constructor, which specifies a semicolon delimited list of Macintosh file types.

For instance, to create a filter that will allow the user to choose files with an .as, .txt, .css, or .html extension, you would use a filter such as:

```
var filter1:FileFilter = new FileFilter("text:", "*.as;*.txt;*.css;*.html");
var file:File = File.documentsDirectory;
file.browseForOpen("Select Text File", new Array(filter1));
```

You can specify a file filter array for any of the file browser methods in AIR.

Deleting Files

As you learned earlier in this chapter, AIR also has access to delete a single file or to recursively delete all the files in a folder. To delete a single file, you need to get a reference to the file, then call its `deleteFile()` method.

```
var myFile:File = File.applicationStorageDirectory.resolvePath("logs/appLog.txt");
myFile.deleteFile();
```

Copying, Moving, or Renaming Files

If you need to copy or move files around on the local system, AIR allows you to do it with the `copyTo()` and `moveTo()` methods. When you are using these methods, you need to define two references: one to the file you want to copy (or move) and one to the folder to which you want the copy or move made. If you want to rename the file as you copy or move it, create the second reference to a file with a new name, not just a folder, and AIR will automatically rename it while it copies or moves the file.

Copy

```
var myFile:File = File.applicationStorageDirectory.resolvePath ("logs/appLog.txt");
var backupFile:File = File.applicationStorageDirectory.resolvePath ("logs/
➥ backup");
myFile.copyTo(backupFile, true);
```

Move

```
var myFile:File = File.applicationStorageDirectory.resolvePath ("logs/appLog.txt");
var backupFile:File = File.applicationStorageDirectory.resolvePath ("logs/
➥ backup");
myFile.moveTo(backupFile, true);
```

Rename

While there is no rename method in the `File` class, you can do a rename by using the move operation to the same directory with a different filename.

```
var myFile:File = File.applicationStorageDirectory.resolvePath ("logs/appLog.txt");
var backupFile:File = File.applicationStorageDirectory.resolvePath ("logs/appLog.
➥ old.txt ");
myFile.moveTo(backupFile, true);
```

Writing ActionScript Objects to the File System

Aside from normal file access, AIR has one more special type of file access: serializing and deserializing ActionScript objects to disk. It does this by using the same AMF (ActionScript Messaging Format) serialized format that is natively available in Flash Player, for communication with a remote server.

NOTE For more information on using AMF to communicate with a server, see Chapter 10, "Understanding Data Services and the Need for Remote Data," and Chapter 11, "Interacting with a Java Server Using Blaze DS."

This is a very useful technique because it gives you the ability to save and reload parts of your application to disk. The next time a user may use the application, you can bring it right back to the same place they left it.

To do this, the `FileStream` class has two methods: One is for reading an object saved to disk, the `readObject()` method. The second method, `writeObject()`, will write the object in memory to disk. These two methods save you from the usual task of converting your data to some intermediate format, like XML, before writing it.

Saving object state

One reason you might use this technique would be if you had an Application model object that controls the state of the application. If you wanted to store the whole application model on the disk so that the next time the user runs the application it returned to the exact state it was in, serializing that model and writing it to disk would make sense. With this technique you can easily save (also referred to as *serialize)* the object directly to a file on the user's machine when you close the application. Also, you can directly read (also referred to as *deserialize*) back in the object when the user opens the application again.

```
private function saveStateObject(myFile:File, data:Object):void{
    var fileStream:FileStream = new FileStream();
    try{
        fileStream.open( myFile, FileMode.WRITE);
        // write the application model to disk.
        fileStream.writeObject( data );
    }
    finally{
        fileStream.close();
    }
}
```

In this example, any arbitrary ActionScript object that is passed to this method will be automatically serialized and written to disk.

To read this file back out, it is just as simple:

```
private function readStateObject(myFile:File):void{
    var fileStream:FileStream = new FileStream();
    try{
        fileStream.open( myFile, FileMode.READ );
        // write the application model to disk.
```

```
        data = fileStream.readObject();
        trace(data.name);
    }
    finally{
        fileStream.close();
    }
}
```

Here, the serialized file is read back from the OS, and the `name` property of the object is read, and then traced to the console.

NOTE While the examples in this book read and write generic ActionScript objects to the file system, it is possible to write strongly typed objects as well. If the class of the object you are writing includes a `[RemoteClass(alias="...")]` metadata tag, like those you will use in Chapter 10, "Understanding the Need for Remote Data," the object will maintain its strong type when it is read back using the `readObject()` method.

Looking at the dpTimeTracker Example

The dpTimeTracker accesses the file system for a few different tasks. In Chapter 3, "Interacting with the Clipboard," and Chapter 4, "Implementing Drag and Drop Between the OS and AIR," you explored how the dpTimeTracker was capable of creating an Excel file from the data in a datagrid. Of course, in order to create a file, the dpTimeTracker application uses the `File` and `FileStream` classes. Likewise, in Chapter 5, "Reading and Writing to a SQLite Database," you learned how the dpTimeTracker uses a SQLite database. Before the application could read from the database, it needed to open the database file, also using the `File` class.

Creating the Excel File

Open the ListToExcelClipboardDragDropHandler.as file from the net/digitalprimates/dragDrop folder. This file was examined in Chapters 3 and 4, explaining how the clipboard and drag-and-drop functionality works. As you learned then, the `createXLS()` method was added as a data handler function for the copy data method, so, when the user copies the data from the datagrid and later pastes it, this function will fire and then create the file. Likewise, this method is also the data handler function for adding the data to the clipboard for drag-and-drop operations. Regardless whether the function was called from a copy or drag operation, this time you will focus on how the Excel file itself is created and written to disk.

```
private function createXLS():Array {
    var file:File = File.createTempDirectory().resolvePath("data-
    ➥ +dateFormatter.format(new Date())+".xls");
    var excelFile:ExcelFile = dgToExcel();
    var fileStream:FileStream = new FileStream();
    fileStream.open(file, FileMode.WRITE);
    fileStream.writeBytes( excelFile.saveToByteArray() );
    fileStream.close();
    return new Array(file);
}
```

When this function is called, it first creates a temp directory, in which it will get a reference to file whose name is "data-" followed by the current date and time, as formatted by a date formatter class. The specified format string is "YYYY-MM-DD-HH-NN-SS" (specified on line 213), which specifies a four-digit year, followed by a two-digit month, followed by a two-digit day, followed by a two-digit hour (in 24-hour mode, so a number from 0 to 23), followed by a two-digit minute in the hour, and ending with a two-digit seconds in the minute. So, if this were run at the stroke of midnight on May 15, 2007, the file name would be "data-2007-05-15-24-00-00." Remember, if a file of that name didn't already exist in the directory (which is likely the case), a new file will be created. Next, the as3xls library is used to create the contents of the Excel file (for more information on the open source as3xls project, see its Google code homepage http://code.google.com/p/as3xls/).

NOTE For more information on the DateFormatter and other Flex Formatters, see *Adobe Flex 3, Training from the Source* by Adobe Press.

This library returns the binary data that will make up the Excel file, as an instance of a class, named `ExcelFile`. Next, a `fileStream` instance is created and used to open the file in the write mode. Next the byte array of the ExcelFile is written to the `fileStream`, using the `writeBytes()` method. Lastly, the `fileStream` is closed, and the file reference is returned so it is available from the clipboard. Now, when a user pastes (or drops) this content into a directory (or desktop), the file will be created in a temp directory and moved to the directory where the user dragged or pasted it.

Reading the SQLite File

As you learned in Chapter 5, before you can work with a SQLite database, you need to have a reference to the database file. In the dpTimeTracker application, this reference is created in the `OpenDatabase` class in the commands/sql directory. When working with the SQLStatements on a SQLite database, you do not need to manipulate the file stream itself. All the interactions with the contents of the file are abstracted into the `SQLStatement` class; all you need is a reference to the file itself.

```
package commands.sql{
    import flash.filesystem.File;
    import mx.rpc.events.ResultEvent;
    import mx.rpc.http.HTTPService;
    import net.digitalprimates.framework.command.SQLCommand;

    public class OpenDatabase extends SQLCommand{
        private var reference:Object;
        private var openMode:String;
        private var autoCompact:Boolean;
        private var pageSize:int;

        override public function execute():void {
            connection.openAsync( reference,openMode,
            ➥ this,autoCompact,pageSize );
        }

        public function OpenDatabase( connection:*,
        ➥ reference:Object = null,
        ➥ openMode:String = "create",
        ➥ autoCompact:Boolean = false, pageSize:
        ➥ int = 1024):void {
            if ( !reference ) {
                var dbFile:File =
                ➥ File.applicationStorageDirectory.resolvePath(
                ➥ "TimeTracker.db");
                this.reference = dbFile;
            } else {
                this.reference = reference;
            }
```

```
                this.openMode = openMode;
                this.autoCompact = autoCompact;
                this.pageSize = pageSize;

                super( connection );
            }
        }
}
```

In Chapter 5, you learned how each of the discrete interactions with the SQLite database can be abstracted into a simple command. The dpTimeTracker uses a command called `OpenDatabase` to create a reference to the database file. The `SQLConnection` class knows how to handle the interactions with the database file, but to work it needs a valid file reference.

In the constructor of the `OpenDatabase` class, the first thing that happens is a check to see if a reference to a database file has been passed in. If it hasn't, a local variable named `dbFile` is used to get a reference to a file named TimeTracker.db in the application storage directory. When this command is executed, the `SQLConnection` class takes the file reference and opens it asynchronously.

Next Steps

In this chapter, you learned how to interact with the file system. In the next chapter, you will learn the various ways in which your AIR application can be customized, using Styles, Skins, and the Native AIR APIs. Once you have an understanding of all the customizations you can make to your application, there are no bounds to the creativity you can bring to an AIR project.

CUSTOMIZING THE LOOK AND FEEL OF AN APPLICATION

CHAPTER 7

One of the most appealing features of AIR is that applications written with it do not need to look like a web application. Existing outside the browser offers a level of creative freedoms that have never before existed for web developers. The Flex framework provides a robust API for controlling the look and feel inside the application window, which is available for applications that run inside or outside a browser. By default, AIR applications use your standard operating *system chrome* (a particular look used for the windows throughout an OS) to style the application window itself. Regardless of your OS of choice, there is a default look and feel for applications on your OS. However, if you want to give your application a completely custom look and feel, you can leverage the additional AIR APIs for controlling elements such as windows, menus, and taskbars.

The native chrome for each OS provides some common elements for minimizing, maximizing, closing, resizing, and moving the application window. With the use of the AIR Windowing API, you can still add all this functionality without needing the system default chrome to provide it; in fact you can completely control the look and feel of your application without the system chrome. Throughout this chapter, you will explore the various techniques and options available for customizing an AIR application.

Understanding the Differences between the Flex and AIR APIs

Native to browser-based Flex applications are two mechanisms for customizing the look and feel: styling and skinning. Styling allows you to modify the appearance of any component through the use of style properties, which can adjust elements such as the font size and background color, among many other predefined style properties. The other way to customize the look is by skinning. Skins are graphics that replace pieces of a visual element. These graphics can be files, such as JPGs, GIFs, and SWFs, or as an ActionScript class, which uses the drawing API.

AIR offers more possibilities, with the addition of its Window, Menu, and TaskAPIs. By combining Flex's robust abilities to completely customize the look and feel of each element with AIR's additional ability to add native style menus, items on taskbars, and complete control over the look and feel of the window chrome itself, the design possibilities for your AIR application are almost limitless.

Using Styles

Each component in the Flex framework has a series of style properties that can be set to control the look and feel of an application. Each style is clearly delineated in the Adobe Flex 3 Language Reference (known as ASDOC) documentation. For these style properties, there are three different approaches to apply styles. The simplest is setting a style on a component directly as an attribute of its MXML tag. Consider this simple example:

```
<?xml version="1.0" encoding="utf-8"?>
<mx:WindowedApplication xmlns:mx="http://www.adobe.com/2006/mxml"
    layout="absolute" >
    <mx:Label text="This is Text" />
</mx:WindowedApplication>
```

When this runs, it will appear like this:

Figure 1: A Simple, unstyled label in an AIR application

With the addition of some inline styles on both the application and the label itself, the result can have a very different look and feel.

```
<?xml version="1.0" encoding="utf-8"?>
<mx:WindowedApplication xmlns:mx="http://www.adobe.com/2006/mxml"
    layout="absolute"
    backgroundColor="#000000">
    <mx:Label text="This is Large Bold White Text"
        color="#ffffff"
        fontWeight="bold"
        fontSize="24"
        fontFamily="Verdana"
        horizontalCenter="0"
        verticalCenter="0"/>
</mx:WindowedApplication>
```

Figure 2: A styled label in an AIR application

Notice that the contents of the application have been changed vastly. From a code perspective, the only difference between the two is some minor styling on the application (by changing the background color) and on the label (by changing the color, size, font, weight, and positioning).

As was mentioned previously, inline MXML styles are just one of the three ways that styles can be set. Another equally valid approach is to set the styles via ActionScript. The `UIComponent` class, which is the superclass to all Flex components, defines a method named `setStyle()` method. This allows for any component, regardless whether it was created via MXML or via ActionScript, to have its styles set. The basic syntax for working with styles using ActionScript is:

```
componentName.setStyle("styleName",newValue);
```

One of the main reasons you might decide to set a style in ActionScript instead of via MXML attributes is the very common case when you are dealing with a component that was created in ActionScript instead of in MXML. Imagine an application that queries a back-end server for a list of credit cards accepted by the application. For each record returned by the server, a radio button will be created on the checkout page. Because these radio buttons were not defined at design time using MXML, but instead were created in ActionScript, there is no MXML tag in which the styles can be set as attributes.

```
private function handleCreditCardList(event:ResultEvent=null):void{
    var aCardsAccepted:Array = event.result as Array;
    for(var i:int=0;i<aCardsAccepted.length;i++){
        var rb:RadioButton = new RadioButton();
        rb.label = aCardsAccepted[i].ccName;
        this.addChild(rb);
    }
}
```

In this example, if you wanted to add a style to each radio button, for instance, to make the font size larger, there is no MXML tag in which you could apply an attribute. Instead, you would need to use the `setStyle()` method. Here is the same example, this time applying a font size of 20 to each radio button.

```
private function handleCreditCardList(event:ResultEvent=null):void{
    var aCardsAccepted:Array = event.result as Array;
    for(var i:int=0;i<aCardsAccepted.length;i++){
        var rb:RadioButton = new RadioButton();
        rb.label = aCardsAccepted[i].ccName;
        rb.setStyle("fontSize",20);
        this.addChild(rb);
    }
}
```

Be careful using setStyle(). Each time setStyle() is called on a component currently shown on the screen, the screen is forced to redraw. You should note that in this example, the style is set before the radio button is added to the display list, so the screen is redrawn only once. If you were to switch the order of the setStyle() and addChild(), this code would become far less efficient.

The third mechanism you can use to set the styles on components is Cascading Style Sheets (CSS). In reality, the style API we've discussed so far (setting styles inline or through the setStyle() method) are both actually using CSS style properties. Extending this metaphor a bit more, you can also build a series of styles in a CSS file and apply those styles to individual components or to all components of a particular class. While Flex does not support the full suite of CSS syntax, it does support both type selectors and class selectors.

A type selector allows for all elements of a particular type (based on a particular ActionScript class in the Flex world) to have a style applied to it. For instance:

```
Button{
      color: #FF0000;
      font-size:20;
}
```

This type selector will set the color of the text on any button in the application to red (#FF0000), and the font size to 20 pts.

NOTE One thing to note is the various syntaxes you have seen in this chapter for the style properties. When you were setting the size of the text inline in an MXML tag, the syntax you used was `<mx:Label fontSize="20"/>`, but the example using the ActionScript class used `font-size:20`. In general, CSS uses hyphens as separators between words in multi-word styles, such as font-size, font-weight, and so on. However, because MXML is an XML-based language, and the XML specification does not allow for hyphens in attribute names, Adobe has generated a series of "ActionScript equivalent" CSS style property names, specifically to allow for the styles to be applied in any of the following ways. When setting the size of text using either `setStyle()` or CSS blocks, both the traditional CSS "font-size" and the ActionScript equivalent ("fontSize") will work interchangeably. However, if applying the style inline in an MXML tag, only the ActionScript equivalent will work.

To use CSS styles, such as a type selector, you will need a Style block. This can be done using the `<mx:Style>` tag. In between the open and close `<mx:Style>` tags, you can add any syntactically valid CSS styles. In the vast majority of cases, these styles will be set from the main application file. Consider this example:

```
<?xml version="1.0" encoding="utf-8"?>
<mx:WindowedApplication xmlns:mx="http://www.adobe.com/2006/mxml"
layout="absolute">
    <mx:Style>
        Button{
            font-size:20;
            font-weight:bold;
            color:#ff0000;
        }
    </mx:Style>
    <mx:Button label="Click Me"/>
</mx:WindowedApplication>
```

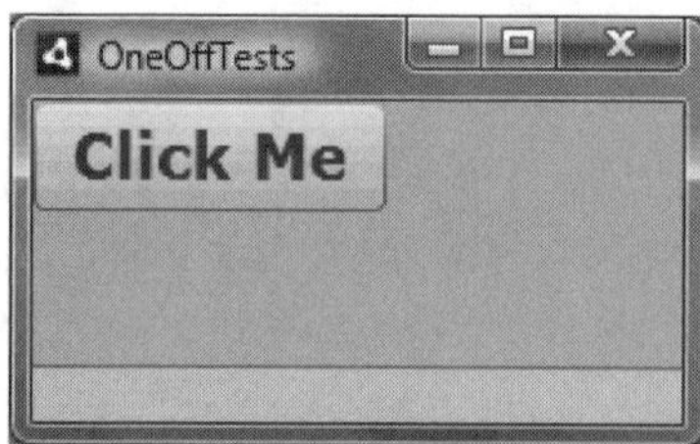

Figure 3: A stylized button

The other element type allowed in a style block is referred to in the CSS world as a *class selector.* A class selector allows you to assign any one or more styles into an arbitrary style name. You can then choose to apply that style on any element in your application.

```
.myBigBoldRedText{
    font-size:20;
    font-weight:bold;
    color:#ff0000;
}
```

A class selector always begins with the dot (.) character and is followed by any arbitrary string. This example defines the `myBigBoldRedText` class selector. To apply this style on an element in your application, you would set the element's `styleName` property equal to `"myBigBoldRedText"`.

```
<?xml version="1.0" encoding="utf-8"?>
<mx:WindowedApplication xmlns:mx="http://www.adobe.com/2006/mxml" >
    <mx:Style>
        .myBigBoldRedText{
            font-size:20;
            font-weight:bold;
            color:#ff0000;
        }
    </mx:Style>
    <mx:Label text="I am styled" styleName="myBigBoldRedText"/>
    <mx:Label text="I am not styled" />

</mx:WindowedApplication>
```

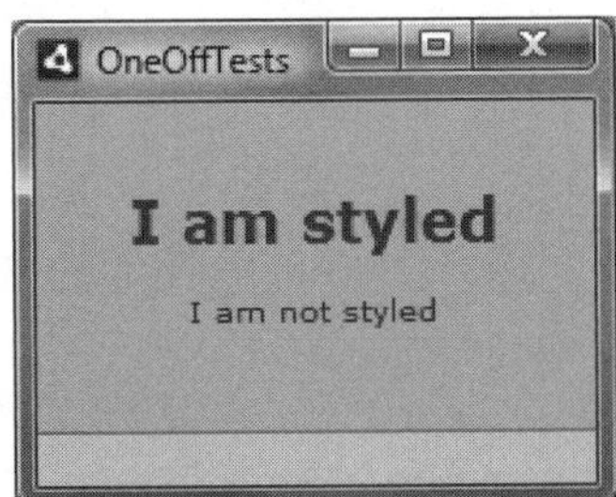

Figure 4: Two labels—the top one styled, the bottom one default style

This example shows two labels—one that has the style applied and one that does not. When this runs, it is easy to see that the top one is much larger, bolder, and redder than the other.

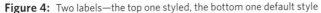

NOTE Flex developers who haven't worked with CSS in HTML recently are frequently confused by the terms *type selector* versus *class selector*. To object-oriented programmers, the term *class* has very specific connotations. However, CSS uses this term differently because CSS is not inherently object oriented. So in CSS, you would use a type selector to refer to any element of a particular ActionScript class. A class selector is used to define an arbitrary grouping of styles.

Frequently, developers do not want to hard code their CSS styles directly into their application, and would prefer to use an external file to house their style sheets. Storing style sheets externally allows for much better re-use of styles across multiple applications. Flex-based AIR applications can do this easily. Rather than having a tag pair for `<mx:Style>`, use a self-closing tag, with the source attribute pointing to an external style sheet. The same syntax rules apply for the external style sheet, but they can now be separated from the application itself.

myStyles.css

```
.myBigBoldRedText{
    font-size:20;
    font-weight:bold;
    color:#ff0000;
}
```

MyApp.mxml

```
<?xml version="1.0" encoding="utf-8"?>
<mx:WindowedApplication xmlns:mx="http://www.adobe.com/2006/mxml" >
    <mx:Style source="myStyles.css"/>
    <mx:Label text="I am styled" styleName="myBigBoldRedText"/>
    <mx:Label text="I am not styled" />
</mx:WindowedApplication>
```

When this runs, it will be identical to the example that had the Style block inline. There is no functional difference between placing your styles inline in a code block versus placing them in an externally referenced Style block. Using an external file is preferable because it enables re-use, but in both cases, the same styles are compiled into the application in the same way.

NOTE Any of the style codes shown in this chapter will allow for styles to be compiled into an application. If you need to load styles at runtime, instead of compiling them in, you can find the syntax for this in Chapter 16, "Customizing the Look and Feel of a Flex Application," in *Adobe Flex 3: Training from the Source* book by Adobe Press.

Using Skins

Another way to change the look of Flex components is with a skin. Each piece of the components in Flex is represented by a skin. For example, the scrollbar is made up of a skin for the up and down buttons, a skin for the thumb (which the user drags), and a skin for the track along which the user can drag the thumb. By replacing these skins with other graphics, you can completely customize the look and feel of a scrollbar. These skins can be provided as graphical files, as a combination of graphics in a SWF, or as ActionScript classes, which use the drawing API.

Aside from having skins to represent the various elements of components, each of the skinned elements usually has several different skins, representing the different states the component may be in. Using the scrollbar example again, the up button actually has four different skins, `upArrowSkin` (which represents the default state of the up arrow button), `upArrowDownSkin` (which is how the button will appear as the user is clicking it), `upArrowOverSkin` (which is the appearance of the button as the user mouses over it), and `upArrowDisabledSkin` (which shows how the button looks if the scrollbar is disabled). There are similarly different states for each of the skinned areas of the scrollbar. Usually if you want a component to have a completely new look, you will need to define all the skins for the states on that specific component.

Graphical skins are a means of specifying a graphical file (such as a PNG, JPG, GIF, or SWF) to be used for one or more of the skin style properties. Usually these are created outside Flex and either compiled or loaded in. Once these images or SWFs for your skin are in the project, they can be used on a component as a skin by declaring them as a style. For instance:

```
<mx:Style>
    Button {
        upSkin: Embed("../assets/myButtonUpSkin.PNG");
    }
</mx:Style>
```

You can also define the skin in ActionScript by using the `setStyle()` method. To do this, you need to declare a variable and embed the skin in it. This variable is then used as the value in the `setStyle()` method.

```
<?xml version="1.0" encoding="utf-8"?>
<mx:WindowedApplication xmlns:mx="http://www.adobe.com/2006/mxml"
    initialize="initButton();">
```

```
    <mx:Script>
        <![CDATA[
            [Embed("../assets/myButtonUpSkin.gif")]
            public var myButtonUpSkin:Class;

            private function initButton():void {
                myButton.setStyle("upSkin", myButtonUpSkin);
            }
        ]]>
    </mx:Script>

    <mx:Button label="My Button" id="myButton"/>
</mx:WindowedApplication>
```

Another way of setting the skin on a button is inline in the MXML declaration of a component.

```
<mx:Button id="myButton" label="My Button"
    upSkin="@Embed(source='../assets/myButtonUpSkin.PNG')"/>
```

Setting skins to be a bitmap graphic is a good way to have a unique design to your component. Another way to accomplish having a new look is with vector graphics. You can define classes for your skins and have them draw themselves however you want. These types of skins are referred to as *programmatic skins.* Programmatic skins offer you great customization possibilities and the ability to do all the work in Flex by just extending one class and one method. Normally, programmatic skins are made by extending the `ProgrammaticSkin` class and then overriding the `updateDisplayList()` method to do all the drawing work. So to make a new skin for your button using a programmatic skin, you would need to create a new class and extend `ProgrammaticSkin`, and then override the `updateDisplayList()` method of `ProgrammaticSkin`. Then inside the `updateDisplayList()` method, you will need to use the graphics object to do your drawing. Here is a simple example of a new programmatic skin class that will make the Button skin just a black rectangle outline.

```
package skins{
    import mx.skins.ProgrammaticSkin;

    public class myButtonProgrammaticSkin extends ProgrammaticSkin{
        override protected function updateDisplayList(unscaledWidth:Number,
        ➥ unscaledHeight:Number):void{
            graphics.lineStyle(1, 0x000000);
```

```
            graphics.drawRect(0, 0, unscaledWidth, unscaledHeight);
        }
    }
}
```

Using these different ways of setting up skins for your components will give them a unique look and feel that can be maintained throughout your application.

Using the Window API

Styles and skins are available to all Flex applications, whether they are deployed to the browser or to the AIR runtime. However, in browser-based applications, there are no styles that will allow you to change how the encompassing browser looks. In an AIR application, you can completely control the look and feel, including controlling the appearance of the application window itself. This is done using the Window API.

By default, all applications in your OS have a particular look to them (known as the *system chrome*). In Windows, applications have a title bar that can be clicked to drag the window, and three buttons on the right side. In the Mac OS, there is also a title bar, with three buttons on the left side. As a desktop developer with AIR, you can choose to use the system chrome or not.

To turn off the system chrome, you will need to both edit the application descriptor and set a style property on your `WindowedApplication` tag. The application descriptor (which was explored in Chapter 1, "Building Your First AIR Application," in the section "Describing Your Application with an Application Descriptor"), has a node called *initialWindow,* which sets a series of instructions for how the application will look and feel as it first starts. If you create a new AIR project in Flex Builder, you will see the initialWindow node default to settings like this:

```
<initialWindow>
    <!-- The main SWF or HTML file of the application. Required. -->
    <!-- Note: In Flex Builder, the SWF reference is set automatically. -->
    <content>[This value will be overwritten by Flex Builder in the output
        app.xml]</content>

    <!-- The title of the main window. Optional. -->
    <!-- <title></title> -->
    <!-- The type of system chrome to use (either "standard" or "none").
        Optional. Default standard. -->
    <!-- <systemChrome></systemChrome> -->
```

```
    <!-- Whether the window is transparent. Only applicable when systemChrome
        is false. Optional. Default false. -->
    <!-- <transparent></transparent> -->

    <!-- Whether the window is initially visible. Optional. Default false. -->
    <!-- <visible></visible> -->

    <!-- Whether the user can minimize the window. Optional. Default true. -->
    <!-- <minimizable></minimizable> -->

    <!-- Whether the user can maximize the window. Optional. Default true. -->
    <!-- <maximizable></maximizable> -->

    <!-- Whether the user can resize the window. Optional. Default true. -->
    <!-- <resizable></resizable> -->

    <!-- The window's initial width. Optional. -->
    <!-- <width></width> -->

    <!-- The window's initial height. Optional. -->
    <!-- <height></height> -->

    <!-- The window's initial x position. Optional. -->
    <!-- <x></x> -->

    <!-- The window's initial y position. Optional. -->
    <!-- <y></y> -->

    <!-- The window's minimum size, specified as a width/height pair,
        such as "400 200". Optional. -->
    <!-- <minSize></minSize> -->

    <!-- The window's initial maximum size, specified as a width/height pair,
        such as "1600 1200". Optional. -->
    <!-- <maxSize></maxSize> -->
</initialWindow>
```

Aside from the content node, all the other nodes in the initialWindow section specifically affect the look and behavior of the application at startup. Notice, however, that the other nodes are all commented out by default, meaning they will be assigned the default values. Many of the nodes are self explanatory, such as minSize, maxSize, width, height, x, and y. Others specify whether the system chrome buttons will be enabled or disabled, such as the minimizable, maximizable, and resizable nodes. The visible node allows for you to build an application that starts with no visible UI at all, but can become visible as it runs (perhaps it has an item in the system tray, or is listening for a particular keyboard shortcut). The systemChrome node accepts one of two values, *standard* or *none,* to determine how the application will appear. If none is used as the systemChrome value, a default Flex chrome look will be used, independent of the OS you are running it on. This Flex chrome can also be disabled with the use of the `showFlexChrome` style property of the `WindowedApplication` class. Lastly, if neither the system chrome nor the Flex chrome is being used, you can choose to make your application transparent by setting the transparent node's value to `true`. If your application is transparent, you will only see the application where a visible element exists. In other words, your application takes the shape of its content, instead of always fitting into a rectangular box. Using this combination (no system chrome, no Flex chrome, and transparent), you can regain complete control over the look of your application.

Figure 5: The dpTimeTracker application initial login screen with a nontraditional rectangular shape

NOTE If you try to set transparent to true **while the systemChrome is still set to** standard**, you will get a compile time error that says that you have an illegal value in the application descriptor. In order for transparent to be set to** true**, the systemChrome must also be set to** none**.**

Working with the NativeWindow class

It is important to note that if you remove the system chrome, your application will not have the minimize, maximize, restore, close, resize, and move controls, which the system chrome natively provides. If you still need this functionality, you can add it in manually to your application, using the methods of the NativeWindow class. This next example shows a simple application that removes all the chrome and adds its window controls to allow for maximize, restore, minimize, close, move, and resize operations.

```
<?xml version="1.0" encoding="utf-8"?>
<mx:WindowedApplication xmlns:mx="http://www.adobe.com/2006/mxml"
    layout="absolute"
    showFlexChrome="false">
    <mx:Script>
        <![CDATA[
          [Bindable]
            private var isMaximized:Boolean = false;
        ]]>
    </mx:Script>
    <mx:ApplicationControlBar fillAlphas="[1,1]"
        fillColors="[#ff0000,#ff0000]"
        mouseDown="nativeWindow.startMove()" dock="true">
        <mx:Button click="nativeWindow.close()" label="Close"/>
        <mx:Button click="nativeWindow.minimize()" label="Minimize"/>
        <mx:Button label="Maximize"
            click="nativeWindow.maximize();isMaximized=true"
            visible="{!isMaximized}"
            includeInLayout="{!isMaximized}"/>
        <mx:Button label="Restore"
            click="nativeWindow.restore();isMaximized=false"
            visible="{isMaximized}"
            includeInLayout="{isMaximized}"/>
    </mx:ApplicationControlBar>
    <mx:HBox width="100%"
        height="20" bottom="0"
```

```
        backgroundColor="#ff9900"
        mouseDown="nativeWindow.startResize(NativeWindowResize.BOTTOM)"/>
</mx:WindowedApplication>
```

At the top of the application is a docked ApplicationControlBar, which is set to be filled with an opaque red color. Notice that the ApplicationControlBar has a `mouseDown` event handler that calls `nativeWindow.startMove()`. This instructs the framework to drag the window with the user's mouse when they mouseover this control bar.

Inside the ApplicationControlBar are four buttons that provide the close, minimize, maximize, and restore functionality. To prevent the maximize and restore buttons from being visible at the same time, a private bindable variable, `isMaximized`, was created as a Boolean. When this is `true`, the maximize button is hidden; when it's `false`, the restore button is hidden. Each of those buttons has a handler for its `click` event. The click handler for the maximize button calls `nativeWindow.maximize()`, and the handler on the restore button calls `nativeWindow.restore()`. They each toggle a Boolean property, to indicate which of these two is the current state. Lastly, at the bottom of the screen an HBox is docked, which is twenty pixels tall and stretches the entire width of the screen. The HBox has a `mouseDown` event handler that uses the `startResize()` method to allow the user to drag up or down to resize the application's height. The `startResize()` method takes a single argument indicating from which edge or corner the resize will occur. The `NativeWindowResize` class has nine constants, indicating the various edges and corners. This example uses the `NativeWindowResize.BOTTOM` constant, which specifies that the resize will occur from the bottom edge, allowing only a vertical resizing.

With the use of these nativeWindow methods, you can add back all the functionality that the system chrome provided while maintaining complete control over the appearance.

Figure 6: Close, Minimize, and Maximize buttons added to the application window

Creating new windows

Another common task in desktop development is the need to spawn a new window for your application. Much like how you can control the look and feel of the initial window, there are also controls you can use for each additional window you create in AIR. This can be done when you create a new NativeWindow. To control the appearance of a window, you will need to define a set of NativeWindowInitOptions that you will then pass into the constructor for a new NativeWindow. These options are the new window's equivalent to the application descriptor. For example, to turn off the system chrome you would set the NativeWindowInitOptions.systemChrome property to NativeWindowSystemChrome.NONE. Likewise, there are options you can set for any of the other properties we discussed earlier.

```
<?xml version="1.0" encoding="utf-8"?>
<mx:WindowedApplication xmlns:mx="http://www.adobe.com/2006/mxml"
    layout="absolute"
    showFlexChrome="false">
    <mx:Script>
        <![CDATA[
          [Bindable]
            private var isMaximized:Boolean = false;
            private function createNewWindow():void{
                var opts:NativeWindowInitOptions =
                ➥ new NativeWindowInitOptions();
                opts.maximizable=false;
                opts.minimizable=false;
                opts.systemChrome=NativeWindowSystemChrome.STANDARD;
                var win:NativeWindow = new NativeWindow(opts);
                win.height=200;
                win.width=200;
                win.title = "this is my new window";
                win.activate();
            }

        ]]>
    </mx:Script>
    <mx:ApplicationControlBar fillAlphas="[1,1]"
        fillColors="[#ff0000,#ff0000]"
        mouseDown="nativeWindow.startMove()" dock="true">
        <mx:Button click="nativeWindow.close()" label="Close"/>
        <mx:Button click="nativeWindow.minimize()" label="Minimize"/>
```

```
        <mx:Button label="Maximize"
            click="nativeWindow.maximize();isMaximized=true"
            visible="{!isMaximized}"
            includeInLayout="{!isMaximized}"/>
        <mx:Button label="Restore"
            click="nativeWindow.restore();isMaximized=false"
            visible="{isMaximized}"
            includeInLayout="{isMaximized}"/>
    </mx:ApplicationControlBar>
    <mx:Button label="new window" click="createNewWindow()"/>
</mx:WindowedApplication>
```

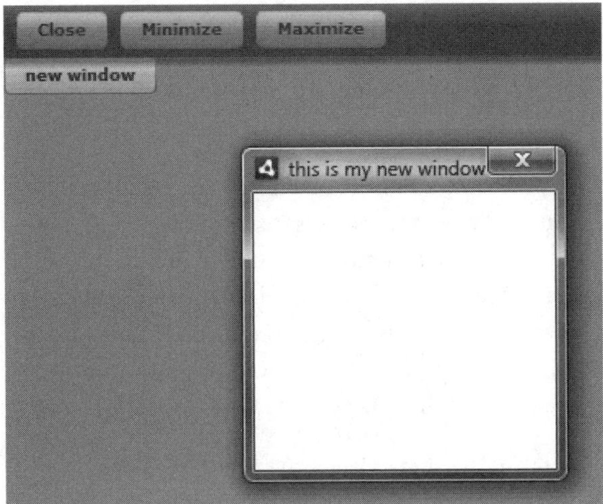

Figure 7: A new window launched from the AIR application

In this example, when you click the new window button, the `createNewWindow()` method is called. First a new `NativeWindowInitOptions` instance is created. The `minimizable` and `maximizable` options are set to `false` (hence there are no minimize or maximize buttons). The system chrome is set to standard, so that the title area, close button, and border will have the standard OS appearance and behaviors. Then, a nativeWindow is instantiated, passing these options into the constructor. After setting a title and size for the new window, it is launched with the `activate()` method.

In this simple example, the new window has no content. In a real-world scenario, a component that subclasses `NativeWindow` would have been created, instead of the NativeWindow itself. This subclass will provide the necessary content.

NOTE Be sure to close any windows created when exiting your application. If the main application window is closed, but a child window remains open, the application will continue to run and consume the end user's system resources.

Working with Menus

Each OS has a series of menus that are common across applications and are known by the users. Likewise, your AIR applications have the ability to create menus, and have them behave identically to the menus native to all other applications in the OS. In the Mac OS, an application's menus are generally found across the top menu of the OS, while in Windows, the menus are usually found within the application window, just below the applications title bar. Like everything else in AIR, you can customize how and where these menus appear, if needed, but it's also important to understand how to use the system defaults.

Menus do a great job for efficiency by providing a rich set of choices in a small screen area, eliminating the need for more buttons or other controls that will take up a lot of space in your application. AIR provides access to a number of different menus in the OS, which can each contain similar or different options, as required by your application. Regardless of where they are located, menus exist to give the user a list of options for a given point in the application. Making the right menu choices available from a particular location can help create the most fulfilling user experience.

Since the majority of the menus in AIR use the `NativeMenu` class, they are drawn entirely by the OS, and not by AIR. These menus exist outside the normal Flash or HTML rendering areas and tend to have a look or feel matching the OS, rather than your application. There are means available to provide customizations to these menus, helping to unify them with your application's look and feel.

Application and Window Menus

The Windows and Mac operating systems each have a built-in mechanism for displaying menus for an application. In the Mac OS, application menus are displayed at the top of the screen when your application is active. For example, if you run the Safari browser, the application menu at the top of the screen would have the title of the application, in this case Safari, and then it would have a list of menus for interacting with Safari. With the application menus, there are some standard menus that you will see without changing anything. You have the ability to add to these menus or to remove items you do not want the user to have access to. Using the application menus is a great way to give some familiarity with our application to Mac OS users.

In Windows, the main menu for an application is displayed inside the application window, below the title bar. Most Windows applications have menus like this, so they should be very familiar to Windows users and usually can be found at the top of any application running in Windows. Unlike the menus in Mac OS, there are no default values, only the items you specifically add. Here is a simple example, showing menu data defined in an XML block:

```
<?xml version="1.0" encoding="utf-8"?>
<mx:WindowedApplication xmlns:mx="http://www.adobe.com/2006/mxml"
    layout="absolute" menu="{nativeMenu}">
    <mx:FlexNativeMenu id="nativeMenu" dataProvider="{menuData}"
        labelField="@label" showRoot="false" />
    <mx:XML id="menuData" >
        <root>
            <menuItem label="File">
                <menuItem label="New"/>
                <menuItem label="Open"/>
                <menuItem label="Close"/>
            </menuItem>
            <menuItem label="Edit">
                <menuItem label="Copy"/>
                <menuItem label="Cut"/>
                <menuItem label="Paste"/>
                <menuItem label="Find"/>
            </menuItem>
            <menuItem label="View">
                <menuItem label="Zoom">
                     <menuItem label="50%"/>
                     <menuItem label="75%"/>
                     <menuItem label="100%"/>
                     <menuItem label="125%"/>
                     <menuItem label="150%"/>
                </menuItem>
                <menuItem label="Options"/>
            </menuItem>
        </root>
    </mx:XML>
</mx:WindowedApplication>
```

The menu data is set as the data provider of an instance of the FlexNativeMenu class, which is assigned an id of nativeMenu. The labelField attribute is used to instruct the nativeMenu to use the label attribute of the XML as the label shown in the menu. The showRoot attribute is set to false, instructing the FlexNativeMenu class to ignore the root node, and instead use the File, Edit, and View menu items as the top level for the menus. Lastly, the nativeMenu is bound to the menu property of the WindowedApplication, which instructs the application to use an OS menu for its rendering. When using Windows, this menu will appear inside the window, just below the title bar; when using Mac OS, it will appear in the top system menu.

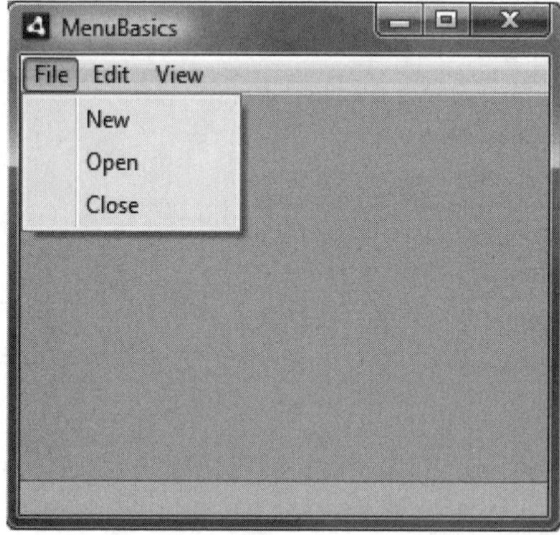

Figure 8: Basic Windows menu

The FlexNativeMenu class, which is used in this example, has a few other services it can provide, one of which is support for keyboard shortcuts.

```
<?xml version="1.0" encoding="utf-8"?>
<mx:WindowedApplication xmlns:mx="http://www.adobe.com/2006/mxml"
    menu="{nativeMenu}">
    <mx:Script>
        <![CDATA[
            import mx.events.FlexNativeMenuEvent;
            private function doItemClick(event:FlexNativeMenuEvent):void{
                trace(event.label);
            }
        ]]>
```

```
    </mx:Script>
    <mx:FlexNativeMenu id="nativeMenu"
        dataProvider="{menuData}"
        labelField="@label"
        showRoot="false"
        keyEquivalentField="@key"
        itemClick="doItemClick(event)"  />
    <mx:XML id="menuData" >
        <root>
            <menuItem label="File">
                <menuItem label="New" key="n" ctrlKey="true"/>
                <menuItem label="Open" key="o" ctrlKey="true"/>
                <menuItem label="Close" key="w" ctrlKey="true"/>
            </menuItem>
            <menuItem label="Edit">
                <menuItem label="Copy" key="c" ctrlKey="true"/>
                <menuItem label="Cut" key="x" ctrlKey="true"/>
                <menuItem label="Paste" key="v" ctrlKey="true"/>
                <menuItem label="Find" key="f" ctrlKey="true"/>
            </menuItem>
    ...
        </root>
    </mx:XML>
</mx:WindowedApplication>
```

This example adds a key attribute to each of the menu item nodes, as well as a ctrlKey="true". The addition of the keyEquilaventField attribute to the FlexNativeMenu instance allows you to add keyboard shortcuts, which can activate the same functionality as choosing the item from the menu. In this example, the keyEquilaventField is set to @key, meaning the system should look for an attribute of the menu item named key, to determine which key will activate that command. By setting the ctrlKey attribute to true, and assigning a key equivalent field, you can define the keyboard shortcut. This means that pressing the Control key along with the specified key (from the key equivalent field) will trigger the item click event and pass along the menuItem that matches that combination; so pressing Ctrl+C will pass exactly the same event object to the doItemClick() method, as if the user had selected the Copy menu item.

NOTE **This example assumes the keyboard shortcuts will only work when pressing the Control key. When using Mac OS, the standard for keyboard shortcuts is the Command key, not the Control key. To create an application that will honor the Control key in Windows and the Command key in Mac, you need to not specify ctrlKey or cmdKey in the data, and instead use the** `keyEquivalentModifiersFunction()`, **like this:**

```
private function getModifierForOS(item:Object):Array{
    var modifiers:Array = new Array();
    if((Capabilities.os.indexOf("Windows") >= 0)){
        modifiers.push(Keyboard.CONTROL);
    } else if (Capabilities.os.indexOf("Mac OS") >= 0){
        modifiers.push(Keyboard.COMMAND);
    }
    return modifiers;
}
<mx:FlexNativeMenu id="nativeMenu"
...
        keyEquivalentField="@key"
        keyEquivalentModifiersFunction="getModifierForOS" />
```

Context Menus

Context menus are menus that appear when the user right-clicks (Cmd-clicks) the application or an object within it. Context menus pop up and give a user a list of options, usually relative to the item on which they clicked. Context menus are an effective way to provide options for a specific item in the application, as users can right-click directly on that item to get to the menu. Each interactive object in AIR has a property called `contextMenu`. You can specify what items should appear in your context menu by adding an instance of the `ContextMenuItem` class to the `customItems` array of a component's context menu class.

```
<?xml version="1.0" encoding="utf-8"?>
<mx:WindowedApplication xmlns:mx="http://www.adobe.com/2006/mxml"
    layout="horizontal" creationComplete="initApp()">
    <mx:Script>
        private function initApp():void{
            list2.contextMenu = buildListContextMenu();
            this.contextMenu = buildAppContextMenu();
        }
```

```
private function buildListContextMenu():ContextMenu{
    var myContextMenu:ContextMenu = new ContextMenu();
    var item1:ContextMenuItem =
    ➥ new ContextMenuItem("Copy Other DataGrid")
    item1.addEventListener(ContextMenuEvent.MENU_ITEM_SELECT,
    ➥ doCopy);
    myContextMenu.customItems.push(item1);

    var item2:ContextMenuItem = new ContextMenuItem("Clear");
    item2.addEventListener(ContextMenuEvent.MENU_ITEM_SELECT,
    ➥ doClear);
    myContextMenu.customItems.push(item2);

    return myContextMenu;

}
 private function buildAppContextMenu():ContextMenu{
    var myContextMenu:ContextMenu = new ContextMenu();
    var item1:ContextMenuItem = new ContextMenuItem("Maximize App")
    item1.addEventListener(ContextMenuEvent.MENU_ITEM_SELECT,
    ➥ doMaximize);
    myContextMenu.customItems.push(item1);

    var item2:ContextMenuItem = new ContextMenuItem("Minimize App");
    item2.addEventListener(ContextMenuEvent.MENU_ITEM_SELECT,
    ➥ doMinimize);
    myContextMenu.customItems.push(item2);

    var item3:ContextMenuItem = new ContextMenuItem("Close App");
    item3.addEventListener(ContextMenuEvent.MENU_ITEM_SELECT,
    ➥ doClose);
    myContextMenu.customItems.push(item3);

    return myContextMenu;

}
private function doMaximize(e:ContextMenuEvent):void{
    this.nativeWindow.maximize();
}
```

```
        private function doMinimize(e:ContextMenuEvent):void{
            this.nativeWindow.minimize();
        }
        private function doClose(e:ContextMenuEvent):void{
            this.nativeWindow.close();
        }
        private function doCopy(e:ContextMenuEvent):void{
            list2.dataProvider = list1.dataProvider;
        }
        private function doClear(e:ContextMenuEvent):void{
            list2.dataProvider = null;
        }
    </mx:Script>
    <mx:List id="list1">
        <mx:dataProvider>
            <mx:Array>
                <mx:String>Red</mx:String>
                <mx:String>Blue</mx:String>
                <mx:String>Green</mx:String>
                <mx:String>Cyan</mx:String>
                <mx:String>Yellow</mx:String>
                <mx:String>Magenta</mx:String>
                <mx:String>Black</mx:String>
            </mx:Array>
        </mx:dataProvider>
    </mx:List>
    <mx:List id="list2"/>

</mx:WindowedApplication>
```

In Figure 9, you can see two context menus in play. When the user right-clicks (Cmd-clicks) the right List box, they see a context menu with options specific to the list ("Copy From Other List" and "Clear"); when the user right-clicks elsewhere in the application, they see options specific to the application (Minimize, Maximize, and Close).

NOTE If you have experience working with context menus in Flash Player, you may notice there is no mention of the built-in items that are always in the context menu. Because AIR is not subject to the same restrictions as Flash, there are no built-in items to consider; the context menu contains only the content you add to it.

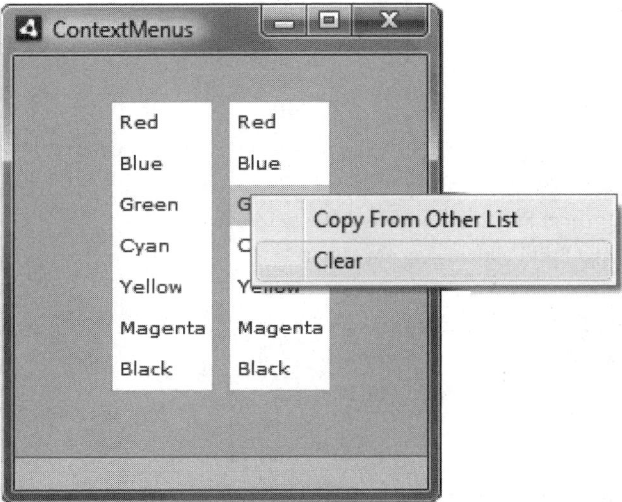

Figure 9: A context menu added to allow the user to copy the data from one List to the other

OS Menus

Another element you can interact with from AIR is the Operating System Menus, such as the Mac OS Dock and the Windows System Tray. AIR provides functionality to allow you to add items to these menus, and optionally, to add a context menu to these, allowing for further actions if the user right-clicks (or Cmd-clicks) them.

Working with these menus is done by creating an icon and adding the icon to the appropriate menu. This provides the user even more control of the application, as they can have a mechanism to interact with it, even if it is neither onscreen nor active.

Because the Mac OS Dock and Windows System Tray have very different behaviors, there are actually separate classes you need to use to interact with them. Regardless of which OS your application is running, you can specify the icon to use by setting the `nativeApplication.icon` property. You should be aware though, that in Windows, this icon is an instance of the `SystemTrayIcon` class, while in Mac OS it's an instance of the `DockIcon` class. Both of these classes inherit from the `InteractiveIcon` class, so there are many common methods and properties of each; however, you should check the `NativeApplication.supportsDockIcon` or `NativeApplication.supportsSystemTrayIcon` property before referring to any specific properties of one of these classes.

```
<?xml version="1.0" encoding="utf-8"?>
<mx:WindowedApplication xmlns:mx="http://www.adobe.com/2006/mxml"
    creationComplete="doInit()">
    <mx:Script>
        <![CDATA[
            private function doInit():void{
                var icon:InteractiveIcon=nativeApplication.icon;
                var iconData:BitmapData = createIcon();
                icon.bitmaps = new Array(iconData);
                if(NativeApplication.supportsSystemTrayIcon){
                    SystemTrayIcon(icon).tooltip =
                        "I'm a happy little AIR app!";
                }
            }
            private function createIcon():BitmapData{
                var canvas:Shape = new Shape();
                canvas.graphics.beginFill(0xffff00);
                canvas.graphics.drawCircle(24,24,24);
                canvas.graphics.endFill();
                canvas.graphics.beginFill(0x000000);
                canvas.graphics.drawEllipse(13,13,9,12);
                canvas.graphics.drawEllipse(27,13,9,12);
                canvas.graphics.endFill();
                canvas.graphics.lineStyle(3,0x000000);
                canvas.graphics.moveTo(11,32);
                canvas.graphics.curveTo(24,46,37,32);
                var result:BitmapData =
                ➥ new BitmapData(48,48,true,0x000000);
                result.draw(canvas);
                return result;
            }
        ]]>
    </mx:Script>
</mx:WindowedApplication>
```

Figure 10: A tooltip in the Windows System Tray

With a Windows SystemTrayIcon, you can add tool tips by simply providing a string to the `tooltip` property. Both SystemTrayIcon and DockIcon also support showing a nativeMenu, by specifying the `menu` property. Other APIs exist to allow you to call attention to the items in the Windows Task Bar, or Mac OS Dock, by either flashing (Windows) or bouncing (Mac). For further information about OS specific functionality, see the AIR Language Reference for the `DockIcon`, `SystemTrayIcon`, and `InteractiveIcon` classes.

Exploring the Customizations in the dpTimeTracker

The dpTimeTracker has a nontraditional look and feel because it turns off the system and Flex chrome, and it is transparent. So all you see of the TimeTracker is the places where it has content. As a result, its shape is nonrectangular. This is handled in both the application descriptor file and as a style of the `WindowedApplication` class. First, look at the CSS file (located in assets/css). Near the top, you will find a block that builds a type selector for the `WindowedApplication` class.

```
WindowedApplication{
    backgroundAlpha: 0;
    horizontalAlign: left;
    showFlexChrome: false;
    verticalGap: 0;
    verticalScrollPolicy: off;
    horizontalScrollPolicy: off;
}
```

Among the styles properties here is the setting of `showFlexChrome` to `false`. Combined with the changes in the application descriptor (TimeTracker2-app.xml), this creates the custom look. Open the descriptor file.

```
<initialWindow>
        <!-- The main SWF or HTML file of the application. Required. -->
        <!-- Note: In Flex Builder, the SWF reference is
            set automatically. -->
        <content>[This value will be overwritten by Flex Builder in the
            output app.xml]</content>
```

```
<!-- The title of the main window. Optional. -->
<!-- <title></title> -->

<!-- The type of system chrome to use (
    either "standard" or "none").
    Optional. Default standard. -->
<systemChrome>none</systemChrome>

<!-- Whether the window is transparent. Only applicable when
    systemChrome is false. Optional. Default false. -->
<transparent>true</transparent>
```

Now look at the initialWindow section. Here, you can see that the `systemChrome` property is set to none, and the `transparent` property is set to `true`. With these in place, the only pieces of the application that can be seen are the application-specific content. There is no rectangular box to surround it or anything else to inhibit its designer's creativity.

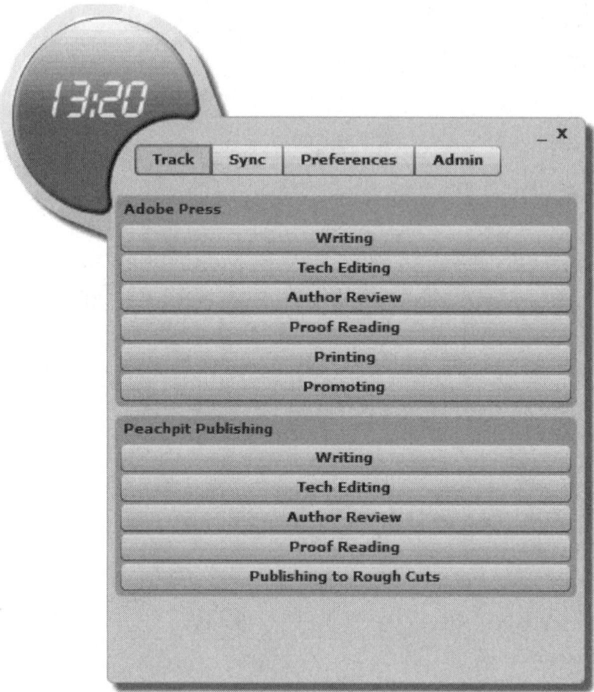

Figure 11: AIR's custom look for the dpTimeTracker application

One of the benefits of not using the system chrome is that the application will appear identical on all operating systems; however, this custom look added a bit of extra complexity for application developers. The interface needed to include a mechanism for minimizing, closing, and moving the application.

Open the TopControlBar.mxml file from the net/digitalPrimates/controls directory. Notice that there are two buttons added at the end that act to provide the minimize and maximize functionality, provided by the `nativeWindow` class.

```
<?xml version="1.0" encoding="utf-8"?>
<mx:HBox xmlns:mx="http://www.adobe.com/2006/mxml"
    width="100%" minWidth="400" height="30" verticalAlign="middle"
    backgroundColor="#dddddd" alpha="1"
    borderColor="#bbbbbb" borderStyle="solid" borderThickness="1"
    paddingLeft="5" paddingRight="5" horizontalGap="5"
    mouseDown="stage.nativeWindow.startMove()">

    <mx:Script>
        <![CDATA[
            import model.AppModel;
            import mx.core.Application;

            [Bindable]
            private var appModel:AppModel = AppModel.getInstance();
        ]]>
    </mx:Script>

    <mx:Image source="assets/images/clock16.png"/>
    <mx:VRule height="20" />
    <mx:Spacer width="10"/>
    <mx:LinkButton label="Track"
        click="Application.application.currentState='Tracking'"
        enabled="{appModel.loggedIn}" />
    <mx:LinkButton label="Sync"
        click="Application.application.currentState='Sync'"
        enabled="{appModel.loggedIn}"/>
    <mx:LinkButton label="Prefs"  enabled="{appModel.loggedIn}"/>
    <mx:LinkButton label="Admin"
        click="Application.application.currentState='Administration'"
        enabled="{appModel.loggedIn}" />
    <mx:Spacer width="100%"/>
```

```
    <mx:Button click="stage.nativeWindow.minimize()"
        styleName="minimizeButton" tabEnabled="false" toolTip="Minimize"/>
    <mx:Button click="NativeApplication.nativeApplication.exit()"
        styleName="closeButton" tabEnabled="false" toolTip="Close"/>
</mx:HBox>
```

When the minimize button is clicked, the call to `nativeWindow.minimize()` handles the actions; likewise, the `click` event handler for the close button calls the method called `nativeApplication.exit()`. Likewise, if you open the VisualTimer.mxml file from the components directory, you can see that the image allows the user to click it and drag the application around the screen. This is necessary because there is no system chrome; the default drag mechanism for an application is not present.

```
<?xml version="1.0" encoding="utf-8"?>
<mx:Canvas xmlns:mx="http://www.adobe.com/2006/mxml" width="165" height="165">
    <mx:Script>
        ...
    </mx:Script>
    <mx:Image source="assets/images/blue_button.png"
        mouseDown="stage.nativeWindow.startMove()"/>
        <mx:Label x="10" text="{timeString}" styleName="timeText" width="70%"
textAlign="center" alpha=".9" verticalCenter="-15"/>
</mx:Canvas>
```

As you can see, you can achieve quite a bit of customization with relatively little code.

Next Steps

Now that you have a solid understanding of many of the fundamentals of an AIR application, you are ready to explore the Presence API. In the next chapter, you will learn how AIR provides an easy approach to detect if the application is online or offline, and a series of events to which you can react to adjust the application's functionality accordingly.

WORKING WITH THE PRESENCE API

CHAPTER 8

Any computer that relies on a network connection runs the risk of losing its connection due to a technical problem or a lack of connectivity. AIR enables applications to handle such cases without interrupting the workflow by means of the Presence API. This chapter will discuss using the `ServiceMonitor` class to determine if a network connection is available, and the `URLMonitor` class to detect if HTTP communication is allowed to a specified address. The chapter will also illustrate how you can use the `SocketMonitor` class to determine if a particular socket is available on a firewalled or router-protected connection. In addition to understanding the classes, this chapter will look at how the dpTimeTracker application uses the Presence API to check if the user has a connection, and if so, check the server to see if there are any updates to the application.

Understanding and Detecting Network Presence

Why is it important to be aware of the connectivity changes on a network? Rich Internet Applications frequently need to download or upload data and communicate with remote servers to operate properly. If the application does not know if it is or is not connected, then the application has no means to react when the connectivity state changes. This could result in the RIA not operating properly, or worse, it can potentially do damage by continuing to run routines over a non-functioning connection with unforeseen consequences, all the while not giving its user a means to ascertain and handle the situation. Needless to say, in the modern business world where precision, timeliness, and security are the driving forces of success, such cases could be show-stopping.

The introduction to this book described the history of computer applications and drew parallels between client server applications and today's Rich Internet Applications. Drawing on that parallel, an RIA will usually suffer from a change in its connectivity in exactly the same way a client/server application would: it would lose its means to acquire and persist data. Interruptions in the connection can be enough to let the application miss updates or refreshes of data, allowing the user to work on corrupted data. AIR applications are not yet capable of eliminating all the risk associated with connectivity, but they offer capabilities to help mitigate this Achilles' heel of traditional web applications. Rather than just prevent the unwelcome consequences of a connection failure in the middle of a business transaction, AIR applications allow for elegant handling of data and workflow should such events happen, providing a smooth continuation of the running routine. AIR allows RIA developers to take charge of events normally outside their influence by providing means to monitor, detect, and manage the changes in the network status without interrupting or slowing down the workflow. In addition, handling the changes in the network status is entirely transparent to the application user thus allowing a more care-free RIA experience.

Detecting a User's Connection

To determine the user's ability to connect to a remote server, there are a few steps that need to be taken. First, you must make the proper classes available to enable network monitoring. Next, you will create an instance of a monitoring class, add listeners to it, and start its monitoring.

Making the Presence API available

To detect the existence of a network connection, or changes to that connection, you can use the AIR Presence API. Before you can use this API, you need to make it available to your application project. If you are using Flex Builder to build your application, no additional work is necessary; however, if you are building an AIR application with the SDK directly, or with a third-party tool, you will need to ensure that the libraries are included. In the frameworks directory of the AIR SDK is the servicemonitor.swf file, which is a separate framework designed to provide you the capability to monitor a network connection.

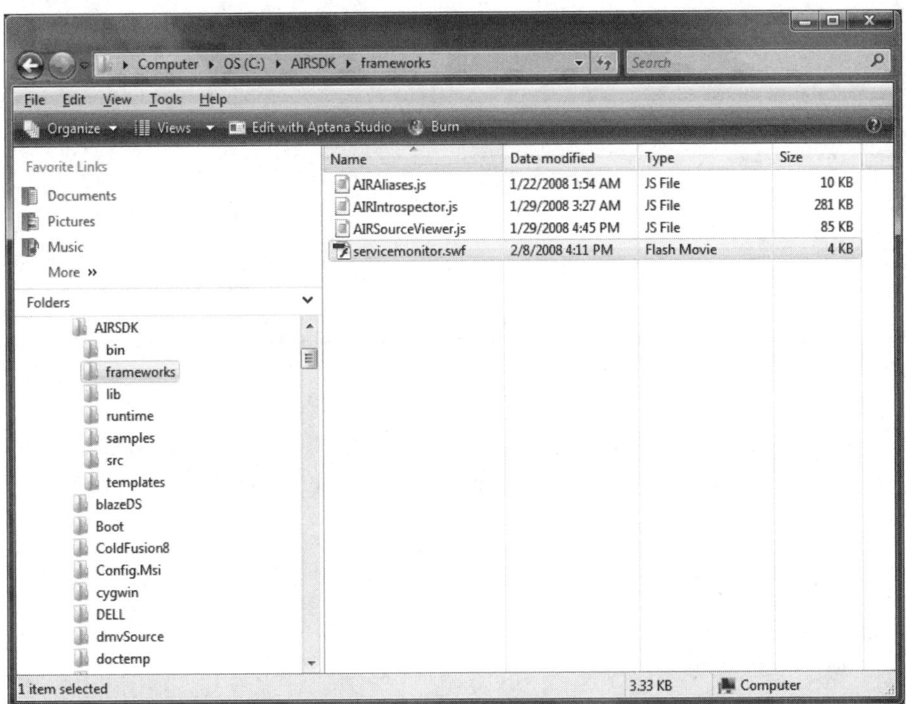

Figure 1: The servicemonitor framework in the AIR SDK

Alternatively, when using Adobe Flex Builder 3, the library file servicemonitor.swc is automatically included for use in connection monitoring applications. This SWC file contains the servicemonitor.swf.

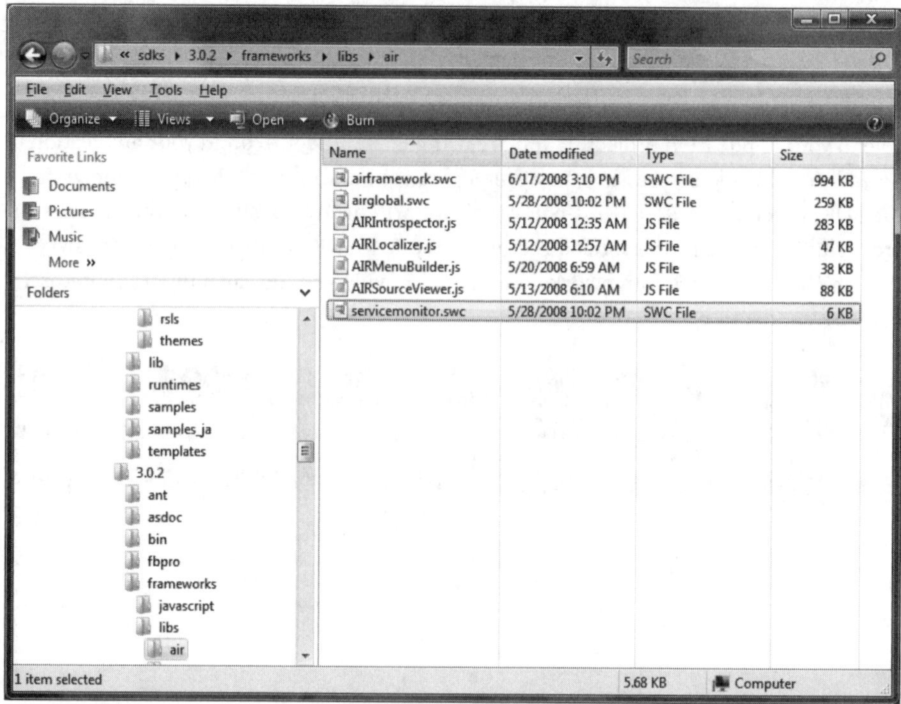

Figure 2: The servicemonitor framework in Flex Builder 3

When creating an AIR project in Flex Builder, this SWC will be included automatically. You can verify it exists by looking at the project build path, from the project Properties panel.

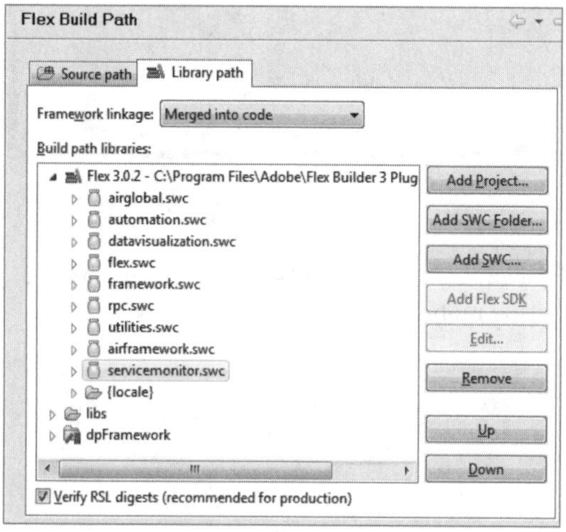

Figure 3: The servicemonitor.swc is automatically included in the Flex build path

When using JavaScript, you should manually add the SWF to the project by copying it into the application project folder and using the HTML Script tag. Also, be sure to put the Script tag with reference to the servicemonitor.swf before declaring the AIRAliases.js file, and remember to package the servicemonitor.swf with the rest of the AIR application when ready to publish.

```
<script src="servicemonitor.swf" type="application/x-shockwave-flash">
</script>
<script src="AIRAliases.js" type="text/javascript">
</script>
```

In this example, you can see one of the additions to WebKit that AIR added; the script bridge that allows for leveraging ActionScript classes directly from JavaScript. Normally, a script tag can only reference a script file, such as JavaScript, but in this example, the first script tag is explicitly including a SWF, which is only possible with the AIR extensions to WebKit. The servicemonitor.swf file contains a `ServiceMonitor` class that implements the framework to enable monitoring of the connection and some basic properties that will become useful when using the two `ServiceMonitor` subclasses also included in it. The real work will be done using the `URLMonitor` and `SocketMonitor` classes; both are discussed further later in this chapter.

Detecting connectivity changes

Once your project has access to the Presence API, the general process for detecting connectivity changes is to instantiate a new monitor instance and supply it correct parameters. Depending on your applications needs, there are a variety of different monitor instances available. For example, an application can have one instance monitoring a connection to a website, and another instance monitoring a specific port on the client machine. To be effective, all the monitor instances should have an event listener to allow the application to react as needed. Finally, it is a developer's responsibility to start the monitoring process. Do not be alarmed if these instructions sound vague at the moment. We will discuss these monitors in-depth and with code samples to demonstrate all the concepts. The following steps are useful to keep in mind when planning network monitoring for an AIR application:

1. Instantiate a new monitor.
2. Pass correct parameters to the monitor instance.
3. Add an event listener to the monitor instance to allow the monitor to catch events directly related to changes in network connection.
4. Start the monitoring process.

Understanding the URLMonitor

Suppose that your RIA needs to frequently make requests to an HTTP server to upload new data or get the latest update. Further assume that it is of critical importance that the application has the latest server data, otherwise the application features may cause harm. What the application *should* do in case the data is clearly out of date is try to update first, and then delay any actions until the update is successful. So, how does the application know when to institute this delay?

AIR provides a `URLMonitor` class to enable the application to monitor a connection to an HTTP server and broadcast events in the case of any changes in network state. If you need this functionality, you must add it to the application using the `URLMonitor` class. As was mentioned earlier, you will need to ensure that your application has access to this class, through the inclusion of the servicemonitor library (either as an SWC or SWF). In order to understand the `URLMonitor` class, provided below is a sample application built in AIR. Listing 1 is a sample AIR application that uses the `URLMonitor` class and follows the four steps from the previous section to monitor a network for changes in status.

Listing 1

```
<mx:WindowedApplication xmlns:mx="http://www.adobe.com/2006/mxml"
    creationComplete="initApp();">
    <mx:Script>
        <![CDATA[
            import air.net.URLMonitor;

            private function initApp() : void{
                var urlMonitor:URLMonitor;
                var urlRequest:URLRequest =
                ➥ new URLRequest( "http://www.adobe.com/");

                urlMonitor = new URLMonitor( urlRequest );
                urlMonitor.addEventListener( StatusEvent.STATUS,
                ➥ statusEventHandler );
                urlMonitor.start();
            }

            protected function statusEventHandler(
            ➥ event:StatusEvent ) : void{
```

Listing 1 (continued)

```
                trace("Current Status : " + event.code );
            }

        ]]>
    </mx:Script>
</mx:WindowedApplication>
```

The URLMonitor class is in the air.net package and has to be imported first. To ensure that monitoring starts as soon as the application starts, the initApp() method is called from the creationComplete event handler of the application.

Inside the initApp() method, an instance of the URLMonitor is created. The constructor requires that a single argument be passed, which is an instance of the URLRequest class. The URLRequest class simply allows for the developer to specify what HTTP address is referenced; in this case the application will attempt to monitor the connection to Adobe's home page, so a full URL address is supplied as an argument to the URLRequest constructor.

The URLMonitor dispatches a StatusEvent.STATUS event any time a change in network connectivity happens. Hence, the event listener for this event must be added to the instance of the URLMonitor.

Finally, the monitoring process must be manually triggered by calling the start() method of the URLMonitor class.

In the handler for the StatusEvent.STATUS event called statusEventHandler, the application examines the received object, which is an instance of the StatusEvent class, and traces out its code property. This property can be one of two String values, represented by the static constants Service.available and Service.unavailable. Running the application and looking at its Output window, it is easy to produce the following output by disconnecting the network cable attached to the computer and then plugging it back in.

```
Current Status : Service.available
Current Status : Service.unavailable
Current Status : Service.available
```

As was mentioned earlier in the chapter, there is no limit on how many monitors you can instantiate at a time. In fact, in order to reliably determine whether or not a particular HTTP server is available, you should use multiple monitors to track changes in connection to key web pages or websites. If you had an application that pulled in weather details from weather.com, live traffic updates from traffic.com, and the latest stock prices from etrade.com, you would likely want to monitor the ability to connect to each of these sites.

Listing 2 demonstrates the same concepts as in Listing 1, except it is written in JavaScript and uses slightly different properties available with the monitor.

Listing 2

```
<html>
<head>
    <script src="servicemonitor.swf" type="application/x-shockwave-flash">
    </script>
    <script src="AIRAliases.js" type="text/javascript">
    </script>
    <script>
    var urlMonitor = null;
    function initApp(){
      var request = new air.URLRequest( 'http://www.adobe.com' );
      urlMonitor = new air.URLMonitor( request );

      urlMonitor.addEventListener( air.StatusEvent.STATUS, statusEventHandler);
      urlMonitor.start();
    }

    function statusEventHandler ( e ){
      var elem = document.createElement( 'div' );
      elem.innerText = urlMonitor.available;
      document.body.appendChild( elem );
    }
    </script>
</head>
<body onload="initApp()">

</body>
</html>
```

In Listing 2, instead of examining `StatusEvent` properties, the application uses the `available` property of the `URLMonitor`. The property is a Boolean value that signifies whether or not a connection is present.

In addition to the properties and methods you see in the code samples here, there are a few other useful members of the `URLMonitor` class.

- `pollInterval`—A Number value that specifies the time interval in milliseconds for polling the server specified by the URL request. If set to zero or unspecified, the server is only polled immediately after the `start()` method is called and when the network connection status changes (for example, when the OS dispatches an event indicating a change in connectivity, as opposed to whether or not a particular URL can be accessed). Note that the `pollInterval` has nothing to do with *when* the `StatusEvent` is dispatched, but rather *how often* the network should be probed for connection changes, so that `StatusEvent` may be dispatched if needed. The default value for `pollInterval` is 0. In the AIR code example in Listing 1, adding `urlMonitor.pollInterval = 100` would test the server every 100 milliseconds. Should the connectivity change, `StatusEvent.STATUS` event will be dispatched.
- `acceptableStatusCodes`—An array listing numeric values for possible successful responses from the URL request. Default values are:
  - 200 (OK)
  - 202 (Accepted)
  - 204 (No content)
  - 205 (Reset content)
  - 206 (Partial content, in response to request with a Range header)

NOTE Independent of the defaults, you can customize this list of acceptable status codes to match the needs of your application.

- `running`—A read-only Boolean value signifying whether the monitor has been started.
- `lastStatusUpdate`—A read-only Date property that holds the time of the last update on the connection status.
- `urlRequest`—A read-only URLRequest object holding the value of the requested URL.
- `checkStatus()`—This protected method works behind the scenes by attempting to contact and query data from the URL listed in the `URLRequest` instance. The method then checks the status code returned against all values listed in `acceptableStatusCodes` property. If the match is found, the available property is set to `true`. In any other case, it sets the `available` property to `false`.

Understanding the SocketMonitor

As applications grow in complexity, it may be necessary for the application to use binary or XML sockets for exchanging data, as opposed to simply using HTTP requests. There are a number of use cases that may require this functionality, such as integrating with third-party tools like Merapi (merapi.googlecode.com); using a remote secure connection or VPN; or including a mail client that uses specific ports on the PC instead of HTTP. In order to establish monitoring on specific ports, the application should use the SocketMonitor class included with the servicemonitor.swf. Listing 3 is a modified version of the AIR example in Listing 1.

Listing 3

```
<mx:WindowedApplication xmlns:mx="http://www.adobe.com/2006/mxml"
  layout="absolute"
  creationComplete="init();">
  <mx:Script>
    <![CDATA[
      import air.net.SocketMonitor;

      private function init() : void
      {
        var socketMonitor: SocketMonitor;
        var host:String = 'messenger.yourdomain.com';
        var port:Number = 5220;

        socketMonitor = new SocketMonitor (host, port);
        socketMonitor.addEventListener( StatusEvent.STATUS, statusEventHandler );
        socketMonitor.start();
      }

      private function statusEventHandler( event:StatusEvent ) : void
      {
        var statusEvent:StatusEvent = event;
        trace("Current Status :: " + statusEvent.code );
      }

    ]]>
  </mx:Script>
</mx:WindowedApplication>
```

Much like the `URLMonitor`, the `SocketMonitor` class must first be imported from the `air.net` package. Its constructor takes two arguments: a String value representing the host endpoint and a Number value that is the port used for communication. In this example, the host is a messenger client that operates on port 5220. The call to the `start()` method is standard to all monitors.

The following properties are available when using the `SocketMonitor` class:

- `pollInterval`—A Number value that specifies the time interval in milliseconds for polling the server specified by the `host` property. If set to zero or unspecified, the server is only polled immediately after the `start()` method is called and when the network connection status changes. Note that the `pollInterval` has nothing to do with *when* the `StatusEvent` is dispatched, but rather *how often* the port should be probed for connection changes so that `StatusEvent` may be dispatched if needed. The `StatusEvent` event is only dispatched right after the `start()` method and any time the connectivity changes. The default value for `pollInterval` is 0. In the AIR example in Listing 1, adding `socketMonitor.pollInterval = 100` would test the messenger client host server every 100 milliseconds. Should the connectivity change, `StatusEvent.STATUS` event will be dispatched.
- `host`—A read-only property that holds the server endpoint that is being monitored.
- `running`—A read-only Boolean value signifying whether the monitor has been started.
- `port`—A read-only property that returns an int representing the port being monitored.
- `checkStatus()`—This protected method works behind the scenes by attempting to connect to the monitored socket to check for the connect event.

Understanding and Detecting User Presence

So far, this chapter has discussed one aspect of building a Rich Internet Application with AIR—its communication with the network. This is one *point of entry* in and out of the application. `URLMonitor` and `SocketMonitor` give us sufficient tools to detect changes in the connectivity so the application can be enabled to respond appropriately.

What about the application user? The user is in direct communication with the application through data input and output, changing options or settings, influencing the flow of events, and so on. It would make sense to enable the application to have awareness of its user's activity or inactivity over a period of time. Much like being aware of changes in the state of connectivity, being informed of whether or not the user has performed any action in a particular unit of time, or being notified of the user becoming active again, may be useful in a variety of ways.

Why Should I Care about User Presence?

There are a number of cases that could require an application being aware of the user's activity. One of the more frequent cases is for applications that are dealing with sensitive data, and require a user login before they can use the application. In these cases, it is not uncommon to force the user to login again after a certain period of inactive time, preventing another user accessing data for which they are not authorized while the primary user is away from their machine. Another case can come as a performance enhancement to processor-intensive applications. Generally speaking, applications that require modest system resources and do not bog the system down over a period of time are considered to be examples of high-quality programming. The application may be computationally intensive through the use of animations to enhance user experience. When the system detects the user has been inactive for a specified period of time, it would be a good design idea to disable the connection until the activity resumes.

Tracking User Presence

To facilitate handling of user presence, AIR delivers a capability to determine when the application user becomes active or inactive. It does so through the use of the `NativeApplication` class, which is available for use in any AIR application. `NativeApplication` is an object created at startup that represents the native AIR application itself. In addition to its other responsibilities, the `NativeApplication` will dispatch two events relevant to the user's activity: `userIdle` and `userPresent`. Before the user is considered to be idle, the application needs to detect no keyboard or mouse activity from them for a period of time. This time period is defined by the `idleThreshold` property of the `NativeApplication` class, which by default is set to 300 seconds (5 minutes). To allow your application to detect the user presence, you need to listen for these two events from the `NativeApplication` instance. The snippet of code in Listing 4 demonstrates the use of these events as well as the correct way to set up the listeners.

Listing 4

```
<?xml version="1.0" encoding="utf-8"?>
<mx:WindowedApplication xmlns:mx="http://www.adobe.com/2006/mxml"
    creationComplete="establishPresenceCheck()">
    <mx:Script>
        <![CDATA[
            private function establishPresenceCheck():void{
                nativeApplication.idleThreshold=10;
                nativeApplication.addEventListener(Event.USER_IDLE,
                ➥ handleUserIdle);
                nativeApplication.addEventListener(Event.USER_PRESENT,
                ➥ handleUserPresent);
            }
               private function handleUserIdle(event:Event):void{
                trace("idle");
            }
            private function handleUserPresent(event:Event):void{
                   trace("present");
            }

        ]]>
    </mx:Script>

</mx:WindowedApplication>
```

NativeApplication provides its instance through the nativeApplication property of the application. Two user presence events that signal a user's inactivity and activity are available to the developer: Event.USER_IDLE and Event.USER_PRESENT. The Event.USER_IDLE event is dispatched when no keyboard or mouse activity is detected in the span of time set by the idleThresholdproperty of NativeApplication class. The Event.USER_PRESENT event is dispatched on the next keyboard or mouse event. The idleThreshold property is set here to be 10 seconds, instead of the default 300.

Building Auto-Update Features into an Application

Now that you have enabled the user to continue work in case the connection fails and made the application more resource efficient when the user is idle, it is time to ensure that the user is running the latest build. It is necessary to keep the application up-to-date because the contents of an update can range from critical bug fixes to new HTTP addresses to monitor. It is also highly recommended to make it a smooth, trivial, and safe task for the application user.

Working with the Updater Class

AIR provides developers with effective means to keep their Rich Internet Applications up-to-date using the `Updater` class located in `flash.desktop` package. In order to update an application to the latest version, the application must create an instance of the `Updater` class and call its only method, `update()`. This method enables the application to point to an AIR file on the computer that is currently running the application and use it as a replacement for the currently running application file.

The developer must keep a few things in mind when working with the `Updater` class. The `Updater` class must be instantiated before calling its `update()` method. To successfully perform an update, the updated application file must reside on the computer where the application is running. The next sections cover the process of updating an AIR application.

Downloading an update

To demonstrate the concept of downloading an update, Listing 5 shows a sample that reads an AIR file from a URL address and saves it to the application storage directory. As you learned in Chapter 6, "Interacting with the File System," the application storage directory refers to the unique location available to each AIR application for persistent personal storage available in the `File` class. The explanation of Listing 5 assumes that you are familiar with `File` and `FileStream` classes from Chapter 6.

Listing 5

```
var urlString:String = "http://dptimetracker.googlecode.com/files/
➥ TimeTracker1.1.air";
var urlReq:URLRequest = new URLRequest(urlString);
var urlStream:URLStream = new URLStream();
var fileData:ByteArray = new ByteArray();
urlStream.addEventListener(Event.COMPLETE, loaded);
urlStream.load(urlReq);
```

Listing 5 (continued)

```
function loaded(event:Event):void {
    urlStream.readBytes(fileData, 0, urlStream.bytesAvailable);
    writeAirFile();
}

function writeAirFile():void {
    var file:File = File.applicationStorageDirectory.resolvePath(
    ➥ "My App v2.air");
    var fileStream:FileStream = new FileStream();
    fileStream.addEventListener(Event.CLOSE, fileClosed);
    fileStream.openAsync(file, FileMode.WRITE);
    fileStream.writeBytes(fileData, 0, fileData.length);
    fileStream.close();
}

function fileClosed(event:Event):void {
    trace("The AIR file is written.");
}
```

First, an instance of `URLRequest` is created to hold the full URL of the updated application file (http://dptimetracker.googlecode.com/files/TimeTracker1.1.air in this case). Then, an instance of `URLStream` is made to download the URL. Also, the application declares a ByteArray object instance called `fileData` to hold the data gathered from the downloaded URL. Then, an event listener is set up to detect when the URL download is finished using an `Event.COMPLETE` event. Finally, the `load()` method is invoked on the `URLStream` instance to begin the download.

When the download is ready, a `readBytes()` method is invoked on the `urlStream` object to read the URL data that was downloaded into the `fileData` object.

NOTE In order for an application to be able to update itself, it needs to be signed by the same certificate that was used to sign the initial version of the application. For more information on digitally signing applications, please see Chapter 13, "Deploying AIR Applications."

Installing an update

Once the updated application file has been downloaded onto the computer, the application is ready to utilize the update() method of the Updater class to bring in a new version. The following sample shows a simple update.

```
var updater:Updater = new Updater();
var airFile:File = File.desktopDirectory.resolvePath("Sample_App_v2.air");
var version:String = "3.02";
updater.update(airFile, version);
```

When the call to update() method occurs, the application exits in a manner similar to how NativeApplication.exit() causes the runtime to close the application. The reason for closing the application is that AIR cannot update a currently running application. When the application successfully updates, it is re-launched using the latest version. The application is re-launched whether or not the update is accomplished. A failed update will simply launch the old version.

NOTE The version passed to the update method must match the version in the new version's application descriptor. If these versions do not match, the installation will fail and will show an error message.

In some cases, the runtime may fail to successfully install the update. For example, if the NativeApplication.applicationID property is different between the current and updated version, then the AIR installer throws an error notifying the user of the difference. Also, calling the update() method when using the AIR debug launcher application throws a runtime exception.

The update will also fail if the application did not specify the version number in the arguments for the update() method. This String variable must match the string in the version attribute of the main application tag of the application descriptor file for the AIR file to be installed. This is done as a security precaution so that the AIR application does not mistakenly install an older version that might contain a security vulnerability that has been fixed in the currently running application (also known as a *downgrade attack).* It is up to the developer to specify the version number, which can be along the lines of "version 5.3" or just "5.3." Please note that the AIR runtime does not validate the version string—it is rather left for the application code to do before the update is attempted. In case the update file is retrieved via the web, it is a good design practice to enable the web service to provide the version number to AIR for use as a version parameter in the update() method. When retrieving the AIR file through other means where the version number is not available, it may be obtained by examining the file as a ZIP archive where the second record is the application descriptor file.

Other common causes of a failed update include the lack of adequate user privileges. Microsoft Windows users are required to have administrative privileges. Mac OS users must have sufficient system privileges to install to an application directory.

Another word of warning is to always check the version number on every re-install attempt. Otherwise, the application may go into an endless loop where it is trying to install an update, fails, and then tries the installation again repeating the circle. A simple way to do this would be to record the version number of a file before the start of an update and then compare it to the version number when re-launching the application.

AIR kindly reduces your work efforts by providing a default interface for updating and installing your application.

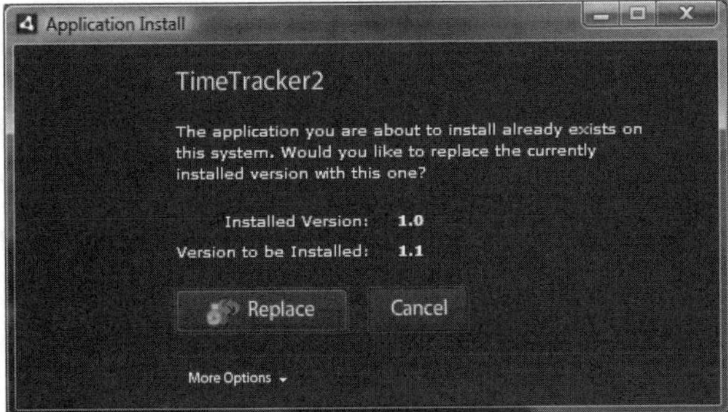

Figure 4: Air default install/update interface

This interface will be used when the first instance of the application is installed on the computer. However, the developer can specify custom interfaces for subsequent updates to the application by setting the customUpdateUI node in the application descriptor file for the currently running application.

```
<customUpdateUI>true</customUpdateUI>
```

When the application is installed and the user opens an AIR application with an application ID and a publisher ID that match the installed application, the runtime opens the application rather than opening the default AIR application installer. When the `NativeApplication.nativeApplication` object dispatches an `invoke` event, the application can decide whether an update is needed using the `Updater` class. If the decision is to update, the application may present its own custom installation interface instead of the default one AIR provides.

Reviewing the Auto-Update Features in dpTimeTracker

In the dpTimeTracker, the application is using a URL monitor to determine whether or not it is capable of connecting to the Google code project, where the application code base lives. If the network is available to that URL, a flag is set to true in the application model, otherwise, its set to false. To see how this is done, open TimeTracker2.mxml, and examine the last two methods of the Script block.

```
private function initApp() : void {
    var urlRequest : URLRequest = new URLRequest("http://www.google.com");
    var urlMonitor : URLMonitor = new URLMonitor(urlRequest);
    urlMonitor.addEventListener( StatusEvent.STATUS, onStatusChange, false, 0,
    ➥ true );
    urlMonitor.start();

    //updating AppModel with local version from TimeTracker2-app.xml
    var appXml:XML = NativeApplication.nativeApplication.
    ➥ applicationDescriptor;
    var ns:Namespace = appXml.namespace();
    appModel.localVersion = appXml.ns::version[0];
}
private function onStatusChange(evt : StatusEvent) : void {
    if (evt.code == "Service.unavailable") {
        appModel.onlineStatus = false;
    } else {
        appModel.onlineStatus = true;
    }

    new UserMessageCommand( "Your connection status has changed to " +
    ➥ (appModel.onlineStatus ? "Online" : "Offline") ).execute();
}
```

As you can see, when the initApp method (which is called from creationComplete) executes, it sets urlMonitor on the URL for the dpTimeTracker application, sets a listener, and starts the monitor. The application also reads the current version number from the application descriptor, and sets it into the application model.

In the event handler for the status event, the evt.code of the StatusEvent object is compared to "Service.unavailable." If the code matches that, the appModel.onlineStatus property is set to `false`; otherwise, it is set to `true`. Either way, the `UserMessageCommand` is used to notify the user of the status change.

The `onlineStatus` property is used in the `Login` class.

```
package modules.authentication{
    import commands.GetCurrentVersionCommand;
    import commands.UserMessageCommand;

    import flash.desktop.Updater;
    import flash.events.Event;
    import flash.events.IOErrorEvent;
    import flash.events.MouseEvent;
    import flash.events.TimerEvent;
    import flash.filesystem.File;
    import flash.filesystem.FileMode;
    import flash.filesystem.FileStream;
    import flash.net.URLRequest;
    import flash.net.URLStream;
    import flash.utils.ByteArray;
    import flash.utils.Timer;

    import helpers.UserHelper;

    import model.AppModel;

    import modules.authentication.commands.AddUserCommand;
    import modules.authentication.commands.AuthenticateCommand;

    import mx.containers.Form;
    import mx.controls.Button;
    import mx.controls.CheckBox;
    import mx.controls.TextInput;
    import mx.rpc.events.FaultEvent;
    import mx.rpc.events.ResultEvent;

    [Event("loginSuccess")]
    [Event(name="newUser")]
    [Event(name="cancelNewUser")]
    public class Login extends Form {
        [Bindable]
```

```
protected var remoteAndLocalSame:Boolean = true;
[Bindable]
protected var appModel : AppModel = AppModel.getInstance();

[Bindable]
protected var enteredUsername:String;
[Bindable]
protected var enteredUsername:String;

public var loginButton : Button;

public var username:TextInput;
public var password:TextInput;
public var serverUsername:TextInput;
public var serverPassword:TextInput;

protected function handleLogin( username:String,
➥ password:String ):void {
    loginButton.enabled = false;

    if( appModel.onlineStatus == true ) {
        var getcurrVersionCommand:GetCurrentVersionCommand  = new
        ➥ GetCurrentVersionCommand();
        getcurrVersionCommand.setCallbacks( handleVersionResult,
        ➥ handleVersionFault ).execute();
    } else {
        authenticateAndContinue( );
        new UserMessageCommand( "you are currently Offline, unable to
        ➥ check for updates" ).execute();
    }
}

protected function authenticateAndContinue() : void {
    var authCommand:AuthenticateCommand = new AuthenticateCommand(
    ➥ enteredUsername, enteredPassword );
    authCommand.execute();

    loginButton.enabled = true;
}
```

```
protected function handleUserNameChange( event:Event ):void {
    enteredUsername = event.target.text;
    if ( remoteAndLocalSame && serverUsername ) {
        serverUsername.text = enteredUsername;

    }
}

protected function handlePasswordChange( event:Event ):void {
    enteredPassword = event.target.text;
    if ( remoteAndLocalSame && serverPassword ) {
        serverPassword.text = enteredPassword;
    }
}

protected function handleRemoteSameAsLocal( event:Event ):void {
    if ( ( event.target as CheckBox ).selected ) {
        remoteAndLocalSame = true;
        if ( serverUsername ) {
            serverUsername.text = enteredUsername;
        }

        if ( serverPassword ) {
            serverPassword.text = enteredPassword;
        }
    } else {
        remoteAndLocalSame = false;

        if ( serverUsername ) {
            serverUsername.text = "";
        }

        if ( serverPassword ) {
            serverPassword.text = "";
        }
    }
}
```

```
protected function createNewUser( username:String, password:String,
    serverUsername:String, serverPassword:String ):void {
    var userExists:Boolean = UserHelper.userExistsInEncryptedStore(
        username );

    if ( !userExists ) {
        var command:AddUserCommand = new AddUserCommand( username,
        ➥ password, serverUsername, serverPassword );
        command.setCallbacks( success, failure );
        command.execute();
    } else {
        appModel.loginState = "userExists";
    }
}

protected function success( data:Object ):void {
    appModel.loginState = "";
}

protected function failure( info:Object ):void {
    appModel.loginState = "userExists";
}

protected function handleAddUserClick( event : MouseEvent ) : void {
    dispatchEvent( new Event( "newUser", false, false ) );
    appModel.loginState='addUserState';
}

protected function handleCreateUserClick(
➥ event : MouseEvent ) : void {
    dispatchEvent( new Event( "cancelNewUser", false, false ) );
    createNewUser( username.text, password.text, serverUsername.text,
        serverPassword.text );
}

protected function handleCancelNewUser( event : MouseEvent ) : void {
    dispatchEvent( new Event( "cancelNewUser", false, false ) );
    appModel.loginState='';
}
```

```
//****************************************
//Version comparision and updating methods
//****************************************

protected function compareVersionAndUpdate( oldVersion: String,
    newVersion: String ) :void {
    if( Number(newVersion) > Number(oldVersion) ) {
        //update is available
        trace( "downloading the new application version from
        ➥ the server");
        new UserMessageCommand( "your application is out of date,
        ➥ downloading new version", 1000 ).execute();
        var pauseTimer : Timer = new Timer( 1000, 1 );
        pauseTimer.start();
        trace("pausing for 1 second so user can see the message" );
        pauseTimer.addEventListener( TimerEvent.TIMER_COMPLETE,
        ➥ pauseTimerCompleteHandler );
    } else {
        //this version is up-to-date
        trace( "aborting update, everything's up-to-date");
        authenticateAndContinue();
    }
}

protected function pauseTimerCompleteHandler(
➥ event : TimerEvent ) : void{
    trace( "pause for message, complete, now updating" );
    downloadUpdate( AppModel.APP_UPDATE_SERVER );
}

private function downloadUpdate(file:String):void {

    var downloadStream : URLStream = new URLStream();
    var fileStream:FileStream = new FileStream();
    downloadStream.addEventListener(Event.COMPLETE,
    ➥ downloadStreamComplete, false, 0, true );
    downloadStream.addEventListener(
    ➥ IOErrorEvent.IO_ERROR, handleIOError);
    downloadStream.load(new URLRequest(file));
```

```
}

private function handleIOError( event : IOErrorEvent ) : void {
    trace( "server URL could not be loaded, IOError " );
    new UserMessageCommand( "the update server specified could not
    ➥ be accessed at this time" ).execute();
    //continue with login since the app can't be updated right now
    authenticateAndContinue();
}

private function downloadStreamComplete( event : Event ) : void {
   var downloadStream : URLStream = event.currentTarget as URLStream;
   var fileStream:FileStream = new FileStream();
   var appData:ByteArray = new ByteArray();

 //Alert the user that a new version is being downloaded and
  //installed now
  downloadStream.readBytes(appData, 0,
  ➥ downloadStream.bytesAvailable);

  var updateFile:File = File.applicationStorageDirectory.resolvePath (
  ➥ "dpTimeTracker.air");
  trace(updateFile.nativePath);
  fileStream.open(updateFile, FileMode.WRITE);
  fileStream.writeBytes(appData, 0, appData.length);
  fileStream.close();
  var appUpdate:Updater = new Updater();
  appUpdate.update(updateFile, appModel.remoteVersion);

}

protected function handleVersionResult(
➥ event : ResultEvent ) : void {
    trace( "version XML has returned,
    ➥ checking current vs. server version");
    //version XML node name goes here
    var returnedXML : XML = event.result as XML;
    appModel.remoteVersion = returnedXML.vNum.toString();
    compareVersionAndUpdate( appModel.localVersion,
    ➥ appModel.remoteVersion);
}
```

```
        protected function handleVersionFault( event : FaultEvent ) : void {
            trace( "getting version has failed, xml not returned" );
        }

        //**********************************
        //End version comparing and updating
        //*********************************
    }
}
```

NOTE **In the real world version of the dpTimeTracker application, the functionality to check for new updates, as well as the functionality to update the application have each been split into their own commands. The version of the application that we use in this book has been simplified, to help more clearly explain the concepts. You can find both the book version, as well as the more complete real world version in the Google Code repository.**

Aside from the login functionality, this class also handles updating the application. When the user clicks the login button, the `handleLogin` method is called. This method checks the application model to determine if the user is online or off. If they are online, the `GetCurrentVersionCommand` class is used to determine the latest available version of the application. Any results from this method are passed to the `handleVersionResult` method (which takes the resulting data and passes it to the `compareVersionAndUpdate` method). The `compareVersionAndUpdate` method checks if the latest version from the server (as stored in the `newVersion` argument to the function) is greater than the current version of the application. If the user needs a new version of the application, a message is shown to the user for one second (with the use of the `Timer` class). At the end of that time, the `pauseTimerCompleteHandler` method is called, which tells the application to download the latest version of the application. When the file is finished downloading, the `downloadStreamComplete` handler fires, which writes the downloaded file to the application storage directory. The last two lines of this method instantiate the `Updater` class and use it to update the application.

```
var appUpdate:Updater = new Updater();
appUpdate.update(updateFile, appModel.remoteVersion);
```

In each of the `else` blocks (if the user doesn't have a connection, or there are now new updates, or an error occurs downloading an update), the `authenticateAndContinue` method is called, which checks the username and password entered, and allows the user to run the application as usual.

As you can see, the dpTimeTracker application uses several of the classes introduced in this chapter, such as `URLMonitor` and `Updater`.

Next Steps

In the next chapter, you will learn about the use of HTML in an AIR application. As you know by now, one of the key strengths of AIR is that it offers the power of desktop application development to developers proficient only in web technologies. While developers used to working in Flash Player have learned to work around the limitations that Flash has for HTML content, AIR has none of these restrictions, and as an AIR developer, you are free to mix HTML and Flash/Flex content in your AIR application.

USING HTML CONTENT IN A FLEX/ AIR APPLICATION

CHAPTER 9

In the previous chapters, we explored how Flex gives you access to the core pieces of the operating system allowing for a true desktop experience. Next, you are going to switch gears and look at what makes AIR such a valuable desktop runtime for the web-based developer.

By choosing to use AIR, you gain the ability to leverage your existing web-based skills and knowledge to create applications for the desktop. This does not limit you to only Flex and Flash because AIR also has the ability to build HTML and JavaScript directly into an application. An AIR application can consist of a seamless blend of Flex and HTML.

This chapter will explore how to use HTML in an AIR application, how to combine SWF-based and HTML content in a single application, as well as the security concerns associated with using web-based content on the desktop.

Introducing WebKit

AIR includes WebKit (www.webkit.org) in order to be able to render HTML and JavaScript content. WebKit is an open-source engine and is the same HTML engine on which Apple's Safari browser is based. Using an established open-source HTML rendering engine provides Adobe with the ability to quickly offer a robust feature set in AIR, as well as a pre-existing development community, to support and aid in application development.

However, there are additional concerns and issues that arise when integrating an HTML engine into a desktop runtime environment. Because a web-based application behaves inherently differently from a desktop application, there are changes necessary to allow HTML content to work effectively in a desktop application.

When including HTML content in a Flex-based AIR application, we need to know how to display and work with the content. There is a control in Flex that can be used to designate an area as a place for HTML content. This control works just like any other display object in Flex, and the same properties, such as `height` and `width`, are available. You can use this control in MXML or ActionScript in the same way that you would use any control.

```
<mx:HTML  id="html"
    width="500" height="500"
    location="http://weather.yahoo.com/forecast/USIL0922.html"/>
```

AIR Extensions to WebKit

The AIR runtime offers a number of extensions to HTML, JavaScript, and CSS to fully translate HTML content to the desktop. These changes include ways to manage and secure content, changes to facilitate communication between ActionScript and JavaScript, and additional options to manage commands that are typically handled by the web browser.

The security of the desktop is one of the most important things to consider when using HTML content on the desktop. Allowing HTML pages or JavaScript code to have access to the desktop but also the ability to receive and send to any remote location poses large security issues. Many of the extensions to the WebKit engine have been made to ensure that AIR applications and their users are safe.

HTML Extensions

When including HTML content in an existing Flex-based AIR application, the HTML is a piece of the larger application. In this regard, the HTML content can be thought of as another component inside a Flex application. However, in the default implementation of WebKit (or any other HTML engine), there is a much less robust event framework than Flex offers, making it difficult to truly work with it as you would any other component. This creates an environment where the HTML content is hanging out by itself and not telling the rest of the application what's happening, which is unlike every other component in Flex. In order to change this, many events have been added in WebKit that allow you to work with the HTML content just like you would any other Flex component.

You can specify event listeners for these events in either ActionScript or JavaScript so that you have greater control in responding to the HTML content. Following are the new events that have been added to HTML content in AIR's implementation of WebKit, including:

- `oncontextmenu`—Dispatched whenever a context menu is opened when a user right-clicks (or Command-clicks on Mac).
- `oncopy`—Dispatched when an object is copied to the clipboard.
- `oncut`—Dispatched when an object is cut to the clipboard.
- `ondominitialize`—Dispatched when the document object model (DOM) of an HTML element (such as a frame or iframe) is created, but before any child elements of it have been created or any scripts are run.
- `ondrag`—Dispatched when a user clicks an element to start a drag operation.
- `ondragend`—Dispatched when an element is released at the end of a drag operation.
- `ondragenter`—Dispatched when an object is dragged over the edge of another object.
- `ondragleave`—Dispatched when an object is dragged off of another object.
- `ondragover`—Dispatched as an object is moved while being dragged over another object.
- `ondragstart`—Dispatched at the start of a drag operation.
- `ondrop`—Dispatched when an object is dropped on another object.
- `onpaste`—Dispatched when content is pasted into an element.

NOTE For information on these and other added events, please see the Flex 3 LiveDocs, available from Adobe (http://livedocs.adobe.com/flex/3/).

Of these new events, the `ondominitialize` event is worth a special note. This event is dispatched by a frame's DOM object, which holds all the elements of a frame, after the window and document objects of the frame have been created but before any scripts have been parsed or any document elements have been created. By listening for this event, you can react early in the frame's life cycle, allowing you the ability to add any objects, variables, or functions to the frame, such that they will be available to any script in that frame's HTML.

Security

AIR uses sandboxes to segment HTML content. Each sandbox is considered its own unique section, and the files in a particular sandbox are granted permissions in relation to each other. Using this approach, files can be easily divided into separate security and access groups. When a file is loaded by AIR, the content is put into a specific sandbox and that file can only call methods and properties of other content loaded in that same sandbox. This is very important because each sandbox is given a level of access, a set of possible actions, and a set of communication rules.

Sandbox Type	Description
Application	Has access to all the AIR APIs, as well as the ability to access the file system.
Local trusted	Has access to the local file system but does not allow access to the other AIR APIs or to remote servers. This is also known as the local-with-filesystem sandbox.
Remote	Only has access to other elements served from the same domain.

There are three main sandboxes, the `application` sandbox, the local trusted sandbox, and the `remote` sandboxes. Any file loaded from the application's installation directory will be placed into the `application` sandbox, and it will receive full access to all of the AIR APIs, as well as be able to access the file system. However, elements in this sandbox cannot access remote servers. Any other files loaded from the local file system are put into the `local-with-filesystem` sandbox. This sandbox grants access to the local file system but does not allow access to the other AIR APIs or to remote servers. Any other file that is loaded from a remote server is loaded into a `remote` sandbox that corresponds to the domain from which the file was loaded. Files in the same `remote` sandbox can communicate with each other, but cannot access properties or methods of content from other `remote` sandboxes.

Understanding the sandboxes for the various types of content is significant, especially if you are building applications that are *mashups* (defined by Wikipedia as a web application that combines data from more than one source into a single integrated tool) and have content from several different sites. When building this style of application, you need to remember which pieces of content are allowed to talk to other pieces of content.

There may be instances when you need a local file to be able to communicate with resources from a `remote` sandbox, such as building a controller to a mashup application. You can achieve this by loading the content into a frame or iframe and specifying the sandbox into which you would like to place the content. The AIR extensions to WebKit include a new `sandboxRoot` attribute of the HTML frame tag, which allows you to specify a sandbox into which the file will be loaded. Another AIR extension to WebKit is the `documentRoot` attribute, which is used to specify an application-specific location to which a URL from the loaded file resolves. With the use of this property, any requests made by clicking a link on a remotely loaded file will be loaded against local versions of the file in the `documentRoot` directory specified, rather than from the remote server.

Consider the example used across Listings 1—3, which uses a local HTML file with an iframe to load a remote file, which has a Google Map, and functionality to add a marker to any arbitrary latitude and longitude. Be aware that you need all three of these files working together in order to see this work.

Listing 1—MyMap.html

```
<!DOCTYPE html PUBLIC "-//W3C//DTD XHTML 1.0 Strict//EN"
  "http://www.w3.org/TR/xhtml1/DTD/xhtml1-strict.dtd">
<html xmlns="http://www.w3.org/1999/xhtml">
  <head>
    <meta http-equiv="content-type" content="text/html; charset=utf-8"/>
    <title>Remote Page with a google map</title>
    <script src="http://maps.google.com/maps?file=api&amp;v=2&amp;key=
    ➥ ABQIAAAA0XeiexVzOKP6Gh9aU6PiiBTfIGA82XDoQXXa7qLAOEAZj7TrchT8vpsvm
    ➥ 6IHeHwxk2m2McWvUn9NOQ"
      type="text/javascript"></script>
    <script type="text/javascript">

    //<![CDATA[
    var bridge;
```

code continues on next page

Listing 1 (continued)

```
    function addMarker(lat,lon){
        var map = new GMap2(document.getElementById("map"));
        map.setCenter(new GLatLng(lat,lon), 16);
        map.setMapType(G_HYBRID_MAP);
        var marker = new GMarker(new GLatLng(lat,lon));
        map.addOverlay(marker);

    }
    function load(){
        bridge = new Object();
        bridge.addMarker = addMarker;
        window.childSandboxBridge = bridge;
        draw();
    }
    function draw() {
        if (GBrowserIsCompatible()) {
            var map = new GMap2(document.getElementById("map"));
            map.setCenter(new GLatLng(42.033357,-87.864854), 16);
            map.setMapType(G_HYBRID_MAP);
        }
    }
    //]]>
    </script>
  </head>
  <body onload="load();" onunload="GUnload();">
    <div id="map" style="width: 500px; height: 300px"></div>
  </body>
</html>
```

Here you can see a fairly straightforward implementation of the Google Maps API. A function has been added named `addMarker`, which takes two arguments: `lat` and `lon`. The method gets a handle on the map, centers it on the latitude and longitude provided, and adds a marker to the map at those coordinates.

The other function to note is the `load` method, which creates a new object named `bridge`, adds the `addMarker` method as a method of the `bridge` object, and sets the `bridge` object as the `childSandboxBridge` of the window.

In order to prevent malicious code from a remote server from being able to adversely affect a machine running AIR, AIR has implemented a strict concept of security sandboxes, such that content in one sandbox can freely interact with other content in the same sandbox, but has very little access to content in other sandboxes. If you need to interact with a function on a remote page, you can make it accessible by placing that function in a sandbox bridge. And as all JavaScript developers know, when interacting with a web page in JavaScript, you use properties and methods of the Document Object Model (DOM). AIR has added new properties to the DOM, called `childSandboxBridge` and `parentSandboxBridge`. By having a remote site explicitly expose a piece of functionality in a `sandboxBridge`, it will be accessible in other security sandboxes.

In Listing 1, the `addMarker` method is explicitly exposed across the `bridge` to allow this application to call the function directly from the AIR application.

Next you will look at the local HTML file shown in Listing 2, which will reference the remote page.

Listing 2—Mashupframe.html

```
<html>
<script>
    function addMarker(lat,lon){
      var childInterface = document.getElementById(
      ➥ "iframecontent").contentWindow.childSandboxBridge;
      childInterface.addMarker(lat,lon);
     }
</script>
<body >
<iframe id="iframecontent" width="100%" height="100%"
    src="http://jefftapper.googlepages.com/MyMap.html"/>
</body>
</html>
```

This HTML file is pretty straightforward. It contains an iframe with the `iframecontent` `id`, which is pointing at the remote HTML page with the Google Map API. A JavaScript function called `addMarker` has the same signature as the remote `addMarker` function. When it runs, it gets a reference on the `childSandboxBridge` from the loaded page and passes the `lat` and `lon` parameters to the remote `addMarker` method that the sandbox exposed. Lastly, look at the MXML file shown in Listing 3 that ultimately demonstrates Flex content in AIR interacting with a remote HTML page.

Figure 1: A simple, Flex-based AIR application page

Listing 3—Main.mxml

```
<?xml version="1.0" encoding="utf-8"?>
<mx:WindowedApplication xmlns:mx="http://www.adobe.com/2006/mxml"
    layout="vertical"
    width="550" height="400">
<mx:Script>
      <![CDATA[
            private function interact():void{
                var domWindow:Object = htmlContent.domWindow;
                domWindow.addMarker(42.033901,-87.866077);
            }
            private function onComplete():void {
                btn.enabled = true;
                btn.label="Add Marker";
            }
      ]]>
    </mx:Script>
```

Listing 3 (continued)

```
    <mx:HTML id="htmlContent"
      width="100%" height="100%"
      location="mashupframe.html"
      complete="onComplete()"
      verticalScrollPolicy="off" horizontalScrollPolicy="off"/>
    <mx:Button click="interact()" id="btn" enabled="false"
        label="Please Wait, loading..."/>
</mx:WindowedApplication>
```

What you see here is a simple Flex-based AIR application page, which has an `<mx:HTML>` tag that can load the local HTML file as well as a button. The `complete` event of the HTML tag fires an `onComplete` method, which enables the button for the user. This is done so that it's not possible to access the function on the remote HTML page until the page is finished loading. Once the button is enabled, and the user clicks it, the `interact` method is called, which gets a handle on the content in the local HTML file (with the use of the `domWindow` property of the `htmlControl`) and calls the local `addMarker` function, passing through some coordinates. When this call is heard by the local HTML file, it in turn passes those coordinates to the remote file. The remote file centers the map at those coordinates and adds a marker to the map.

As noted earlier, by default HTML files may only communicate with other resources that are in the same sandbox (remember that all files loaded from the same domain are placed inside the same `remote` sandbox so they can communicate with each other). Developers who are used to working with AJAX (Asynchronous JavaScript and XML) are used to loading data into their page via the JavaScript XMLHttpRequest (XHR) API. Natively, AIR will attempt to prevent any cross-sandbox XHR requests. If you need to re-enable this functionality, you use with the `allowCrossDomaininXHR` attribute of a frame or iframe, which AIR added as an extension to WebKit. If this attribute is set to `true`, the loaded content will be able to make XHR requests not only to the server from which it came, but also to other remote servers. Allowing cross-domain XHRs can be very dangerous, as the HTML file will accept requests made from any location. This opens the door for malicious attacks on your HTML pages and leaves the possibility for data to be injected into your application. Therefore, you should include the `allowCrossDomaininXHR` attribute in a frame tag only when it is absolutely necessary.

If you are building an AIR application that uses AJAX to make HTTP requests to retrieve XML, you can still do this from AIR. To make a data request, you would create a new XMLHttpRequest object. This is an object provided by AIR for making data requests from files. Following is a sample XMLHttpRequest call.

```
request = new XMLHttpRequest();
request.open("GET", "http://xml.weather.yahoo.com/forecastrss?p=
➥ USIL0922&u=f", true);
xmlhttp.onreadystatechange = function() {
      // do something
}
xmlhttp.send(null);
```

The same sandbox restrictions discussed earlier still apply to XMLHttpRequests. Earlier, you saw how you can use the `childSandboxBridge` to expose content in a child page. Likewise, you can allow a child to interact with the parent by using the `parentSandboxBridge`. To set up a parent sandbox bridge, you will need to inject code into the remote page. The `ondominitialize` event (another AIR addition to WebKit) fires as soon as the remote content's DOM is available, but before any code runs on that page. Having an event that fires at this time can allow you to set a property, which the remote page can use to access a sandbox bridge to interact with the parent.

JavaScript in WebKit

When an application is built for the desktop, it is important to ensure that the user is safe and that there is no possibility for the application's code to be manipulated. As we've already seen, AIR modified WebKit to use sandboxes to provide the required security when using HTML in the desktop environment. Next, you will explore some of the other changes AIR has made to WebKit, specifically focusing on how JavaScript has been changed.

Earlier, you learned that AIR uses the concept of a sandbox to determine what JavaScript may be executed for each HTML. The `application` sandbox encompasses any content installed with an AIR application. This sandbox provides access to the runtime environment. To prevent malicious hijacking of the user's system, dynamic creation and execution of JavaScript code is severely restricted, only allowing it from files also in the `application` sandbox. Alternatively, you can place the local files in the `local-with-filesystem` sandbox, where they can have access to the local file system but not the AIR APIs. All files loaded from the network are loaded into a `remote` sandbox limited to the domain from which it was loaded, although you can use the `sandboxRoot` and `documentRoot` properties to map pages to a specific sandbox.

Many of the JavaScript restrictions exist to prevent the dynamic creation of code that may compromise the system, so the `eval()` function has been severely limited. You can use the `eval()` function after a page load is complete, but any evaluation that results in executable code will throw a security error. For further security, external scripts can only be loaded by an HTML file that is mapped to a non-application sandbox.

AIR API Access from JavaScript

In the same ways that AIR exposes integration with the OS to Flex-based applications, the same level of integration can be used from HTML applications. The implementation for this functionality is fundamentally different when accessed from JavaScript than it is from ActionScript, so you need a different strategy. With the extensions to the JavaScript functionality in WebKit, AIR provides the HTML content with the ability to access the same APIs you have learned about throughout this book.

When using JavaScript, you will be able to interact with the AIR runtime through the window object. AIR has added several properties to the window object that allow JavaScript to use the AIR and Flash APIs. Among these new properties are the `window.nativeWindow`, `window.htmlLoader`, and `window.runtime` properties. Each one of these properties provides access to the underlying elements of AIR.

The `window.nativeWindow` property provides control over window-specific properties such as `size` and `visibility`, as well as allowing access to window methods and events such closing, moving, or resizing the window. For example:

```
window.nativeWindow.close();
```

The `window.htmlLoader` property gives you access to the HTMLLoader object defined in AIR (through either the `HTMLLoader` class in Flash-based applications, or the `htmlLoader` property of the `<mx:HTML>` tag). This allows control over the appearance and behavior of the loaded HTML content.

Finally, the `window.runtime` property allows the use of classes from the AIR and Flash APIs. For example, to create a new File reference from JavaScript in AIR, you would use:

```
var testFile = new window.runtime.flash.filesystem.File();
```

This allows you to access the features that AIR offers, such as access to the file system; use of local SQL databases; and control of application appearance and menus, clipboard access, native drag and drop, and others. To ease the process and not require developers to type in the full package (`window.runtime.flash.*`), a JavaScript file called AIRAliases.js has been included with the AIR SDK. This file provides a way to quickly access the various pieces of the AIR API from within JavaScript. The AIRAliases.js file contains alias definitions for many runtime classes so that you can access them with far less required typing. For example:

`window.runtime.flash.desktop.NativeApplication`
can be accessed as
`air.NativeApplication`,

`window.runtime.flash.filesystem.FileStream`
is available as
`air.FileStream`,

`window.runtime.flash.data.SQLDatabase`
is available as
`air.SQLDatabase`,
and so on.

These are just a few of the many aliases provided by the AIRAliases.js file. The entire list is available in the file itself, as well as in the *Adobe AIR Language Reference for HTML Developers* documentation (http://help.adobe.com/en_US/AIR/1.1/jslr/).

To include the AIRAliases.js file in your own custom HTML pages, you simply need to add the following script reference in your HTML file.

```
<script src="AIRAliases.js"></script>
```

ActionScript Objects in JavaScript

Using JavaScript, you can not only access the AIR APIs, but can also interact with any ActionScript classes, including those you create yourself. For example, if you had an application that used both Flex and HTML to display information about cars, you could define an ActionScript class to create a custom Car datatype (known as a valueObject), which might look like this:

```
package valueObjects {
    public class Car {
        public var make:String;
        public var model:String;
        public var year:Number;
    }
}
```

Of course, from the Flex side, this valueObject becomes available by just importing the class and using it. To instantiate this class from JavaScript, you need to do two things. First, you need to set the `runtimeApplicationDomain` for the HTML control that has loaded the HTML page to the domain that contains the class definitions. For example, you could set the `runtimeApplicationDomain` to the primary application domain like this:

```
html.runtimeApplicationDomain = ApplicationDomain.currentDomain;
```

Once you set `runtimeApplicationDomain` to the proper domain, you can then instantiate the custom class inside JavaScript, as the following code illustrates:

```
var carClass = new window.runtime.valueObjects.Car();
```

JavaScript DOM from ActionScript

Likewise, you can also access any of the variables, functions, or display elements available from the JavaScript DOM from ActionScript as well. Once the HTML control has dispatched its `complete` event, you know that all the objects in the HTML content have been loaded and are available. You may have some luck trying to access objects in the HTML content before the `complete` event has been dispatched, but there is a good chance that the object will not have been parsed or created yet, and you will likely receive a runtime error.

To access any object inside an HTML page, you can use the `domWindow` property of the HTML control. This property is a reference to the global window object in JavaScript. For example, to read the value of a variable `foo` defined in JavaScript, you would inspect the `domWindow.foo` property of your HTML control.

Similar to accessing variables, you can access display objects as well, using the same syntax that JavaScript developers are used to: the `getElementById` method on the JavaScript window. This method returns a reference to the display object with the specified `id`, and then you may access the content of the display object by inspecting the object's `innerHTML` property.

Listing 4 is a simple example of accessing the various types of JavaScript objects from ActionScript:

Listing 4

```
function onInit():void {
    var html:HTML = new HTML();
    html.width = 500;
    html.height = 500;
    html.addEventListener(Event.COMPLETE, handleComplete);
    var xhtml:XML =
        <html>
            <script>
                weather = "raining";
                function getForecast() {
                    return weather;
```

code continues on next page

Listing 4 (continued)

```
                }
            </script>
            <body>
                <p id="weatherman">What's the forecast for today, Jim?</p>
            </body>
        </html>;
    html.htmlText = xhtml.toString();
}

function handleComplete(event:Event):void {
    trace(html.domWindow.weather); // raining
    trace(html.domWindow.document.getElementById("weatherman").innerHTML);
    trace(html.domWindow.getForecast());
}
```

It is also possible to modify the values of any HTML object in ActionScript using the same strategy as in Listing 4. If you wanted to change the weather to "sunny," you would use the following code:

```
html.domWindow.weather = "sunny";
```

HTMLLoader

The HTMLLoader object exists to allow you to load HTML content into a Flash-based (as opposed to a Flex-based) AIR application. To use it, add an instance of the HTML-Loader directly to a container just like any other child. In Flex-based applications, you are more likely to use the `HTML` class, rather than the `HTMLLoader` class, since Flex containers require that their children all extend UIComponent. The HTMLLoader does not extend UIComponent and is therefore not natively suitable for use in Flex applications.

If you are working in a Flex-based AIR application and find the need to interact directly with the HTMLLoader instance that is wrapped in the `HTML` class, you can do so with the use of the public `htmlLoader` property.

When using the HTML control, an HTML page can be loaded by assigning the page URL to its `location` property. However, when using the HTMLLoader control directly, a page is loaded by passing a URLRequest object, which contains the URL of the page to be loaded, to the `load()` method of the HTMLLoader object. For example:

```
var html:HTMLLoader = new HTMLLoader();
var url:URLRequest = new URLRequest("http://www.digitalprimates.net/ ");
html.load(url);
```

It is also possible to render an HTML string directly instead of loading a fully formed page. If you have a string variable that contains a snippet of HTML, and pass it to the `loadString()` method of HTMLLoader or set it as the `htmlText` property of the HTML control, the control will render just the specified string.

Working with Events

The HTML control dispatches a variety of ActionScript events to which event listeners can be registered in the typical ActionScript style.

```
html.addEventListener( "htmlDOMInitialize", htmlDOMInitializeHandler );
```

or

```
<mx:HTML htmlDOMInitialize="htmlDOMInitializeHandler(event)"/>
```

The HTML control is capable of dispatching these events:

- `complete`—Dispatched when loading is complete.
- `htmlDOMInitialize`—Dispatched when the DOM of a frame or iframe is created, but before any elements are created or scripts are parsed.
- `htmlRender`—Dispatched when the HTML content is rendered onscreen.
- `locationChange`—Dispatched when the `location` property is changed.
- `uncaughtScriptException`—Dispatched when a JavaScript exception occurs but is not caught.

DOM Events

You can also listen for JavaScript (or more accurately DOM) events from ActionScript and/or Flex in an AIR application as well. To accomplish this, you may either add a callback function for the specific event or use the `addEventListener()` function to register a listener function. For example:

- HTML

  ```
  <html>
      <a href="#" id="testClick">Click</a>
  </html>
  ```

- ActionScript using a callback function

```
function completeHandler(event:Event):void {
    html.window.document.getElementById("testClick").onclick = handleClick;
}
function handleClick():void {
    trace("In handleClick");
}
```

- ActionScript using `addEventListener()`

```
function completeHandler(event:Event):void {
    var testClick:Object = html.window.document.getElementById("testClick");
    testClick.addEventListener("click", handleClick);
}
function handleClick ():void {
    trace("In handleClick");
}
```

Remember that it is important to wait until the HTML control has dispatched the complete event so you know that the HTML objects have been instantiated.

Handling Events in JavaScript

It is also possible to respond to events, regardless whether they are initiated in the DOM or in the Flex side of the AIR application, directly in the JavaScript code. To do so, you would use the same strategy that you would in ActionScript: add an event listener to the appropriate object using the `addEventListener()` function. For example, if you wanted to listen for the `move` event that is dispatched whenever the application window is moved, you would do this:

```
<script>
function onInit() {
    window.nativeWindow.addEventListener(
    ➥ air.NativeWindowBoundsEvent.MOVE, handleMove);
}
function handleMove(event) {
    air.trace( event.x + ", " + event.y );
}
</script>
```

Just like in ActionScript, the listener function will implicitly be passed a parameter containing the event object with the information specific to the event.

One thing to be careful of when manually adding event listeners to your HTML content is that you need to manually remove them if you want the HTML content to be available for garbage collection. (For a great overview on memory management and garbage collection in Flex, see Chapter 26, "Profiling Flex Applications," of the *Adobe Flex 3, Training from the Source* book by Adobe Press.) If the HTML content is removed for any reason, such as the window closing or the file being unloaded, these event listeners continue to persist, and they prevent the removed content from being available for garbage collection. It is very important to remove event listeners so that the garbage collector can pick up the objects that are no longer used. Stray objects in memory are often referred to as a *memory leak* in an application, and can degrade the performance of the application over time. To make these elements eligible for garbage collection, event listeners that you added should be removed when the HTML content is either unloaded or when the window object is closed. If you do not remove the event listeners, the garbage collector will see that the object still has references to it and so the object would not be cleaned up. Here, you can see some simple strategies for removing event listeners.

```
<script>
    window.onunload = cleanUp;
    window.nativeWindow.addEventListener(air.Event.CLOSING, cleanup);

    window.nativeWindow.addEventListener(air.NativeWindowBoundsEvent.MOVE,
        handleMove);
    function cleanUp()
    {
        window.nativeWindow.removeEventListener(
        ➥ air.NativeWindowBoundsEvent.MOVE, handleMove);
}
</script>
```

Alternatively, you may want to remove an event listener when it is no longer useful. For example, when a window is fully loaded, the `complete` event is dispatched, which happens only once. There is really no need to keep that event listener around any longer, so it can be safely removed once it has executed.

```
<script>
    window.htmlLoader.addEventListener("complete", handleComplete);
    function handleComplete(event) {
        // handle the loading
        window.htmlLoader.removeEventListener("complete",  handleComplete);
    }
</script>
```

JavaScript Exceptions

Should an exception be thrown from JavaScript and not handled with a try/catch statement, the HTML control will dispatch an `uncaughtScriptException` event. By default, this event will output the JavaScript error message into the FlexBuilder Output View, however you can determine exactly what you want it to do by adding an event listener for this event.

An event listener can be registered in ActionScript in exactly the same way you would listen for any other ActionScript event, or it can be registered in JavaScript on the `window.htmlLoader` object.

```
<script>
    window.htmlLoader.addEventListener("uncaughtScriptException",
    ➥ htmlErrorHandler);
</script>
```

Controlling HTML Content

You can control HTML content, just as you can any other element in Flex, such as moving, resizing, rotating, or otherwise manipulating the display area of the content. Because the HTML control extends the `UIComponent` class and therefore retains all of its functionality, you can manipulate it just like any other UIComponent.

Scrolling

The `HTMLLoader` class does not provide a default means to implement scrolling, while the `HTML` class, which is a wrapper to the HTMLLoader, does include the scrolling functionality. You can manually add scroll bars to the HTMLLoader, if your application requires that functionality. To do this, you would need to manipulate the `scrollH` and `scrollV` properties based on the size of the content, which you can determine by the `contentWidth` and `contentHeight` properties. The `scrollH` and `scrollV` properties control the amount, in pixels, that the HTML content is scrolled, and the `contentWidth` and `contentHeight` properties represent the width and height of the HTML content inside the HTMLLoader. This is different from the `width` and `height` properties that represent the actual width and height of the HTMLLoader on the stage. If scrolling is necessary, the `contentWidth` or `contentHeight` properties will be larger than the `width` and `height` properties of the control. The `scrollH` and `scrollV` properties are offsets from the size of the HTMLLoader, because the size is the default visible space of the container. So, if your HTMLLoader has a height of 400 and a `contentHeight` of 600, setting the `scrollV` property to 1 would show pixels 1–401 of the HTML content. Therefore, to scroll to the bottom of the page you would use the following code:

```
html.scrollV = html.contentHeight-html.height;
```

However, because scrolling behavior is built into the Flex HTML control, a scroll bar will automatically be generated and is available for use without you having to write any additional code. It is still possible to scroll the content programmatically by using the `verticalScrollPosition` and `horizontalScrollPosition` properties of the HTML control, which work in the same way for all Flex controls that have scroll bars.

Working with the History List

Just like its counterpart in a web browser, as new pages are loaded into an HTML control, AIR automatically maintains a history of these pages. Paralleling the browser functionality, you can access this history with the use of the `window.history` object. This history object provides information on the previously loaded pages and the position of the current page in the history list, and offers the ability to navigate through the pages in the history list, which is crucial if you are looking to implement a next and back button on the HTML control.

Each item in the history list is an instance of the `HistoryListItem` class. The class provides several properties that describe the HTML page it represents, including:

- `isPost`—A Boolean property that returns `true` if the item was an HTTP Post and `false` if it was any other type of HTTP request (such as GET, PUT, and so on).
- `originalUrl`—The URL of the page as it was requested from the AIR application. If there were any redirects on the page, this URL will still represent the original requested URL.
- `title`—The title of the HTML page.
- `url`—The actual URL of the loaded page. Unlike the original URL, if the server requested a redirect, this property contains the URL of the page that was actually loaded, not the page that was requested.

To get items from the history object, you can call the `getHistoryAt` method of the HTML control, which will return the specified `HTMLHistoryItem` object. You can use the `historyPosition` and `historyLength` properties of the HTML to see the position of the currently viewed page in the history list, as well as the total number of pages in the history.

Three methods have been defined to facilitate moving through the history. Calling `historyBack()` will move one position backward, if possible, and calling `historyForward()` will move one position forward, if possible. Using the `historyGo()` method will move a specified number of pages. If the value passed to the `historyGo()` method is positive, the HTML will navigate that many pages forward in the history list; if the value is negative, the HTML will navigate that many pages backward in the history list. If the move is to the zero or last position, it will stop moving. To reload the current page, you could call the `historyGo()` method with a value of 0 or call the `refresh()` method of the HTML control.

Using HTMLHost

In a traditional browser environment, JavaScript offers several ways to control the window into which the HTML content has been loaded. A similar set of methods is available in AIR. The original JavaScript methods are not actually available—only the modified version provided by AIR. For example, in a traditional browser-based application, JavaScript can change the value of a browser's status bar by using the `window.status` property; however, an AIR application does not natively have a status bar, therefore this property does not behave in the same way. Instead of discarding these common JavaScript APIs, AIR provides a simple way to override the default functionality and behavior for these various properties and methods.

By default, the following JavaScript properties and methods are disabled when an HTML control is created:

- `window.status`
- `window.document.title`
- `window.location`
- `window.blur()`
- `window.close()`
- `window.focus()`
- `window.moveTo()`
- `window.moveBy()`
- `window.open()`
- `window.resizeTo()`
- `window.resizeBy()`

You can use these properties and methods if you need to, but before you can, you will need to enable them by specifying an `HTMLHost` for your application. The `HTMLHost` defines how these methods and properties will work. In a pure browser-based environment, the browser is the whole application, and so these methods and properties apply directly to the browser. In an AIR application, you have the freedom to determine what these properties and methods mean in terms of your application. In order to use this, you will need to create an instance of the HTMLHost class and assign it to the htmlHost property of your HTML control. When calling the constructor of the HTMLHost class, you can pass in a Boolean value, indicating if you want the HTMLHost to use its default behaviors. If you don't provide a value, it will be set to true. If you want to customize the behaviors of the htmlHost, you should pass a value of false, which will then allow you to provide your own custom functionality. For example, you could display an Alert to the user whenever the window.status property is changed. To do this, you would create a new subclass of HTMLHost. Inside this subclass, you would specify the functions that you want to override, and provide your own functionality.

```
package {
    import flash.html.*;
    import mx.controls.Alert;

    public class StatusHost extends HTMLHost {
        public function StatusHost(defaultBehaviors:Boolean=false){
            super(defaultBehaviors);
        }
        override public function updateStatus(value:String):void {
            Alert.show("Change in status - " + value);
        }
    }
}
```

Then, in your main file you would do this:

```
var html:HTML = new HTML();
html.width = 500;
html.height = 500;
html.htmlHost = new StatusHost();
html.location = "helloWorld.html";
addChild(html);
```

Using a similar strategy, you can override the behavior for any of the properties or methods that HTMLHost supports. Here are a few more samples of how to override the behaviors in HTMLHost.

To handle the window.location being changed:

```
override public function updateLocation(value:String):void
{
    htmlLoader.load(new URLRequest(value));
}
```

To handle the window.close() method being invoked:

```
override public function windowClose():void
{
    htmlLoader.stage.nativeWindow.close();
}
```

To handle the window.document.title being changed:

```
override public function updateTitle(value:String):void
{
    Alert.show("Requesting to change title to: " + value);
}
```

Opening HTML Content in the OS Default Browser

As you would expect from a desktop application, you can choose to have HTML content launched in the OS native browser or directly in your application. By calling the navigateToURL method from your application, the URL will be opened in the default browser for the user's OS. This can be very useful in providing some functionality not natively available from AIR. For instance, AIR has no native capability to open a user's email client; however, a browser does, and will do so, when a link with a mailto attribute is encountered. Likewise, some browsers are capable of opening Microsoft Word when a user clicks a link for a .doc or .rtf document, opening Microsoft Excel for an .xls document, and so on.

NOTE The navigateToURL method requires a URLRequest object as a parameter, and the URLRequest object specifies the location to load in the web browser.

When using the navigateToURL function, the locations that may be loaded are restricted depending on the sandbox of the file that is calling the function. These security restrictions prohibit certain URL schemes from being used for the destination of the web browser.

Only the following URL schemes are allowed:

- In the `application` sandbox:
  - http:
  - https:
  - file:
  - mailto:
  - app:
  - app-storage:
- In the `local-with-filesystem` sandbox:
  - file:
  - mailto:
- In the `remote` sandbox:
  - http:
  - https:
  - mailto:

The URL provided should be constructed just like it would be inside a web browser. The mailto scheme will direct the request to the system's default mail application.

Adding PDF Content

Using the HTMLLoader and the Adobe Reader browser plug-in, AIR can render PDF files directly into your AIR application. Because a PDF file will be shown in the context of an HTMLLoader component, the PDF content may be sized and positioned just like any other content in an HTMLLoader. Likewise, you can control the PDF content in the same ways that you would an HTMLLoader.

Detecting PDF Capabilities

Before PDF content can be rendered in AIR, the user must have a PDF reader installed on their system, because AIR uses the Adobe Reader browser plug-in to render the

PDF files. Therefore, the user is required to either have Adobe Reader or Adobe Acrobat version 8.1 or higher installed to allow for the rendering of PDF content in an AIR application.

It is important to be sure that a user is capable of displaying PDF content before attempting to load it. You can check the users' ability to render PDF files by checking the `pdfCapability` property of an HTML control or an HTMLLoader object. This property will have one of four values, each of which is represented by a static constant from the `HTMLPDFCapability` class.

- `STATUS_OK`

  A sufficient version of Acrobat Reader is installed.

- `ERROR_INSTALLED_READER_NOT_FOUND`

  No version of Acrobat Reader is installed.

- `ERROR_INSTALLED_READER_TOO_OLD`

  A version of Acrobat Reader is installed, but it is too old.

- `ERROR_PREFERRED_READER_TOO_OLD`

  A sufficient version of Acrobat Reader is installed, but an older version of Acrobat Reader is configured to handle PDF content.

Here is a snippet of code that can be used to ensure that the user can properly display PDF content:

```
if(html.pdfCapability == HTMLPDFCapability.STATUS_OK)
{
    trace("PDF content can be displayed");
}
```

Loading PDF Files

You use the same method to load PDF files as you do for loading HTML files. The URL of the PDF file is passed to the `load()` method of the HTMLLoader, or to the `location` property if you are using the `<mx:HTML>` control.

```
var pdf:HTML = new HTML();
pdf.height = 500;
```

```
pdf.width = 500;
if(pdf.pdfCapability == HTMLPDFCapability.STATUS_OK)
{
    pdf.location = "http://help.adobe.com/en_US/AIR/1.1/devappshtml/
    ➥ devappshtml.pdf";
}
```

You can even use JavaScript to control the PDF just like in a typical HTML file. Extensions in Acrobat Reader allow JavaScript to control page navigation, magnification, and multimedia events, and to process forms.

Knowing PDF Limitations in AIR

While PDF content can be rendered inside of AIR, there are several known issues. The PDF content will not display if the NativeWindow that contains the PDF content is transparent. Likewise, the PDF content will not display if any of the visual properties of the HTMLLoader have been changed; this includes the `filters`, `alpha`, `rotation`, or `scaling` properties. Also, the stage of the application may not be in full-screen mode, and the stage's `scaleMode` property must be set to `StageScaleMode.NO_SCALE`.

Another important caveat to keep in mind is that the display order of the objects on the display list will act differently when PDF content is being displayed. The PDF content will display properly inside of the HTMLLoader, however it will always be on the top of the other display objects in AIR.

If a link is clicked that leads to a bookmark in the PDF file, the display will scroll to the proper place in the PDF content as expected. However, clicking links inside of a PDF file that lead to a different location (even if that location is a new window) will redirect the HTMLLoader object that contains the PDF file to the location of the link.

Exploring the Use of HTML in the dpTimeTracker Application

The help system in dpTimeTracker has been implemented as a series of HTML files that are loaded into an HTML control, in a separate application window.

To begin exploring how the dpTimeTracker application uses HTML, open the TimeTracker2.mxml file, and notice the `launchHelp` method defined in the script block.

```
private function launchHelp():void{

    var win:HelpSystem = new HelpSystem();
    win.height=300;
    win.width=400;
    win.title = "dpTimeTracker Help";
    win.open();
}
```

This method creates a new instance of the `HelpSystem` class, sets its `height`, `width`, and `title`, and then opens it in a new window. Next, look at the HelpSystem.mxml file located in the help package.

```
HelpSystem.mxml
<?xml version="1.0" encoding="utf-8"?>
<mx:Window xmlns:mx="http://www.adobe.com/2006/mxml" layout="absolute"
    showFlexChrome="true">
    <mx:HTML location="help/main.html" width="100%" height="100%"/>
</mx:Window>
```

As you can see, this class is nothing but a simple Window subclass, containing an HTML control. The HTML control is assigned a location, which points at the root help file, main.html. Next, look at the main.html file, also in the help package.

```
main.html
<!DOCTYPE HTML PUBLIC "-//W3C//DTD HTML 4.01//EN" "http://www.w3.org/TR/html4/
strict.dtd">
<html>
    <head>
        <meta http-equiv="Content-Type" content="text/html; charset=iso-8859-1" />
        <title>dpTimeTracker Help</title>
        <LINK rel="stylesheet" href="help.css" type="text/css">
            </head>
    <body>
        <h1 align="center">dpTimeTracker Help</h1>
        <table width="100%">
            <tr>
                <td width="150">
                    <a href="login.html" class="links">Login</a><Br/>
                    <a href="newUser.html" class="links">
                        Creating a New User</a><Br/>
                    <a href="login.html" class="links">Tracking Time</a><Br/>
```

```
                <a href="newUser.html" class="links">Syncing Time</a><Br/>
                <a href="login.html" class="links">Preferences</a><Br/>
                <a href="newUser.html" class="links">Administration</a><Br/>

            </td>
            <td>
                <h1>dpTimeTracker</h1>
                <h2>(c) 2008 Digital Primates IT Consulting Group</h2>
                <p>Welcome to dpTimeTracker<br/>
                Use the links on the left side to navigate through this
                    interactive help system.</p>
            </td>
        </tr>

    </table>
  </body>
</html>
```

Again, nothing terribly surprising, this is a pretty simple and straightforward HTML file, containing a title, a series of links, and a content area, where the help files will be rendered. Also, a style sheet, help.css, is included to consistently style all the HTML content throughout the help system. Once the help system launches, the user can click any of the links to navigate to the specific help topic. Take a quick look at help.css in the help directory.

```
/* CSS file */
body{
    font-family:sans-serif;
}
a{
    font-size:small;
    text-decoration:underline;
}
h2{
    font-weight:bolder;
    font-size:smaller;
}
```

You can see that the help.css file defines type selectors of the body, links (a) and h2 sections of code. With these defined, all the HTML content throughout the help system can have a consistent look.

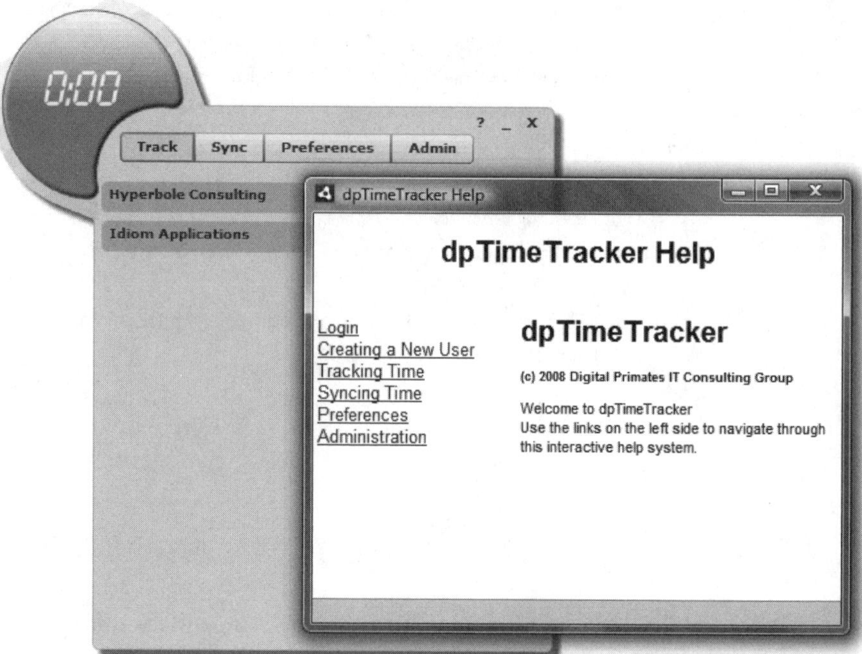

Figure 2: Time Tracker Help

Next Steps

Now that you are well-versed in the fundamental APIs of AIR and know how to add other non-Flash content, such as HTML and PDF, you are ready to learn how to integrate your application with a back-end server. In the next chapter, you will learn why a server is needed and how to integrate live dynamic data from a server into your application.

UNDERSTANDING THE NEED FOR REMOTE DATA

CHAPTER 10

Flex developers are accustomed to on-demand delivery of their applications over the Internet or through an intranet. AIR applications, once installed, launch from the local machine, leading many developers to wonder if the use of AIR means they no longer need a server. This chapter examines why servers remain useful to AIR developers and how to use HTTPService, Web Services, and the AMF protocol to exchange data between your AIR application and the outside world.

Why Use a Server?

Perhaps a more fitting question is, "Why not use a server?" If you find that you require applications that can neither access data from other machines or networks nor share the data that is generated from using the application, then you may be happy with a local application reading and writing local data, as discussed in Chapter 6, "Interacting with the File System."

Most applications, however, are far more interesting when they can be updated with remote data, can publish data, and can make the same application data available anywhere.

When making this decision for your application, you should ask yourself, "Will I ever need to use this application with my data when I'm away from my desktop?" and "Will I ever need to publish my data or share it with others?"

If the answer is yes, you should design your application to use a server. In this chapter, you will learn about the different kinds of servers available so you can decide which is most appropriate for your application.

What Kind of Server Can You Use?

You have a variety of servers available to you. Servers can be local (running on the same machine as your AIR application) or remote (running across a network or the Internet).

Later in this chapter, you will learn about service layers and stubs, which grant you the ability to develop your application without regard to the exact type of server you will eventually use. This separation of concerns will allow you to concentrate on your application logic and defer server implementations until later, even at runtime!

Downloading files

For decades, data has been exchanged between applications using flat files. While this approach is popular, likely due to human comfort factors such as being able to look at the file system and seeing your data, it comes with a number of disadvantages.

For example, both the producer application and consumer application must agree on a file format, a format that may not adhere to any standard format. If the producer application changes the format, the consumer applications must all be updated, recompiled, and redeployed.

Also, files are not guaranteed to be portable across systems. As you learned in Chapter 6, different OSs use different carriage returns and line feeds. Further, files must be managed in some way, either by the producer application, the consumer application, or even a third application that must be created specifically to handle the life cycle of the files.

Finally, in order for the consumer applications to process the new data, they must be informed of its existence. This implies the need for another layer of notification complexity: How does the system processing the data know that the data is ready? Is it based on a schedule? Does the program periodically check for the existence of the data? This additional layer simply adds complication and work. Many of these shortcomings are addressed by other communication methods.

Using Request/Response (RPC)

The RPC (Remote Procedure Call) service provides asynchronous access to external data. The service lets you make a request for data from a remote service. The remote service processes the request and returns the data to your AIR application at a later time.

There are several implementations of RPC, such as SOAP (Simple Object Access Protocol), REST (Representational State Transfer), XML, and AMF (Action Messaging Format). On the client side, you would use a WebService, HTTPService, or RemoteObject component. In reality, all of these services make use of the HTTP (Hypertext Transfer Protocol) for data transfer.

You can use HTTP as an RPC service by returning a file from the remote server and reading the contents of the file into your AIR application. For example, you could write an AIR application that processes expense reports created in a spreadsheet and saved as a CSV (comma separated values) file.

While HTTP transfer can be used to exchange any type of data, it is most useful when working with XML via SOAP- or REST-based services.

SOAP

SOAP is used to exchange XML messages between two running processes, such as an application and a web service. It is typically run over a network via an HTTP protocol. In practice, SOAP requests tend to be heavy and expensive: when a request is created, it is marshaled into a larger XML message before it is sent to the server. Even for the smallest request, the XML message is quite verbose. For the returned message, which can contain a large amount of XML data, using a SOAP message structure makes sense. But the cumbersome nature of the send request caused SOAP to lose out, in favor of REST.

The benefit of SOAP for business applications is that the XML surrounding the message describes the message in the detail necessary that any programming language that can use SOAP (including Java, C#, PHP, Ruby, Python, and many others) can completely understand the message, including the data types of all the data being transferred. It is this platform-neutral nature of SOAP-based web services that has led to their widespread use in business applications today.

To make requests to a SOAP-based WebService, you can use the `<mx:WebService>` tag. When using this tag, you will need to provide at least three pieces of information: the URL for the WebService WSDL file (Web Service Descriptor Language), an `id`, and a handler for the result event.

```
<mx:WebService id="musicService"
    wsdl="http://www.radioFreeAstoria.net/astistService.wsdl"
    result="handleResults(event)"/>
```

Here, you can see a very simple example that defines a WebService, with an `id` of `musicService`, which points at a WSDL file on a fictional radioFreeAstoria server. When results are received, they are routed through the `handleResults()` method.

In order to make a request to this WebService, you will use the service's `id` as an object, and call a method name, which is made available from that service. For instance, if you wanted to call a method called `getSongsForArtist()`, which requires that you pass an artist name and returns an array of songs for that artist, you might use:

```
musicService.getSongsForArtist("The Beatles");
```

NOTE For more information about WebService, SOAP, WSDL, as well as other properties, methods, and events for the WebService class, please see the *Adobe Flex 3: Training from the Source* book by Adobe Press.

REST/XML

A REST service is one from which data can be requested via HTTP and the data is returned in a simple XML message. In this way, REST servers offer an advantage over SOAP, in that the request message is usually much smaller.

REST services are inherently stateless in that with each request to the server, the client must provide all the information necessary to fulfill the request, including identification of the client if the server is architected to maintain state.

When dealing with REST-based requests, state can only be maintained on the server, and only as long as a mechanism for identifying returning clients is implemented. This is frequently done with the use of a unique identifier for each client that is sent to the server with each request.

A big advantage to REST servers is that the request/response mechanism is easily understood by anyone accustomed to web development. A user gesture such as the click of a hyperlink generates a request, and a response follows. Even though the website has no notion that the same user is clicking, the sequence of actions on the client can be interpreted at the server as repeated requests by the same user, so it can maintain the state.

With REST, the server is essentially exposing its API (Application Programming Interface) and making it available through common mechanisms such as HTTP and XML. For example, you could write an AIR application that uses the API of a site that stores statistics on bands and their music. Your first call to the REST server could request the names of the albums for a band. Your next call could request the names of the songs from a particular album. Though the REST server would have no notion that your client application is the one making the two calls, your application would have a notion of the relationship among band albums and songs, and could present that information to the user in an organized fashion.

To make HTTP requests for XML or any other data, you can use the `<mx:HTTPService>` tag.

When instantiating an HTTPService, you will at least want to give the service an `id`, specify a URL, and specify a handler for the result event. Consider this example:

```
<mx:HTTPService id="gradeService"
    url="http://www.myuniversity.edu/services/gradeService.xml"
    result="handleResults(event)" />
```

Here, a service is defined with the `id` of `gradeService`, which points to an XML file. When the result comes back, a method called `handleResults()` will be called. In order to make the request, the `send()` method of the service needs to be called.

NOTE For more information about HTTPService and the other properties, methods, and events for it, please see the *Adobe Flex 3: Training from the Source* book by Adobe Press.

Action Messaging Format (AMF)

AMF is a binary format that uses a similar set of RPC services to those used by SOAP and other HTTP requests for exchanging data between an application and a server. Unlike the SOAP or REST services described earlier, the data transmitted between client and server is sent as fully realized ActionScript objects, serialized into a binary format, allowing for a much more efficient communication. The reason for this efficiency is twofold. First, because the data transmitted is binary, it is much smaller, and therefore travels over the wire faster. Secondly, the data received from the server is already a fully realized ActionScript object, so it is not necessary for the client to parse XML data into objects; the data arrives in a form ready to be used.

In AIR, the `RemoteObject` class is used to access data on the remote server via the AMF protocol. A `RemoteObject` is simply a means of accessing classes on another server.

For example, you could be attending a university that has published an API to their ColdFusion server for students to retrieve their class schedules, grades, and other information. You want to write an AIR application that reads all the grades for a particular student from all of their classes and tracks their progress across semesters. The `RemoteObject` declaration might look like this:

```
<mx:RemoteObject id="gradesSvc"
    destination="ColdFusion"
    source="University.cfcs.Grades"
    result="saveGradesResult(event)"
    showBusyCursor="true" />
```

This creates a remoteObject component with an `id` of `gradesSvc`, which points to the Grades ColdFusion component on the server. The destination does not define the server as ColdFusion; the type of service is defined in a configuration file (`services-config.xml`), or, as you will learn later in this chapter, it can be defined in ActionScript.

Just like the SOAP- and HTTP-based services, calls made through the `RemoteObject` class are made asynchronously. That is, the request is made and processing continues without getting the results back immediately. To handle the results when they come back, you define a result handler. In this example, the result handler named `saveGradesResult` is called once the server has responded with data. The type of event you will receive is an instance of `mx.rpc.events.ResultEvent`.

In order for a remoteObject to be used, an AMF Gateway is needed on the server. Adobe has a number of products that include an AMF Gateway, including ColdFusion, BlazeDS, and LiveCycle Data Services. Chapter 11, "Communicating with Adobe BlazeDS," discusses configuring AIR to talk to these servers.

In Flex, to invoke a ColdFusion CFC, you would start by specifying the RemoteObject, such as in this example:

```
<mx:RemoteObject
    id="addressBookService"
    destination="ColdFusion"
    source="AddressBook.cfcs.PhoneNumber">
    <mx:method name="retrievePhoneNumber"
        result="usePhoneNumber(event)"
        fault="Alert.show(event.fault.message)" />
</mx:RemoteObject>
```

You have created a remote object component that points to a ColdFusion component called PhoneNumber. Though the `destination` is listed as "ColdFusion," this is only a descriptive name. To verify the actual server technology used, you would look in the services-config.xml file.

To invoke your new remote method, you simply call it using the `id` you created, like this:

```
<mx:Button
    id="phoneBtn"
    label="Retrieve Phone Number"
    click="addressBookService.retrievePhoneNumber()" />
```

If the server call executes successfully, your result handler, `usePhoneNumber`, will be invoked with an event that contains the following result:

```
public function usePhoneNumber(event:ResultEvent) : void {
    Alert.show(event.result as String);
}
```

Real-Time Messaging Protocol (RTMP)

The Real-Time Messaging Protocol (RTMP) is used to broadcast messages between a server and Flash Player. Much like a RemoteObject, RTMP transmits data via AMF, but the difference is that a stateful connection is maintained between the client and server, allowing the server to push data to the client, while the use of RemoteObject only allows the server to respond to a request from the client. This is why it is referred to as a real-time protocol; either side (client or server) can send a message at any time. It is highly optimized and can support many simultaneously connected clients.

RTMP has the ability to traverse firewalls through HTTP tunneling and can also run securely over an https connection. It maintains a persistent connection so audio and video data can be streamed smoothly to clients. Because the RTMP has a small header for each chunk of data it transmits, overhead is low, aiding in performance.

The RTMP requires a special server in order to be able to use it, such as the Adobe Flash Media Server, Adobe LiveCycle Enterprise Server (LCES), or third-party servers such as Red5 and WebORB.

To use the RTMP features of LCES, you can use the `Producer` and `Consumer` classes. These classes work on a publish and subscribe mechanism, which is an asynchronous way of sending messages.

In typical publish and subscribe, the publishers and subscribers are decoupled, meaning that they are not aware of each other. Publishers create messages and put them onto a stream, while subscribers sign up for certain kinds of messages and then sit back and receive them.

You would use such a mechanism when you want a scalable messaging system where the publishers and subscribers needn't be aware of each other. You would likely want to avoid such a mechanism when you need a guarantee that the subscribers will receive the messages sent.

In the Flex producer and consumer model, messages are sent on a channel specified by the `destination` property. When the consumer receives a message, it invokes the handler specified in its `message` property.

The following code demonstrates a simple producer and consumer example. The producer sends out a message, and the consumer receives it and writes it to the console. First, the following MXML defines the components:

```
<mx:Consumer id="consumer" destination="motd"
    message="motdHandler(event.message)" />
<mx:Producer id="producer" destination="motd" />
```

The consumer might handle the message like this:

```
import mx.messaging.messages.AsyncMessage;
import mx.messaging.messages.IMessage;

protected function motdHandler(message:IMessage) : void {
    trace(message.body.motd);
}
```

While the producer might produce the message like this:

```
protected function sendMotd() : void {
    var message:IMessage = new AsyncMessage();
    message.body.motd = "Soup is good food.";
    producer.send(message);
}
```

The IMessage interface has a property called body, which is of type `Object`. This allows you to dynamically create properties on that Object, such as `motd`. As long as the consumer knows to look for that property, the message can be processed once it is received.

The same producers and consumers can be used with BlazeDS messaging, even though Blaze doesn't specifically use RTMP. This is explained in more detail in the next chapter.

Sockets

Another mechanism for real-time messaging between client and server is with the use of sockets. Sockets are used as a direct, two-way connection between two applications or processes. Establishing a socket connection gives you only a pathway to transfer data; the socket does not inherently care what is being transmitted. Thus, data can be exchanged in binary or text format, and all details of formatting are defined by the server providing the socket.

In AIR, a socket connection can be created with either of the two socket classes provided: the `XMLSocket` or `BinarySocket` class. The primary difference between the two is that the `XMLSocket` expects that strings will be passed, while the `BinarySocket` is expecting that the data transferred are binary objects.

Continuing the university grade example from earlier, you now want to connect to your high school's server and include your grades there in your AIR application. Your high school offers only a socket connection. You might write a custom ActionScript class like this:

```
class HighSchoolGradesSocket extends Socket {
    protected var response:String = "";
    protected var studentID:String;

    public function HighSchoolGradesSocket(host:String, studentID:String,
    ➥ port:uint=80) {
        super(host, port);
        this.studentID = studentID;
```

```
            configureListeners();
        }

        protected function configureListeners():void {
            addEventListener(Event.CONNECT, socketConnectHandler, false, 0,
            ➥ true);
            addEventListener(ProgressEvent.SOCKET_DATA, socketDataHandler,
            ➥ false, 0, true);
            addEventListener(IOErrorEvent.IO_ERROR, socketIoErrorHandler,
            ➥ false, 0, true);
            addEventListener(SecurityErrorEvent.SECURITY_ERROR,
            ➥ socketSecurityErrorHandler, false, 0, true);
            addEventListener(Event.CLOSE, socketCloseHandler, false, 0, true);
        }

        protected function socketConnectHandler(event:Event):void {
            var message:String = "GET &studentID=" + studentID + "/\n";

            try {
                writeUTFBytes(message);
            }
            catch (error:IOError) {
                trace("Could not connect: " + error);
            }
        }

        protected function socketDataHandler(event:ProgressEvent):void {
            var responsePart:String = readUTFBytes(bytesAvailable);
            response += responsePart;
        }
    }
```

You can create your new class like this:

```
var hsGradesSocket:HighSchoolGradesSocket =
➥ new HighSchoolGradesSocket('grades.valleyRidgeHS.com',
➥ 'tim.smith.2073', 8080);
```

Some of the event handlers were left out of the example. You will need to listen for all these events and, on an error, decide how to handle it.

Note that in order to use Flex to access data through a socket, the server must define a cross-domain policy file. Socket policy files differ from document policy files, but the concept is the same. A socket policy file might look like this:

```
<?xml version="1.0"?>
<cross-domain-policy>
    <allow-access-from domain="*" to-ports="80,8080"  />
</cross-domain-policy>
```

This file would allow access from all domains and socket-based connections on ports 80 through 8080, inclusive, from Flex clients.

Using Design Patterns when Working with a Server

As you begin to build larger-scale applications, it helps to have an understanding of some common design patterns. The RPC services themselves implement a pattern known as the Asynchronous Token pattern. There are other patterns you may use to build your applications, to help make them more maintainable and easier to use.

Role of AsyncToken

The Asynchronous Token (frequently referred to as the AsyncToken) pattern is a design pattern for passing data from the execution of an asynchronous request to the result or fault handlers for the same asynchronous request.

When several asynchronous requests are made, there's no guarantee on the order in which the responses will occur, due to the asynchronous nature of the request. When you handle the returned data, you will often need to match the response with the request that made it so you can know what to do with the returned data, or how to handle a failure from the server.

This is the problem that the AsyncToken pattern helps to solve. A reference to a new instance of a token is returned to you from the `execute()` method. You are free to add whatever data you want to this token, and this instance is guaranteed to be returned to you in the response or failure method. This allows you to match up your responses with your requests.

Role of Service Interfaces

Frequently, development of client applications happens at the same time as the development of the server and the services. To allow the client-side developers to work (even though the actual services are not yet available), it's not uncommon to use stub data to simulate the data that will be returned from the server. When you are doing this, it is important to structure the incoming and outgoing data to closely mirror what the server will use when it is done. To aid in this, client and server-side developers will frequently agree upon an interface that lists the methods available from the server, the data that can be passed to each method, and the data types each method will return. By having an agreed-upon interface for how the client and server will communicate, the application can initially be built out against stub data, and real-world data can be plugged in without too much additional work when it becomes available.

Role of Stub Data

Stub data allows you to fake server calls and concentrate on writing the client portion of your application. When developing a multitiered application, it is useful to code to an agreed-upon interface between the client and server. This way, the developers creating the client-side code can work independently of those creating the server-side code. When the client-side and server-side teams are ready for the two tiers to communicate, there will be a natural fit. Think of the first trans-American rail lines: one team started in the east, the other in the west, and when the two teams met, their "interface"—the gauge of the rail—allowed the track to be completed and for trains to travel over it.

When developing to stub data, you will write code that implements a stub interface and will return some data to your application. Most likely, this will be data you code directly into the stub layer.

Once you are ready to communicate with the real server, you would swap out your stub layer and swap in the server layer. If you coded your application to the interface, this process should be relatively easy.

Let's say you are building an application that generates an application tip on demand. Your interface might look like this:

```
public interface IApplicationTipServices {
    function getTip():AsyncToken;
}
```

Your stub might look like this:

```
public class StubApplicationTipService implements IApplicationTipServices {
    private var responder:IResponder;
    private var service:StubDataService;

    public function StubApplicationTipService( responder:IResponder,
        service:StubDataService ) {
        this.responder = responder;
        this.service = service;
    }

    public function getTip():AsyncToken {
        var token:AsyncToken;

        token = service.result( StubDataBuilder.generateTip() );
        token.addResponder(responder);
        return token;
    }


    public class StubDataBuilder {
        public static function generateTip():String {
        var tip:String = 'Always save before quitting';

        return tip;
    }
}
```

When the time comes to swap in another service layer, all you need to do is replace your `StubDataBuilder` with a different data builder (one that retrieves data from the server) and then write a new `generateTip()` method. Because you've coded to an interface, the rest of your application does not need to change.

Role of a ServiceFactory

A `ServiceFactory` is a singleton class that returns an object representing your remote service. The object you get back implements a specific interface rather than being of a certain class type.

This distinction is important to understand, because it's the key concept in being able to swap out services throughout development with minimal disruption to the development process. As discussed earlier, the client and server teams can agree on an interface between the tiers and capture that "software contract" in an interface. All remote services will implement that interface, just as the client code will be written to use that interface.

How does the client code use that interface? First, the `ServiceFactory` is a singleton, so an instance can be retrieved at any time. From that instance, methods can be invoked without regard to which object at runtime will be fulfilling that request.

As an example, let's assume you are writing a route-planning application that allows a user to enter a starting point and a destination and then press a button to calculate the miles between them.

While your analysis team is busy deciding which of the mapping services provided by vendors, Google and Yahoo, is more suited for the project, your development team has decided to limit the risk by defining a generic mapping interface that will work with the API from either vendor.

Your interface might look like this:

```
public interface IDistanceComputable {
    function distanceShortestRoute( begin:Location, end:Location):Number;
    function distanceQuickestRoute( being:Location, end:Location):Number;
}
```

Your client code might look like this:

```
public class GetQuickestRouteCommand extends CommandAdapter {
    override public function execute():void {
        asyncToken = ServiceFactory.getDistanceComputableService(this).
        ➥ distanceShortestRoute( begin, end );
    }
}
```

And to tie it all together, your `ServiceFactory` might look like this:

```
public class ServiceFactory {
    private static var _googleServiceCache:HTTPService;
    private static var _yahooServiceCache:HTTPService;
    private static var _stubServiceCache:StubDataService;
```

```
    public static function getDistanceComputableService(
    ➥ resp:IResponder ):IDistanceComputable {
        switch ( ConfigModel.service ) {
            case 'google':
                return new GoogleMapService( resp, _googleServiceCache );
                break;
            case 'yahoo':
                return new YahooMapService( resp, _yahooServiceCache);
                break;
            case 'stub':
                return new StubMapService (resp, _stubServiceCache );
                break;
        }
        return null;
    }
}
```

Note that regardless which service you actually use, the client code you use to get that shortest route distance is the same. In the section on stub data, you learned how to write your own fake data service while your server team finishes their work with the Google and Yahoo mapping services.

Further, which service is used is determined by how the ConfigModel object is configured. During development, the service might be determined at compile time. But there's no reason why the service couldn't be changed at runtime. There are a variety of reasons this could happen: user preference, one of the mapping services goes down or has a long response time, and so on.

Frequently, `ServiceFactory` will read the properties it uses to instantiate the proper class, based on variables it reads from a configuration file or a ConfigModel. Look at a sample `ServiceFactory` class.

```
package services{
    import mx.messaging.channels.AMFChannel;
    import mx.rpc.IResponder;
    import mx.rpc.remoting.mxml.RemoteObject;

    import net.digitalprimates.framework.services.StubDataRpcService;


    public class ServiceFactory{
```

```
public var _cfChannelSet:ChannelSet;
public var _flexChannelSet:ChannelSet;

// cached services
private static var _serviceFactory:ServiceFactory;
private static var _authService:RemoteObject;

private static var USE_STUB_DATA:Boolean;

public static function getInstance():ServiceFactory {
    if (_serviceFactory == null) {
        _serviceFactory = new ServiceFactory(
        ➥ new SingletonEnforcer());
    }
    USE_STUB_DATA = ConfigModel.USE_STUB_DATA;
    return _serviceFactory;
}

public function ServiceFactory(enf:SingletonEnforcer)  {
    var _cfChannel:Channel = new AMFChannel(ConfigModel.CFCHANNELID,
    ➥ ConfigModel.CFAMFENDPOINT);
    _cfChannelSet = new ChannelSet();
    _cfChannelSet.addChannel(_cfChannel);

    var _flexChannel:Channel = new AMFChannel(
    ➥ ConfigModel.FLEXCHANNELID, ConfigModel.FLEXAMFENDPOINT);
    _flexChannelSet = new ChannelSet();
    _flexChannelSet.addChannel(_flexChannel);
}

public static function getAuthService(
➥ resp_:IResponder):ISampleService {
    if (!USE_STUB_DATA)  {
        if (_authService == null) {
            _authService = new RemoteObject('ColdFusion');
            _authService.channelSet =
            ➥ ServiceFactory.getInstance().cfChannelSet;
            _authService.source =
            ➥ "net.digitalprimates.services.AuthService";
            _authService.showBusyCursor = true;
```

```
                }
                return new SampleServiceRemote(resp_, _authService);
            } else {
                var _stubService:SampleServiceLocal =
                ➥ new SampleServiceLocal();
                return new SampleServiceLocal (resp_, _stubService);
            }
        }
    }
}
class SingletonEnforcer{

}
```

As you can see, the service factory is defined as a singleton, meaning that only one instance of the class can exist. Since ActionScript 3.0 does not provide the ability to have a private constructor, a workaround is used to enforce the singleton—a private class, which can only be called from the `ServiceFactory` class. The private class `SingletonEnforcer` is defined in the same file as `ServiceFactory`, but it is defined after the closure of the package block. This ensures that this class only can be called by the other classes in this file, of which there is just one—`ServiceFactory`. Since calling the constructor of `ServiceFactory` requires an instance of `SingletonEnforcer`, and `SingletonEnforcer` can only be called by `ServiceFactory`, you can reasonably ensure that other developers will not be able to instantiate the class on their own. The only way other classes in the application can work with this class is through a call to the static `getInstance()` method. Aside from checking if an instance exists and creating it if it doesn't, the `getInstance()` method also sets the local `USE_STUB_DATA` property, based on the property from the ConfigModel.

The next thing to notice is that the constructor for the class builds two instances of the `ChannelSet` class, each of which uses an AMFChannel whose properties (`id` and `uri`) are passed through to the AMFChannel constructor. Details of the `Channel` and the `ChannelSet` classes are described in the "BlazeDS Architecture Basics" section of Chapter 11.

The `getAuthService()` method is what will ultimately create and return an instance of the `remoteObject` class, which knows how to call the AuthService object on the server. You'll notice that the first thing this class does is check if the system is using live data or stub data. As was discussed earlier, the use of stub data is great for development, especially if developing offline or before the server-side methods are complete. However, before deploying, it is necessary to turn off the stub data and compile and test with real live data. The ConfigModel (populated from variables in an XML file) has a property called useStubData, which indicates if ServiceFactory methods should contact the server or work against local "dummy" data. If the system is using stub data, an instance of the SampleServiceLocal is returned; otherwise an instance of SampleServiceRemote is returned. It is important to note that both the SampleServiceLocal and SampleServiceRemote are implementations of ISampleService, so, regardless of which one is in use, the developers can know that a predetermined set of methods are available. Next, an overview of the ISampleService interface is in order.

```
package samples.serviceFactory.services{

    import mx.rpc.AsyncToken;

    public interface ISampleService{
        function getUserById(id:String):AsyncToken;
    }
}
```

A straightforward interface, this defines a single method, getUserByID, which takes an id as a string and returns an AsyncToken. The use of the AsyncToken allows the framework the ability to know which call a given result matches, as described earlier in this chapter. The local version of the service returns a dummy data version of the User class, while the remote version returns a live version of the User class. Since both versions are built to use the same interface, it is easy to switch between developing against live data versus developing against stub data.

Using Remote Data in the dpTimeTracker Application

One of the features of the dpTimeTracker application is its ability to synchronize the collected timesheet data back with a server. Based on the initial requirements of the application, it was designed to be able to sync data with a server-based product called Harvest (http://www.getharvest.com/).

Exploring the Synchronization with Harvest

In Chapter 5, "Reading and Writing to a SQLite Database," you learned how the application uses commands to encapsulate common functionality. The same command pattern is used to allow the application to interface with remote data. In the application, when data needs to be synchronized back to a server, all the application developer needs to do is call the SyncToHarvestCommand class. Start by looking at this class.

```
package modules.timeSync.commands {
    import model.beans.TimeEntry;

    import net.digitalprimates.framework.command.CommandAdapter;

    import services.ITimeTrackerServices;
    import services.ServiceFactory;

    public class SyncToHarvestCommand extends CommandAdapter {
        private var entry:TimeEntry;

        public function SyncToHarvestCommand( entry:TimeEntry ) {
            this.entry = entry;
            super();
        }

        override public function execute():void {
            var ro : ITimeTrackerServices;
            ro = ServiceFactory.getTimeTrackerService(this);
            ro.updateTimeEntries( entry );
        }

    }
}
```

Structurally, this class is very similar to the commands you saw in Chapter 5. The class has a constructor, which takes some specific data (in this case an instance of the TimeEntry class). The only other method in the class is the execute() method. Inside the execute() method, there is a call to the ServiceFactory to get the Harvest service, which returned an implementation of the ITimeTrackerServices interface. Finally, the timeEntry instance is passed to the updateTimeEntries method of the object returned from the ServiceFactory. Next, look at the ITimeTrackerServices interface.

```
package services{
    import model.beans.TimeEntry;

    import mx.rpc.AsyncToken;
```

```
    public interface ITimeTrackerServices{
        function updateTimeEntries ( entry:TimeEntry ) : AsyncToken;
        function addTimeEntry ( entry : TimeEntry ) : AsyncToken;
        function authenticate( un:String, pw:String ):AsyncToken;
        function getPersonInformation( username:String ):AsyncToken
        function getClientsAndProjects( username:String ):AsyncToken;
    }
}
```

The updateTimeEntries method is defined in the interface. Since the ITimeTrackerServices method is defined to return an instance implementing this interface, you know as a developer that the updateTimeEntries method will always be available whenever you call the getTimeTrackerService method. Since this method is generic, it is capable of returning any class that implements the ITimeTrackerServices interface, regardless where the actual data is coming from. Even better, since the application ships with an implementation of the interface to allow for integration with Harvest, it can be used as a road map to integrate with any other third-party timetracking applications. If you need to integrate with another system, such as Microsoft SharePoint or Intuit's QuickBooks, you can learn about their APIs and add a new service to take data from dpTimeTracker and share it with these systems.

Next, look at the getTimeTrackerService static method of the ServiceFactory class, which is located in the services package.

```
public static function getTimeTrackerService( resp_: IResponder )
    :ITimeTrackerServices {
        switch( ConfigModel.service) {
        case 'harvest':
            return getHarvestService(resp_);
            break;
    }
    return null;
}
```

Clearly, this is a simple method that looks in the ConfigModel to determine how the system is going to synchronize time entries. Currently, this is built to only support Harvest, but it's easy to add additional switches to the case statement to support other systems. So, if the config model indicates that the system will synchronize to Harvest, the getHarvestService method is returned; otherwise, the method returns null. Next, look at the getHarvestService method in the ServiceFactory class.

```
public static function getHarvestService( resp_ : IResponder )
➥:ITimeTrackerServices{
    if( !_harvestServiceRequestProxy ){
        var encoder:Base64Encoder = new Base64Encoder();
        encoder.encode( ConfigModel.HARVEST_USERNAME + ":" +
        ➥ ConfigModel.HARVEST_PASSWORD );

        var header:URLRequestHeader = new URLRequestHeader("Accept",
        ➥ "application/xml");
        var header1:URLRequestHeader = new URLRequestHeader("Content-Type",
        ➥ "application/xml");
        var header2:URLRequestHeader = new URLRequestHeader(
        ➥ "Authorization", "Basic " + encoder.toString() );

        _harvestServiceRequestProxy = new URLRequest(
        ➥ ConfigModel.HARVEST_URL + "/daily/add" );
        _harvestServiceRequestProxy.method = URLRequestMethod.POST;
        _harvestServiceRequestProxy.requestHeaders.push(header);
        _harvestServiceRequestProxy.requestHeaders.push(header1);
        _harvestServiceRequestProxy.requestHeaders.push(header2);
    }

    return new HarvestTimeTrackerService(resp_, _harvestServiceRequestProxy );
}
```

The first thing this method does is check if the `_harvestServiceRequestProxy` exists. This is a variable that is used to cache the settings for how the application connects to the Harvest service. So, if the variable doesn't exist, it is created and set with the proper properties. Regardless whether it was created earlier or is being created now, the proxy object is passed on to a new instance of the `HarvestTimeTrackerService` class.

The Harvest APIs require that certain HTTP headers are passed with each request, including the Accept, Content-Type, and Authorization headers. Both the Accept and Content-Type headers are passed the XML mime type of "application/xml." The third header (stored in a variable called `header2`) added is a Base64Encoded variable of the user's username concatenated with a colon, followed by the user's password. This string is encoded using the Base64Encoder and passed as the Authorization header.

The rest of this method creates a new `URLRequest` instance, passes it the URL for the Harvest server, and specifies the method of the request to be "post" (represented by the static constant `URLRequestMethod.POST`.) Lastly, the three headers are added to the requestHeaders property of the _harvestServiceRequestProxy object. This object is passed on to the new instance of the HarvestTimeTrackerService class.

Lastly, open the HarvestTimeTrackerService class.

```
package services.harvest{
    import flash.net.URLRequest;

    import model.AppModel;
    import model.beans.Category;
    import model.beans.Project;
    import model.beans.TimeEntry;

    import mx.rpc.AsyncToken;
    import mx.rpc.IResponder;

    import net.digitalprimates.framework.adapters.URLLoaderAdapter;

    public class HarvestTimeTrackerService implements ITimeTrackerServices{
        private var request : URLRequest;
        private var responder : IResponder;

        protected var appModel : AppModel = AppModel.getInstance();

        public function HarvestTimeTrackerService(
        ➥ res:IResponder,req:URLRequest ){
            this.request = req;
            this.responder = res;
        }

        public function updateTimeEntries( entry:TimeEntry ) : AsyncToken{
            request.data = convertToHarvestXML(entry);
            return new URLLoaderAdapter( responder ).load(request);
        }
...
        private function convertToHarvestXML(timeEntry: TimeEntry) : XML  {
                var tmpString:String = '';

                tmpString = '';
```

```
            tmpString += '<?xml version="1.0" encoding="UTF-8"?>
            ➥ <request>';
            tmpString += '<notes>' + timeEntry.description + '</notes>';
            tmpString += '<hours>' + ((timeEntry.netTime/1000)/60) +
            ➥ '</hours>';

            for( var j:int=0; j<appModel.projects.length; j++ ) {
                var project:Project = appModel.projects.getItemAt( j )
                ➥ as Project;

                if( project.projectID == timeEntry.projectID ) {
                    tmpString += '<project_id>' + project.remoteID +
                    ➥ '</project_id>';
                    break;
                }
            }

            for( j=0; j<appModel.categories.length; j++ ) {
                var category:Category =
                ➥ appModel.categories.getItemAt( j ) as Category;

                if( category.categoryID == timeEntry.categoryID ) {
                    tmpString += '<task_id>' + category.remoteID+
                    ➥ '</task_id>';
                    break;
                }
            }

            tmpString += '<spent_at>' + new Date() + '</spent_at>';
            tmpString += '</request>';

            return new XML( tmpString ) ;

        }
    }
}
```

This class has the implementation details for sending data to Harvest. Notice the `updateTimeEntries` method, which takes an instance of the `TimeEntry` class. The `timeEntry` instance is passed to the `convertToHarvestXML` method, which takes all the elements from the TimeEntry instance and describes them in the REST XML structure that the Harvest server is expecting.

This should give you a sense of how the application pulls together a series of design patterns, including AsyncToken, ServiceFactory, and Command, to abstract the communication with the server. With this abstraction, developers needing to use the service can call a simple command and have the work done for them, without having to understand the details of the Harvest API.

Exploring the Versioning System

As was discussed in Chapter 8, "Working with the Presence API," the dpTimeTracker application checks a server to see if it has the latest version each time a user logs in. To find and invoke this service, the same mechanisms are used in that a module of the application calls a command, the command has an execute() method that calls the ServiceFactory, and the ServiceFactory ultimately instantiates the class that is responsible for calling the server. Recall from Chapter 8 that the Login class calls the GetCurrentVersionCommand when the user starts the login process. Open the GetCurrentVersionCommand class from the root commands directory.

```
package commands{
    import net.digitalprimates.framework.command.CommandAdapter;

    import services.ServiceFactory;
    import services.remote.IVersionServices;

    public class GetCurrentVersionCommand extends CommandAdapter {

        override public function execute() : void {
            var ro : IVersionServices;
            ro = ServiceFactory.getCurrentVersionService(this);
            ro.getCurrentVersion();
        }

    }
}
```

The GetCurrentVersionCommand is an incredibly simple class; it has only one method: execute(). The method defines a variable named ro, which is data typed as an implementation of the IVersionServices interface. The variable ro is then set to be equal to what is returned from the call to the static getCurrentVersionService method of the ServiceFactory class. Lastly, the getCurrentVersion method is invoked on the ro object. Next, take a quick peek at the IVersionServices interface.

```
package services.remote{
    import mx.rpc.AsyncToken;

    public interface IVersionServices {
        function getCurrentVersion() : AsyncToken
    }
}
```

An incredibly simple interface, any implementing class must include a single method called getCurrentVersion(). Much like the methods from the ITimeTrackerServices interface you explored earlier, the getCurrentVersion method of this interface also returns an AsyncToken. As discussed earlier, the AsyncToken pattern is implemented by all of the RPC services. The ServiceFactory class has a static method named getCurrentVersionService method that instantiates a class, which knows how to communicate with the server, sets its properties, and returns the instance.

Next Steps

Now that you understand the need for remote data, the mechanisms available for communicating with the server, and how a series of design patterns can help this communication, you are ready to delve deeper into your understanding of server communications. In the next chapter, you will learn about data messaging and nuances for interacting with the BlazeDS server.

COMMUNICATING WITH ADOBE BLAZEDS

CHAPTER 11

The previous chapter explored reasons why your application may want to communicate with a server and further demonstrated abstracting that layer of communication to decouple your application's visual components from the server technology.

That theme will continue in this chapter as you explore Adobe BlazeDS, an open-source, Java-based solution provided by Adobe for interacting with server data. BlazeDS was developed to facilitate an easier, faster, and cleaner approach to integrating with server-side data than previously available. The intended results are more engaging RIA experiences achieved by reducing the time required to develop data-intensive applications and increasing the runtime performance through new communication techniques and smarter data formats.

BlazeDS is a huge topic that could easily fill a book by itself. Further, BlazeDS is built upon Java, a topic that fills many more books. Therefore, this chapter will limit its scope by focusing on two major BlazeDS topics, the enhanced Remote Procedure Call (RPC) capabilities provided to your application when running BlazeDS, and the extremely powerful messaging functionality that allows your application to send and receive messages to other clients and servers, allowing the creation of collaborative applications. A number of Java Enterprise Edition (EE) topics and references will be made. While there is an attempt to provide a basic definition, a more detailed one is beyond the scope of this chapter.

If you are relatively new to Java, you should be able to gain a basic understanding of configuring and using BlazeDS in this chapter, but learning more about Java EE will be the only way to gain mastery of the material.

The Role of BlazeDS

As RIAs have evolved, they have become more complex and more data-intensive. Often companies find themselves needing to recreate existing business logic in new ways to facilitate its use by RIAs and, even after this additional work, the existing data connectivity options do not always perform sufficiently to handle this new data.

The way in which RIAs access server-side data also tends to be inconsistent and sometimes exceedingly complex. This lack of a standard methodology means new developers joining a team have a large learning curve, and applications can become very difficult to debug.

Finally, the traditional web application and early RIAs tended to rely exclusively on a client-initiated data model; that is, the client was responsible for initiating all requests for data. If data changed on the server side, the change would not be reflected in the client's data model until a future request from the client to the server updated the data. The reliance on this client-initiated model led to various implementations of polling and to overly creative schemes to solve a basic problem: servers and other clients could not easily notify each other of changes.

BlazeDS solves a majority of these issues by providing a consistent, high-performance method of connecting clients and servers. It eases the constraints on integrating existing services and Java EE infrastructure by providing simplified access to server-side Java from the client.

BlazeDS also provides the capability for server-side data push over standard HTTP 1.1, in addition to providing automated and transparent `failover` (the ability to choose a new protocol when one fails to connect) to a variety of polling options if the client is unable to allow server-side push due to firewall or network restrictions. BlazeDS builds on that infrastructure to offer full publish and subscribe messaging capabilities. This allows a server to notify its clients of changes as they occur, and allows multiple clients to notify each other of important events and send along relevant data.

Collectively, these technologies allow the developer to standardize their approach to creating timely, data-intensive applications and open a whole new tool set to create innovative next-generation clients.

How to Get BlazeDS

It is not necessary to install BlazeDS to use this chapter or examine the sample application. However, doing so will allow you to examine the configuration files and settings in more detail than can be covered in the chapter.

Adobe offers a BlazeDS turnkey that is a BlazeDS server configured with a handful of small applications to provide a deeper understanding of the product. If you do choose to download and install BlazeDS, we recommend using this version while learning.

BlazeDS is an open-source project maintained by Adobe Systems, Inc., and you can find it for download at the Adobe open-source portal at opensource.adobe.com. The direct URL to the BlazeDS project is http://opensource.adobe.com/blazeds/ and the direct link to the turnkey BlazeDS server is http://opensource.adobe.com/wiki/display/blazeds/download+blazeds+trunk.

BlazeDS Architecture Basics

BlazeDS is a basic implementation of an Enterprise Service Bus (ESB). An ESB can be thought of as very convenient plumbing that allows applications to communicate with each other and other available services while reducing the number of discrete connections that need to be made. The following diagram demonstrates communication points between applications without an ESB:

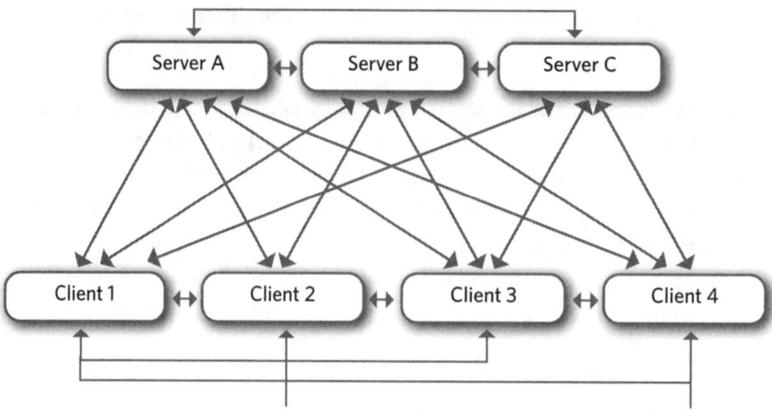

Figure 1: Application communication without an ESB

With an ESB, this diagram could be simplified to appear more like the following:

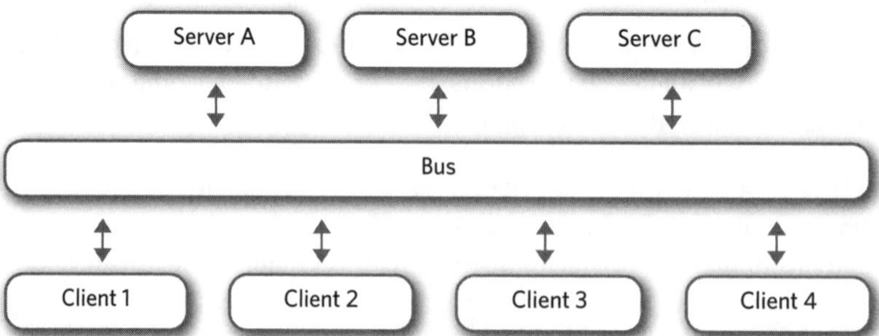

Figure 2: Application communication with an ESB

The ESB serves as a common connection point for all parties in this diagram. Messages from one participant are routed across the ESB to others as needed. This diagram shows the reduction of connection complexity, but using an ESB also provides another huge gain—protocol abstraction.

In the first diagram, either every client and server has to communicate using the same protocol, or alternatively, each client and server must understand and be able to communicate with every other protocol in use. This is rarely feasible in practice.

Most systems are heterogeneous, that is, composed of new and legacy components, newer clients, and chunks of code written by "some developer who used to work here." The ESB model facilitates this real-world scenario by allowing each party to connect using its own protocol or method, and then using an adapter to translate requests to and from a common format for transmission across the bus. This moves the complexity of multiple protocols and systems away from the clients, servers, and applications, and into a centralized location for management.

Successfully working with BlazeDS requires an understanding of a few key terms. They are presented here starting at the client side and moving toward the BlazeDS server.

- **Destination**—A destination is a virtual location on the BlazeDS server that accepts connections. The destination provides a convenient and abstracted way of discussing and referring to a combination of protocols, ports, formats, and configuration data. As you will see later in this chapter, AIR refers to these destinations inside your code, preventing the need to hardcode URL ports and other information about the server's location and configuration.
- **Producer**—A producer is responsible for creating a message that will be sent to a destination.
- **Consumer**—A consumer subscribes to a destination. When messages are sent to that destination, the consumer will receive them.
- **Messages**—In the context of this chapter, we will refer to a message as any data transferred to and from a BlazeDS destination. Even RPC services like HTTPService and RemoteObject use messages behind the scenes. Messages are routed over channels.
- **Channels and Endpoints**—Channels and endpoints are responsible for serializing and deserializing your message into the appropriate format and protocol when moving a message between the client and server.
- **Adapter**—Adapters translate requests from the universal format of the bus to the format required by various services.

In the following sections, you will explore basic configurations of these terms to clarify their meaning and the way in which they work together.

Configuration Files

BlazeDS uses a series of configuration files to configure all the needed components to make a destination. These files are found under the WEB-INF\flex folder of the application. For example, in the default BlazeDS turnkey installation, these files would be found in the /install_root/tomcat/webapps/blazeds/WEB-INF/flex folder from your root drive.

The main configuration file is named services-config.xml. This file defines the channels and endpoints supported by this server and includes three additional configuration files named proxy-config.xml, remoting-config.xml, and messaging-config.xml. This chapter will address the main services-config.xml file and the remoting-config.xml file throughout the Remote Procedure Calls section. Then we will address the messaging-config.xml file later in this chapter when you learn to configure publish/subscribe messaging.

Examining the services-config.xml file first, you will see that it is a well-formed XML file that starts with the <service-config> node as the root. Within the file, there are nodes for services, security, channels, logging, and system.

The services node includes the proxy-config.xml, remoting-config.xml, and messaging-config.xml files previously mentioned. This will configure the services available within this BlazeDS application.

The security node configures the authentication type and level needed before a client can access services available in this application.

The channels node configures the acceptable protocols and port by which a client can communicate with this application.

The logging node allows you to configure the type, amount, and final destination of any logging that happens on the BlazeDS server. A great tip while developing against a BlazeDS server is to change the logging that is sent to the *console* (command window where BlazeDS is run) from Error to Debug. This will provide a vast amount of useful information and help to save you from the inevitable typos and mistakes that are made when configuring BlazeDS. Listing 1 shows a logging node with console output set to Debug instead of the default Error.

Listing 1

```
<logging>
    <target class="flex.messaging.log.ConsoleTarget" level="Debug">
        <properties>
            <prefix>[BlazeDS] </prefix>
            <includeDate>false</includeDate>
            <includeTime>false</includeTime>
            <includeLevel>false</includeLevel>
            <includeCategory>false</includeCategory>
        </properties>
        <filters>
```

Listing 1 (continued)

```
            <pattern>Endpoint.*</pattern>
            <pattern>Service.*</pattern>
            <pattern>Configuration</pattern>
        </filters>
    </target>
</logging>
```

Finally, the system node sets various system settings, including the ability to automatically redeploy (reload) BlazeDS if you make a change to one of these configuration files. That option is turned off by default in the test drive version.

These configuration files will be modified throughout the remainder of this chapter to allow clients to call services on the server and enable messaging between clients.

Remote Procedure Calls

Remote Procedure Calls (RPC) allow your application to execute a method on a remote computer. They simply allow you to interact with a remote server to send or retrieve data. AIR and BlazeDS together offer three main approaches for communication with the server.

The first is the `HTTPService` class, which sends and retrieves information over HTTP without a prescribed data format. The HTTPService tag is most often used to send and receive XML data.

The second is the WebService, which also sends and receives XML over HTTP; however, the XML used is required to conform to a specific protocol: SOAP. SOAP is most commonly used to invoke a server-side method and potentially return data to the client using this protocol. It is an extensible platform and language-independent approach that can be successfully used to communicate across a variety of platforms.

Finally, the `RemoteObject` class allows you to interact directly with server-side Java objects. It can be used to execute methods of objects and receive results. Unlike SOAP, RemoteObject generally uses a binary protocol named AMF (Action Message Format), which is significantly less verbose and faster than SOAP to package and transfer to the client. Unfortunately, the RemoteObject tag is not available for every platform. BlazeDS makes this technology available for Java servers, and there are implementations for ColdFusion, .NET, and PHP that are well known at the time of this writing. Fortunately, Adobe has opened the specification for AMF, so it is likely that implementations will exist for every major server technology in the future.

While BlazeDS enhances the ability to use any of these services with Flex or AIR, this section will concentrate on the power provided by the combination of BlazeDS and the RemoteObject tag.

Configuring BlazeDS to Use RemoteObjects

One of the major advantages of using BlazeDS is the use of destinations, introduced earlier. Destinations allow a single point of management for all services and provide additional features such as the ability to proxy requests from different domains, handle client authentication, logging, and configure URLs using server-side XML files. Most importantly, they decouple this information from your application, meaning that your applications no longer need to contain hard-coded URLs and protocol information.

Creating a destination for an RPC call requires examining and potentially modifying the services-config.xml file and making a new entry in the remoting-config file. Examining the services-config.xml file will reveal a channels node, as mentioned earlier. That channels node further contains one or more channel-definition nodes, which are used to define the acceptable combinations of port, protocol, and settings when communicating with BlazeDS.

Depending on the version of BlazeDS you chose to download, it will look similar to Listing 2:

Listing 2

```
<channels>
    <channel-definition id="my-amf" class="mx.messaging.channels.AMFChannel">
        <endpoint url=
            "http://{server.name}:{server.port}/{context.root}/
            ➥ messagebroker/amf"
                class="flex.messaging.endpoints.AMFEndpoint"/>
  </channel-definition>

  <channel-definition id="my-secure-amf"
    class="mx.messaging.channels.SecureAMFChannel">
    <endpoint url="https://{server.name}:{server.port}/{context.root}/
    ➥ messagebroker/amfsecure"
        class="flex.messaging.endpoints.SecureAMFEndpoint"/>
```

Listing 2 (continued)

```
    <properties>
      <add-no-cache-headers>false</add-no-cache-headers>
    </properties>
  </channel-definition>
</channels>
```

These channel-definitions allow for two protocols when communicating with BlazeDS: AMF (Action Message Format) and Secure AMF (secure socket version of AMF).

The first channel definition instructs any client attempting to communicate with BlazeDS that it is allowed to send messages in AMF, over HTTP, and back to the same server, port, and context root where it was retrieved. In other words, an application found at http://www.digitalprimates.net/blazeDS/nothingHere.swf would attempt to communicate back to www.digitalprimates.net using HTTP, on port 80, using the context root of BlazeDS. This channel-definition is assigned an `id` named my-amf for reference in later configuration.

The second channel definition instructs any client attempting to communicate with BlazeDS that it is allowed to send messages in AMF, using *https*, back to the same server, port, and context root where it was retrieved. This channel definition is assigned an `id` named my-secure-amf for reference in later configuration.

When you specify a destination, you can choose to use either of these channels or tell BlazeDS clients to first attempt to use one, and only use the second if the first is unavailable. In other words, your client could attempt to send data securely; however, if this was not an option due to network configuration, they could use the non-secured route.

Next, a destination needs to be created inside the remoting-config.xml file that will use one or more of the available channels.

Depending on the version of BlazeDS you chose to download, the remoting-config.xml file will look similar to Listing 3:

Listing 3

```
<?xml version="1.0" encoding="UTF-8"?>
<service id="remoting-service"
    class="flex.messaging.services.RemotingService">
```

code continues on next page

Listing 3 (continued)

```
    <adapters>
        <adapter-definition id="java-object"
            class="flex.messaging.services.remoting.adapters.JavaAdapter"
            default="true"/>
    </adapters>

    <default-channels>
        <channel ref="my-amf"/>
    </default-channels>

</service>
```

The file starts with a service node and contains nodes for adapters and default-channels. The adapters node contains one or more adapter-definition nodes. These definitions indicate the available adapters, which you may remember are minimally responsible for translating to and from the common format of the message bus to more specific or legacy formats.

In this case, the adapter-definition defines a JavaAdapter that understands how to invoke methods of and retrieve results from a Java object. This adapter is set to the default adapter for this service.

The next node is the default-channels node. In this case it dictates that every destination defined in this file will use my-amf by default, which is the unsecured AMF channel defined in the services-config.xml file. Individual destinations can override this default.

Defining a destination in this file is an easy process of adding a new node named destination.

```
<destination id="dateSample">
    <properties>
        <source>java.util.Date</source>
    </properties>
</destination>
```

This destination node defines a new destination named dateSample. It also defines a property of the destination called `source`. The `source` in this case is `java.util.Date`, which is the Java `Date` class. This destination does not currently define a channel to use, so it will use the default-channel by default.

Effectively, this destination indicates that a client may call methods and access properties of the `java.util.Date` class remotely using AMF over HTTP.

Using the Destination in a Client

Developers that create web-based applications using Flex have an advantage over AIR developers when developing the client. When creating the client in Flex, you can import the settings defined in the services-config.xml file using a `-services` command in the compiler options.

Unfortunately, when developing an AIR client, you need to specify more of this configuration information manually. This process can be done using MXML or ActionScript and can happen statically or based on configuration information you might retrieve from a web service or by other means.

The AIR application in Listing 4 calls the `getTime()` method of the `java.util.Date` class on `creationComplete` and displays the result in an Alert. The channel information is defined in MXML:

Listing 4

```
<?xml version="1.0" encoding="utf-8"?>
<mx:WindowedApplication xmlns:mx="http://www.adobe.com/2006/mxml"
    creationComplete="getServerTime()">
    <mx:Script>
        <![CDATA[
            import mx.rpc.events.FaultEvent;
            import mx.rpc.events.ResultEvent;
            import mx.controls.Alert;
            private function handleResult( event:ResultEvent ):void {
                Alert.show( String( event.result ), 'Date in ms' );
            }

            private function handleFault( event:FaultEvent ):void {
                Alert.show( String( event.fault ),
                ➥ 'Fault contacting Server' );
            }

            private function getServerTime():void {
                ro.getTime();
            }
        ]]>
    </mx:Script>
```

code continues on next page

Listing 4 (continued)

```
    <mx:RemoteObject id="ro"
        destination="dateSample"
        result="handleResult(event)"
        fault="handleFault(event)">
        <mx:channelSet>
                <mx:ChannelSet>
                  <mx:channels>
                        <mx:AMFChannel id="myamf" uri="http://
                        ➥ localhost:8400/blazeds/messagebroker/amf"/>
                    </mx:channels>
                </mx:ChannelSet>
        </mx:channelSet>
    </mx:RemoteObject>
</mx:WindowedApplication>
```

In the application in Listing 5, the channel information is constructed in ActionScript instead of MXML, but accomplishes the same goal:

Listing 5

```
<?xml version="1.0" encoding="utf-8"?>
<mx:WindowedApplication xmlns:mx="http://www.adobe.com/2006/mxml"
    creationComplete="getServerTime()">
    <mx:Script>
        <![CDATA[
            import mx.messaging.channels.AMFChannel;
            import mx.messaging.Channel;
            import mx.messaging.ChannelSet;
            import mx.rpc.events.FaultEvent;
            import mx.rpc.events.ResultEvent;
            import mx.controls.Alert;
            private function handleResult( event:ResultEvent ):void {
                Alert.show( String( event.result ), 'Date in ms' );
            }

            private function handleFault( event:FaultEvent ):void {
               Alert.show( String( event.fault ),
               ➥ 'Fault contacting Server' );
           }
```

Listing 5 (continued)

```
            private function getServerTime():void {
                var cs:ChannelSet = new ChannelSet();
                var amfChannel:Channel =
                    new AMFChannel("my-amf",
                    ➥ "http://localhost:8400/blazeds/messagebroker/amf" );

                cs.addChannel( amfChannel );
                ro.channelSet = cs;

                ro.getTime();
            }
        ]]>
    </mx:Script>
    <mx:RemoteObject id="ro"
        destination="dateSample"
        result="handleResult(event)"
        fault="handleFault(event)"/>
</mx:WindowedApplication>
```

If the BlazeDS server and client are configured properly, the application will display a pop-up window with the server's date expressed in milliseconds.

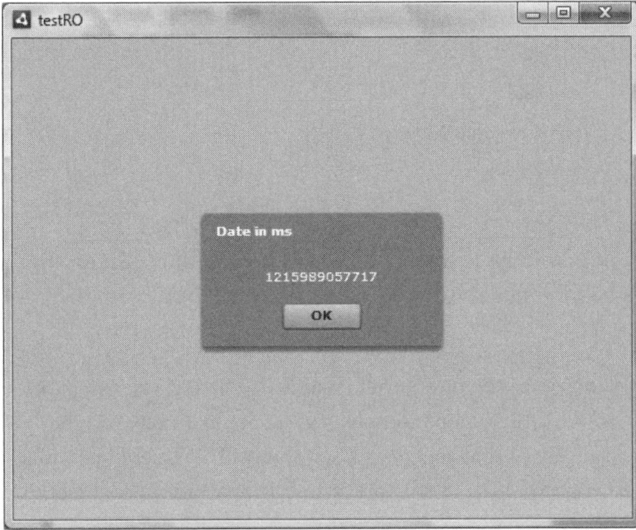

Figure 3: Server's time returned to the client via AMF

One important requirement that BlazeDS places on the Java classes that it uses in this manner is an empty constructor. As you may have noticed from the code, you never directly instantiated the Java `Date` class but rather simply called a method on it. BlazeDS instantiates this class for you and does not pass arguments when it does so, therefore any class you wish to instantiate in this manner must have an empty constructor.

For simplicity of configuration, we chose a built-in Java class to call in this case, however, you are free to create and call any Java class you configure on the server.

Mapping Java and ActionScript Types

One of the goals of BlazeDS is to enable reuse of existing infrastructure written in Java. The previous example demonstrated calling a simple method, `getTime()`, on a date object instantiated on the server and retrieving the result. However, you will usually need to pass arguments to a method call as well, which requires a greater understanding of how ActionScript and Java types map to each other. The following table represents the most common conversions, but a complete list is available in the BlazeDS developer's guide.

Java	ActionScript
String, char, char[]	String
int, short, byte	int
Boolean	Boolean
double, long, float	Number
Date	Date
Collection	ArrayCollection
Map	Object

This means that passing an ActionScript Number object to a Java method requesting a double is valid. Further, if a Java method returns a Collection, it will be represented as an ArrayCollection in AIR.

This knowledge significantly increases the number of Java methods that you can call; however, some methods accept or return more complex types. For example, you may have a Java method named `saveUser()` that accepts a User object. This User object may contain a series of properties related to the user and even additional complex objects.

To transmit an instance of a User object to Java, first you must create a custom ActionScript class with the same properties and types in ActionScript. Then you would use a special metadata tag named RemoteClass to map the ActionScript class to the Java class on the server. For example:

```
package samples.vo {

    [Bindable]
    [RemoteClass(alias="net.digitalprimates.vo.User")]
    public class User {

        public var userId:int;
        public var firstName:String;
        public var lastName:String;
        public var office:String;
        public var phoneNumber:String;
    }
}
```

This ActionScript class, when sent back to BlazeDS, will automatically become an instance of the `net.digitalprimates.vo.User` class, defined on the server. Further, anytime BlazeDS sends the result of a method call back to the client that contains an instance of the `net.digitalprimates.vo.User` class, it will become a `samples.vo.User` ActionScript object.

There are a few important items to remember when using this technique. First, you must ensure that the properties and types match exactly or risk that BlazeDS will be unable to convert the object. Second, by default, every property in the ActionScript object will be sent to the Java server when the user object is passed. Should you wish to prevent a given property from being sent with the object, there is an additional metadata tag that can be used per property called `[Transient]`. For example:

```
package samples.vo {

    [Bindable]
    [RemoteClass(alias="net.digitalprimates.vo.User")]
    public class User2 {

        public var userId:int;
        public var firstName:String;
        public var lastName:String;
        public var office:String;
        public var phoneNumber:String;
        [Transient]
        public var phoneNumber2:String;
    }
}
```

In this case, the `phoneNumber2` property will not be sent to the server when the remainder of the object is sent.

Finally, all the examples in this chapter use the default serialization/deserialization capabilities of AIR and BlazeDS. While it is beyond the scope of this chapter to teach, you can define your own serialization and deserialization routines to have extremely granular control over the objects as they are transmitted. To use this functionality, your ActionScript object must implement the flash.utils.IExternalizable interface, and your Java object must implement the java.io.Externalizable interface.

Publish/Subscribe Messaging

Publish/Subscribe messaging allows your application to create, send, and receive messages asynchronously. Other clients and servers can subscribe to receive any messages you publish, and in turn you can subscribe to receive their messages. Coupled with the BlazeDS advanced streaming and polling capabilities, this feature allows your clients to reach a new level of interactivity with servers and each other.

Similar to the RPC services in the previous section, messaging services use a destination. The two roles we are concerned with when discussing messaging are publishers and consumers. Clients become consumers of a given destination, and when a new message is published to that destination every consumer receives a copy. Clients and servers can be both consumers and publishers at the same time, and there is no formal limit on the number of destinations that can be consumed.

Each message is composed of a header and body. The header contains information to identify the message as well as any information used to route the message. The body contains any data accompanying the message. For example:

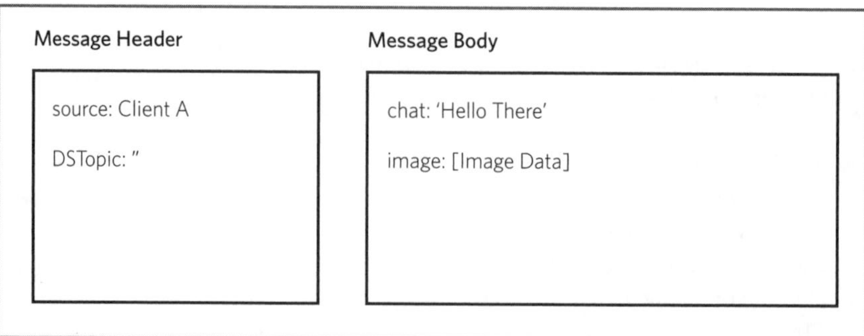

Figure 4: Message envelope example with header and body

The messaging capability in BlazeDS uses adapters much like the RPC service. Several types of messaging adapters are available for BlazeDS including: The ActionScript adapter, which is a lighter-weight messaging adapter providing the ability to route messages between clients, the ColdFusion Event Gateway Adapter used to interact with ColdFusion servers, and the JMS (Java Message Service) adapter, which provides enterprise-level support and participation in full Java messaging.

Configuring BlazeDS to Use Messaging

Much like the RPC configuration noted previously, configuring BlazeDS messaging requires examining and modifying several configuration files on the BlazeDS server. The two files about which we are most concerned in this section are the services-config.xml file and the messaging-config.xml file. As a reminder, these files are found under the WEB-INF\flex folder of the application. For example, in the default BlazeDS turnkey installation, these files would be found in the /install_root/tomcat/webapps/blazeds/WEB-INF/flex folder from your root drive.

Previously in this chapter, you examined the services-config.xml file to identify and understand the channels for AMF and Secure AMF. This section will add to that knowledge introducing two new channels: Streaming AMF and Polling AMF.

Streaming AMF

Streaming AMF uses HTTP 1.1 to keep the connection between the client and server open. This means that the server is able to send messages to the client without the client manually re-initiating communication. This is extremely important when dealing with messaging, as a new message may be published by a client or server at any time. If your client is able to use streaming, that message will be immediately forwarded to the client.

To configure streaming, you need to add another channel-definition under the channels node in the services-config.xml file.

```
<channel-definition id="my-streaming-amf"
    class="mx.messaging.channels.StreamingAMFChannel">
        <endpoint url=
            "http://{server.name}:{server.port}/{context.root}/
            ➥ messagebroker/streamingamf"
            class="flex.messaging.endpoints.StreamingAMFEndpoint"/>
</channel-definition>
```

This block enables a Streaming AMF channel for use in your destinations named my-streaming-amf.

NOTE Each of the channel-definitions described so far in this chapter have many configuration options that allow you to customize the way the channel works. This chapter describes the most basic implementation. The BlazeDS developers guide has a full description of the options.

Unfortunately, streaming has some limitations. First, streaming cannot be used in an environment where a proxy server is the client's only connection to the Internet. Generally, a proxy server's job is to forward requests from clients to servers and potentially cache those results for future requests. This is not compatible with streaming, where a connection is maintained. Second, network configuration and firewall settings within an organization may limit traffic and disallow streaming. Finally, streaming may not be used if the only access to BlazeDS is through the web tier. To facilitate streaming, the BlazeDS server must be able to directly communicate with the client. In an environment where all requests first pass through the web server, the streaming option will not work.

While streaming is still a viable and useful option, these limitations would likely cause most developers to ignore its powerful capabilities. Fortunately, BlazeDS provides a way to deal with these circumstances called *failover*. Your server and client can be configured to first attempt to use streaming; however, if streaming cannot work correctly for a given client, the client will then attempt another protocol to accomplish this goal. This second protocol is usually Polling AMF.

Due to the protocol abstraction discussed earlier in this chapter, Client A may connect to the server via streaming, while Client B may only be able to handle polling. This means that each client can connect in the strategy that provides the best individual experience without downgrading the performance of any other client. As you will see shortly, BlazeDS provides this service without the need for additional development on your part.

Polling AMF

Polling AMF provides a great fallback when streaming is unavailable. Due to its polling nature, it will be slower for clients to receive a message than its streaming counterpart and the load on both the server and clients is higher as they are constantly re-connecting to check if new data has arrived. However, this protocol makes it possible to interact with clients through messaging in environments where streaming is simply not feasible.

The polling channel provides significant configurability to optimize polling for your particular application. In a production environment, these values need to be optimized for your server.

Depending on the version of the BlazeDS server you downloaded from Adobe's site, the Polling AMF channel definition may already exist in the services-config.xml file. If not, you will need to add it to the channels node so that it is available for failover when your messaging destination is configured.

```
<channel-definition id="my-polling-amf"
    class="mx.messaging.channels.AMFChannel">
    <endpoint
        url= "http://{server.name}:{server.port}/{context.root}/
        ➥ messagebroker/amfpolling"
        class="flex.messaging.endpoints.AMFEndpoint"/>
    <properties>
        <polling-enabled>true</polling-enabled>
        <polling-interval-seconds>4</polling-interval-seconds>
    </properties>
</channel-definition>
```

This channel-definition allows the client to poll the server. The properties specify that it will reconnect with the server every four seconds to check for new messages. This channel-definition will be referred to as my-polling-amf when used later. At this point, the channels node of the services-config.xml file would look like Listing 6:

Listing 6

```
<channels>
    <channel-definition id="my-amf"
        class="mx.messaging.channels.AMFChannel">

        <endpoint
            url="http://{server.name}:{server.port}/
            {context.root}/messagebroker/amf"
            class="flex.messaging.endpoints.AMFEndpoint"/>
  </channel-definition>

    <channel-definition id="my-secure-amf"
        class="mx.messaging.channels.SecureAMFChannel">
```

code continues on next page

Listing 6 (continued)

```
        <endpoint
            url="https://{server.name}:{server.port}/{context.root}/
            ➥ messagebroker/amfsecure"
            class="flex.messaging.endpoints.SecureAMFEndpoint"/>

    <properties>
      <add-no-cache-headers>false</add-no-cache-headers>
    </properties>
    </channel-definition>

    <channel-definition id="my-streaming-amf"
        class="mx.messaging.channels.StreamingAMFChannel">

        <endpoint
            url="http://{server.name}:{server.port}/{context.root}/
            ➥ messagebroker/streamingamf"
            class="flex.messaging.endpoints.StreamingAMFEndpoint"/>
    </channel-definition>

    <channel-definition id="my-polling-amf"
        class="mx.messaging.channels.AMFChannel">

        <endpoint
            url="http://{server.name}:{server.port}/{context.root}/
            ➥ messagebroker/amfpolling"
            class="flex.messaging.endpoints.AMFEndpoint"/>

        <properties>
            <polling-enabled>true</polling-enabled>
            <polling-interval-seconds>4</polling-interval-seconds>
        </properties>
    </channel-definition>
</channels>
```

There are a few important things to note in this channels block. First, you did not have to remove the AMF channels earlier to add the streaming channels in this section. These channels provide options for the clients to connect, and you can have as many as you would like. Second, each channel definition needs a unique `id` so that it can be referred to uniquely when creating destinations.

The next step to enable messaging on BlazeDS is to add a messaging adapter and destination to the messaging-service.xml file.

Examining the messaging-config.xml file, you will see that it is a well-formed XML file that starts with the <service> node as the root. Within the file, there are nodes for adapters and default-channels. To enable messaging, you will also add a new node for a destination. Overall, this file should look very similar to the remoting-config.xml file as they are both service definitions.

The default version of this file included with the BlazeDS download has an adapter node that defines an ActionScript messaging adapter and has the definition for a JMS adapter, although it is not enabled by default.

```
<adapters>
    <adapter-definition id="actionscript"
        class="flex.messaging.services.messaging.adapters.ActionScriptAdapter"
        default="true" />
    <!- <adapter-definition id="jms"
        class="flex.messaging.services.messaging.adapters.JMSAdapter"/>-->
</adapters>
```

The sample applications in this chapter use the ActionScript adapter, which is a great general-purpose messaging adapter. From the BlazeDS and client perspective, the JMS adapter will work in an identical fashion; however, the JMS adapter requires a significant amount of effort to set up JMS on the Java server, which is well beyond the scope of this book.

Next, you will need to add a destination to the messaging-config.xml file. This destination will use the ActionScript adapter and specify the my-streaming-amf channel as its primary method of communication and the my-polling-amf channel as a secondary method.

```
<destination id="chatDestination">
    <channels>
        <channel ref="my-streaming-amf"/>
        <channel ref="my-polling-amf"/>
    </channels>

    <adapter ref="actionscript"/>
</destination>
```

This destination demonstrates using the adapter named actionscript and specifying that the my-streaming-amf channel is your first choice, with the my-polling-amf channel as a second choice. This destination specifically notes both the adapters and channels, regardless of the default options set on the entire service.

Using the Destination in a Client

The client in this case is a very simple and ubiquitous chat client with absolutely no configuration options. Chat applications are frequently used to demonstrate this functionality as they fall into the category of "simplest thing that could possibly work."

The complete client is provided in Listing 7, and then the individual aspects will be explained following the listing:

Listing 7

```
<?xml version="1.0" encoding="utf-8"?>
<mx:WindowedApplication xmlns:mx="http://www.adobe.com/2006/mxml"
    layout="vertical" creationComplete="setupApp()">
    <mx:Script>
        <![CDATA[
            import mx.messaging.events.MessageEvent;
            import mx.messaging.messages.AsyncMessage;

            private function submitText():void {
                var asyncMessage:AsyncMessage = new AsyncMessage();
                asyncMessage.body.text = message.text;
                producer.send(asyncMessage);
                message.text = "";
            }

            private function handleMessage( event:MessageEvent ):void {
                chat.text += event.message.body.text + "\n";
            }

            private function setupApp():void {
                consumer.subscribe();
            }
        ]]>
    </mx:Script>
```

Listing 7 (continued)

```
        <mx:ChannelSet id="messageChannelSet">
            <mx:channels>
                <mx:StreamingAMFChannel id="streamingAmf"
                    uri="http://localhost:8400/blazeds/messagebroker/
                    ➥ streamingamf"/>
                <mx:AMFChannel id="pollingAmf" pollingEnabled="true"
                    uri="http://localhost:8400/blazeds/messagebroker/
                    ➥ amfpolling"/>
            </mx:channels>
        </mx:ChannelSet>

    <mx:Producer id="producer"
        destination="chatDestination"
        channelSet="{messageChannelSet}"/>

    <mx:Consumer id="consumer"
        destination="chatDestination"
        channelSet="{messageChannelSet}"
        message="handleMessage(event)"/>

    <mx:TextArea id="chat" width="100%" height="100%" editable="false"/>
    <mx:HBox width="100%">
        <mx:TextInput id="message"/>
        <mx:Button click="submitText()"/>
    </mx:HBox>
</mx:WindowedApplication>
```

This client creates a very simple user interface with a TextArea to show the results of the chat, a TextInput in which to type in a new message, and a button to submit that message to other users.

A ChannelSet named messageChannelSet is defined in MXML (it could have also easily been defined in ActionScript) for both the producer and consumer to use. It specifies to use streaming as the primary method when connecting to the server, and, if this is not feasible, to use polling. This ChannelSet is then used in the Producer and Consumer tags along with the destination name.

When the application's `creationComplete` event occurs, the `subscribe()` method of the Consumer is called. At this point, the application begins listening for new messages.

When a new message arrives, the `handleMessage` event handler is called, and the new message is displayed in the TextArea.

Finally, when the button is clicked, the `submitText()` method is called, which creates a new message, adds the text from the TextInput to the message, and sends it to the server for distribution to any consumers that have subscribed.

This basic example is the foundation of all messaging. Clients subscribe to consume messages. Producers create those messages. The messages can contain any type of data. When a new message arrives, the client does something with that message.

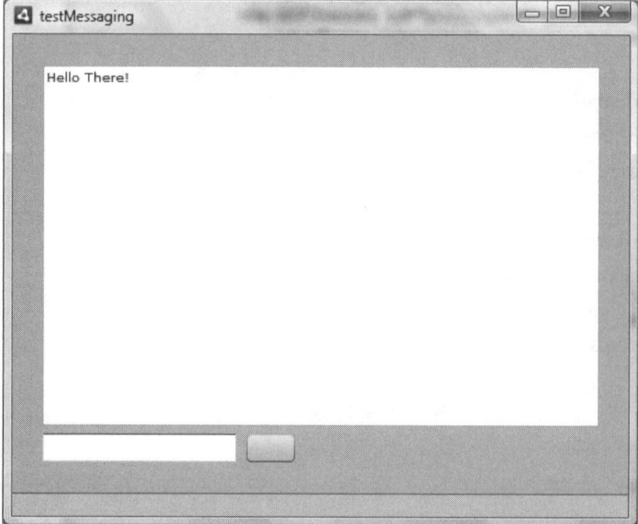

Figure 5: Publish subscribe messaging chat

Filtering with selectors

Consuming messages is a wonderful way to make highly interactive and responsive clients. However, it is unlikely that your client will need or want to receive every message sent by a producer. Therefore, you are provided with two methods to be more specific about the types of messages you do wish to receive.

The first method works with both ActionScript and JMS messaging adapters. It is called *message filtering* and uses a property of the consumer named `selector`. When messages are produced, extra information can be placed inside the message header. The `selector` property then takes a string that is a SQL92 conditional expression. It can access that additional header information to decide if the consumer should receive a given message. For example, when the message is sent, it includes extra header information, as in Listing 8:

Listing 8

```
private function submitText():void {
    var asyncMessage:AsyncMessage = new AsyncMessage();
    asyncMessage.body.text = message.text;
    asyncMessage.headers = new Array();
    asyncMessage.headers["sourceID"] = "23";
    producer.send(asyncMessage);
    message.text = "";
}
```

Consumers can now filter on this `sourceID` to ensure that they only receive a subset of the available messages.

Listing 9

```
<mx:Consumer id="consumer"
    destination="chatDestination"
    channelSet="{messageChannelSet}"
    message="handleMessage(event)"
    selector="sourceID = '23'"/>
```

The `selector` property of the consumer can be changed at runtime, however, the consumer will need to re-subscribe if this occurs. Using the example in Listing 9, the `handleMessage` event handler would only be called when the incoming message had a `sourceID` of 23 in the header.

Using subtopics

Subtopics are another way that you can be more granular in the way you publish and consume messages. Unfortunately, this method only works with the ActionScript messaging adapter and will not work with the JMS adapter.

To use subtopics, a change needs to be made to the messaging-config.xml file. An <allow-subtopic> node needs to be added to the destination on the server. This node enables the server logic necessary to manage topics and deliver only applicable messages to the client.

The modified destination in the messaging-config.xml file looks like the example in Listing 10:

Listing 10

```
<destination id="chatDestination">
    <channels>
        <channel ref="my-streaming-amf"/>
        <channel ref="my-polling-amf"/>
    </channels>

    <adapter ref="actionscript"/>

    <properties>
        <server>
            <allow-subtopics>true</allow-subtopics>
        </server>
    </properties>
</destination>
```

After this change, the server is ready to accept messages with subtopics. Publishing messages with subtopics is a very easy task. Both the Producer and Consumer instances have a `subtopic` property that can be set. By default, the subtopic uses a period as a separator, much like a Java dot path. The following is a modified version of the producer in Listing 7 that publishes to a subtopic:

```
<mx:Producer id="producer"
    destination="chatDestination"
    channelSet="{messageChannelSet}"
    subtopic="net.digitalprimates.chat"/>
```

This producer now sends messages with this subtopic information. The messages will only be received by consumers with a matching subtopic. To make a consumer explicitly consume this subtopic, it would also have a `subtopic` property like the following example:

```
<mx:Consumer id="consumer"
    destination="chatDestination"
    channelSet="{messageChannelSet}"
    message="handleMessage(event)"
    subtopic="net.digitalprimates.chat"/>
```

The consumer can also use wildcards to consume a variety of subtopics. In the following example, the consumer would receive any messages under the net.digitalprimates topic.

```
<mx:Consumer id="consumer"
    destination="chatDestination"
    channelSet="{messageChannelSet}"
    message="handleMessage(event)"
    subtopic="net.digitalprimates.*"/>
```

Collectively these options provide greater granularity and the ability to reduce traffic to the client, which simply wastes processing time by dealing with unnecessary messages.

Using MultiTopic Consumers and Producers

Now that you understand the concepts of subtopics, it is time to introduce the MultiTopic consumer and producer. Put simply, these are like the producer and consumer classes you examined earlier; however, they are able to handle multiple topics at one time.

The `MultiTopicProducer` class has a method named `addSubtopic()` that accepts a string and adds that subtopic to the list of subtopics where messages will be sent.

```
addSubtopic(subtopic:String):void
```

Alternatively, you can also set the `subtopics` property of the class, which accepts an ArrayCollection and can be used with databinding. Setting the `subtopics` property with an ArrayCollection full of subtopics is equivalent to calling `addSubtopic()` for each member of the ArrayCollection.

The `MultiTopicConsumer` has a method named `addSubscription()`, which takes two arguments: a subtopic and a selector. This specifies the subtopics this consumer should receive along with any selectors that should be applied.

```
addSubscription(subtopic:String = null, selector:String = null):void
```

These tags have a significant advantage over using multiple producer or consumer tags. First, they offer a single point of subscription. Second, they ensure that you only receive one copy of a message, even if your combination of subscriptions would normally yield multiple copies.

Listings 11–13 demonstrate a complete client that builds upon the client chat application in previous examples and illustrates a complete `MultiTopicConsumer` use case. In this application, multiple users can still chat using text over one subtopic: however, they can also drag images from their desktop to the application to share with other users using a second subtopic.

The code exists in three separate files. The first is TextProducer, which encapsulates the TextInput, Button, and Producer, which sends the text to the server. The second is ImageProducer, which encapsulates the logic for accepting an image dragged from the desktop to the application and the Producer responsible for sending that image to the server.

The final file is the WindowedApplication, which contains an instance of both TextProducer and ImageProducer. It also contains a text field for showing the text information, an image field for displaying any image that arrives over messaging, and a `MultiTopicConsumer` instance that listens to both subtopics for new information to arrive.

Listing 11—TextProducer

```
<?xml version="1.0" encoding="utf-8"?>
<mx:HBox xmlns:mx="http://www.adobe.com/2006/mxml">
    <mx:Script>
        <![CDATA[
            import mx.messaging.ChannelSet;
            import mx.messaging.messages.AsyncMessage;

            [Bindable]
            public var messageChannelSet:ChannelSet;

            private function submitText():void {
                var asyncMessage:AsyncMessage = new AsyncMessage();
                asyncMessage.body.text = message.text;
                producer.send(asyncMessage);
                message.text = "";
            }

        ]]>
    </mx:Script>
    <mx:Producer id="producer"
        destination="chatDestination"
        channelSet="{messageChannelSet}"
        subtopic="net.digitalprimates.chat"/>

    <mx:TextInput id="message"/>
    <mx:Button click="submitText()" label="Send Message"/>
</mx:HBox>
```

Listing 11 is simply a reorganization of the previous code. When the user enters text and presses the button, it is sent along to the net.digitalprimates.chat subtopic of the chatDestination.

Listing 12—ImageProducer

```
<?xml version="1.0" encoding="utf-8"?>
<mx:Canvas xmlns:mx="http://www.adobe.com/2006/mxml"
    backgroundColor="0xFF0000"
    nativeDragEnter="handleDragEnter(event)"
    nativeDragDrop="handleDragDrop(event)">

    <mx:Script>
        <![CDATA[
            import mx.messaging.ChannelSet;
            import mx.messaging.messages.AsyncMessage;

            [Bindable]
            public var messageChannelSet:ChannelSet;

            private function handleDragEnter( event:NativeDragEvent ):void {
                    if ( event.clipboard.hasFormat(
                    ➥ ClipboardFormats.FILE_LIST_FORMAT ) ) {
                            NativeDragManager.acceptDragDrop(
                            ➥ event.target as InteractiveObject );
                    }
            }

            private function handleFileRetrieved( event:Event ):void {
                var stream:FileStream = event.target as FileStream;
                var byteArray:ByteArray = new ByteArray();

                stream.readBytes( byteArray );

                var asyncMessage:AsyncMessage = new AsyncMessage();
                asyncMessage.body.image = byteArray;
                imageProducer.send(asyncMessage);
            }
```

code continues on next page

Listing 12 (continued)

```
            private function handleDragDrop( event:NativeDragEvent ):void {
                if ( event.clipboard.hasFormat(
                ➥ ClipboardFormats.FILE_LIST_FORMAT ) ) {
                    var fileList:Array = event.clipboard.getData(
                    ➥ ClipboardFormats.FILE_LIST_FORMAT ) as Array;
                    var file:File = fileList[ 0 ];

                    if ( file ) {
                        var stream:FileStream = new FileStream();
                        stream.openAsync( file, FileMode.READ );
                        stream.addEventListener(Event.COMPLETE,
                        ➥ handleFileRetrieved );
                    }
                }
            }
        ]]>
    </mx:Script>
    <mx:Producer id="imageProducer"
        destination="chatDestination"
        channelSet="{messageChannelSet}"
        subtopic="net.digitalprimates.image"/>

    <mx:Label text="Drag Images Here"/>
</mx:Canvas>
```

Listing 12 is more complex than Listing 11 as it builds upon the topics you have learned in previous chapters. The user is allowed to drag an image file from their desktop to this component. When that occurs, the File API loads the data from that image from the local hard drive. Once the data is loaded successfully, it is sent along to the net.digitalprimates.image subtopic of the chatDestination. Notice that there is very little difference in how this message is sent versus the text message.

Listing 13—WindowedApplication

```
<?xml version="1.0" encoding="utf-8"?>
<mx:WindowedApplication xmlns:mx="http://www.adobe.com/2006/mxml"
    layout="vertical" creationComplete="setupApp()"
    xmlns:components="components.*">
    <mx:Script>
```

Listing 13 (continued)

```
        <![CDATA[
            import mx.messaging.MultiTopicConsumer;
            import mx.messaging.events.MessageEvent;
            import mx.messaging.messages.AsyncMessage;

            private var consumer:MultiTopicConsumer;

            private function handleMessage( event:MessageEvent ):void {
                switch ( event.message.headers.DSSubtopic ) {
                    case "net.digitalprimates.chat" :
                        chat.text += event.message.body.text + "\n";
                        break;

                    case "net.digitalprimates.image" :
                        image.load( event.message.body.image );
                        break;
                }
            }

            private function setupApp():void {
                consumer = new MultiTopicConsumer();
                consumer.destination = "chatDestination";
                consumer.channelSet = messageChannelSet;
                consumer.addEventListener(MessageEvent.MESSAGE, handleMessage
);
                consumer.addSubscription( "net.digitalprimates.chat" );
                consumer.addSubscription( "net.digitalprimates.image" );

                consumer.subscribe();
            }
        ]]>
    </mx:Script>
        <mx:ChannelSet id="messageChannelSet">
            <mx:channels>
                <mx:StreamingAMFChannel id="streamingAmf"
                    uri="http://localhost:8400/blazeds/messagebroker/
                    ➥ streamingamf"/>
                <mx:AMFChannel id="pollingAmf" pollingEnabled="true"
```

code continues on next page

Listing 13 (continued)

```
                        uri="http://localhost:8400/blazeds/messagebroker/
                        ➥ amfpolling"/>
                </mx:channels>
            </mx:ChannelSet>

        <mx:HBox width="100%" height="100%">
            <mx:TextArea id="chat" width="100%" height="100%" editable="false"/>
            <mx:Image id="image" width="150" height="150"/>
        </mx:HBox>

        <mx:HBox width="100%">
            <components:TextProducer width="100%"
                messageChannelSet="{messageChannelSet}"/>
            <components:ImageProducer width="150"
                messageChannelSet="{messageChannelSet}"/>
        </mx:HBox>
    </mx:WindowedApplication>
```

Listing 13 uses both the TextProducer and ImageProducer components. On startup, the `setupApp()` method is called. This method creates a `MultiTopicConsumer` and adds a subscription for both net.digitalprimates.chat and net.digitalprimates.image. The `subscribe()` method of the `MultiTopicConsumer` is then called to begin receiving messages.

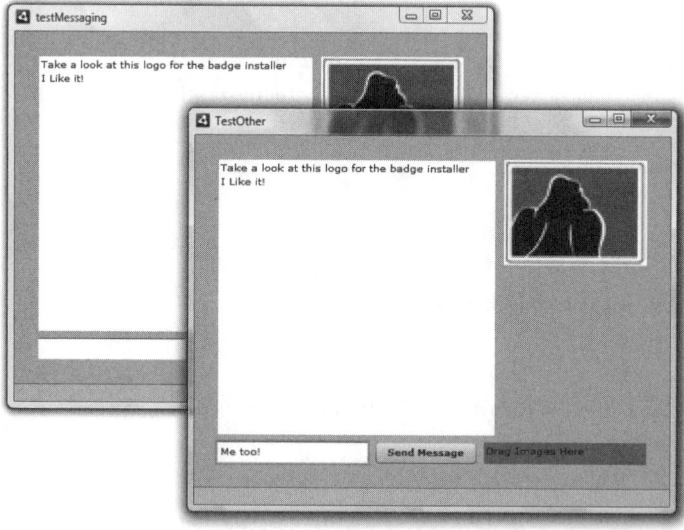

Figure 6: Sending chat and image data through messaging

When messages are sent to either of those subtopics, the `handleMessage()` event handler is called and passed the MessageEvent that occurred. The handler examines the header to determine if the message arrived from the image or chat subtopic. If the subtopic was for text, it displays the newly arrived data in the text field in the same way as the previous messaging examples in this chapter. If the newly arrived data was an image, it displays it in the image tag.

BlazeDS and LiveCycle Data Services

BlazeDS is related to a product from another Adobe product line named LiveCycle Enterprise Services (ES). This section briefly explains the relationship as developers new to these technologies can quickly become lost in the range of features, names, and buzz words used when describing the differences between these two products.

LiveCycle ES is a product line intended to facilitate enterprise-level projects. It is composed of many products designed to handle problems in the areas of content services, process management, document output, information assurance, and, finally, data capture. Each of these topics is broken down into products or services that address key customer concerns.

BlazeDS is not directly related to LiveCycle ES as a whole, but rather to a product within the Data Capture area of the LiveCycle ES product line named LiveCycle DataServices, which facilitates communication between RIAs and servers. To further complicate matters, Adobe breaks LiveCycle DataServices into two products: LiveCycle DataServices Community Edition and LiveCycle DataServices ES.

LiveCycle DataServices (DS) Community Edition is essentially a commercial version of BlazeDS. Adobe offers the Community Edition as a subscription service. It packages the certified builds of BlazeDS along with Adobe support, meaning that you will receive a tested and released version of the product in addition to any patches, fixes, and upgrades for the duration of your subscription. Effectively, you'll receive the benefits of the open-source BlazeDS project and will also receive Adobe support for critical applications.

This edition is a good choice if your business environment demands commercial software, as opposed to open-source software, and you anticipate the need for ongoing support.

LiveCycle DataServices ES uses the infrastructure offered by BlazeDS as building blocks to provide higher-level data functionality. It offers all of the features of BlazeDS plus a new high-performance protocol named RTMP (Real-Time Messaging Protocol), data paging, streaming, and dataset synchronization (which allows multiple clients to automatically keep a large dataset in sync as changes occur). It also offers direct support for occasionally connected clients, integration with portals, and full integration with the remainder of the LiveCycle product line.

You can think of BlazeDS as building blocks that can be used by a developer to construct any type of object. LiveCycle DataServices ES can be thought of as a castle made from those same blocks.

Next Steps

At this point, you have an understanding of the BlazeDS RPC and messaging services and the differences between BlazeDS and LiveCycle Data Services. Taking the time to download and install the BlazeDS test drive server and work through the examples provided in it will solidify both this knowledge and demonstrate some of the additional functionality not contained within this chapter.

TESTING AIR APPLICATIONS WITH FLUINT

CHAPTER 12

All applications contain bugs. The larger the application, the more bugs the application is likely to contain. Bugs in your AIR application generally occur as a result of mistakes during the development process; however, they can also occur due to bugs in the Flex framework, the AIR runtime, or the compiler that transforms your source into executable code.

In the course of creating software, developers continually test it to some degree. They write code, they compile it, and they test it to ensure it functions as expected. However, these tests generally lack two important components. First, this type of on-demand testing is generally used to test a very small and specific feature as it is being developed. It rarely represents a very comprehensive test. Second, the tests lack reproducibility. For example, once you test that the login form of your application works, it is unlikely that you will retest it while working on some other feature. This leaves open the possibility that a later change in the code will break a feature written earlier.

Automated testing helps to solve these issues. It provides a framework in which the developer writes a series of tests, either before, during, or after development depending on your development methodology. All of these tests can then be continually and easily re-executed and expanded upon during the development and testing cycles to achieve both comprehensive test coverage of the code and continual retesting of any application changes.

Types of Testing

Application testing is a very broad concept that encompasses a variety of techniques and testing styles. It can range from low-level tests that require knowledge of the inner workings of the code to usability testing, designed to ensure that the system's intended users can comprehend and interact with the system effectively. This chapter deals with only two types, unit and integration testing.

NOTE Different development methodologies dictate different approaches to writing tests. For example, advocates of test-driven development (TDD) choose to write their tests first, and then write the actual code that will be tested. This chapter will just demonstrate techniques for testing; it is up to you to apply them to a specific methodology.

Unit tests are designed to test the accuracy of the smallest pieces of an application. In object-oriented programming, this usually means a single method of an object. This type of test is written by a developer and requires knowledge of the inner workings of the code.

To test a method in your code, every Boolean decision in that method needs to be evaluated. Every decision in your method needs two tests, one for the true outcome and one for the false. The implication is that every single method in your code will require several unit tests to ensure accuracy.

```
function returnFlexOrAIR( flex:Boolean ):String {
    if ( flex ) {
        return 'Flex';
    } else {
        return 'AIR';
    }
}
```

This method requires two unit tests, one where the `flex` argument is passed true, and one where it is passed false. Clearly this means a large number of tests will need to be written and maintained for any system with even marginal complexity.

However, the benefits of these tests outweigh the associated costs. With a valid set of unit tests in place, debugging time tends to be significantly reduced, as you have known good elements of the system that do not need to be continually re-examined. Further, if unit tests are kept up-to-date as you discover bugs, you can eliminate the common practice of inadvertently re-causing an already fixed bug. Finally, a series of unit tests can execute tests much faster than a developer, meaning you spend less time repeatedly clicking around an application to test your code, while actually gaining better test coverage.

By definition, unit tests are intended to test the smallest pieces of the system. Errors can still occur when you combine these pieces to create functionality. This is the realm of integration testing, which is designed to test how already tested units of code combine and interact together.

Flex and AIR are event-based languages with a fair amount of asynchronicity. Unlike unit tests, integration tests must be able to deal with this asynchronous nature to be successful. Additionally, because several components are being integrated together, there are often a series of steps required to create or configure these components before the actual test begins. This makes creating integration tests more complicated; however, integration testing techniques can allow the developer to programmatically test user interface components and system functionality.

Absent from this chapter is solid information on functional testing. Several vendors have products that integrate with Adobe Flex to provide visual test recording and replay. All of these tools work to some degree, however, at the time of writing, most still have significant issues to be resolved. In particular, none seem to grasp the idea that asynchronicity is important in Flex, nor do they seem to work outside of the web browser in AIR.

Testing Frameworks

There are several testing frameworks available for Flex and ActionScript, all of which can also be used with AIR. The most notable frameworks are listed here:

- **FlexUnit**—Original Flex/ActionScript 3.0 unit testing framework designed and implemented by Adobe and community members. It mimics JUnit (the standard unit testing framework for Java) functionality and provides a solid unit testing base. As of this writing, this project has not been updated in some time.

- **Visual Flex Unit**—Based on FlexUnit but adds the ability to do visual assertion, which aides in UI testing. It does so by comparing image snapshots of the screen.
- **ReflexUnit**—Metadata driven testing framework for Flex 2 and Flex 3 that has stronger asynchronous support than FlexUnit, including the ability to run asynchronous tests in parallel. The project promises Eclipse plug-ins in future releases and provides a solid base for unit testing.
- **FUnit**—Metadata driven testing framework for Flex 2 and Flex 3. The project has a lot of potential, but it is currently in the alpha stage with no apparent support for asynchronous tests.
- **ASUnit**—Unit testing framework that supports Flash Player 6, 7, 8, and 9. Good unit testing solution and should be a strong consideration if you are doing both Flex- and Flash-based projects.
- **Fluint** (formerly dpUInt, renamed in the 1.0 release)—Based on the style of FlexUnit, however, rewritten for better asynchronous support and support for testing UI components. Fluint supports both unit and integration testing and introduces the concept of sequences to support multistep asynchronous tests.

The examples in this chapter demonstrate using Fluint for testing. The basic unit test concepts are applicable, with differences in syntax, to any of the frameworks mentioned in the previous list; however, Fluint also supports integration testing, which is imperative for providing more complete testing of AIR applications.

Understanding Fluint

The Fluint (**Fl**ex **U**nit and **Int**egration) testing framework is open-source. It is licensed under the MIT License, a free software license originating at the Massachusetts Institute of Technology, designed for creating unit and integration tests for Flex and Flex-based AIR projects. During its lengthy beta program, it was referred to as dpUInt (digital primates Unit and Integration).

It is based loosely on the concepts of FlexUnit and JUnit but provides enhanced asynchronous support, a graphical way to see the success or failure of your tests, and integration with continuous build systems. Specifically, it allows multiple simultaneous asynchronous operations, asynchronous setup and teardown (which will both be explained in detail later in the chapter), and asynchronous returns before method body completion. Collectively, these enhancements facilitate full support for UI component testing and testing of code written in various Flex frameworks, such as Adobe Consulting's Cairngorm project.

Installing Fluint

The dpTimeTracker project contains the appropriate library, test runner, and sample tests to use Fluint. Later in this chapter, we will explore some of these tests. This section will explore retrieving, building, and adding Fluint to your own project.

Fluint is hosted at Google Code, Google's open-source project hosting service. The URL for this project is http://fluint.googlecode.com/. The project consists of a library that contains the base classes and code, which find and organize your tests, and a test runner that executes those tests and provides visual feedback.

You have two choices when using Fluint. You may simply download a precompiled version of the project library as an SWC, which is an archive file for Flex code and assets, or you may download the source code and build Fluint yourself. The first option is much easier; however, the second provides you with the full source should you wish to dig deeper into the code.

Installing the pre-compiled library

Create a new project, or open an existing project, where you would like to use Fluint for testing. Then visit the Google code project site at http://fluint.googlecode.com/ and click the Downloads tab at the top of the page. Choose the link for the fluint_v1.swc, and download it to the libs directory of your project.

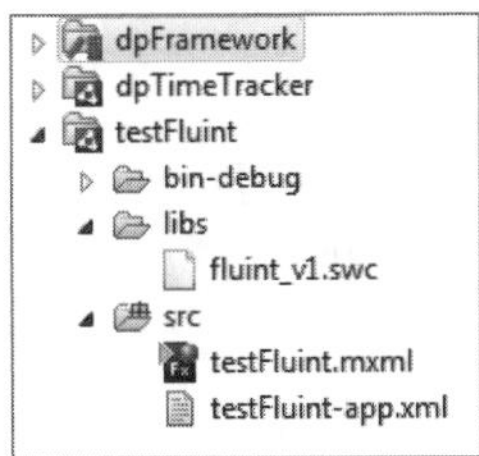

Figure 1: Adding Fluint to a project as a SWC

Any SWC files in the libs directory are automatically available to Flex Builder during the compilation process. This single step makes all test classes associated with Fluint available for your use.

Building the library

Retrieving the source code to build Fluint yourself requires a Subversion client. Subversion (SVN) is a version control system widely used in closed- and open-source projects. Explaining SVN and the setup of that client is beyond the scope of this book, however, there are many useful tutorials online.

If you have an SVN client installed, then visit the Google code project site at http://fluint.googlecode.com/ and click the Source tab. You will be provided with directions for synchronizing directly with the SVN repository, which will ensure continual access to the latest versions and bug fixes. After you synchronize the source code, you will need to import the project into Flex Builder. To accomplish this, use the following steps:

1. From the Flex Builder menu, select File > Import.
2. Select Other.
3. Expand the General item.
4. Choose Existing Projects into Workspace.
5. Click the Browse button next to the "Select root directory" field, and browse to the location where you downloaded the Fluint classes.
6. Click the Select All button and then click Finish.

   Next, use the source to add Fluint testing support to your existing project:

7. From the menu, choose Project properties > Flex Build Path.
8. Click the Library Path tab.
9. Click the Add Project button.
10. From the pop-up menu, select the library project that was just created, and click OK.
11. Click OK on the Properties panel to close it.
12. From the Project menu, choose Clean.
13. Ensure that both your project and the Fluint library project are selected and then click OK.

When the build completes, you will be ready to begin creating test cases using the Fluint framework.

Framework Terminology

Before creating your first test, you need to understand some terminology in reference to the Fluint testing framework. In Fluint, a developer needs to understand test suites, test cases, and test methods, which are represented inside the framework by three classes named `TestMethod`, `TestCase`, and `TestSuite`.

Test Method

A test method is the smallest unit of the testing process. A test method executes code and checks the outcome. At the end of the test method, the developer generally makes an assertion, stating the expected outcome of this executed code. The expected value may be true or false, null or not null, perhaps even equal to another variable. If the assertion is valid, the test passes. If the assertion does not logically work (for example, you assert that the outcome should be false but it is really true), the test fails. You may call the `fail()` method at any time, if the result of a location in the code or state is simply a failure.

The following methods are used to make these assertions at the end of your test method in Fluint:

- `assertEquals()`—Accepts two parameters and is a valid assertion if the two values are equal. This is the equivalent of the "==" operator in ActionScript.
- `assertStrictlyEquals()`—Accepts two parameters and is a valid assertion if the two values are strictly equal. This is the equivalent of the "===" operator in ActionScript. It works in an equivalent way to `assertEquals()`, but data types are not converted before the comparison. Therefore, to be true, both the values and data type must be the same.
- `assertTrue()`—Accepts a single parameter and is a valid assertion if the value is `true`.
- `assertFalse()`—Accepts a single parameter and is a valid assertion if the value is `false`.
- `assertNull()`—Accepts a single parameter and is a valid assertion if the value is `null`.
- `assertNotNull()`—Accepts a single parameter and is a valid assertion if the value is not `null`.

Unit test methods execute specific methods in an object. The focus of each test is very narrow, and developers rely upon many tests to adequately cover the functionality of an object. Ideally each unit test makes only a single assertion. This is a point of contention among developers and testers, as many feel that making multiple assertions in a single test is an appropriate practice. Generally, however, a single assertion per method ensures the best granularity in resolving test failures and hence is a recommended practice.

Test Case

A test case is a collection of test methods that share a common test environment, also referred to as a *test fixture*. Each test case has a `setUp()` and `tearDown()` method, which are responsible for respectively creating and destroying that test environment.

For example, if you wanted to write a series of test methods to test the Flex `Timer` class, they could all exist in a single test case. In the `setUp()` method, you would create a `Timer` instance. In the `tearDown()` method, you would stop the timer and remove references so it can be garbage collected. Each test method would then exercise a behavior or method of the timer.

If your test case has two test methods, the Fluint framework would execute the test case in the following way:

```
setUp();
testMethod1();
tearDown();

setUp();
testMethod2();
tearDown();
```

The `setUp()` method executes before each of your test methods, and the `tearDown()` method runs after each test method. By default, all test methods in your test case need to begin with a lowercase "test," so `testTimer` and `testEvent` are valid test method names, but `TestOne` and `oneTest` are not. There is no formal limit on the number of methods you can use in a single test case.

As the developer, you are responsible for ensuring that any objects created or properties set in the `setUp()` method are reversed or destroyed in the `tearDown()` to ensure that the next test method has a valid environment to begin.

Test Suite

A test suite is a collection of test cases. The Fluint framework contains a test suite named `FrameworkSuite`, which is responsible for testing the framework. The suite contains test cases pertaining to different aspects of the library, such as asynchronous tests or `UIComponent` tests. Each of those test cases then contains test methods that share a common setup to be executed.

Test Runner

A test runner is a Flex or AIR application that executes the test methods in your suites and cases. Tests are often run during development on the desktop of the developer's machine. In this case, a user interface that reports errors and failures visually can be useful. However, tests are also often run from a server via an automated build system. In this case, the user interface may not matter at all and an XML output is significantly more helpful.

Fluint does not prescribe a specific user interface, but rather provides a series of components that can be used together in either a Flex or AIR project to provide whichever pieces of the user interface are required for your preference. These components include a tree that displays the test suites, test cases, and test methods along with their success or failure, and a visual progress bar that tracks progress as tests execute along with nonvisual components that create XML files with test results.

Listing 1 shows a simple test runner implementation that executes the existing framework tests:

Listing 1

```
<?xml version="1.0" encoding="utf-8"?>
<mx:WindowedApplication xmlns:mx="http://www.adobe.com/2006/mxml"
    xmlns:dp="http://www.digitalprimates.net/2006/mxml"
    layout="absolute"
    creationComplete="startTestProcess(event)"
    width="100%" height="100%">

    <mx:Script>
      <![CDATA[
          import net.digitalprimates.fluint.unitTests.frameworkSuite.
          ➥ FrameworkSuite;
```

code continues on next page

Listing 1 (continued)

```
        protected function startTestProcess( event:Event ):void {
            var suiteArray:Array = new Array();
            suiteArray.push( new FrameworkSuite() );
            testRunner.startTests( suiteArray );
        }
    ]]>
  </mx:Script>
  <dp:TestResultDisplay width="100%" height="100%"/>
  <dp:TestRunner id="testRunner"/>

</mx:WindowedApplication>
```

This simple test runner, which is also available from the download page of the Google code project, creates a `TestResultDisplay` and `TestRunner` in the main application. When the `creationComplete` event fires, an instance of the `FrameWorkSuite` class is pushed onto an array and passed to the `startTests()` method of the `TestRunner` instance. This sample test runner creates a tree-based test browser and a visual progress bar that tracks the progress of tests as they execute. Tests that succeed are represented by a green indicator, and tests that fail are represented by a red indicator. Any of these indicators can be selected to further investigate information about a test success or failure.

In the simplest use case, this test runner example would be added to the Flex project you wish to test. It references components provided by the library, but exists in the Flex project. When executed, this test runner will run through the tests created to test the framework.

Creating Basic Unit Tests

Creating unit tests in the Fluint framework is a relatively simple process. However, as the number of unit tests grows in your project, keeping tests organized can become a challenge. This section explains both how to create test cases and methods, and provides a suggested method of organizing your test directories. This can be modified to suit your specific needs.

Creating Test Cases and Methods

Creating tests involves the creation of the test methods, test cases, and test suites. The easiest place to start this process is with the creation of the test case. Each test case exists as its own class and must extend net.digitalprimates.fluint.tests.TestCase, which provides the core functionality for creating and executing the tests. Each test case will define one or more test methods that share a common test environment (also called a *fixture*).

Listing 2 shows a simple math test case with a single test method:

Listing 2

```
package testing.myFirstTestSuite.testCases {
    import net.digitalprimates.fluint.tests.TestCase;

    public class SimpleTestCase extends TestCase {
        public function testMath():void {
            var x:int = 5 + 3;
            assertEquals( 8, x )
        }
    }
}
```

While simplistic, this test shows that the + operator in ActionScript correctly adds two small positive integers. You assert that the result of this math operation should be equal to 8. If *x* is equal to 8, the test will pass, else it will fail.

Before this test case can be executed, it must be added to a test suite. Each test suite exists in its own class file. The constructor of that class uses a method named addTestCase() to indicate that specific test cases should be part of the suite. The addTestCase() method takes one parameter, an instance of a test case. The following code shows an example test suite:

```
package testing.myFirstTestSuite {
    import net.digitalprimates.fluint.tests.TestSuite;

    import testing.myFirstTestSuite.testCases.SimpleTestCase;

    public class MyFirstTestSuite extends TestSuite {
        public function MyFirstTestSuite() {
            super();

            addTestCase( new SimpleTestCase() );
        }
    }
}
```

This code defines a new test suite named MyFirstTestSuite and uses the addTestCase() method to add a test case to the suite, SimpleTestCase. As you develop your own tests, your test suites will likely contain many tests. Each will be added by a call to the addTestCase() method. Creating a test runner to execute suites is the final step required to begin testing. The following code shows an example of a very simple application to run tests:

```
<?xml version="1.0" encoding="utf-8"?>
<mx:WindowedApplication xmlns:mx="http://www.adobe.com/2006/mxml"
    xmlns:dp="http://www.digitalprimates.net/2006/mxml"
    layout="absolute"
    creationComplete="startTestProcess(event)"
    width="100%" height="100%">

    <mx:Script>
        <![CDATA[
        import testing.mySecondTestSuite.MySecondTestSuite;
        import testing.myFirstTestSuite.MyFirstTestSuite;

        protected function startTestProcess( event:Event ):void {
            var suiteArray:Array = new Array();
            suiteArray.push( new MyFirstTestSuite() );
            testRunner.startTests( suiteArray );
        }
        ]]>
    </mx:Script>
    <dp:TestResultDisplay width="100%" height="100%"/>
    <dp:TestRunner id="testRunner"/>

</mx:WindowedApplication>
```

This application consists of two components, the TestResultDisplay and TestRunner. When the creationComplete event occurs, the startTestProcess method creates an array containing an instance of a test suites, MyFirstTestSuite. It then passes that array to the startTests() method of the TestRunner instance. This instructs the test runner to execute the test suite, test cases, and test methods. Any number of test suites can be added to this array before execution.

Organizing Test Directories

By convention, tests are kept within a nested set of directories that contains both the suite and test case files. The following suggestions work well to keep tests organized even in very large environments:

- Each test suite should have its own directory.
- The suite definition (subclass of the `TestSuite` class) should reside in the test suite directory.
- In the directory for the test suite, there should be a tests directory.
- In the tests directory, store your test cases (subclasses of the `TestCase` class) for the test suite.
- Any additional classes needed to accomplish testing can be stored in further subdirectories.

For example:

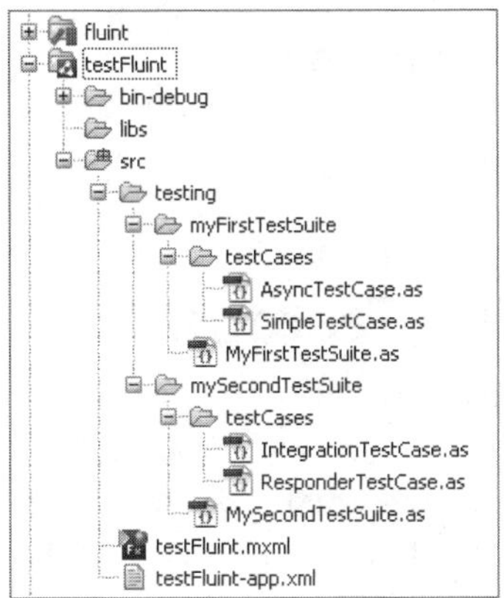

Figure 2: Sample test directory structure

In the figure, a directory named testing is created. Inside testing, a directory is created for each test suite in the project. These directories contain an ActionScript class, which inherits from `TestSuite` and defines the test cases included in the suite, in addition to a directory named testCases. Finally, the test cases in each of these suites are defined in classes inheriting from `TestCase`, which exist in the testCases directory.

This directory structure is merely a suggestion and not enforced by the framework. You are free to rework this to fit your needs.

Creating Asynchronous Tests

An asynchronous test is a test that depends on an action that may not happen synchronously. An excellent example of this is an `HTTPService`. For example, you make a call to the server and request data. When the data is available, you are notified via an event. However, the original method initiating the server call will have completed long ago before the data arrives.

Many of the common properties set on UIComponents in Flex are actually asynchronous. When setting a property on a given control, often the intended value is stored in a private variable internal to the control and applied later by the Flex framework. Inherently, this means you need strong asynchronous capabilities to test these features.

As with all test cases, an asynchronous test case exists as its own class and must extend `net.digitalprimates.fluint.tests.TestCase`. This test case will also make use of the `setUp()` and `tearDown()` methods mentioned earlier to create a test environment for these tests.

To simulate asynchronous events without the need for services or understanding the complexity of UIComponents, the following example uses timers. This example will help to illustrate the major points while keeping the code understandable.

Each test case will define one or more test methods that share a common test environment.

Implementing Simple Setup and Teardown

The `setUp()` method is defined in the `TestCase` class. You override the `setUp()` method to create an environment in which your test methods will execute. The `tearDown()` method reverses any items created in the `setUp()` method to ensure that the system is back to a normal state before proceeding to the next test method. Remember, `setUp()` runs before each test method, and `tearDown()` runs after each test method.

The following example shows a test case using the `setUp()` and `tearDown()` methods.

```
package testing.myFirstTestSuite.testCases {
  import net.digitalprimates.fluint.tests.TestCase;

public class AsyncTestCase extends TestCase {
    import flash.utils.Timer;
    import flash.events.TimerEvent;
```

```
    private var timer:Timer;

    override protected function setUp():void {
      timer = new Timer( 100, 1 );
    }

    override protected function tearDown():void {
      timer.stop();
      timer = null;
    }

    public function testTimerLongWay():void {
    }
  }
}
```

The class definition for AsyncTestCase defines a new private variable named `timer` of type Timer and overrides the `setUp()` method to instantiate this timer. The arguments passed to the timer's constructor instruct it to complete 100 milliseconds after it is started and only trigger once. The `tearDown()` method is also overridden to stop the timer and set the timer reference to `null` when the test is complete. This allows the timer to be garbage collected after each test.

Creating a Simple Asynchronous Test Method

This example has a single test named `testTimerLongWay()`. This method will set up an asynchronous test in the most verbose way to clearly illustrate each step. Future methods will demonstrate an abbreviated approach.

Listing 3

```
public function testTimerLongWay():void {
    var asyncHandler:Function =
    ➥ asyncHandler( handleTimerComplete, 500, null, handleTimeout );
    timer.addEventListener(TimerEvent.TIMER_COMPLETE, asyncHandler,
    ➥ false, 0, true );
    timer.start();
}
```

This function calls a special method of the TestCase named asyncHandler to create an instance of a class (the AsyncHandler class) that waits for an event to occur. The first parameter of the asyncHandler method is the event handler to notify if the test succeeds as planned (the asynchronous event is received). The second parameter is the number of milliseconds to wait, in this case 500, before declaring the test a failure. The third parameter is a generic object for passing additional data called passThroughData, which will be explored in detail shortly. The last parameter is the timeout handler. This is the method that will be called if the timeout (500ms) is reached before the asynchronous handler is called.

The next line in the function adds an event listener to the timer instance to listen for a TIMER_COMPLETE event. If this event occurs before 500ms elapse, the handleTimerComplete() method passed to asyncHandler will be notified. The final line starts the timer. As this method completes, the code inside the TestCase class also automatically starts the failure timer for the asynchronous event.

NOTE This event listener is using weak references. This concept is important but beyond the scope of this chapter to explain. If you do not thoroughly understand this concept, there are many great articles written on the topic as well as a full lesson in the *Adobe Flex 3: Training from the Source* book that covers garbage collection and the profiler. It is worth exploring.

When a method completes without any errors being thrown or any assertions that prove false, it is considered a success. Without the call to asyncHandler() in this method, Fluint would immediately mark this test a success. The presence of the asyncHandler() informs the TestCase that it needs to wait for either the TIMER_COMPLETE event or the 500ms timeout to occur before deciding if the test case was a success or failure.

The asyncHandler() method referenced two additional methods, the handleTimerComplete() method and the handleTimeout() method. The following example demonstrates the method signature and content of these two methods.

```
protected function handleTimerComplete( event:TimerEvent,
➥ passThroughData:Object ):void {
}

protected function handleTimeout( passThroughData:Object ):void {
    fail( "Timeout occurred before event");
}
```

The `handleTimerComplete()` method accepts two parameters, the event object that will be generated when the event occurs, and any `passThroughData` that was sent to the `asyncHandler()` method call. In this case, the `passThroughData` is null. The `handleTimeout()` method accepts only a single parameter, the `passThroughData`, as this method is called when the event fails to occur in the specified period of time.

If the `handleTimerComplete()` method is called, no additional code is executed. Whenever a test method ends without an error or untrue assertion, it is considered a success. However, in the `handleTimeout()` method, the `fail()` method of the `TestCase` instance is called, passing it a message about the failure. This method marks the test method as a failure and allows the framework to proceed to the next test method.

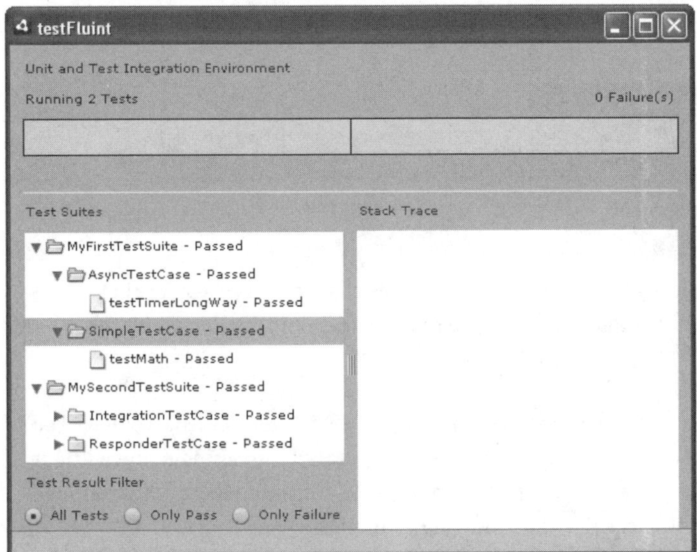

Figure 3: Test Runner displaying the success of the two test methods

When the test runner executes, it will execute each of the two test methods currently defined. Using the code so far in this chapter, it will display two successful test methods, the simple math test and the asynchronous test in Listings 2 and 3.

If you were to change the timer instantiation in the `setup()` method to trigger in 1000ms instead of in 100ms, the test would fail as the timer events would occur after the specified timeout. The output of the test runner in that situation would look like the following figure.

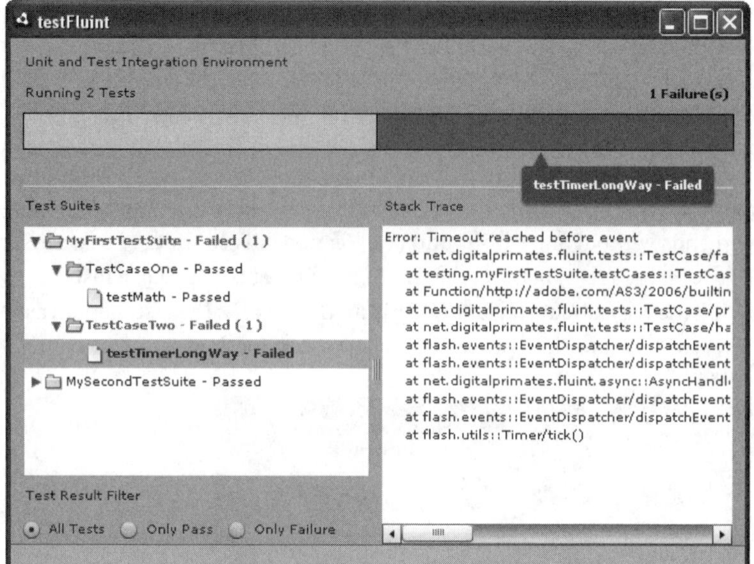

Figure 4: Test Runner displaying the failure of an asynchronous test

NOTE The basic visual test runner used in this chapter allows you to click any failed test in the top progress bar to receive more information about the failure.

In Listing 3, the creation of the `asyncHandler()` and the `addEventListener()` occurred on separate lines of code, however, they can be incorporated into a single line without the need to declare a separate instance first. In practice, many of your asynchronous event handlers will look more like the following example:

```
public function testTimerShortWay():void {
    timer.addEventListener(TimerEvent.TIMER_COMPLETE,
    ➥asyncHandler( handleTimerComplete, 500, null, handleTimeout ),
    ➥false, 0, true );
    timer.start();
}
```

It is important to note that this test method reuses both the `eventHandler` and `timeoutHandler` from Listing 3. You should see significant reuse in well-crafted handlers as you continue to develop test methods.

Using Pass-Through Data

The passThroughData argument of the asyncHandler method provides a dynamic way to ensure reuse of event and timeout handlers. Any data passed into the handler via the passThroughData argument will be passed to either the eventHandler on success or the timeoutHandler on a timeout.

Building on the previous example, here is another Timer test that uses the timer's current repeatCount property. The following code illustrates the testTimerCount() method.

```
public function testTimerCount() : void {
    var o:Object = new Object();
    o.repeatCount = 3;

    timer.repeatCount = o.repeatCount;
    timer.addEventListener(TimerEvent.TIMER_COMPLETE,
    ➥asyncHandler( handleTimerCheckCount, 500, o, handleTimeout ),
    ➥false, 0, true );
    timer.start();
}
```

The method creates a generic object and adds a property called repeatCount to that object. The repeatCount property of the timer is set to the value contained in this object. This causes the timer to count down three separate times before the TIMER_COMPLETE event occurs.

The previous examples always passed a null to the passThroughData argument of the asyncHandler() method, however, this time the argument contains the object o that was created at the beginning of the method. The asyncHandler() method calls handleTimerCheckCount() if the TIMER_COMPLETE event occurs, or handleTimeout() if the timeout is reached first.

The handleTimerCheckCount() method verifies that the timer executed the specified number of times.

```
protected function handleTimerCheckCount( event:TimerEvent,
➥passThroughData:Object ):void {

    assertEquals( ( event.target as Timer ).currentCount,
    ➥passThroughData.repeatCount );
}
```

The `handleTimerCheckCount()` method calls `assertEquals()` passing the `currentCount` property of the `Timer` instance and the `repeatCount` property of the pass-through data. If these two properties are equal, the test succeeds.

An important concept to note is that this method constitutes a generic handler function that uses data created during the test. This same handler could be used for many different tests. More examples of this concept plus asynchronicity during setup and teardown will be reviewed when UIComponents are tested in the next sections.

Creating Integration Tests

Creating integration tests within a complex asynchronous environment is never an easy process; however, the facilities provided within Fluint make it more feasible. This section explains both the foundation for creating text fixtures with asynchronous UIComponents and two separate strategies for writing these integration tests.

It should be noted that this section deals with integration tests generally from a UIComponent level, however, the concepts apply regardless if your testing domain applies to components, services, or simply combinations of classes.

Creating a Simple UIComponent Test

As you begin creating more complicated asynchronous tests, you will have a need for a more complex testing environment as well. One level of complexity that becomes immediately clear is the need for asynchronicity in both the `setUp()` and `tearDown()` methods. One major feature of the Fluint entire framework is the ability to test `UIComponent` class derivates of arbitrary complexity. In Flex, UIComponents inherently have asynchronous aspects.

When you add a TextInput to your application, it is not immediately drawn on the screen, nor is its internal state completely stable. The TextInput, let alone more complicated controls such as ComboBox, go through a complex internal process of setup before they are ready for user interaction. This process involves creating children, measurement, and layout, as well as committing any properties to the control that were specified at creation or immediately after. Until this entire process is complete, any tests you write against this component will likely be invalid. Dependent upon the speed of your machine and other tasks running, each time you run your test the control could be in a slightly different state.

To be consistent, you need to wait until the component is valid and the state is known before you begin testing it. This is the point of asynchronous setup and (potentially) asynchronous teardown: to ensure that the components under testing are in a known and valid state before continuing.

Overriding the setup and teardown behavior

This example uses the TextInput component. It is a relatively simple UIComponent (from a testing perspective) and very familiar to most users. The test case creates a `TextInput` in `setUp()` and waits until the TextInput instance dispatches the `creationComplete` event (meaning it has been created and initialized) before executing the test methods. Examine Listing 4:

Listing 4

```
package testing.mySecondTestSuite.testCases {
    import net.digitalprimates.fluint.tests.TestCase;

    import mx.controls.TextInput;
    import mx.events.FlexEvent;
    import flash.events.Event;

    public class IntegrationTestCase extends TestCase {
        private var textInput:TextInput;

        override protected function setUp():void {
            textInput = new TextInput();
            textInput.addEventListener(FlexEvent.CREATION_COMPLETE,
            ➥ asyncHandler( pendUntilComplete, 1000 ), false, 0, true );
            addChild( textInput );
        }

        override protected function tearDown():void {
            removeChild( textInput );
            textInput = null;
        }
    }
}
```

The class defines a private variable named `textInput` to refer to the `TextInput` instance created in the `setUp()` method. After the `TextInput` instance is created, an event listener is added for the `creationComplete` event. Similar to the previous asynchronous calls, an `asyncHandler` is created, which calls `pendUntilComplete()` if the event occurs within 1000 milliseconds.

The `pendUntilComplete()` method is an empty method of the `TestCase` class. You are free to specify your own method instead; however, as with the previous tests, the lack of an error or failure indicates success, so an empty method simply allows the framework to continue.

Next, the `TextInput` instance needs to be added to the display list. Currently, the `TextInput` exists in memory, but until it is added to the display list, it does not begin the process of creating any children, performing any layout, or actually dealing with properties set on the component. UIComponents are added to the display list by becoming a child of an object already on the display list, such as the application or a container. The `TestCase` class is not a UIComponent itself, nor does it exist on the display list; however, it does provide a façade for adding these children to a special singleton container defined in the `TestRunner` called `testEnvironment`. All the basic child manipulation methods are supported in this facade. These include:

`addChild()`	`getChildAt()`
`addChildAt()`	`getChildByName()`
`removeChild()`	`getChildIndex()`
`removeChildAt()`	`setChildIndex()`
`removeAllChildren()`	`numChildren()`

You are also responsible for cleaning up the test case when a test method is finished executing. In this case, the `TextInput` instance needs to be removed from the display list and made eligible for garbage collection. This is accomplished using the `removeChild()` method and by setting the `textInput` property to `null`.

Writing the test method

The test method for this UIComponent will set the `htmlText` property and later check to ensure that the `text` property was set properly as a result. Many of the UIComponents in Flex set a private variable internal to the control when you set one of their many properties. Later, in a method called `commitProperties()`, they often deal with this change and apply it as needed to the control. Unfortunately, this means that writing to a property and immediately reading from it only tests your machine's ability to read and write memory. To truly ensure that a value has been committed to a control, we often need to wait for an event before reading it.

Examine the following testSetHTMLTextProperty() method:

```
public function testSetHTMLTextProperty() : void {
    var passThroughData:Object = new Object();
    passThroughData.propertyName = 'text';
    passThroughData.propertyValue = 'digitalprimates';

    textInput.addEventListener( FlexEvent.VALUE_COMMIT,
    ➥ asyncHandler( handleVerifyProperty, 500, passThroughData,
    ➥ handleEventNeverOccurred ), false, 0, true );
    textInput.htmlText = passThroughData.propertyValue;
}
```

This method uses passThroughData and the short method of adding an asyncHandler discussed previously. It creates and instantiates a new object called passThroughData, then creates a property in that object named propertyName and sets its value to text. Next, it creates a property named propertyValue and sets its value to digitalprimates.

The method adds an event listener to the TextInput instance for the event named FlexEvent.VALUE_COMMIT. When this event occurs, the test case will call a method named handleVerifyProperty. If the event does not occur, it will call handleEventNeverOccurred. The timeout property of the asyncHanlder() method specifies 500ms for this event to occur and provides the passThroughData object created earlier as the passThroughData parameter.

On the next line, the method sets the htmlText property of the TextInput instance to the value specified in the passThroughData object. If the TextInput behaves correctly, the text property should reflect the correct value after the VALUE_COMMIT event.

Using the asyncHandler(), the method informed the test case that it should wait for either the VALUE_COMMIT event or the 500ms timeout to occur before attempting to decide if the test case was a success or failure. Without the call to asyncHandler, this particular test method would be marked a success as soon as the method body finished executing.

Creating a reusable handler method

The eventHandler property of the asyncHandler() method specifies that handleVerifyProperty() should be invoked if the event occurs within the specified period of time and that `handleEventNeverOccurred()` should be called if the event does not occur in a timely manner. These methods can be examined in the following code:

```
protected function handleVerifyProperty( event:Event,
➥ passThroughData:Object ):void {
    assertEquals( passThroughData.propertyValue,
    ➥ event.currentTarget[ passThroughData.propertyName ] );
}

protected function handleEventNeverOccurred( passThroughData:Object ):void {
    fail('Pending Event Never Occurred');
}
```

The `handleVerifyProperty()` method represents an extremely generic way to verify a property on an object. In the handler, the method calls `assertEquals()` passing the `propertyValue` property of the `passThroughData` object as the first argument. For the second argument, the `propertyName` property of the `passThroughData` object is used along with the `event.currentTarget` to retrieve the current value from the `TextInput` instance. Effectively, this is a very generic and reusable way to write this same statement:

```
    assertEquals( passThroughData.propertyValue, textField.text );
```

In this case, the test method ensures that when the value digitalprimates is set on the `htmlText` property of the `TextInput` instance, it can be read correctly from the `text` property. This test case demonstrates the foundation for integration testing with UIComponent instances. In the next sections, we will dive further into testing using UIComponent subclasses and discuss sequence testing.

Working with Test Sequences

Even relatively simple tests for a complicated component can quickly become tedious to write. For example, to test a login form that has username and password text inputs and a button for submitting the values requires setting the username and the password, waiting until they are committed to their respective controls, clicking the button, and watching for the login event. Then you can check the current values against the initially set values.

Using the asynchronous approach we have discussed so far, this would require five to seven distinct methods to implement this single test. This would be repetitive and error-prone work.

Sequences are an attempt to reduce the pain associated with constructing these tests. They provide a simpler method of defining the steps that need to happen in order, and potentially asynchronously, before an assertion can occur. Like all unit and integration tests, a sequence is designed to test exactly one thing at a time, but it acknowledges that many steps may need to occur before the assertion.

This example will create a single test for a login form. The login form will be a custom MXML component. The test case will instantiate the component in the `setUp()` method and wait until the `creationComplete` event fires before beginning the test.

The test will set the username and password. Once the values have been committed, it will simulate the login button click and wait for a custom login event to be broadcast. Once that event is received, it will check that the password contained in the event matches the password entered in the field.

Creating the login form

The login form in this case is a custom MXML component. Typically this type of form would exist somewhere in your project and would be tested via these classes. In this case, the login form broadcasts a `TextEvent` named `loginRequested` when the button is clicked. Examine the code in Listing 5 before examining the test methods.

Listing 5

```
<?xml version="1.0" encoding="utf-8"?>
<mx:Panel xmlns:mx="http://www.adobe.com/2006/mxml" layout="vertical"
    title="Please Login" height="168">
    <mx:Metadata>
        [Event(name="loginRequested", type="flash.events.TextEvent")]
    </mx:Metadata>

   <mx:Script>
        <![CDATA[
            protected function handleLoginClick( event:Event ):void {
                dispatchEvent( new TextEvent( 'loginRequested',
                ➥ false, false, passwordTI.text ) );
            }
        ]]>
    </mx:Script>
```

code continues on next page

Listing 5 (continued)

```
    <mx:Form width="100%">
        <mx:FormItem label="Username" required="true">
            <mx:TextInput id="usernameTI"/>
        </mx:FormItem>
        <mx:FormItem  label="Password" required="true">
            <mx:TextInput id="passwordTI" displayAsPassword="true"/>
        </mx:FormItem>
    </mx:Form>
    <mx:HBox width="100%" horizontalAlign="center">
        <mx:Button id="loginBtn" label="Login"
            click="handleLoginClick( event )"/>
    </mx:HBox>
</mx:Panel>
```

When the `loginBtn` Button instance broadcasts a `click` event, the `handleLoginClick()` method dispatches a new `TextEvent` named `loginRequested` that contains the text in the password `TextInput`. This isn't a great real-world use case for the `TextEvent`, but it will work for demonstration purposes. Testing this form will minimally involve populating the password field and causing the `Button` instance to emit a `click` event.

Setting up the test case

The test case will need an overridden `setUp()` and `tearDown()` method similar to the `TextInput` test case in Listing 5.

```
package testing.mySecondTestSuite.testCases {
    import mx.events.FlexEvent;

    import net.digitalprimates.fluint.tests.TestCase;

    import testing.mySecondTestSuite.testCases.mxml.LoginForm;

    public class SequenceTestCase extends TestCase {
        private var form:LoginForm;

        override protected function setUp():void {
            form = new LoginForm();
            form.addEventListener( FlexEvent.CREATION_COMPLETE,
            ➥ asyncHandler( pendUntilComplete, 100 ), false, 0, true );
```

```
            addChild( form );
        }

        override protected function tearDown():void {
            removeChild( form );
            form = null;
        }
    }
}
```

In this case, an instance of the LoginForm is created and added as a child in the setUp() method. The tearDown() method makes this instance eligible for garbage collection.

Writing the test sequence steps

Testing sequences live in a test method, just like all of the other tests explored in this lesson so far. They are able to use passThroughData and eventually timeout or call an event handler. However, their syntax is significantly different as they hide a fair amount of complexity from the developer.

Sequences are composed of two types of operations:

- **Actions**—which modify values, dispatch events, or accomplish other goals
- **Pends**—which cause the sequence to wait for some event to occur or action to complete before continuing

The following is an example sequence for testing a form:

```
public function testLogin():void {
    var passThroughData:Object = new Object();
    passThroughData.username = 'myuser1';
    passThroughData.password = 'somepsswd';

    var sequence:SequenceRunner = new SequenceRunner( this );

    sequence.addStep( new SequenceSetter( form.usernameTI,
    ➥ {text:passThroughData.username} ) );
    sequence.addStep( new SequenceWaiter( form.usernameTI,
    ➥ FlexEvent.VALUE_COMMIT, 100 ) );
```

```
    sequence.addStep( new SequenceSetter( form.passwordTI,
    ➥{text:passThroughData.password} ) );
    sequence.addStep( new SequenceWaiter( form.passwordTI,
    ➥FlexEvent.VALUE_COMMIT, 100 ) );

    sequence.addStep( new SequenceEventDispatcher( form.loginBtn,
    ➥new MouseEvent( 'click', true, false ) ) );
    sequence.addStep( new SequenceWaiter( form, 'loginRequested', 100 ) );

    sequence.addAssertHandler( handleLoginEvent, passThroughData );

    sequence.run();
}
```

Initially, the method creates a generic object for passThroughData and sets a username and password property to myuser1 and somepsswd. This object will be used later for comparison to ensure that the form functions properly.

Next, the method creates a new SequenceRunner. This object is responsible for ensuring that the steps in the sequence are followed in order and that the sequence waits, when necessary, for the previous step to complete before proceeding to the next.

The addStep() is called on the sequence to define the type and order of steps.

The first step is defined by a new instance of the SequenceSetter class. The new SequenceSetter is used to set one or more properties on a specific target.

```
public function SequenceSetter( target:IEventDispatcher, props:Object )
```

The first parameter to the SequenceSetter constructor is the target where the properties will be set. The second parameter is a generic object with name/value pairs that represent these properties. This line specifically sets the text property of the username TextInput inside the form to the value defined in the username property of the passThroughData object.

The next step creates and adds a new SequenceWaiter to the sequence. The new SequenceWaiter instructs the sequence to pause until a specific event occurs.

```
public function SequenceWaiter( target:IEventDispatcher, eventName:String,
➥timeout:int, timeoutHandler : Function = null )
```

The first parameter to the SequenceWaiter constructor is a target, which must implement the IEventDispatcher interface. All Flex UIComponents implement this interface;

it simply ensures that the target can broadcast events. The second is the name of the event that will occur. The third parameter is the number of milliseconds to wait for that event, before timing out. There is an optional fourth parameter, which is a method to call if the expected event does not occur before the timeout. If you do not provide this method, the sequence code uses a default version built into the framework. This line specifically tells the sequence to wait for the username `TextInput` inside the form to broadcast a `valueCommit` event, indicating that the `text` property has been committed, before proceeding to the next step.

In general, the `valueCommit` event usually means that a given property is stable inside a control. This, like most things, is not only up for argument but also varies slightly between controls. The larger point here is that these sequence tests are, almost by definition, clear box tests. You need to know how the control works to accomplish this type of testing. Those with intimate knowledge of the framework may note that, with `TextInputs`, the `valueCommit` doesn't actually guarantee much when setting the `text` property. While true, the `valueCommit` example is only meant to be an illustration from which to learn, not a complete test suite.

Next, the method repeats the same procedure for the password field, ensuring that the value is committed before the sequence is continued.

The method then adds an instance of the `SequenceEventDispatcher` class to the sequence. This class dispatches an event on a specific target to simulate an action.

```
public function SequenceEventDispatcher( target:EventDispatcher,
➥ eventToBroadcast:Event )
```

The constructor for this class takes two parameters. The first is the target, which must be an `IEventDispatcher` from which you wish to broadcast an event. The second is an instance of an `Event` object that you wish to broadcast. Practically, this step causes the login button inside of the form to broadcast a `click` event as though a user had clicked the button. The `LoginForm` that you created earlier calls a function to broadcast a custom event once that button is clicked.

The method then instructs the sequence to wait until the form broadcasts a `loginRequested` event before proceeding with the sequence.

Next, an `assertHandler` is added to the sequence. An `assertHandler` is a method that will be called when the end of the sequence is reached, so that the developer can perform any asserts and ensure that the test succeeded.

```
public function addAssertHandler( assertHandler:Function,
➥ passThroughData:Object ):void;
```

The first parameter of addAssertHandler() is the method to be called. The second is the passThroughData. The method signature for an assertHandler is the same as the other asynchronous handlers created in previous sections.

```
public function handleEndOfSequence( event:Event,
➥ passThroughData:Object ):void;
```

The first parameter is an event object, and the second parameter is the passThroughData for that test.

Finally, the sequence is started from the beginning. The SequenceRunner will follow each of these steps until any step fails or the end of the sequence is reached. If the end is reached, the method defined in the addAssertHandler will be called and the passThroughData will be sent along. If one of the steps fails, the timeout handler associated with that step will be called. If a timeout handler is not defined, the TestCase class contains a default implementation that will inform you of the failure.

The method referenced in the addAssertHandler() method is defined in the following code. If the end of the sequence is reached, this method is invoked to determine if the sequence failed or succeeded.

```
protected function handleLoginEvent( event:TextEvent,
➥ passThroughData:Object ):void {
    assertEquals( passThroughData.password, event.text );
}
```

The assertEquals() will check that the text property of the TextEvent matches the password put into the password field. If they match, the process of adding a password to the form's password field, clicking the login button, and broadcasting an event with the password included works.

Exploring other sequence steps

In addition to the sequence steps listed in the previous section, the Fluint framework also provides a SequenceBindingWaiter. The SequenceBindingWaiter is used to wait for a property to change on a given object before continuing. This is most useful when using databinding in your system and a given operation updates a data model.

```
public function SequenceBindingWaiter( target:IEventDispatcher,
➥ propertyName:String, timeout:int, timeoutHandler : Function = null )
```

The first argument is the object where the property is defined. The second is the name of the property that is expected to change, followed by the timeout in milliseconds and an optional timeout handler function.

All sequence steps implement one of two interfaces, ISequencePend or ISequenceAction. If you were to create your own type of sequence step, and implement one of these interfaces, the Fluint framework would understand how to let the sequence participate in this same process by waiting or invoking the action.

Hopefully, you see the power that sequences can bring to writing maintainable tests. The next sections will apply sequences to responders, which can be used when testing many aspects of Flex and associated Flex frameworks such as Adobe Consulting's Cairngorm project.

Working with Responders

Events are one way that Flex and AIR controls use to handle asynchronicity; responders are another. Many of the service classes inside Flex and AIR, which include classes such as HTTPService, RemoteObject, and even SQLCommand, return or use an asynchronous token when they invoke a remote method. This token is then used by Flex, and in particular by Flex framework developers, to monitor the status of the call and react when the call succeeds or fails.

The asynchronous token has a method named addResponder(). This method accepts a single parameter, which is an object that implements the mx.rpc.IResponder interface. This dictates that the object must have two methods, one named result that accepts a single object named data, and one named fault that accepts a single object named info. One of these two methods will be called when the service succeeds or fails to retrieve data.

An instance of the responder could be used to gather the result of an HTTPService call like this:

```
public function exampleOne():void {
    var httpService:HTTPService = new HTTPService();
    var asyncToken:AsyncToken;
    var myResponder:Responder = new Responder( handleResult, handleFault );

    asyncToken = httpService.send();
    asyncToken.addResponder( myResponder );
}

public function handleResult( data:Object ):void {
    trace("Success");
}
```

```
public function handleFault( info:Object ):void {
    trace("Failure");
}
```

More commonly, however, the responder that implements the IResponder interface is a completely separate class:

```
public function testResponder():void {
    var httpService:HTTPService = new HTTPService();
    var asyncToken:AsyncToken;
    var myCommand:IResponder = new FileSaveCommand();

    asyncToken = httpService.send();
    asyncToken.addResponder( myCommand );
}
```

Many Flex frameworks, most notably the Cairngorm framework, depend on responders for key functionality. Therefore, the ability to test with responders is requisite of any testing framework.

To test a service that uses responders, you can use one new method, asyncResponder, and one new class, TestResponder.

The asyncResponder() method is similar to the asyncHandler() method used earlier in this chapter but is intended for use with responders.

```
public function asyncResponder( responder:*, timeout:int,
➥ passThroughData:Object = null,
➥ timeoutHandler:Function = null ):IResponder
```

The asyncResponder() method accepts a traditional IResponder or an ITestResponder as the first argument. The difference between these two interfaces is the number of arguments the result and fault functions accept.

If the first argument is an IResponder, the result and fault functions are expected to each accept one argument:

```
function result(data:Object):void;
function fault(info:Object):void;
```

If the first argument is an ITestResponder, the result and fault functions each accept an additional parameter for the passThroughData, making them more useful for testing purposes.

```
public function fault( info:Object, passThroughData:Object ):void;
public function result( data:Object, passThroughData:Object ):void;
```

The new TestResponder class implements ITestResponder and still accepts the two functions, a result and fault, which will be called in the event of either a success or failure from the service.

```
public function TestResponder( result:Function, fault:Function )
```

Using this new method and class, you can test the result of an HTTPService using an asynchronous token in the following way:

```
public function testHTTPResponder():void {
    var httpService:HTTPService = new HTTPService();
    httpService.url = "http://www.google.com/crossdomain.xml";
    httpService.resultFormat = "e4x";

    var asyncToken:AsyncToken;
    var responder:IResponder = asyncResponder(
    ➥ new TestResponder( handleResult, handleFault ), 3000 );

    asyncToken = httpService.send();
    asyncToken.addResponder( responder );
}

protected function handleResult( data:Object, passThroughData:Object ):void {
    trace("It's all good");
}

protected function handleFault( info:Object, passThroughData:Object ):void {
    fail("Received fault from Server");
}
```

As mentioned earlier, many frameworks, such as Adobe Consulting's Cairngorm project, also use responders extensively. While an explanation of Cairngorm is beyond the scope of this book, the following brief example of testing a delegate class is included to demonstrate the power of testing with responders.

```
public function testDelegate():void {
    var someVO:SomeVO = new SomeVO();
    someVO.myName = 'digitalprimates';
    someVO.yourAddress = '1@2.com';

    var responder:IResponder = asyncResponder(
    ➥ new TestResponder( handleResult, handleFault ) , 3000, someVO );
```

```
    var delegate : MyDelegate = new MyDelegate( responder );

    delegate.addSomeData( someVO );
}

protected function handleResult( data:Object, passThroughData:Object ):void {
    assertEquals( data.myName, passThroughData.myName );
}

protected function handleFault( info:Object, passThroughData:Object ):void {
    fail("Received fault from Server");
}
```

NOTE For a full tutorial of using Fluint with Cairngorm, please refer to the Fluint Google code site at http://fluint.googlecode.com/.

Next Steps

Fluint is an evolving project that is now actively being developed by the Flex community. New features that may improve your ability to write tests in a faster and easier way are being added constantly, so be sure to continue to check the documentation and examples on the Fluint site (http://fluint.googlecode.com/).

Remember, creating solid unit and integration tests will ultimately save time during development, refactoring, and most certainly when you need to revise code late in the process. Using the tools available to you in Flex and AIR for testing, you can create stable and testable applications.

DEPLOYING AIR APPLICATIONS

CHAPTER 13

Chapter 1, "Building Your First AIR Application," briefly explained the basics of creating an AIR file using a Hello World application. This lesson will re-address the same topic in more detail as well as discuss methodologies for packaging database files and other assets along with your AIR application.

The goal of this discussion in Chapter 1 was to enable you to work with AIR applications quickly. The goal of this chapter is to teach you to package and deploy final form applications that can be distributed to users through various means, some of which allow the AIR runtime to be installed at the same time.

Using a Digital Certificate

Signing your AIR application with a digital certificate is a requirement of deploying an AIR application. The act of signing this application provides two very legitimate benefits and a few softer assurances. The hard benefits fall into the categories of *authentication* and *integrity.*

An application can contain the name of the person or company that produced it on a splash screen or in some other area. However, the end user of that application cannot rely upon that information. There is no guarantee that the information displayed on that screen was created by the named individual. For example, you could create an AIR application and create an Adobe splash screen; however, this does not actually mean the application was created by Adobe. This is the first benefit provided by a digitally signed application—*authentication.* The end user can be guaranteed that the person or company who created the application is, in fact, who they claim to be.

Once an application is released online, it can be downloaded by anyone. This also means that, with some effort, anyone can modify an application that has already been released. For example, it would take minimal efforts for a developer with proper knowledge to make a copy of the executable for Microsoft Word or a similar product, make changes, and attempt to redistribute it. This is the second benefit provided by digitally signed applications—*integrity.* The end user can be guaranteed that the application has not been modified since the time it was signed. In other words, the application is the original version that the developer or company intended to distribute.

There are also some less technical benefits that are gained by application signing. First, individuals generally feel better installing an application from a known entity. Rather than installing a random application from an unknown developer, they are installing an application that an identifiable individual or company created.

Second, as a developer, signing all of your applications can help you build a brand. Every person that installs the application sees your name and understands that you are the developer. Over time, the simple fact that the application was created by you can instill additional trust.

Unfortunately, the previous statements are only true if you take the time to procure a digital certificate from a recognized certificate authority. AIR allows you to sign applications with a self-signed certificate, which is a certificate that you create and certify on your own. Much like the previous splash screen example, this type of certificate doesn't inspire a great deal of confidence, as anyone can create a certificate and claim to be anyone else. A certificate authority is an organization that researches and guarantees your identity to others.

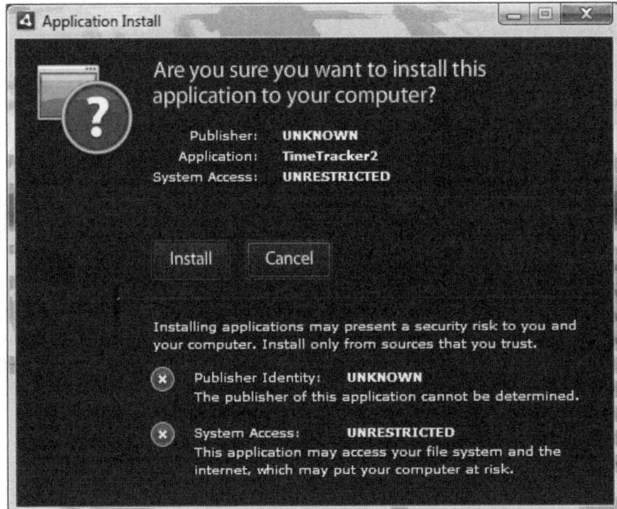

Figure 1: A self-signed application being installed by a user

A good analogy is that of a passport. A self-signed certificate is much like attempting to pass through an airport with a handwritten note asserting that you are in fact who you claim to be. You are unlikely to board a plane in this manner. Conversely, an airport security agent accepts that you are in fact who you claim to be when you present a valid passport. This is because they trust the organization that issues the passport to have performed the relevant work to ensure your identity.

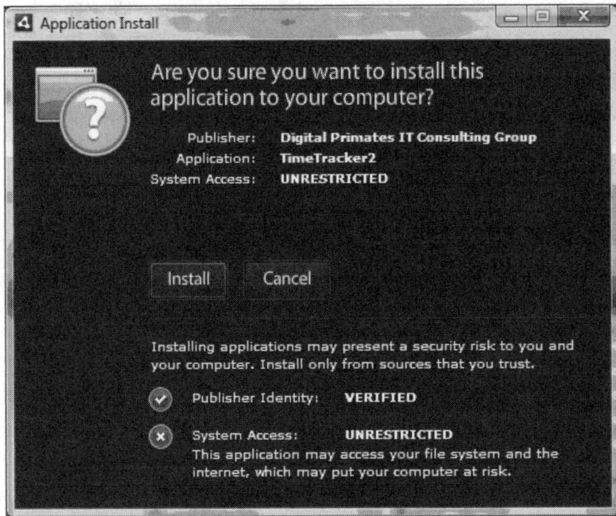

Figure 2: An application with a verified publisher being installed by a user

Self-signed certificates are a very useful way to test your applications; however, before they are deployed for the first time, they should have a valid digital signature guaranteed by a recognized authority. While this is important for all of the reasons mentioned earlier, it is also imperative if you ever plan to update your application. The Adobe AIR updater will only update an existing application to a newer version if both versions are signed with the same certificate. If you initially deploy your application with a self-signed certificate and then later attempt to update to a version signed by a certificate authority, the update will fail. The user will have to manually uninstall the self-signed version and reinstall the new version.

While you can use any certificate authority (CA) for this purpose, the two most common authorities that provide an applicable certificate for signing AIR applications are Thawte and VeriSign. Once purchased, this type of certificate can be used for all your AIR applications. The next section explains the basic steps of creating and purchasing a certificate from Thawte.

Purchasing a Thawte Certificate

Thawte sells a certificate specifically for Adobe AIR developers. It also tends to be the least expensive option among the larger certificate authorities. Purchasing a certificate from Thawte requires the use of Mozilla Firefox. You cannot purchase the certificate using Internet Explorer.

While it is not necessary to purchase a certificate when you begin developing, it is important to allow sufficient time before you intend to deploy your application. The process of obtaining a certificate involves providing initial information to Thawte, allowing them to ask for additional information, and then waiting until they have verified your identity. This can take multiple days, so do not wait until the very last moment to start the process.

You can purchase a certificate from the Thawte website (www.thawte.com). The type of certificate you need to purchase is referred to as a *Code Signing* certificate. As of the time of writing this book, there is a link directly on the main page to purchase this certificate.

Once you select the certificate, you will be presented with a series of choices regarding the use of your certificate; one of these options is an Adobe AIR developer certificate.

These certificates are sold in one-year and two-year enrollment periods. The two-year period is less expensive per year. If you plan to have AIR applications that you will update in the future, you will need to continue to renew and keep this certificate active.

You will be asked for information regarding your organization name, organizational unit, country code, state or province, city or town, web server domain, contact, and identification information. The Thawte site does a good job of providing help on each of these terms; however, this is the information that Thawte will use to verify your organization's identity, so it needs to be 100% accurate.

Once you have submitted all the required information, you will receive progress updates and information requests from Thawte. When all these details have been resolved, you will receive an email allowing you to obtain your certificate.

Using Firefox, you will obtain your certificate from Thawte's site. This automatically installs the certificate into Firefox. You will need to export this certificate to use it with Flex Builder or the command line tools.

Figure 3: Fetching a certificate from Thawte's website

To export the certification, from the Firefox menu, choose Tools > Options > Advanced. Click the Encryption tab followed by the View Certificates button.

Select the certificate you just purchased and click the Backup button. This backup is a P12 file that can be used by the Adobe tools. P12 files, or PKCS12 (Personal Information Exchange Syntax Standard) files are formats for storing certificates that can be used for signing files, email, and other documents. Specify a location you will remember, as you will need it when you export release versions of your software.

Figure 4: Exporting a P12 file using Firefox

When you attempt to save this file, Firefox will ask you to enter a new password to guard against the unauthorized use of this certificate. Flex Builder and the AIR tools will ask for this password when exporting an application. Your certificate will then be saved and ready to use.

Configuring Application Options

In Chapter 1, you learned about a few of the application properties that can be configured via the application's XML descriptor file, including the application's id and name. Chapter 7, "Customizing the Look and Feel of an Application," further explored this file, modifying the setting in the initialWindow node of this file to customize the look and feel of the application's window.

This section will address additional detail and introduce new nodes specified in this descriptor file that affect the application interaction with the user's machine during installation and execution.

Installer Text

The first two nodes were introduced in Chapter 1: name and description. The name and description are displayed by the installer during the installation process. This minimal descriptor file uses simple strings to define these properties:

```
<?xml version="1.0" encoding="utf-8" standalone="no"?>
<application xmlns="http://ns.adobe.com/air/application/1.1">
    <id>net.digitalprimates.airBook.Calculator</id>
    <filename>Calculator</filename>
    <version>1.0</version>
    <name>My Calculator</name>
    <description>An application for mathematics</description>
    <initialWindow>
        <content>Calculator.swf</content>
        <visible>true</visible>
    </initialWindow>
</application>
```

This is perfectly acceptable, however, AIR 1.1 allows you to internationalize your installation by providing an XML list of names and descriptions instead of simple strings. For example:

```
<?xml version="1.0" encoding="utf-8" standalone="no"?>
<application xmlns="http://ns.adobe.com/air/application/1.1">
    <id>net.digitalprimates.airBook.Calculator</id>
    <filename>Calculator</filename>
    <version>1.0</version>
    <name>
        <text xml:lang="en">My Calculator</text>
        <text xml:lang="it">La Mia Calcolatrice</text>
    </name>
    <description>
        <text xml:lang="en">One language is never enough</text>
        <text xml:lang="it">Una sola lingua non è mai abbastanza</text>
    </description>
    <initialWindow>
        <content>Calculator.swf</content>
        <visible>true</visible>
    </initialWindow>
</application>
```

In this case, an English and Italian name and description are provided. The `lang` attribute for each text element specifies the language in a language code. For more information, please refer to RFC4646 (http://www.ietf.org/rfc/rfc4646.txt).

The AIR runtime will attempt to find the closest matching language to the user's system during the installation process. If a match cannot be found, the first entry is used. This information is only used during installation and does not have any effect on the application itself.

Installation Directory and Menu Location

The next two nodes are also optional but provide additional control over the location of the installed application on the user's computer and the location where the AIR application appears in the Windows Start menu.

The installFolder node specifies a subdirectory under the default installation directory for your operating system where the application will reside. For example:

```
<installFolder>Calculator</installFolder>
```

This node will cause this application to be installed in the C:\Program Files\Calculator directory on a Windows machine and in the /Applications/Calculator directory on a Mac. You may also provide a nested subdirectory to the installer, for example:

```
<installFolder>MyTools/Calculator</installFolder>
```

If you do not provide an `installFolder`, the AIR installer uses the name node's value for the directory name.

The `programMenuFolder` only has an impact for Windows users currently. It specifies the folder under the Programs menu of the Start Menu where a shortcut to the application should be placed.

File Types

The fileTypes node of the application descriptor allows you to register file types with your AIR application. For example, when you choose a .txt file from your operating system, it knows to open an associated program that can display and potentially edit text.

Your AIR applications have this same capability. When you install an AIR application, you can associate multiple file types that will cause your AIR application to open when chosen. For example:

```
<fileTypes>
    <fileType>
        <name>net.digitalprimates.airBook.CalculatorFormula</name>
        <extension>frm</extension>
        <description>Calculator Formula File</description>
        <contentType>application/xml</contentType>
    </fileType>
    <fileType>
        <name>net.digitalprimates.airBook.CalculatorMemory</name>
        <extension>mem</extension>
        <description>Calculator Memory File</description>
        <contentType>application/xml</contentType>
    </fileType>
</fileTypes>
```

The name and extension are the only required nodes. The description is used by the operating system to provide a human readable description to the user. Finally, the `contentType` is the MIME type of the file.

NOTE For more information about MIME types, please refer to http://www.iana.org/assignments/media-types/.

During installation, AIR will attempt to associate each of these file types with the AIR application, if that file type is not already registered to another application. The installer will not override any registrations by default.

Once these file types are registered with the operating system, you can open your AIR application by selecting a saved file with the specified extension. If the registered AIR application is already open when you select a registered file, AIR does not open a second instance. Instead, the `NativeApplication` object of the existing instance dispatches an event named invoke, which your application can use to determine an appropriate course of action.

Browser Invocation

Related files provide one method to launch your AIR application; another is browser invocation. Browser invocation refers to the ability for a web page running in the web browser to launch an installed AIR application on the user's computer. This could be useful in a variety of means, perhaps when a user attempts to download an application they have already installed or as part of a coordinated effort to display a file retrieved from a website in an AIR application.

By default, browser invocation of your AIR applications is disabled. To enable it, you must include the following node in your application xml descriptor:

```
<allowBrowserInvocation>true</allowBrowserInvocation>
```

To learn more about all invocation methods, visit the Adobe AIR 1.1 help documentation at http://help.adobe.com/en_US/AIR/1.1/devappshtml/WS5b3ccc516d4fbf351e63e3d118676a5d46-8000.html.

Icons

The AIR installer allows you to specify an icon that the operating system will use to represent your AIR application. This icon is specified via the icon node in the application's XML descriptor file. You can specify different icons for various resolutions using this XML structure. Your icons must be in PNG format and must be exactly the size specified in the XML. For example:

```
<icon>
    <image16x16>assets/icons/calc16.png</image16x16>
    <image32x32>assets/icons/calc32.png</image32x32>
    <image48x48>assets/assets/icons/calc48.png</image48x48>
    <image128x128>assets/icons/calc128.png</image128x128>
</icon>
```

The icon image is a relative path from the application root directory. If you don't specify all of the sizes, AIR attempts to scale the image for you. It also automatically converts the PNG file to the appropriate file type for the user's operating system.

You may also specify icons for each file type that you choose to associate with your AIR application using the same syntax. You simply include an icon node under each fileType node. For example:

```
<fileType>
    <name>net.digitalprimates.airBook.CalculatorFormula</name>
    <extension>frm</extension>
    <description>Calculator Formula File</description>
    <contentType>application/xml</contentType>
    <icon>
        <image16x16>assets/icons/formula16.png</image16x16>
        <image32x32>assets/icons/formula32.png</image32x32>
        <image48x48>assets/assets/icons/formula48.png</image48x48>
        <image128x128>assets/icons/formula128.png</image128x128>
    </icon>
</fileType>
```

The operating system will then display this icon for each of the specified file types.

Assembled

The final assembled application descriptor file using the option in this chapter would appear like the following example:

```
<?xml version="1.0" encoding="utf-8" standalone="no"?>
<application xmlns="http://ns.adobe.com/air/application/1.1">
    <id>net.digitalprimates.airBook.Calculator</id>
    <filename>Calculator</filename>
    <version>1.0</version>
    <name>
        <text xml:lang="en">My Calculator</text>
        <text xml:lang="it">La Mia Calcolatrice</text>
    </name>
    <description>
        <text xml:lang="en">One language is never enough</text>
        <text xml:lang="it">Una sola lingua non è mai abbastanza</text>
    </description>
    <initialWindow>
        <content>Calculator.swf</content>
        <visible>true</visible>
    </initialWindow>
    <allowBrowserInvocation>true</allowBrowserInvocation>
    <installFolder>MyTools/Calculator</installFolder>
    <programMenuFolder>MyTools/Calculator</programMenuFolder>
    <icon>
        <image16x16>assets/icons/calc16.png</image16x16>
        <image32x32>assets/icons/calc32.png</image32x32>
        <image48x48>assets/assets/icons/calc48.png</image48x48>
        <image128x128>assets/icons/calc128.png</image128x128>
    </icon>
    <fileTypes>
            <fileType>
                    <name>net.digitalprimates.airBook.CalculatorFormula</name>
                    <extension>frm</extension>
                    <description>Calculator Formula File</description>
                    <contentType>application/xml</contentType>
                    <icon>
                        <image16x16>assets/icons/formula16.png</image16x16>
```

```
                <image32x32>assets/icons/formula32.png</image32x32>
                <image48x48>assets/assets/icons/formula48.png
                </image48x48>
                <image128x128>assets/icons/formula128.png
                </image128x128>
            </icon>
        </fileType>
        <fileType>
            <name>net.digitalprimates.airBook.CalculatorMemory</name>
            <extension>mem</extension>
            <description>Calculator Memory File</description>
            <contentType>application/xml</contentType>
            <icon>
                <image16x16>assets/icons/mem16.png</image16x16>
                <image32x32>assets/icons/mem32.png</image32x32>
                <image48x48>assets/assets/icons/mem48.png</image48x48>
                <image128x128>assets/icons/mem128.png</image128x128>
            </icon>
        </fileType>
    </fileTypes>
</application>
```

Packaging an AIR Application

Packaging your AIR application into an .air file for distribution is the next step. This file format is used for distributing your AIR application. The .air file format is really a compressed ZIP file containing the components of your application, which is the SWF file if you are using Flex and any assets. It can be opened with any standard unzip utility.

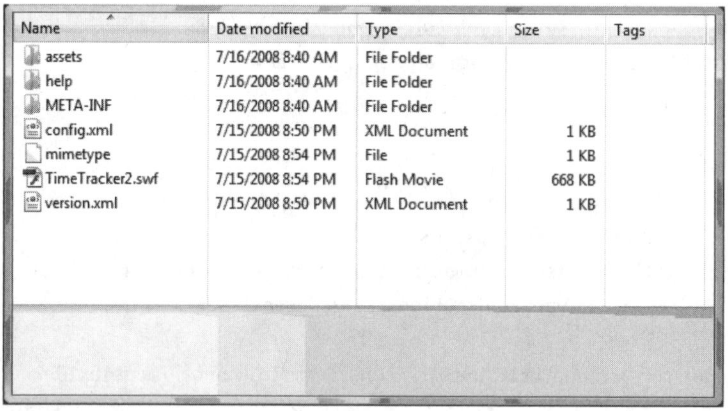

Name	Date modified	Type	Size	Tags
assets	7/16/2008 8:40 AM	File Folder		
help	7/16/2008 8:40 AM	File Folder		
META-INF	7/16/2008 8:40 AM	File Folder		
config.xml	7/15/2008 8:50 PM	XML Document	1 KB	
mimetype	7/15/2008 8:54 PM	File	1 KB	
TimeTracker2.swf	7/15/2008 8:54 PM	Flash Movie	668 KB	
version.xml	7/15/2008 8:50 PM	XML Document	1 KB	

Figure 5: Unzipped .air file for dpTimeTracker

In this .air file, you will see your application and assets along with a META-INF directory. This directory is a concept borrowed from the JAR (Java ARchive) file format and is used to keep your files separate from any files required by AIR. The META-INF directory contains the application's XML descriptor file along with the digital signature for the application, contained in a W3C (World Wide Web Consortium) XML signature format.

Creating your own .air file is a simple process using either Flex Builder or the command line.

Packaging with Flex Builder

Once your application is ready to deploy, you need to package it. From the Flex Builder menu, choose Project > Export Release Build.

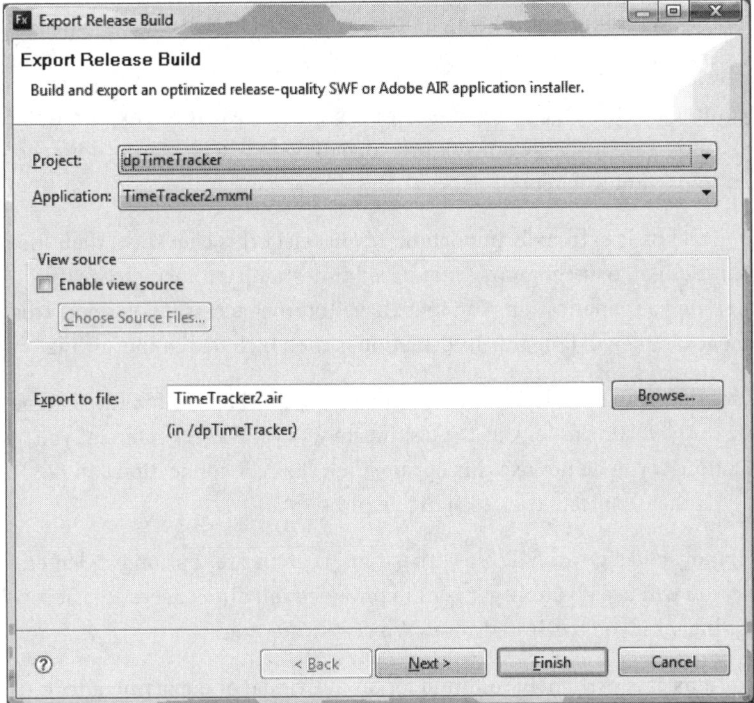

Figure 6: The Export Release Build dialog box in Flex Builder

The Export Release Build dialog box will confirm both the project and main application to export along with the name of the .air file you wish to create. If you are creating an application for demonstration or educational purposes, the Enable view source checkbox will include a copy of your actual source code along with the project deployment. This allows users of the application to view the source if they wish to learn more about how the application was written.

Clicking Next will bring you to the Digital Signature page.

Signing an AIR application

Digitally signing your AIR application allows the user to both authenticate the publisher and to verify the integrity of the application, as you learned previously in this chapter. The Digital Signature page of the Export Release Build dialog box will aid you in this process.

In the Digital Signature page of the Export Release Build dialog box, you will need to navigate to the location where you stored your exported digital certificate. This is the P12 file that you exported from Firefox if you followed the steps in this chapter when purchasing your certificate.

The password required on this page is the password you created when you exported the certificate from Firefox, not the password you provided Thawte when creating your certificate. This is an important difference.

The Timestamp checkbox is extremely important. If you select this checkbox, then the AIR packaging utilities will contact an Internet-based timestamp authority to verify the time when signing your application. You must have Internet access if you select this checkbox, or the packaging will fail. This information is then included in the .air file.

If you use the Timestamp option, then an AIR application signed in this manner can be installed anytime in the future, as long as the certificate was valid at the moment you signed the application. If you do not use this option, then the AIR application can no longer be installed if the certificate used to sign it expires.

By default, the "Export and sign an AIR file with a digital certificate" option is selected. This is the option you will use if your organization provides you direct access to their certificate for signing, or if you registered your own certificate.

In larger organizations, it is extremely common for an individual or department to oversee the secure certificates, and individual developers are not allowed access to that certificate or the password to use it. In that case, select the other radio button, "Export an intermediate AIRI file that will be signed later."

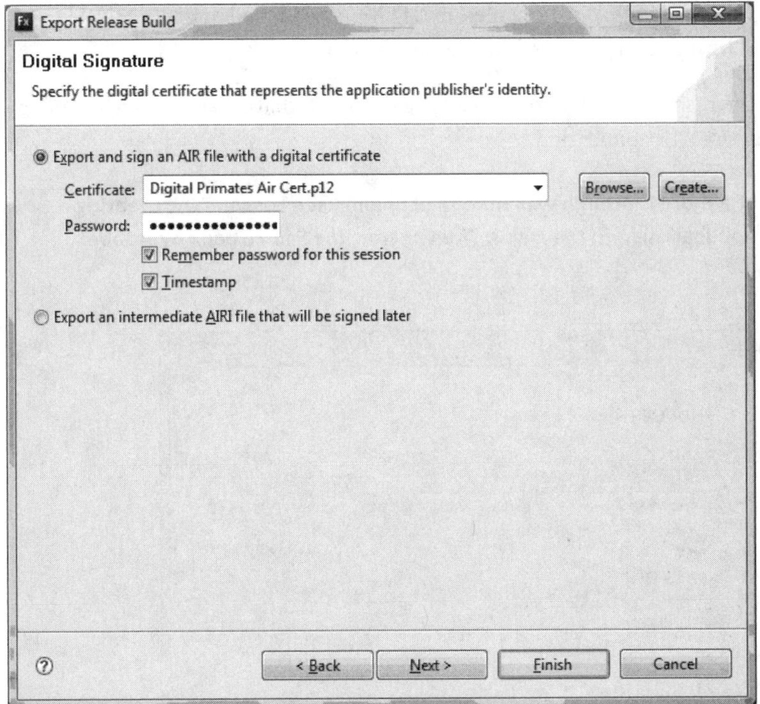

Figure 7: Specifying a Digital Signature in Flex Builder

This option allows you to export a file that contains all the relevant pieces of your application but has not yet been signed. This intermediate file cannot be used by the AIR runtime and hence cannot be distributed. This option allows the developer to control the contents of the .air file and ensure that all relevant pieces are included. The output file (.airi) of this step is then passed along to the individual or group responsible for the certificate to sign before deployment. We will discuss signing an AIRI file later in this chapter.

Including files and assets

Applications often have additional assets that must be included when the AIR application is distributed. These assets could include images that are loaded at runtime, Flex modules that are dynamically loaded, or, in the case of the dpTimeTracker, the help files for the system.

The help files are loaded from the local computer in an HTML window when the user requests help. When deploying this application, these files must be included, or the user will receive an error message. As these files are HTML and loaded dynamically, Flex does not include (link) them in the application by default.

Therefore, it is the responsibility of the developer to ensure that these files are included when packaging the AIR application.

NOTE For a more thorough explanation of linking, see Lesson 20, "Creating Modular Applications," in the *Flex 3: Training from the Source* book by Adobe Press.

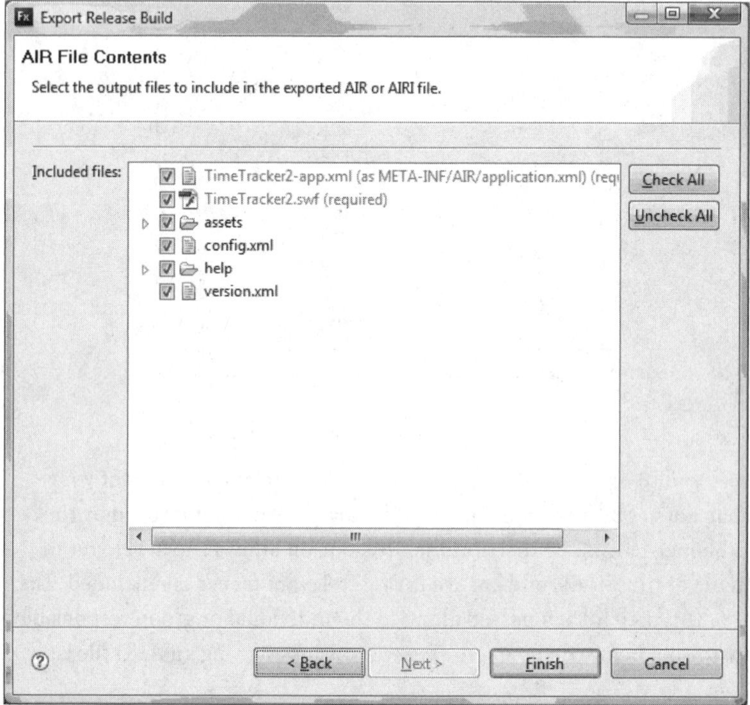

Figure 8: Including additional assets

The AIR File Contents window allows you to select whole directories or single additional files that will be included in the compressed .air file when it is deployed. Certain files (the TimeTracker2.swf and TimerTracker2-app.mxml files in this case) are required and cannot be removed from the final file.

There is one more very important and slightly confusing thing to note about the way this window works. It only shows assets and files that are not already linked into the project. For example, if Flex understands that you need image 123.jpg (either due to an

`[Embed]` directive in your code or use of this file in an included cascading style sheet), it will not appear in this list as it is already built into the final SWF file. This dialog only displays assets in your project that Flex is not planning to include and that need your intervention to include.

NOTE You must manually include an icon file specified for the application or associated files in this manner.

Including a database

In Chapter 5, "Reading and Writing to a SQLite Database," you learned to create a database and tables using SQL statements. This is an effective technique, but it leads to a fairly lengthy set of commands that need to be executed when the database is created. This is especially true if the database contains any default data.

Another more maintainable choice is to create a template database. This template database can be a SQLite database file that is included in your .air file using the technique learned in the previous section.

When the AIR application is installed, this database will be copied into the application directory. Each time the installed application starts, you can check for the existence of the database file in the application storage directory, using the `File` APIs discussed in Chapter 6, "Interacting with the File System." If the database does not exist, you can copy it from the application directory to the application storage directory using the `File` API. This provides you with the ability to make a single template database complete with tables and any preloaded data that will be the starting point for your application.

The dpTimeTracker application chooses not to use this technique because its emphasis is on teaching the SQL commands required for database manipulation.

Packaging with the Command Line

You can deploy your application using the command line instead of the Flex Builder export tools for additional control, flexibility, or simply to avoid using Flex Builder. The concepts in this section are also applicable to developers using Ant or an automated build system. Both of these methods are ways to automate project build and deployment.

To accomplish this task from the command line, you will need to use the ADT (Air Developer Tool), which is a Java application. Like all of the command line tools distributed with Flex and AIR, ADT requires some setup on your system before it can be used.

If you have not performed this setup, before continuing refer to the Adobe LiveDocs help file, "Setting up the Flex 3 SDK," which can be found at http://livedocs.adobe.com/flex/3/html/help.html?content=setup_Flex_1.html.

NOTE Even if you are only using the command line tools, refer to the section, "Packaging with Flex Builder," in this chapter for explanations and information not repeated in this section.

The basic syntax required to package and sign an AIR application on the command line is:

```
adt -package SIGNING_OPTIONS output_file_name app_xml [files_and_dirs ... ]
```

`SIGNING_OPTIONS` are the options to specify the location and type of the *keystore* (a database of keys that contain the signing certificate). To sign an AIR application with the Thawte certificate discussed previously, the options would be:

```
-storetype pkcs12 -keystore /location/of/file/myThawteCert.p12
```

output_file_name is the name of the AIR file (or AIRI intermediate file) that will be created as a result of this process.

app_xml is the path to the application.xml file that describes the AIR application and indicates the location of the main piece of content, for example, the SWF file in a Flex application. You can use relative or absolute paths for this argument.

files_and_dirs is a list of files and/or directories, delimited by whitespace, that need to be included in the .air file. This is equivalent to the AIR File Contents window in Flex Builder. The argument is always a relative path, not an absolute path. When a directory is listed, with the exception of files marked as hidden by the operating system, all the files and directories in it are recursively added.

CAUTION It is easy to make a mistake and accidently include the keystore when adding directories. This invalidates most of the security that AIR has in place, so be absolutely sure not to include the P12 file when creating your AIR file.

There are two other relevant arguments that can be used when including files. First is the `-C` option, which changes the working directory. The `-C` option can be used repeatedly in this syntax to "bounce" between different directories on the file system, including specific files that are not necessarily relative to your project directory.

The second option is the –e option, which allows you to specify a directory where a file will be placed inside the resultant .air file. By default, the relative path between your project directory and any files included is maintained. Files included from the assets directory will remain in the assets directory by default.

The following syntax demonstrates compiling the dpTimeTracker application using the command line instead of Flex Builder.

```
adt -package -storetype pkcs12 -keystore "/someFolder/
Digital Primates Air Cert.p12" TimeTracker2.air TimeTracker2-app.xml
TimeTracker2.swf assets config.xml help version.xml
```

When you run this command, your password for the certificate will be requested. If you wish to provide that password as part of the command, you can use the `-storepass` option after the `-keystore` argument.

There is one frustrating caveat for new users. This command must be run from the directory where the file specified in the <content> node of the application descriptor XML file exists. In other words, this must be run from the location where both the application descriptor XML file and the SWF file exist.

If you intend to use the command line tools, refer to the Adobe LiveDocs help file, "Packaging an AIR Installation File Using the AIR Developer Tool (ADT),"which can be found at http://livedocs.adobe.com/air/1/devappshtml/help.html?content=CommandLineTools_3.html, for a complete listing of all available options.

You can also create an .airi file from the command line for later signing. You can accomplish this by using the `-prepare` option instead of the `-package` option used in the previous example:

```
adt -prepare TimeTracker2.airi TimeTracker2-app.xml TimeTracker2.swf assets
config.xml help version.xml
```

The resultant AIRI file is not ready for distribution but is packaged and can be signed by the proper authority.

Signing an Intermediate File

Signing an intermediate (.airi) file requires using the same `adt` command, but with a `-sign` option.

The syntax for this command is:

```
adt -sign SIGNING_OPTIONS airi_file output_file_name
```

SIGNING_OPTIONS are the options to specify the location and type of the keystore. For more detail, please refer to the first example under "Packaging with the Command Line" in this chapter.

airi_file is the name of the .airi file created by either Flex Builder or the command line tools.

output_file_name is the final name of the .air file you wish to distribute.

To sign the intermediate file for the dpTimeTracker application, you would use the following syntax:

```
adt -sign -storetype pkcs12 -keystore "/someFolder/Digital Primates Air Cert.p12"
TimeTracker2.airi TimeTracker2.air
```

Migrating an AIR File

There are a small number of instances when you may want to change the certificate used to sign your AIR application. For example, you may start with a self-signed certificate and later wish to re-sign it with a purchased certificate, or you may decide to change from Thawte to VeriSign as your certificate vendor. In these cases, you can use the -migrate option of the adt command to migrate from one certificate to another.

```
adt -migrate SIGNING_OPTIONS original_air_file_name new_air_file_name.
```

SIGNING_OPTIONS are the options to specify the location and type of the keystore. For more detail, please refer to the first example under "Packaging with the Command Line" in this chapter.

original_air_file_name is the name of the .air file signed with the original certificate.

new_air_file_name is the name of the .air file that will be created with the new certificate.

For example:

```
adt -migrate -storetype pkcs12 -keystore "/someFolder/
Digital Primates Air Cert.p12" TimeTracker1.air TimeTracker2.air
```

CAUTION While this command will allow you to migrate your AIR application from one certificate to another, the update rules discussed previously in this chapter still apply. If you change certificates, users must uninstall and reinstall the application. The automatic update will not work when the certificate is changed.

Distributing an AIR Application

Now that you can package and sign an AIR application, it is time to discuss distribution methods. AIR files can be distributed in a multitude of ways, including posting on a website, using CDs, or even sending email. All of these options will work seamlessly if the user already has AIR installed on their system. The AIR runtime will recognize the file and allow the user to install it.

Unfortunately, if the user does not have the AIR runtime installed, their system will not recognize the .air file type and the application will not install. In this case, the user would need to know to first install the AIR runtime.

There are two main ways to solve this issue. First, if you are creating a media for distribution such as a CD, you can create an installer program that first installs AIR and then your application. You will need to apply for a license to redistribute the AIR runtime, but afterwards you can create a seamless experience for your users.

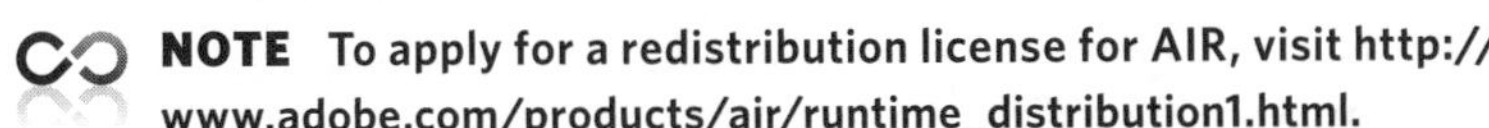

NOTE To apply for a redistribution license for AIR, visit http://www.adobe.com/products/air/runtime_distribution1.html.

The other option is to use the seamless badge install option over the web. In the next section, we will cover the seamless badge install and then briefly discuss MIME types should you wish to distribute the AIR application as a direct download.

Using the Seamless Badge Install

The seamless badge install allows a user to potentially install both Adobe AIR and your application at the same time, without manually saving and running the AIR file from their machine. To facilitate this process, it uses a special SWF file developed by Adobe called badge.swf.

The example files and necessary components to use the badge are distributed with the Flex SDK. If you use the Flex SDK from the command line, these files can be found in the samples/badge directory at the location where you installed the SDK. If you are using Flex Builder, these files can be found at /sdks/3.0.0/samples/badge relative to the directory where Flex Builder is installed. On a Windows machine, this path is C:\Program Files\Adobe\Flex Builder 3.

As of the time of writing this book, version 3.0.0 was the currently released SDK that accompanied Flex Builder. This may change, so always look for the latest version number inside the sdks directory when looking for these files.

Once you have located these samples, you will find several files pertaining to the seamless install. For now, you need to be concerned with the following files:

- AC_RunActiveContent.js—JavaScript code to interact with the browser during the download process
- badge.swf—Compiled Flash application that works with Flash Player to facilitate download
- default_badge.html—Sample HTML file that demonstrates using the badge

The installation badge that you will be working with in this section is designed to aid in the installation of Adobe AIR and your application from a web page. Due to the way Flash Player security works, the badge.swf file behaves differently if you access it from your local file system, or from a web server. Therefore, these files need to be placed on a web server to work with and test them.

To customize this default installer to deploy your application, rename the default_badge.html to a new file name that is more appropriate to your application. The name is unimportant, but it should continue to end in .html or .htm, depending on your web server and configuration.

Now open the file in a text editor. In this file, there are a series of parameters set as FlashVars (Flash Variables) that need to be modified to work with your application. The variables are set inside a function called `AC_FL_RunContent()`. In the default file, it will appear at approximately line 59. The line should read:

```
'flashvars','appname=My%20Application&appurl=myapp.air&airversion=
1.0&imageurl=test.jpg',
```

There are up to six different parameters that can be contained within this single line of code. Some of these parameters are necessary to allow proper functioning of the installation badge. Others can be modified to simply change the visual appearance.

- `appname` (required)—The name of the application. This name is displayed by the badge.swf file when the AIR runtime is not yet installed.
- `appurl` (required)—Must be an absolute URL to the AIR application required for download. The badge.swf makes a second connection when it is time to download this AIR application, so this must be an absolute, not relative URL.
- `airversion` (required)—This is the version of AIR required to correctly run your application. Right now, valid choices are “1.0” or “1.1”.

- `imageurl` (optional)—The URL of an image to display in the install badge.
- `buttoncolor` (optional)—A hex color for the color of the button prompting the user to download.
- `messagecolor` (optional)—A hex color for the text displayed below the download button when the AIR runtime is not yet installed.

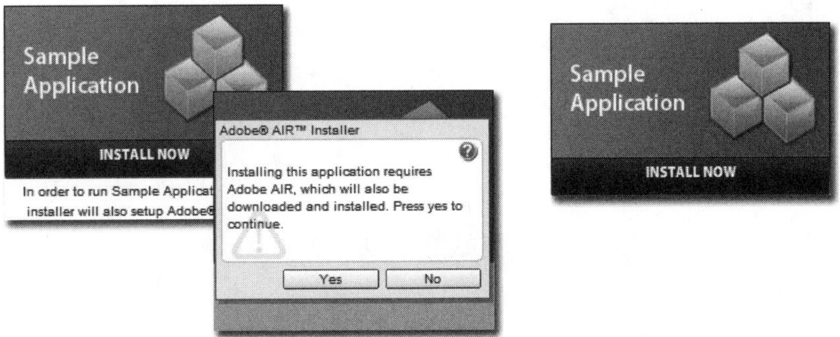

Figure 9: Install Badge shows both when AIR is not installed and when it is installed on the user machine, respectively.

The installation badge must be at least 217 by 180 to fit the required content; however, using the `width` and `height` parameters, you can increase this size as desired.

If this file is deployed to a web server, and your AIR application is available at the specified URL, you should be able to navigate to this web page and experience the seamless install. If you already have AIR installed, you may wish to uninstall it now to understand the entire user experience.

Customizing the Badge

The installation badge can be completely customized by someone with Flash experience. While it is well beyond the scope of this book to teach Flash or the Flash environment, critical information needed to modify that badge will be provided here for any adventurous spirits who wish to pursue this avenue.

Included in the files found in the samples/badge directory under the SDK file named badge.fla. An FLA file is the format that the Flash IDE uses. If you have Flash installed on your system, you can open this file and make any visual changes you desire.

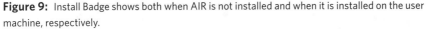

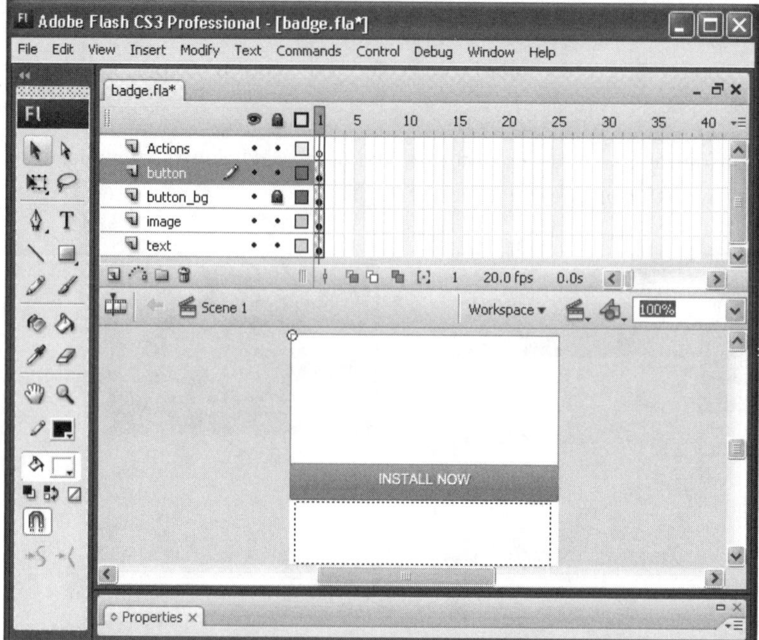

Figure 10: Editing the badge.fla file inside Flash CS3 Professional

However, the types of changes you can make to the badge.swf application go well beyond simple visual changes. You can enhance this file significantly to make the download and install experience even better for the user.

The badge.fla file contains the visual components, but the actual code for the badge functionality is contained in both an ActionScript base class in the AIRBadge.as file and another SWF file named air.swf, which is loaded when the badge.swf loads. This ActionScript class has several functions; one is called when the air.swf successfully downloads and is ready: `onInit()`. The other is called when the button is clicked: `onButtonClicked()`. There are also a few functions for validating URLS and other utility functions.

 **NOTE The air.swf file is hosted by Adobe (http://airdownload.adobe.com/air/browserapi/air.swf). It interacts with the browser and AIR to provide additional functionality.**

Some of the functionality provided by the air.swf file is the ability to determine if AIR is installed on the machine or if it can be installed at all. You can also check if an application is already installed, install an application, and even launch an application that has already been installed.

These functions are provided by the air.swf file, meaning that you can load the air.swf file into your own Flash application, and create a totally custom experience for your users.

Figure 11: A customized installation badge

Using Express Install

One final but very important note is that the installation badge will only work on Flash Player versions 9.0.115 and above. If your user has an older version of Flash Player, they will either need to install AIR manually before continuing, or you can force the user to update Flash Player. The user's Flash Player version can be updated in a minimally intrusive way using a feature called Express Install. Once the Flash Player upgrade is complete, the AIR and AIR application process can restart, allowing seamless installation.

This method requires some additional code from Adobe referred to as the Flash Player detection kit. While explaining the use of this kit is beyond the scope of this book, it is a useful process if your application is likely to be downloaded by individuals with older Flash Player versions.

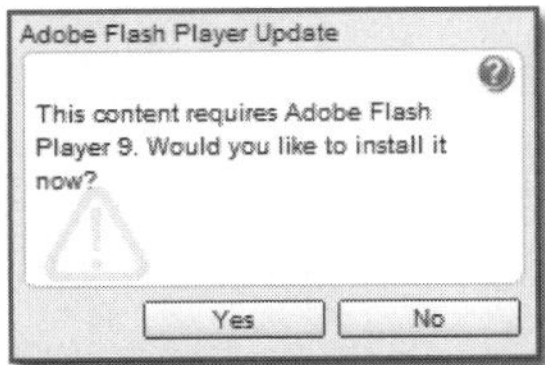

Figure 12: The Flash Player Express Install dialog

A great article on the need for Flash Player detection and instructions explaining how to use Flash Player Express Install can be found at http://www.adobe.com/devnet/flash/articles/fp8_detection.html.

Using Pre-Customized Badges

As of the time of writing this book, there are several projects providing new and innovative types of installation badges. One such project was created by Grant Skinner and may be integrated into a future version of AIR. It pre-integrates the Flash Player Express Install features along with an installation process that takes full advantage of the features available in the air.swf.

You can find more information about this install badge at the Adobe Labs site (http://labs.adobe.com/wiki/index.php/AIR_Badge).

Next Steps

You now have a good understanding of packaging, signing, and deploying AIR applications. As AIR continues to be adopted, more examples of custom installation options will become available online. Continue to watch for these, and examine the code Adobe distributes to stay on the cutting edge of this topic.

UNDERSTANDING AIR SECURITY

CHAPTER 14

As you have discovered throughout the chapters in this book, Adobe AIR gives developers from a web application or RIA background the ability to create highly interactive and powerful applications that are deployed to the user's computer. This simple statement reveals a fundamental point of the utmost importance: these applications have left the relative safety of the web browser and now exist on the user's machine. They now have access to the file system, databases, and other system resources that they never before had. Consequently, as the developer of these applications, you need to leave the mindset of the web browser behind as well.

AIR applications can be powerful. When written poorly, they can permit someone with malicious intent to steal or destroy data, take over a computer, and ultimately destroy the ability of that machine to function in a usable fashion. The AIR runtime imposes security constraints that reduce the likelihood of these events occurring, but ultimately, as the developer, it is up to you to work within these constraints and guidelines to protect the end users of your application.

Web and Desktop Security Differences

Even developers are users of Internet and desktop applications. You may write software, but you also use software written by others. Perhaps without consciously realizing it, you make a lot of choices and have a lot of expectations about how software will work and what it might be able to do to your system. These choices and expectations are certainly influenced by the publisher of the software and your previous experiences with similar software; however, ultimately the method in which the software was deployed makes a huge difference.

With few exceptions, people generally feel safe visiting a website. This is not to say security threats do not exist in this environment, but overall, people are comfortable with the buffer the web browser provides. This buffer keeps websites and applications feeling rather remote compared to a word processing or development tool on your machine, but it also provides a feeling of safety, regardless of the individual that created the original content. Those of you from a web development background know that when a web browser delivers a web page or Internet application, it is often delivered in pieces; that is, different scripts are included on different pages, and often additional code, modules, or libraries are downloaded as you move into new areas of applications. This additional code and scripting doesn't often factor into your perception of security; it is simply a fact of life for web-based applications.

Consider for a moment how contrary that is to the desktop application experience. In general, people do not feel safe downloading and installing an executable file on their desktop unless it is from a well-known publisher. Once a piece of code is downloaded, users generally have to agree or acknowledge some risk simply to install it at all. Individuals who do download and install arbitrary code on their machines often suffer the fate of viruses and trojans, and are usually heartily chided for agreeing to install something they didn't trust. There is absolutely no expectation of safety when downloading and running an application.

Further, if you download a product and it wishes to install additional code, modules, fonts, clipart, and so on, it would likely be considered a bad application if it did not first re-ask your permission to do so. This is exactly the opposite of a web-based application, which is continually reconstructing code or adding new pieces as you navigate.

All of this equates to two very large problems. Developers constructing AIR applications are deploying their application in a way that users do not inherently trust, however, they are used to constructing their applications in a way that was only acceptable due to the high trust of the web browser. Further continuing to follow many of the practices and techniques used to construct applications within the safety of the web browser would expose the users of these applications to undue risk when the application runs as a desktop application.

Ultimately, this means that developers need to learn a new set of rules and techniques, but most importantly, they need to understand that there are extremely valid reasons for the security layers that AIR imposes. Working within these new rule sets and not attempting to work around the AIR security is the only way to ensure that your desktop application will not become the gateway for a hacker to explore your end user's computer.

AIR Security Specifics

Before diving into how AIR security works, it is important to understand that the AIR security model is still subject to the operating system security model. The operating system ultimately governs how the user interacts with AIR and with AIR applications. For instance, an AIR application will only be allowed to read or write files from a location if the operating system grants the user running that application those permissions.

Windows provides some additional control for administrators over the user's interaction with AIR in the form of three registry keys found under HKey_Local_Machine\Software\Policies\Adobe\AIR.

- **AppInstallDisabled**—Can contain the values 0 or 1. A value of 0 means that application installation and uninstallation is allowed, whereas a 1 disallows this feature.
- **UntrustedAppInstallDisabled**—Can also contain a 0 or 1. This key relates to the digital certificates discussed in Chapter 13, "Deploying Air Applications." If the value of this key is 1, then applications signed with a self-signed certificate cannot be installed. Only applications signed with a trusted certificate can be installed.
- **UpdateDisabled**—Also contains a 0 or 1. This key relates to the AIR runtime, and not the applications installed on your machine. If the value 1 appears in this key, then the AIR runtime cannot be updated.

Keeping these restrictions in mind, the following sections will demonstrate the additional security (beyond the operating system) provided by the AIR runtime.

Sandboxes

At the heart of the AIR security model is the concept of sandboxes. Sandboxes are simply logical groupings of files in an AIR application based on their original location. Different sandboxes are allowed different types of access to system, remote, and local resources. While communication between sandboxes is tightly controlled, files in the same sandbox are allowed to interact with each other freely.

AIR uses five main types of sandboxes:

- **Application**—The application sandbox contains any code that lives in the application's installation directory. Items in this directory were likely installed with the original .air file or a subsequent update and have full access to call any method of the AIR APIs.

  The AIR/Flex help files identify the methods that can only be called in the `application` security sandbox by placing an AIR logo next to their name.

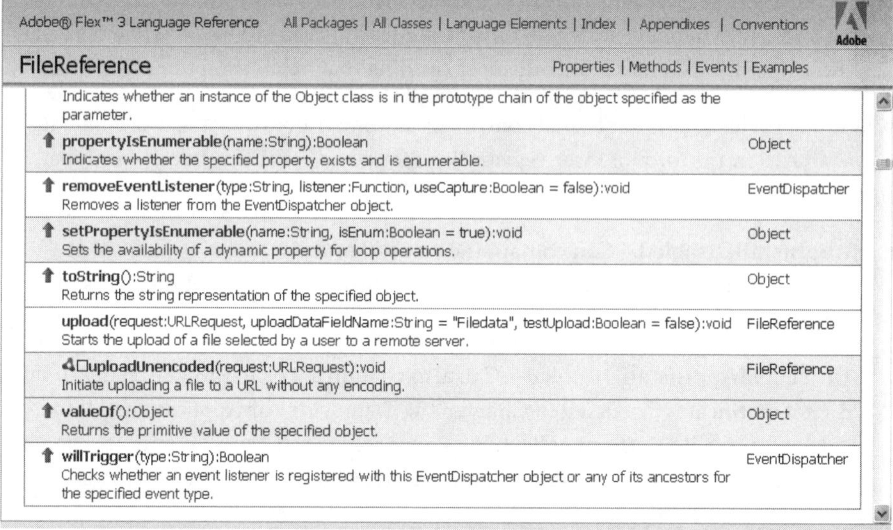

Figure 1: AIR Help files indicating that the `uploadUnencoded()` method may only be called in the `application` sandbox

  AIR applications are often highly interactive applications that take advantage of installed content and on-demand content from the Internet and other sources. As such, they are rarely composed of just files in the `application` sandbox. Files that are not installed with the application will exist in one of four different sandboxes, dependent on their origin. Collectively the sandboxes are simply called *non-application* sandboxes.

- `remote`—Files placed into the `remote` sandbox are downloaded from the Internet to the user's computer. Your application may have many `remote` sandboxes, each based on the domain of the file's original location. In other words, files downloaded from http://www.digitalprimates.net will exist in a different `remote` sandbox than files downloaded from http://blogs.digitalprimates.net.

  There are additional rules when content is loaded from a secure domain such as https://www.digitalprimates.net. To separate all of these files into `remote` sandboxes, AIR normally uses DNS (Domain Name Service) information. However, this information is not secure and is subject to being spoofed by individuals with malicious intent. When a file is downloaded via https, AIR can use the domain's secure certificate to verify the domain information. Therefore to maintain a high level of security, files downloaded from http://www.digitalprimates.net will, by default, not be able to access files downloaded from https://www.digitalprimates.net. However, files from https://www.digitalprimates.net can access files from http://www.digitalprimates.net.

- `local-with-filesystem`—By default, SWF or JavaScript files loaded from any location (on the user's hard drive or a shared drive over a network) other than the application directory are loaded into this sandbox. Files in this sandbox may read other files on the local hard drive but may not communicate over the network or make any type of request to a server.

- `local-with-networking`—Files loaded into this sandbox are allowed to communicate freely over a network and make server requests. However, they are not allowed to read any local files. Only SWF content can exist in this sandbox.

- `local-trusted`—Files in the `local-trusted` sandbox are files designated by the user as safe and can both read local files and communicate on the network. However, these files still will not have full access to the AIR APIs granted by the `application` sandbox.

If you attempt to call a method or access a property of the AIR API that is restricted to the `application` sandbox from any of the non-application sandboxes, AIR will throw a `SecurityError`.

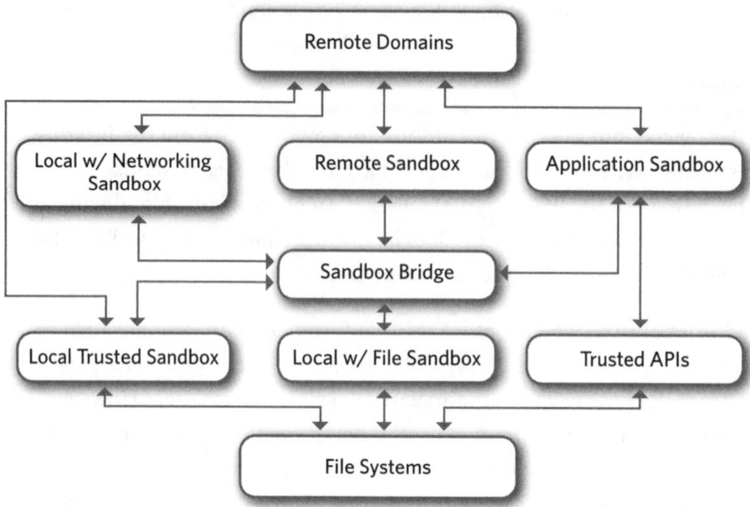

Figure 2: Air security sandbox diagram

This image demonstrates the relationship of the various sandboxes and how they communicate with each other to provide complete application capabilities. Taking the time to understand this relationship will help immensely as you write complicated applications.

Restrictions on the Application Sandbox

To keep the user's system secure, there are also some important restrictions placed on AIR content in the `application` sandbox. These restrictions mainly ensure that files installed in the application directory on startup do not accidently or purposefully grant unauthorized access to items that were not present during installation.

Flex/ActionScript

Flex and Flash developers should be accustomed to working in the Flash Player sandboxes. All the rules from that environment, including cross-domain talking, still apply; however there are several new limitations imposed on Flex and ActionScript. They include the following.

No access to persistent cache

When using Flex 3 with Flash Player 9 update 3 and later, Flash Player could download, save, and reuse a copy of the Flex framework as a library. This meant that many Flex applications could be reduced in size, by factoring the needed framework code into a library. AIR does not allow this feature. Doing so would effectively add code to the `application` sandbox after installation.

HTML content in an ActionScript TextField

When displaying HTML content in an ActionScript TextField component that resides in the `application` sandbox, `<img/>` tags are completely ignored. This is designed to prevent some types of phishing attacks.

Dynamic code with ActionScript

Flex has a class named `Loader` with a method named `loadBytes()`. This method allows the developer to create SWF content from a byte array. Unfortunately, this means that an application could load content from a remote server and then pass the content through this method to create executable code.

The `loadBytes()` method, however, is also extremely useful when creating images, sounds, and other binary assets. As such, this feature is still allowed, but by default, the `loadBytes()` method does not let you load SWF content—only images. The `loadBytes()` method takes two parameters: the first is a byte array, and the second is an instance of a `LoaderContext` class. When using AIR, you can override the default behavior and allow AIR to load executable code by setting the `allowLoadBytesCodeExecution` property to `true` on the `LoaderContext` instance.

HTML/JavaScript

There are many more restrictions placed on HTML and JavaScript interactions within the `application` security sandbox to overcome potential security holes created by dynamic code generation and manipulation.

This book is mainly about working with Flex and AIR applications. The following information is provided for you, should you be attempting to use HTML content in AIR as well. However, teaching the JavaScript and HTML interaction is beyond the scope of this book. If you are not familiar with the terms that follow, or if you are working with

Advanced HTML/JavaScript content, a book specifically on that subject may be warranted. At the time of this writing, the only known, well-reviewed resource specifically for HTML/JavaScript developers is the *Adobe AIR for JavaScript Developers Pocket Guide*, by Chambers, Dura, Georgita and Hoyt. It can be found online at http://onair.adobe.com/files/AIRforJSDevPocketGuide.pdf. This resource is currently only available for AIR 1.0, and it is unknown at this time if it will be kept up-to-date with future revisions.

Dynamic code with JavaScript

The largest restrictions placed on JavaScript in the `application` sandbox deal with dynamic code generation. AIR restricts, but does not eliminate, the use of dynamic code generation inside the `application` sandbox. Instead, these methods can be used while the application code is loading (in the `onload` handler), but not during the remainder of the application's execution. This means that these methods can be used after the onload event is broadcast from the body element and before the `onload` handler finishes executing.

Following are several ways dynamically generated code is often created, all of which are disallowed after the `onload` handler finishes:

- Using the `eval()` function to turn a string into an executable object. This prohibition includes function definition and invocation, property sets and reads, and object literal setters and getters. However, you are allowed to use the `eval()` function to evaluate simple literals:

  ```
  eval("1+2")
  ```

NOTE For a complete list of allowed and disallowed items, refer to "HTML Security" in *Developing Adobe AIR 1.1 Applications with Adobe Flex 3*. This can be found at http://help.adobe.com/en_US/AIR/1.1/devappsflex/WS5b3ccc516d4fbf351e63e3d118666ade46-7f11.html.

- Inserting script tags with help of `innerHTML` or DOM functions. These script tags often have a `src` property that refers to a file outside the `application` sandbox or inline code.

- Calling `document.write()` or `document.writeln()` methods.

- Passing a string to be evaluated as opposed to a function name to the first parameter of either the `setInterval()` or `setTimeout()` function.

- Passing JavaScript to the URL scheme. For example:

```
<a href="javascript:doSomething('withThis')">Click Me</a>
```

XMLHttpRequest

HTML content in the `application` sandbox is disallowed from using synchronous XMLHttpRequest methods to load data from outside the application while the application is still loading.

Windowing

Content in the `application` security sandbox can call the `Window.open()` method to display content. However, if the content it displays is not from any non-application security sandbox, then the window title will always be preceded with the name of the main application and a colon: `( MyApp: )`

You are also disallowed from moving the window in such away as to hide the `( MyApp: )` portion.

Permissions for Non-Application Sandboxes

Many of the items disallowed for content in the `application` security sandbox are perfectly allowable for files in non-application sandboxes. However, there are additional restrictions that pertain to this group as a whole and to individual members of the group (such as `local-with-filesystem`).

Content in the non-application sandbox cannot directly call methods or access properties of content in the `application` security sandbox. It is also unable to directly invoke any methods restricted to the `application` sandbox by the AIR API.

Unlike code in the `application` security sandbox, code in the non-application security sandbox can use the `eval()` and related techniques to generate code at any time, without restriction.

XMLHttpRequest

Use of XMLHttpRequest methods is also changed in these sandboxes. These methods can be used at any time in the non-application sandboxes, however, by default, they are not allowed to load data from any domain other than the domain where the content originated. Both the frame and iframe tags include an `allowcrossdomainxhr` attribute, which, when set to `true`, will override this default.

Windowing

Finally, content in non-application security domains can only call the `Window.open()` method in response to an event caused by keyboard or mouse interaction. In other words, a window cannot be opened on startup, by a timer, or at any arbitrary time in the code. This prevents dynamically loaded code from creating deceptive login and other windows.

Violating any of these security restrictions will result in the JavaScript error, "Adobe AIR runtime security violation for JavaScript code in the application security sandbox."

Cross-Sandbox Communication

As mentioned earlier, AIR applications often take advantage of installed content and on-demand content from the Internet and other sources. However, to be truly interactive, content in the various sandboxes discussed so far must be able to communicate in some capacity. To facilitate this effort in a secure way, AIR offers a concept called sandbox bridges.

Sandbox bridges provide security by defining and limiting the methods that can be called across the sandboxes. When used carefully and appropriately, this methodology allows a great deal of security while still allowing communication in critical areas. Care must still be taken by the developer to ensure that methods called via the sandbox bridge do not give undue access to code running from non-application sandboxes.

The following code demonstrates two separate applications, ParentApp, which is the parent application, and ChildApp, which is the child application. ParentApp has a label that initially displays the text "Start Up".

```
<?xml version="1.0" encoding="utf-8"?>
<mx:WindowedApplication xmlns:mx="http://www.adobe.com/2006/mxml"
layout="absolute" creationComplete="initMe()">
    <mx:Script>
        <![CDATA[
            import flash.display.Loader;
            import flash.net.URLRequest;

            private var childApp:Loader;
```

```
            private function initMe():void {
                var urlRequest:URLRequest = new URLRequest("ChildApp.swf")

                var bridge:LabelUpdateBridge = new LabelUpdateBridge( this );

                childApp = new Loader();
                childApp.contentLoaderInfo.parentSandboxBridge = bridge;
                childApp.load( urlRequest );

                this.rawChildren.addChild( childApp );
            }
        ]]>
    </mx:Script>
    <mx:Label id="lbl" text="Start Up" top="60" left="25"/>
</mx:WindowedApplication>
```

On creationComplete, ParentApp creates a new instance of the LabelUpdateBridge() class and passes it a reference to the application. This class will be examined in a moment. Next, a new Loader class is instantiated to load ChildApp. The Loader has a property named contentLoader Info, which is an instance of the LoaderInfo class. The instance of the LoaderInfo object will later be available to the child application.

The LoaderInfo object has two interesting properties, one named parentSandboxBridge and one named childSandboxBridge. The parentSandboxBridge is used here to provide a bridge from the child to the parent for calling methods. The child can in turn set the childSandboxBridge to provide a bridge for the parent to call methods on the child.

Only the parent can set the parentSandboxBridge property, and only the child can set the childSandboxBridge property, else a SecurityError is thrown.

The ChildApp is a Flex application that calls the methods of the LabelUpdateBridge class when the button is clicked.

```
<?xml version="1.0" encoding="utf-8"?>
<mx:Application xmlns:mx="http://www.adobe.com/2006/mxml" layout="absolute"
    width="110" height="30">
    <mx:Script>
        <![CDATA[
            private function handleButtonClick( event:MouseEvent ):void {
                var labelInterface:Object =
                ➥Object( loaderInfo ).parentSandboxBridge;
```

```
                labelInterface.setLabelValue( "AIR" );
                trace( labelInterface.getLabelValue() );
            }
        ]]>
    </mx:Script>
    <mx:Button label="Change Label" click="handleButtonClick(event)"/>
</mx:Application>
```

When the button is clicked, the handleButtonClick() method is called. It obtains a reference to the parentSandboxBridge from the application's loaderInfo object. In this case, the ChildApp is a Flex application, so it is unaware of the parentSandboxBridge property. Casting it as an object prevents the Flex compiler from complaining, allowing you to access this property and retrieve the LabelUpdateBridge. Next, the set method is used to set the label in the parent application to "AIR," and then finally trace the new value out to the console.

The LabelUpdateBridge class defines the methods the child is allowed to call on the parent.

```
package {
    import mx.core.WindowedApplication;

    public class LabelUpdateBridge {
        private var myapplication:ParentApp;

        public function setLabelValue( value:String ):void {
            myapplication.lbl.text = value;
        }

        public function getLabelValue():String {
            return myapplication.lbl.text;
        }

        public function LabelUpdateBridge( application:ParentApp ) {
            myapplication = application;
        }
    }
}
```

The methods in this bridge allow us to update and retrieve the value of the label without actually allowing the child any access to the objects in the parent application.

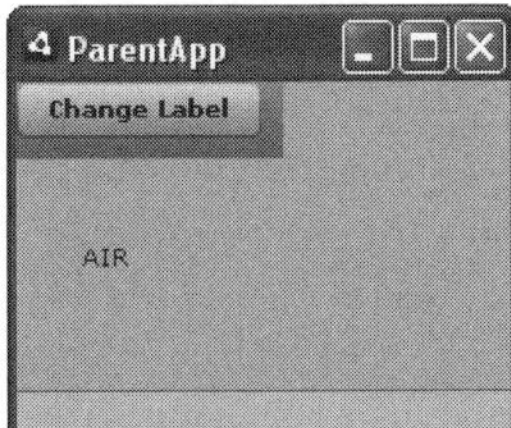

Figure 3: Sandbox bridge at work

Bridges also work in the same way for HTML content as they do for SWF content. AIR adds properties named `parentSandboxBridge` and `childSandboxBridge` to the window object of child frames. For example:

```
var bridge = {};
bridge.getLabelValue = function(){
    return someObject.someProperty;
}

window.childSandboxBridge = bridge;
```

Data moving between the child and parent via the sandbox bridges is serialized. This means that all data is passed by value and not by reference. Further, the data will be untyped after the transfer and cannot be complex object types.

While the sandbox bridge does a tremendous job of forcing developers to isolate their code for security purposes, it is still up to the developer to grant minimal access to content in the `application` security sandbox. You should not create overly broad APIs that take variables or call any method you would like. You must create narrow and specific APIs to ensure that security is maintained.

Finally, if possible, favor using the `childSandboxBridge` over the `parentSandboxBridge`. This means that the higher security code in the `application` security sandbox will be allowed to access methods in the lower security non-application sandbox, but not the other way around.

The Encrypted Store

Using the File and SQLite APIs, you now have the unprecedented ability to store information on a user's machine. However, the type of information and how it is stored still needs careful consideration.

Storing login credentials or personal information, such as identification numbers or credit information, on a local machine in a standard file or SQLite database is making it available for anyone to see. Your AIR application is only one way that this information can be accessed; once it is on the file system, any application with permission can open it.

AIR provides a potential solution for some use cases called the *encrypted local store.* The encrypted local store ties into the DPAPI (Data ProtectionAPI) on Microsoft Windows and the KeyChain on Mac to provide an encrypted and secured way to store some information. Every AIR application and user of your system will be able to retrieve their own local store.

For example, suppose you have two users of the time clock AIR application: Mike and Jeff. Any information stored by Jeff when using the time clock application will not be readable by Mike. Further, when using a different AIR application, Jeff would be unable to read his own information as stored by the time clock. The encrypted local store is only available to the `application` security sandbox.

This is an ideal method to store sensitive information, and it has a generous total capacity of 10 megabytes. This amount is sufficient as the information kept in this store is generally small and should not consist of an entire database or the like.

The `EncryptedLocalStore` class has a few static methods to allow manipulation of the data.

```
setItem(name:String, data:ByteArray, stronglyBound:Boolean = false):void
```

The `setItem()` method accepts a string, which acts as an object key. The data, which is in the form of a ByteArray, is the next parameter and finally a Boolean called `stronglyBound`.

The `stronglyBound` parameter determines which applications are allowed to access encrypted data. By default, the publisher ID of the application is used to determine uniqueness. This means that two applications with the exact publisher ID of "MyCalculator" would be able to access each other's data. Setting this parameter to `true` goes further by not only using the publisher ID of the application to guard the store, but actually uses a hash of the application itself. This is a very useful and secure option to ensure that no other application can read your data. However, if your application changes for any reason, for instance an upgrade, the data will be irretrievable.

```
getItem(name:String):ByteArray
```

The getItem() method accepts the same string as setItem() and returns the ByteArray stored in the encrypted store.

```
removeItem(name:String):void
```

The removeItem() method accepts the same string as setItem() and removes the data from the store.

```
reset():void
```

The reset() method clears the entire store of data.

Encrypted Store in the Time Tracker Application

The dpTimeTracker application makes use of the encrypted store to store the user's login credentials and queries the store to verify these credentials upon login. The dpTimeTracker was meant to be used in an environment where a single Windows username might grant access to the system, but different users would log in and out of the application throughout the day. Therefore, a <user/> XML node is stored for each potential user in the application along with their user id and other critical information.

The <user/> node has the following format:

```
<user>
        <id/>
        <username/>
        <password/>
        <serverUsername/>
        <serverPassword/>
</user>
```

The username and password grant access to the application. The server username and password are stored if the user is synchronizing their time data to a service such as Harvest.

Looking at the UserHelper.as file in the helpers package of the application, you will see several functions used to work with the encrypted store. For a high-level overview of the process, examine the addUserToEncryptedStore() method:

```
public static function addUserToEncryptedStore( id:String,
➥ username:String, password:String, serverUsername:String="",
```

```
    ➥ serverPassword:String="" ):void {
    var users:XML = getUsersFromStore();

    //compose a new user xml node
    var user:XML = <user/>;
    user.appendChild( "<id>" + id + "</id>" );
    user.appendChild( "<username>" + username + "</username>" );
    user.appendChild( "<password>" + password + "</password>" );
    user.appendChild( "<serverUsername>" + serverUsername +
    ➥ "</serverUsername>" );
    user.appendChild( "<serverPassword>" + serverPassword + "</serverPassword>" );

    //append it to our users xml
    users.appendChild( user );

    writeUserToStore( users );
}
```

The method takes all of the critical user information, retrieves the existing users from the store using a method named `getUsersFromStore()`, makes the appropriate changes, and then writes the users back to the store using the `writeUserToStore()` method.

Examine the `getUsersFromStore()` method next:

```
private static function getUsersFromStore():XML {
    var encryptedUsers:ByteArray = EncryptedLocalStore.getItem("users");
    var users:XML = <users/>;

    if ( encryptedUsers ) {

        encryptedUsers.position = 0;
        encryptedUsers.uncompress(CompressionAlgorithm.DEFLATE);
        encryptedUsers.position = 0;

        // read XML Object
        users = encryptedUsers.readObject();
    }

    return users;
}
```

The method retrieves an item named users from the encrypted store. The data retrieved will be a ByteArray. If there is user data in the ByteArray, decompress it using a method of the `ByteArray` class and then use the `readObject()` method to turn the ByteArray back into XML.

The `writeUserToStore()` method performs the opposite function.

```
private static function writeUserToStore( users:XML ):void {
    //compress and store it in the encrypted store
    var bytes:ByteArray = new ByteArray();
    bytes.writeObject(users);
    bytes.position = 0;
    bytes.compress( CompressionAlgorithm.DEFLATE );
    EncryptedLocalStore.setItem("users", bytes);
}
```

This method takes a valid user's XML object, writes it into a ByteArray, compresses it, and saves it back to the encrypted store for future reference.

```
public static function usernamePasswordMatch( username:String,
➥password:String ):Boolean {
    var users:XML = getUsersFromStore();
    var user:XML = getUserXML( username, users );

    if ( user && ( user.password == password ) ) {
        return true;
    }

    return false;
}
```

When a user logs in, the ByteArray is retrieved from the encrypted store; then it is decompressed, and the code browses the XML for a matching username and password. The benefit of this approach is that the usernames and passwords for both the local application (and perhaps even more importantly for the remote server) are stored in an encrypted and safe fashion.

Worst Practices

Every application you write will need to exercise and obey these security constraints and APIs in different ways. Instead of recommending a series of practices to follow, this is a list of things to avoid at all cost as they may well compromise your application and, more importantly, your user's machine.

Using Input or Dynamic Data as Parameters

You are taking a large risk anytime you accept user input and pass it directly along to any API, but this is particularly true now that your application will have direct access to someone's computer.

Using SQL injection

In Chapter 5, "Reading and Writing to a SQLite Database," you learned briefly about a SQL injection attack. This attack occurs when a user intentionally enters malicious text into an input of some type (URL parameter, TextInput, and so on). This input is then passed along to the database and executed. For example, suppose you have a SQL query that returns all the records for a given user based on a user ID.

```
SELECT * FROM AccountHistory WHERE UserID = textInput.text;
```

This is a simplistic example, but if a user enters the number *5* in the textInput field, the following statement will be passed to the database for evaluation:

```
SELECT * FROM AccountHistory WHERE UserID = 5;
```

This query will return the user's account history and display it in a datagrid. However, if the user chose to enter the text *5 or 1=1*, then the following statement will be passed to the database for evaluation.

```
SELECT * FROM AccountHistory WHERE UserID = 5 OR 1=1;
```

In this case, all of the account history for every user in the system will be returned and displayed. This is a basic example, but it demonstrates the types of things you need to consider when writing applications.

Allowing file manipulation

A similar attack can be used with the File API. Take the example of an offline photo book application that reads an XML file from a remote location. That file contains a list of filenames for each file and a URL of the file to download it.

For example:

```
<images>
    <image>
        <fileName>mypic1.jpg</fileName>
        <url>http://www.digitalprimates.net/photos/somepic.jpg</url>
    </image>
</images>
```

The application will download and store this photo. This is fine unless this single XML file were hacked or manipulated. The following code is a somewhat fictitious example:

```
<images>
    <image>
        <fileName>somethingBad.exe</fileName>
        <url>http://www.somesite.net/somethingAwful.jpg</url>
    </image>
    <image>
        <fileName>C:\ProgramData\Start Menu\Programs\Startup\runMe.lnk</
fileName>
        <url>http://www.somesite.net/windowsShortcut.lnk</url>
    </image>
</images>
```

This example probably wouldn't work with even minimal security in place. However, it demonstrates that using dynamic data as direct input to these types of APIs exposes a single point of attack where someone with malicious intent could take over any machine running your application.

Allowing code injection

Building on the previous example, imagine a very dynamic application that chooses to not just load images but to load SWF content using the `loadBytes()` method of the `Loader` class. Once again, corrupting or attacking a single point (the location where the XML file or other data file resides) could result in exposing all users of your application to security issues.

This particular example is much worse. If your application uses the `loadBytes()` method and a malicious individual manages to substitute their own SWF file for yours, there is very little to stop them from causing serious damage.

Try not to load executable code with this method if possible. If you must, certainly do not use user input or the result of a data call to determine the SWF file to load.

Betraying Trust in Your AIR Package

Users will need to trust your application to install it. If they do install it, try not to disappoint them by doing the following things.

Self-signing your application

Purchasing a certificate is an extra expense, and you may be tempted to skip this step, but there are many valid reasons to go through this extra hurdle. Sign your applications with a real certificate, and demonstrate to your users that you care about the integrity of your code and their computer.

Including untrusted or unused files in the AIR file

Every file and piece of code in your AIR application is a potential place where a bug or security hole exists. These files will have full access to the AIR APIs, so do not include any files that you do not trust implicitly. Further, do not include anything extraneous that you may or may not use in the future. These are all potential locations for a security failure.

Forgetting about upgrading your application

Take the extra time to write update procedures into your application, and check for updates on a regular basis. One possible attack against an AIR application is to downgrade it to a previous version. It is not uncommon to discover an error or security issue in your application and publish a new version.

However, when the AIR application updater runs, it merely ensures that the version you are installing is different than the one installed. It does not know that version 3.01a is actually newer than version 2.02b. Therefore, it could let a user downgrade to a version that has a known bug. Not checking if your application is the latest version and not prompting the user to upgrade enables this possibility.

Next Steps

You now have a basic understanding of the AIR APIs; some thoughts on an application framework; and the ability to create, test, and interact with AIR. The next step is building applications and discovering the areas that you personally find interesting and want to learn more about. Enjoy.

GETTING STARTED WITH AIR

APPENDIX A

You can create AIR applications using an IDE such as Adobe Flex Builder 3 (for SWF-based content) and Aptana (for HTML-based content), or using a set of command line tools. While the majority of this book assumes you are working with Flex Builder, this appendix shows how to install both Flex Builder and command line tools.

AIR Tools

There are two key components to AIR—the runtime and the Software Development Kit (SDK). The runtime is needed to run any AIR application, but the SDK is needed only by AIR application developers.

The first step in using or building an AIR application is to have its runtime available. The runtime acts as a virtual machine for AIR applications, providing a base layer between the application and your operating system. It is this runtime that allows the same AIR application to run identically across all supported operating systems.

Runtime System Requirements

The minimum requirements to run AIR are:

Windows:	Macintosh:
1GHz or faster	PowerPC G4 1GHz or Intel Core Duo 1.83GHz or faster
512MB RAM	512MB RAM
Windows 2000 SP4 or XP SP2 or Vista	OSX 10.4.910 or 10.5.1 (PowerPc)
	OSX 10.4.9 or 10.5.1 (Intel)

NOTE At the time this book was written, support for the AIR runtime on Linux was not yet available. While this has been promised for a near future release, its system requirements are not yet known, as it is not yet supported.

Installing the AIR Runtime

Most end users will have the runtime installed automatically when they install their first AIR application. However, developers may often find it necessary to install the runtime independently.

Installing on Windows

1. Download the AIR runtime installer for Windows from the Adobe site (http://www.adobe.com/go/getair).
2. Double-click the AdobeAIRInstaller.exe file. An installation progress window displays.
3. When the installation is complete, click Finish.

Installing on Mac OS

1. Download the AIR runtime installer for Macintosh from the Adobe site (http://www.adobe.com/go/getair).
2. Double-click the AIR.pkg file. The Install Adobe Integrated Runtime 1.0 window displays.
3. Click the Continue button in the lower-left corner of the window. The Select a Destination page of the installer displays.
4. Select the destination volume, and click the Continue button. The Easy Install button displays.
5. Click the Easy Install button in the lower-left corner of the window. If the installer displays an Authenticate window, enter your Mac OS username and password.
6. After the installation completes, click the Close button in the lower-right corner of the installation window.

Getting the SDK

The SDK is required to build AIR applications.

The Adobe AIR SDK provides the tools necessary to build and deploy Adobe AIR applications, including the schema and template for the application.xml manifest file, AIR APIs, Adobe AIR application install badge, AIR Debug Launcher (ADL), and AIR Developer Tool (ADT). You can download the SDK from www.adobe.com/products/air/tools/sdk/. The downloaded file is a compressed archive (.zip on Windows, .dmg on Mac) that you can extract to a directory on your machine.

TIP **If you plan on working with the command line tools of the SDK, it is recommended that you extract the files into an AIRSDK subdirectory that does not have spaces in its name. If you use a directory with spaces (such as program files), you will need to escape out any spaces in the command line arguments.**

Getting Flex Builder

Flex Builder 3 includes the AIR SDK, as well as a full IDE for building web- or desktop-based Flex applications. While the Flex SDK and AIR SDK are freely available, Flex Builder 3 is a commercial product that you can purchase from Adobe. You can download a free 30-day trial of Flex Builder from http://www.adobe.com/cfusion/entitlement/index.cfm?e=flex3email.

NOTE **If you are running Flex Builder 3.0, you will need to follow the instructions in this appendix to allow you to build AIR 1.1 applications. If you are running Flex Builder 3.01 or later, these updates are already included.**

By using the SDK via Flex Builder, the process of compiling and deploying applications is much simpler, because it is all done through the IDE where the application is developed (as opposed to requiring you use the command line tools). While it is possible to interact with ADL and ADT from the command line, using the SDK installed with Flex Builder, you will find it much easier to use the tools within Flex Builder.

NOTE **There are also plug-ins for Dreamweaver, Flash Studio, and third-party tools such as Aptana to ease the process of interacting with the AIR SDK.**

Flex Builder 3 is available in either standalone mode or as a plug-in for Eclipse for the Windows, Macintosh, and Linux platforms. For more information on installing Flex Builder 3, see *Adobe Flex 3, Training from the Source*, by Adobe Press.

CONSIDERATIONS FOR WORKING WITH AIR 1.1

APPENDIX B

At the time this book was written, Adobe had released AIR 1.1, and, although the tools for writing an AIR 1.1 application have been released, they are not yet packaged in a single convenient installer. There are a few things you will need to understand to be able to create an AIR 1.1 application.

To determine whether you need to follow the steps in this appendix, you need to know which build of Flex Builder you have. Open Flex Builder, and from the top menu, choose Help > About Adobe Flex Builder 3. If the version number in the bottom right corner is 3.0.1.#### (where #### is any group of numbers), you are running the updated 3.0.1 version and do not need to execute any of the steps in this appendix. If the version number is 3.0.####, you are running a version that requires you perform the following steps.

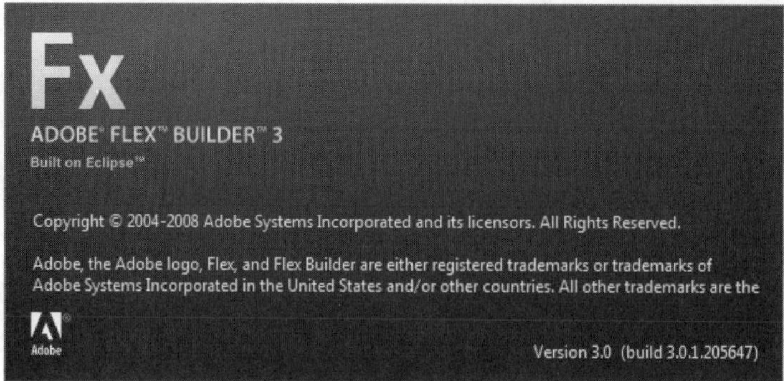

Figure 1: Flex Builder version 3.0.1 - appendix steps unnecessary

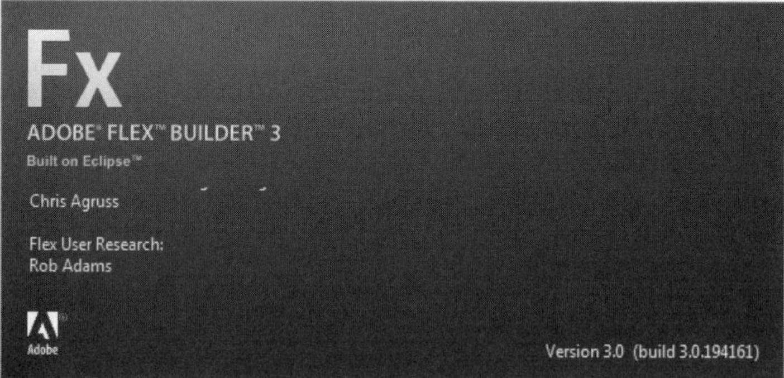

Figure 2: Flex Builder version 3.0 - appendix steps necessary

Updating the Flex SDK

The version of the Flex SDK that is currently shipping with Flex Builder 3 is the Flex 3.0 SDK, which includes full support for AIR 1.0. If you are looking to build an AIR 1.1 application, you will need the Flex 3.0.2 SDK or later, which can be downloaded from http://opensource.adobe.com/wiki/display/flexsdk/downloads. On this page, under the Flex SDK Downloads heading, you will see links to download the Free Adobe 3 Flex SDK, the Open Source Flex SDK, or the Adobe Add-ons for Open Source Flex SDK. You should choose the Free Adobe Flex SDK, as it contains both the open source SDK and the add-ons.

The updated SDK will be downloaded as a compressed archive (ZIP file). Flex Builder 3.0 includes an sdks directory, which, by default, has a 2.0.1 and 3.0.0 directory. You will want to create a 3.0.2 subdirectory there, and extract the downloaded SDK there.

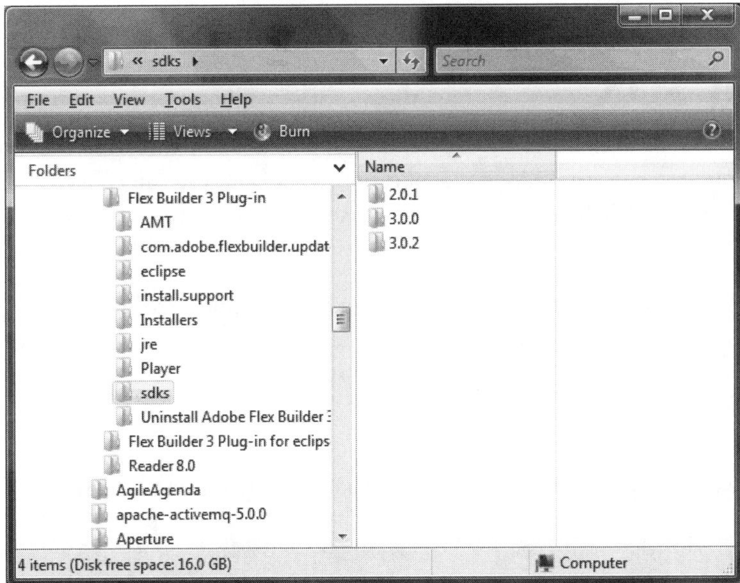

Figure 3: The sdks directory structure

To use AIR 1.1 with the dpTimeTracker application, you will need to take an additional step to make the data visualization classes (which the application uses) available.

NOTE If you want to create an AIR 1.1 application that doesn't use any of the charting or advanced datagrid features, you won't need to take this step, but because dpTimeTracker uses the AdvancedDataGrid, you will need to do this if you wish to compile the application for yourself.

Since the 3.0.2 SDK does not include the data visualization classes, you will need to manually copy over the six items in the following list from the 3.0.0 directory to the equivalent 3.0.2 directory:

- frameworks\libs\automation.swc
- frameworks\libs\datavisualization.swc
- frameworks\locale\en_US\automation_agent_rb.swc
- frameworks\locale\en_US\automation_ rb.swc
- frameworks\locale\en_US\datavisualization_rb.swc
- frameworks\locale\ja_JP\

Instructing Flex Builder 3 to Use a Different SDK

You may have noticed that Flex Builder 3 natively has support to allow you to choose which SDK you want to use to compile your application. By default, you can choose between the 2.0.1 and 3.0.0 SDK, although support exists to allow you to add a new SDK as well.

The ability to add a new SDK to FlexBuilder is provided from the main Preferences panel.

1. With a Flex Project open in FlexBuilder, choose Window > Preferences from the top menu.

2. From the Preferences panel, choose Flex > Installed Flex SDKs from the left pane.

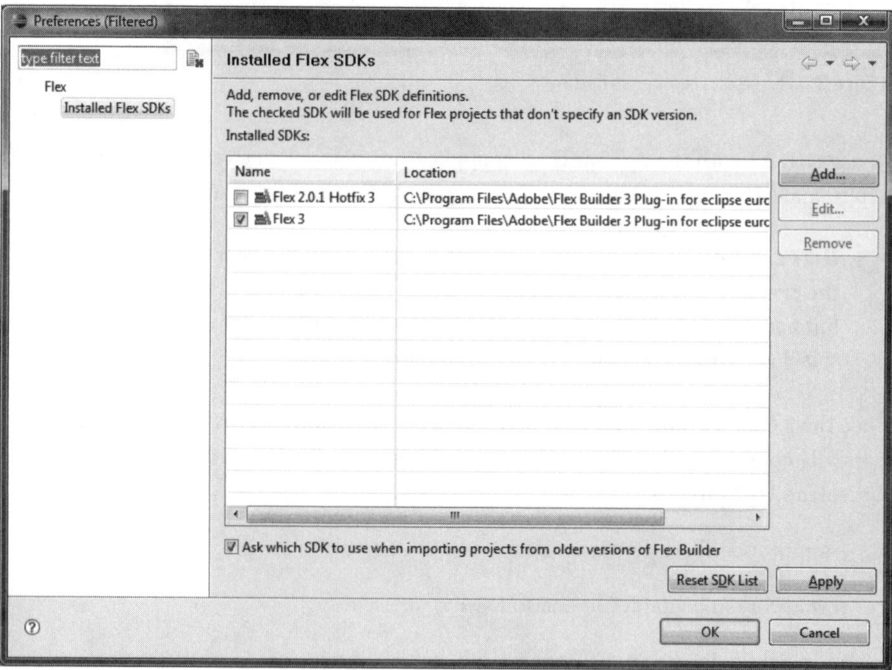

Figure 4: Reviewing the installed SDKs

3. Click the Add button on the right side of the panel.

4. Click the Browse button to browse to the location where you extracted the Flex 3.0.2 SDK. (Following the earlier figures, the location would be C:\Program Files\Adobe\Flex Builder 3 Plug-in\sdks\3.0.2\.)

5. Enter **Flex 3.0.2** as the name of the new SDK.

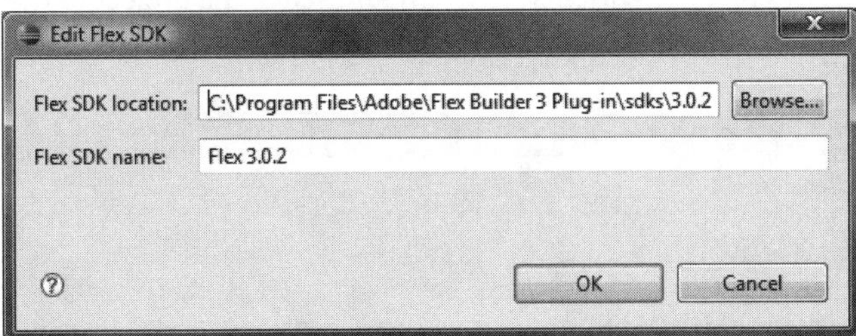

Figure 5: Adding a new SDK

6. Click OK to close the Add Flex SDK dialog box. You will be returned to the screen listing the available SDKS, with your newly added SDK in the list.

7. Select the checkbox next to the Flex 3.0.2 listing to make 3.0.2 the new default SDK.

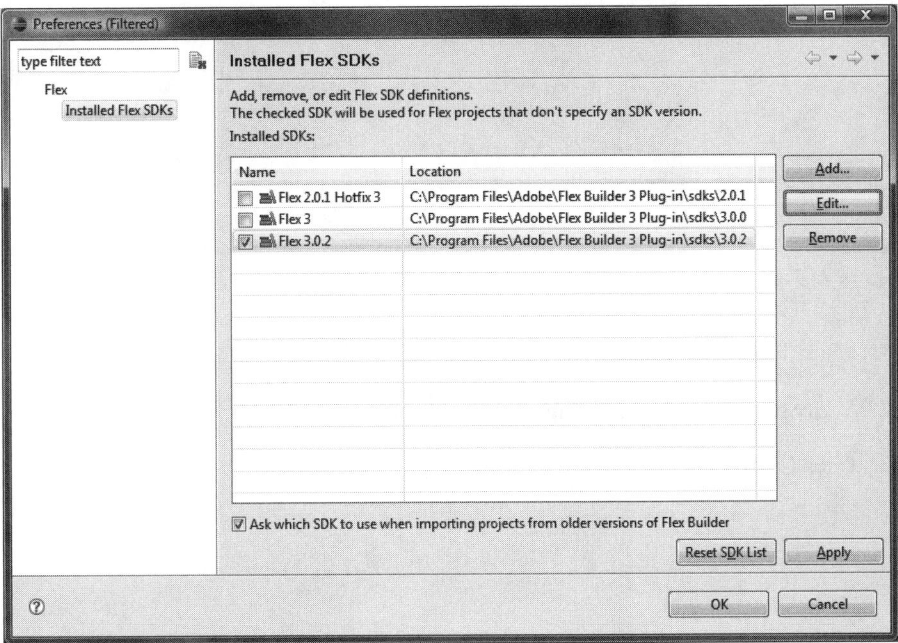

Figure 6: Setting Flex 3.0.2 as the default SDK

8. Click Apply.

9. Click OK to close the Installed Flex SDKs panel.

   Next, you will want to ensure that your project is using the new SDK.

10. Open the project Properties panel (right-click or Command-click the project in the files list, and choose Properties from the context menu).

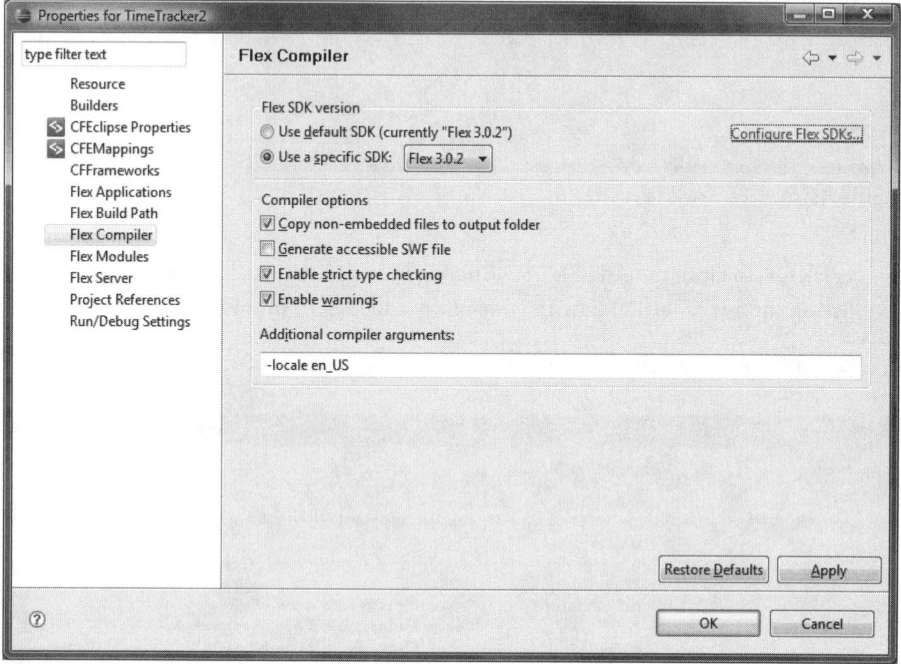

Figure 7: The Flex compiler panel for choosing the specific SDK for a project

11. Click the Flex Compiler link in the left pane.

12. Verify that the project is using the Flex 3.0.2 SDK.

13. Click OK to close the Properties panel.

Modifying the Application Descriptor

Even though FlexBuilder is now set to use the new SDK, which can support AIR 1.1, any new AIR applications created by FlexBuilder will still be created as AIR 1.0 applications. To change an application to use the AIR 1.1 framework instead, you will need to manually modify the application descriptor for any new applications. This is as simple as changing the namespace defined in the root node of the application descriptor. Flex Builder will define the root nodes namespace like this:

```
xmlns="http://ns.adobe.com/air/application/1.0"
```

Instead, you will need to change the 1.0 in the namespace to instead be 1.1:

```
xmlns="http://ns.adobe.com/air/application/1.1"
```

Once this is done, you are ready to create an AIR 1.1 application.

Index

A

B

C

D

E

F

G